THE NEW BOOK OF KNOWLEDGE ANNUAL

1978

HIGHLIGHTING EVENTS OF 1977

THE NEW BOOK OF KNOWLEDGE ANNUAL

THE YOUNG PEOPLE'S BOOK OF THE YEAR

Grolier
INCORPORATED
DANBURY, CONNECTICUT

ISBN 0-7172-0609-2
The Library of Congress Catalog Card Number: 40-3092

CONTENTS

CONTRIBUTORS

BROOKS, Hugh C.
St. John's University (New York City); Fellow, African Studies Association   DJIBOUTI

CASTINO, Ruth Agar
Author, *Spinning and Dyeing the Natural Way*
                                        THE DYER'S ART

CHAZAUD, Jacques
Illustrator; book designer; author and designer of many maze books
          Artwork for A TREE HOUSE MAZE

COLOS, Francois
Illustrator; photographer; contributor to national and international publications. Awards: Art Director Club; Society of Illustrators; Nikon International Contest
          Artwork for PREDICTING EARTHQUAKES

CORWIN, Judith Hoffman
Illustrator; contributor to national and international publications
          Artwork for EMBROIDER A POCKETBOOK

CRONKITE, Walter
CBS News Correspondent
                              OUR CHANGING WORLD

DODSON, Bert
Illustrator
          Artwork for THE DEATH PENALTY: YES OR NO?

DOMOFF, Daniel J.
Consulting editor, Educational Developmental Laboratories, McGraw-Hill Book Company
          SOCCER: THE NEW KICK IN NORTH AMERICA

FRENCH, Bevan M.
Program Chief, Extraterrestrial Materials Research Program, National Aeronautics and Space Administration, Washington, D.C.
                    WHAT'S NEW ON THE MOON?

GARCIA, Tom
Illustrator
          Artwork for IS ANYBODY OUT THERE?

GOLDBERG, Hy
Co-ordinator of sports information, NBC Sports
                                        SPORTS

GOLDSMITH, Harry
Former patent counsel
                    ENERGY-CONSERVATION PATENTS

GRIMM, Michele and Tom
Writers and photographers; authors, *Basic Book of Photography; Hitchhiker's Handbook; My Brown Bag; Twisters; Florida; What Is a Seal?*
                              PAMPERED PETS
          SKATEBOARDING: SURFING ON WHEELS

HAHN, Charless
Stamp Editor, *Chicago Sun-Times*
                              STAMP COLLECTING

HAIMOWITZ, Benjamin
Science writer   AND THEN THERE WERE SOME
                    THE ALASKA PIPELINE
                    A MEDICAL MYSTERY

HARP, Sybil C.
Editor, *Creative Crafts* magazine
          CRAFTS: A WORLD THAT KEEPS ON GROWING

HARVEY, Paul
Illustrator: art director; film director; designer. Awards: 40 national and international citations
          Artwork for THE LONG AND THE SHORT OF IT

HOFFMAN, Jared
High school student; Assistant Editor, *Children's Express;* contributor, *The New York Times;* speaker at the Sixth International Smithsonian Institution Symposium   CHILDREN'S EXPRESS

KULL, David
Science writer   Space Briefs
The Cruelest Winter
The Largest Space Museum in the World

KURTZ, Henry I.
Editor, *Columbia Today;* author, *John and Sebastian Cabot; Captain John Smith;* contributor, *History Today* and *American History Illustrated* magazines   The Queen's Jubilee
The Flight of the Lone Eagle
The Battle of Saratoga

LEWIS, Shari
Puppeteer and author, *The Kids-Only Club Book;* president, American Center of Films for Children
Start a Kids-Only Club

MARGO, Elisabeth
Author, *Taming the Forty-niner*
A Basketmaker's Story

McVICKER, Charles
Illustrator; painter; president, Society of Illustrators; member, American Watercolor Society
Artwork for The Secret of the Ghost Town
Backstroker's Challenge

METZGER, Juan E.
Chairman, Dannon Milk Products
Yogurt—A Natural Food

MISHLER, Clifford
Publisher, *Numismatic News Weekly*
Coin Collecting

MORSCHAUER, Joseph
Science writer   The Water Crisis

PAYNE, Robert
Author, *Mao Tse-tung; A Rage for China; The Life and Death of Adolf Hitler*   Mao Tse-tung

PRICE, Harvey
Chief Scout Executive, Boy Scouts of America
Boy Scouts

SEIBELS, Robert E.
Curator of Birds, Riverbanks Zoological Park, Columbia, South Carolina
The Riverbanks Birdhouse

SHAW, Arnold
Author, *The Rockin' 50's; Honkers and Shouters: The Rhythm and Blues Years; The Rock Revolution; The World of Soul; The Street That Never Slept*   The Music Scene

SKODNICK, Ruth
Statistician
International Statistical Supplement

STEIN, Sara Bonnett
Author, *Great Pets!; Kids' Kitchen Takeover*
Make Your Own Vivarium

STROUGHTER, Carol B.
Girl Scouts of the U.S.A
Girl Scouts and Girl Guides

SWAN, Susan
Illustrator, children's books and educational materials. Awards: Citation of Merit, Society of Illustrators 15th Annual Exhibition; A.I.G.A. Certificate of Excellence (1973)
Artwork for Discovering Your Roots

TESAR, Jenny
Consultant, Curriculum Concepts, Inc.
Predicting Earthquakes
Cartoons! Cartoons! Cartoons!
Discovering Your Roots
Green Animals

ZAMORA, Shirley A.
Program specialist, Office of Program Development, Children's Center, Forest Haven, Washington, D.C.   Occupational Therapy

OUR CHANGING WORLD

Like any other year, 1977 had its share of political, economic, and social problems. But it was also a year full of positive change and great progress as well.

Surprising events in the troubled Middle East led to real hope for a settlement of the 30-year Arab-Israeli dispute. In late November, Egyptian President Anwar el-Sadat traveled to Israel on a historic peace-seeking mission. As the world looked on with elation and disbelief, Sadat extended the hand of friendship to his nation's longtime foe. That encounter led to another historic visit, that of Israeli Prime Minister Menahem Begin to Egypt, during which the two leaders agreed to continue talks, and pledged to seek peaceful solutions to the deep-rooted problems that divide Arabs and Jews.

The United States, too, moved to ease tensions with neighboring countries. Shortly after his inauguration, President Jimmy Carter began to open channels of communication with Cuba. It was a first step toward re-establishing the diplomatic ties that had been broken in 1961, when Cuban Premier Fidel Castro allied his nation with the Communist bloc. And in September, the United States signed new treaties with Panama, in an attempt to resolve the long-standing dispute over control of the Panama Canal. The treaties provide for full Panamanian sovereignty over the canal by the year 2000.

Many nations underwent changes in leadership in 1977. An important change occurred in India, where parliamentary elections resulted in the ouster of Indira Gandhi, who had been prime minister for eleven years. Mrs. Gandhi's popularity had waned because of her harsh measures to silence political opponents. Her defeat was welcomed by those who want to see India maintain its democracy.

In southern Africa, blacks made some gains and suffered some reverses in their efforts to achieve equality with the white minorities. In Rhodesia, white and black leaders met to discuss ways to establish black majority rule in that nation. The prospects for change weren't as good in South Africa. In a vote for whites only, Prime Minister John Vorster, a staunch opponent of full rights for the nation's 18,600,000 blacks, overwhelmingly won re-election. But it was hoped that world opinion would eventually pressure the South African government into extending civil liberties to the nation's blacks.

The energy crisis loomed as large as ever in 1977. One of the worst winters on record led to a massive fuel shortage in the United States. But efforts were under way to solve the problems. President Carter created a Department of Energy and submitted a comprehensive energy program to Congress. But at year's end, Congress was still debating most of the program's important points. And the completion of the Alaska Pipeline during the year has made it possible to bring crude oil from northern Alaska to a point from which it can be shipped to refineries throughout the United States. Scientists are also continuing their efforts to develop new sources of power— among them, solar and nuclear power.

As 1977 drew to a close, prospects for solving some of the world's major problems seemed bright. There was good reason to hope that 1978 might be an even better year.

WALTER CRONKITE

10 A British company announced that it was producing a pocket-size television set that may be the beginning of a new era in communications. The tiny TV, called Microvision, has a 2-inch (5-centimeter) screen, weighs less than 2 pounds (1 kilogram), and is about the size of a paperback book.

14 Robert Anthony Eden, Earl of Avon, died at the age of 79. Eden was prime minister of Britain from 1955 to 1957. He was secretary of state for foreign affairs for more than 12 years, including the critical years from 1940 to 1945 covering most of World War II.

17 Gary Mark Gilmore, a convicted murderer, was executed in Utah. It was the first time a prisoner had been executed in the United States since 1967. More than 350 convicts in the nation's prisons had been sentenced to die; they waited while the question of capital punishment—whether certain prisoners should be executed—was being argued in the nation's courts and legislatures.

Microvision, the new television set that will fit in your pocket.

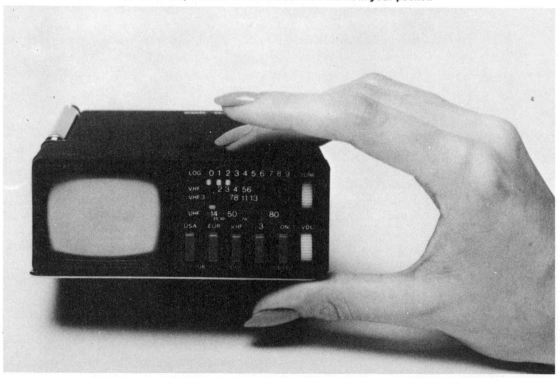

Changing of the guard: Former President Gerald R. Ford and President James E. Carter, Jr., during the inaugural address.

18 Investigators at the Center for Disease Control in Atlanta, Georgia, announced that they had found the cause of "legionnaires' disease." The mysterious type of pneumonia had killed 29 people and sickened 152 others who had been in Philadelphia in 1976 during an American Legion convention there. The cause of the disease was a very unusual bacterium.

20 James E. Carter, Jr., was sworn in as the 39th president of the United States, and Walter F. Mondale was sworn in as the 42nd vice-president. In his brief inaugural address, the new president told the nation: "Your strength can compensate for my weakness, and your wisdom can help to minimize my mistakes. Let us learn together and laugh together. . . ."

21 On his first full day in office, President Carter fulfilled a campaign pledge by granting a full and unconditional pardon to Vietnam War draft evaders not involved in any violent offense against the draft. The pardon affects about 11,000 men who had fled or who had in other ways refused to enter the armed forces during the Vietnam War. It does not include another 100,000 men who had entered the armed forces and then deserted.

FEBRUARY

6 Queen Elizabeth II of England observed the 25th anniversary of her accession to the throne following the death of her father, George VI. Silver Jubilee celebrations will be held throughout the year in Britain and the other Commonwealth nations.

7 The Soviet Union launched Soyuz 24 with two cosmonauts, Viktor V. Gorbatko and Yuri Glazkov, aboard. The Soyuz spacecraft later docked with a Salyut space station that had been orbited in June, 1976.

12 The month-long Second World Black and African Festival of Arts and Culture came to an end. The festival was held at 12 different locations in Nigeria, and it brought together 17,000 artists, dancers, and intellectuals from 50 nations. The performers included belly dancers from Egypt; stilt walkers from Guinea; a steel band from Trinidad and Tobago; Yoruba drummers of Nigeria; dancers from Uganda, Somalia, Senegal, Sudan; and Stevie Wonder from the United States. The purpose of the festival was to "promote black and African artists, performers, and writers, and facilitate their world acceptance. . . ."

18 The United States space shuttle was flight-tested for the first time. The shuttle is designed to be rocketed into earth orbit, and then to return to earth and land like a plane. In this test the shuttle was carried piggyback, on top of a jumbo jet, to an altitude of 16,000 feet (4,900 meters). It is expected that shuttles will ferry men and equipment to orbiting space stations and satellites in the 1980's

21 José Serrano, a New York City construction worker, received a kidney transplant from a Russian donor. The kidney had been flown over from the Soviet Union as part of an agreement between Soviet and American doctors to make body organs available to each other, whenever possible, for transplant operations.

22 For the first time, a Canadian prime minister addressed a joint session of both houses of the U.S. Congress. In the speech, Prime Minister Pierre Elliott Trudeau said: "Canada's unity will not be fractured." He was referring to the separatist movement in Quebec, which desires independence for that province.

The Second World Black and African Festival of Arts and Culture was held in Nigeria. More than 50 nations sent performers, including stilt walkers from Guinea (*above*) and dancers from Burundi (*below*).

4 A severe earthquake hit the Rumanian city of Bucharest and a large surrounding area, killing about 1,500 people, injuring more than 11,000, and leaving tens of thousands homeless.

9 President Jimmy Carter announced the end of the 17-year ban on American travel to Cuba, as well as the end of the bans on travel to Vietnam, Cambodia, and North Korea.

18 President Marien Ngouabi of the central African nation of Congo was assassinated. President Ngouabi had ruled Congo since 1968. (On April 3, Colonel Joachim Yombi Opango was named president.)

20 Five days of voting in parliamentary elections ended in India. The returns brought about the defeat of Indira Gandhi, prime minister since 1966, and the Congress Party she headed. It was the first time the Congress Party had failed to win control of the government since India became an independent nation in 1947. (On March 24, Morarji R. Desai, 81-year-old head of the Janata Party, was sworn in as India's fourth prime minister.)

The collision of two jumbo jets on Tenerife caused the highest death toll in aviation history.

25 A 12-day United Nations conference on the world's water crisis ended. Delegates from more than 100 countries had gathered in Mar del Plata, Argentina, to consider how to control drought, floods, pollution, and disease through better water management.

27 Two 747 jumbo jets collided and burst into flames on the foggy runway of Los Rodeos Airport on the Canary Island of Tenerife. The crash of the American-owned and Dutch-owned jets resulted in the deaths of 582 people, the highest death toll in aviation history. Sixty-two people survived.

30 The National Aeronautics and Space Administration (NASA) announced the discovery of at least five rings around the planet Uranus. The rings, which resemble those around the planet Saturn, were discovered earlier in the month by scientists who were looking at Uranus through a telescope aboard a high-flying airplane. This is how the discovery was made: As the planet passed in front of a star, the bright starlight dimmed several times before it was completely eclipsed by the planet; the starlight then dimmed again at the very end of Uranus' passage. This dimming effect indicated that something was orbiting Uranus (other than its five known moons), thus partially blocking out the starlight. The regularity of the dimming indicated rings rather than a great many small moons.

A drawing of the newly-discovered rings around the planet Uranus.

5 Willy Adams became the first Eskimo in the Canadian Parliament. He will represent the Northwest Territories in the Senate. He was appointed by Governor General Jules Léger, upon the recommendation of Prime Minister Pierre Elliott Trudeau.

9 A Soviet fishing vessel was seized by the U.S. Coast Guard for violating the rules governing the new American 200-mile fishing zone. Under these rules, the United States licenses foreign fishing within this zone; but it strictly regulates the species and the number of fish that can be caught. The cargo of the Soviet ship contained more than was permitted of a regulated species, which made the catch illegal. A few days later, the Soviet Union announced that it would abide by the new rules.

11 After a 30-year absence, some of the people of Enewetak were back in their homeland. Enewetak, an atoll of tiny islands in the Pacific Ocean, is part of a trust territory administered by the United States since World War II. All the inhabitants of these islands were relocated by 1948 when the United States began nuclear testing on the atoll. The United States has begun testing the entire area for radiation; cleaning and rehabilitating the land; and planting food-bearing trees. It is doing this so that eventually more Enewetakese may return.

Enewetakese celebrate their return to their homeland.

Willy Adams: The first Eskimo in Canada's Parliament.

19   The U.S. Supreme Court ruled, by a vote of 5–4, that the spanking of students by teachers or school officials was not a violation of the pupils' constitutional rights.

20   President Jimmy Carter presented a national energy plan to Congress. The objectives of this plan are to decrease America's dependence on imported oil; to have enough oil should a world oil shortage develop in the future; and to develop new sources of energy. He set forth the following energy goals for 1985:

to reduce the yearly growth of the demand for energy.
to reduce oil imports.
to reduce the consumption of gasoline.
to establish a reserve of petroleum that would be enough for a ten-month supply.
to increase coal production.
to insulate 90 percent of U.S. homes and all new buildings.
to use solar energy in more homes.

To reach these goals, President Carter set forth a combination of price regulations, increased taxes, income tax credits, and tax refunds. The plan was sent to Congress for its deliberation.

4 Former president Richard Nixon was closely questioned by TV interviewer David Frost. The broadcast was seen by 45,000,000 Americans, one of the largest audiences ever to watch a television news interview. Nixon admitted that he had made misleading statements about the Watergate affair and had "let the American people down." But he insisted that he hadn't committed any criminal or impeachable offense. (Four more Nixon-Frost interviews followed.)

10 Joan Crawford, 69, American motion picture star, died. Miss Crawford, a screen star since the 1920's, won a 1945 Academy Award for her performance in *Mildred Pierce*.

17 In parliamentary elections in Israel, the Likud Party won the most seats. It was a major defeat for the Labor Party, which had dominated the government since the founding of Israel in 1948. (On June 21, Menahem Begin, leader of the Likud, became prime minister. Begin, a strong advocate of keeping Israeli-occupied Arab land, said that he would work hard to prevent another Arab-Israeli conflict.)

A political cartoon of the Richard Nixon–David Frost interviews.

On May 27 in the Netherlands, the South Moluccan terrorists released all the children they had been holding hostage for four days.

23 In the Netherlands, South Moluccan terrorists seized many hostages, to draw world attention to their demand for an independent homeland of the South Moluccas islands. These islands were once Dutch possessions, but are now part of Indonesia. In a co-ordinated action, one group of terrorists hijacked a train with more than 50 passengers, while a second group seized 106 children and 5 teachers in their elementary school. Thus began the largest mass-kidnapping in modern times. (On May 27, all the children and one teacher were released after many of them had become ill. On June 11, a platoon of Dutch marines stormed the train and rescued the hostages, killing six of the terrorists and two of the hostages. The remaining teachers at the school were rescued by another group of marines.)

30 Aboard Viking 1 on the planet Mars, all the instruments that had been monitoring for biological signs of life were shut off. Similar instruments on Viking 2 had been shut off on May 28. Both Vikings had landed on Mars in 1976. Although they found no signs of life, they will continue to send back pictures and meteorological information.

10   James Earl Ray, the convicted assassin of Martin Luther King, Jr., escaped from the maximum-security prison in Tennessee where he was serving a 99-year term. (He was recaptured on June 13, not far from the prison.)

15   In the first free parliamentary elections since 1936, Spain voted for members of the Cortes, the Spanish parliament. The party of Premier Adolfo Suárez González won the greatest number of seats.

16   Wernher Von Braun, 65, German-born scientist, died. A pioneer in rocket development and space travel, he designed the V-2 missile for Germany during World War II. He went to the United States in 1945. There, he directed the project that sent the first U.S. satellite into orbit, in 1958. He also was in charge of developing the Saturn V rocket, which sent the first men to the moon in 1969.

16   In parliamentary elections held in Ireland, the government headed by Prime Minister Liam Cosgrave was defeated. Cosgrave had been prime minister since 1973. (On July 5, Jack Lynch became prime minister.)

Dr. Wernher Von Braun, who died in June, was a pioneer in space exploration.

The good works of Bishop John Nepomucene Neumann are depicted in eight stained glass windows at St. Peter's Church in Philadelphia.

19 John Nepomucene Neumann, a 19th-century bishop of Philadelphia (Pennsylvania), was declared a saint by Pope Paul VI. Bishop Neumann, who died in 1860, thus became the first male saint of the United States. He was born in Bohemia and moved to the United States at the age of 25. Known as the "Little Bishop" to his flock, he devoted himself to the poor and to education.

27 The Republic of Djibouti became Africa's 49th independent country. The tiny nation, which was formerly known as the French Territory of the Afars and the Issas, had been under French rule for 115 years. Hassan Gouled became the republic's first president.

2 Vladimir Nabokov, 78, Russian-born author, died. Nabokov, who left Russia after the Communist Revolution, was world famous for such books as *Lolita* and *Pale Fire*.

5 In Pakistan, the Army seized power in a bloodless coup and overthrew the government of Prime Minister Zulfikar Ali Bhutto. The coup followed two months of political violence. General Mohammed Zia ul-Haq, the chief of staff of the army, imposed martial law, but announced that elections would soon be held.

13 North Koreans shot down a U.S. helicopter, killing three crewmen, and wounding and capturing a fourth. The helicopter was said to have strayed by mistake into North Korean territory from the demilitarized zone. (On July 16, the North Koreans returned the bodies of the dead men along with the captured crewman. But they refused to return the helicopter, on the grounds that it had violated North Korean airspace.)

Muddy waters swirl through a residential area of Johnstown, Pennsylvania, where severe flooding caused the deaths of 68 people.

A great many stores were looted and wrecked during the massive power failure and blackout in New York City.

13 New York City suffered a massive power failure and blackout. It lasted as long as 25 hours in some areas. Whole neighborhoods were wrecked and looted in the darkness. Damage amounted to millions of dollars, and 3,700 people were arrested for looting and other crimes.

20 An all-night rainfall caused severe flooding in and around Johnstown, Pennsylvania. Sixty-eight people died. It was the worst catastrophe the town had suffered since the great Johnstown flood of 1889 in which more than 2,200 people died.

21 In Sri Lanka, Prime Minister Sirimavo Bandaranaike and her governing Freedom Party were heavily defeated in parliamentary elections. The victorious party was the United National Party, headed by Junius R. Jayawardene. Bandaranaike, one of the few women in the world to hold such high office, had been prime minister for a total of 12 years since 1960.

AUGUST

3   Archbishop Makarios III, 63, president of Cyprus, died. A prelate of the Greek Orthodox Church, Makarios became the first president of Cyprus when the country became independent in 1960.

4   A Department of Energy was added to the U.S. Cabinet. It was the first addition to the Cabinet in eleven years. The new department will work on solving energy-policy problems. It will also consolidate the functions of the many energy agencies scattered throughout the government. James R. Schlesinger was named secretary of the new department. (With the Department of Energy, there are twelve departments in the U.S. Cabinet.)

11   David Berkowitz, a 24-year-old postal worker, was arrested near New York City as the alleged "Son of Sam," who killed six people and wounded seven in a year-long series of attacks.

12   The *Enterprise*, the first re-usable space shuttle, passed another major test. Manned by two pilots, the shuttle was carried piggyback on a jumbo jet to an altitude of about 24,000 feet (7,315 meters). The *Enterprise* was then separated from the jet, and the pilots glide-landed it on a dry-lake runway in the Mojave Desert.

16   Elvis Presley, 42, "the king of rock 'n' roll," died. He was the idol of millions of teenagers in the 1950's, and his many gold records included "Hound Dog" and "Blue Suede Shoes." Presley also starred in about 25 motion pictures.

16   The *Arktika*, a Soviet nuclear-powered icebreaker, became the first surface ship to smash through the huge sheets of ice to reach the North Pole. The North Pole was reached by dogsled by Robert E. Peary in 1909; by air by Admiral Richard E. Byrd in 1926; and under the ice by a U.S. nuclear submarine in 1958. With its three nuclear icebreakers, the Soviet Union hopes to be able to keep shipping lanes across the top of the world open.

19   Groucho Marx, 86, comedian of stage, film, and television, died. Groucho was famous for his bushy, arched eyebrows and the cigar always in his mouth. He first won fame as one of the Marx Brothers team. Later he starred on his own television show, "You Bet Your Life."

The space shuttle *Enterprise* is carried piggyback on a jumbo jet (*above*), and successfully separates from the jet (*below*).

20 The first of the Voyager spacecraft was launched on a course that will take it to the outer reaches of the solar system. If all goes well, it will travel past the planets of Jupiter and Saturn, and perhaps Uranus in 1986. (A second Voyager was launched on September 5, 1977.)

2 Ethel Waters, American singer and actress, died. She first gained fame as a singer, with such songs as "Stormy Weather," and later became a major star of nightclubs, radio, television, stage, and motion pictures.

6 Canada changed its road signs to the metric system as part of its program of complete metrication by 1980. The shift to metric measurements was begun in 1970 and the changeover has been introduced gradually. This leaves the United States as the last major nation that still uses the English system of measurement.

7 U.S. President Jimmy Carter and Omar Torrijos Herrera, Panama's head of government, signed new Panama Canal treaties. Under the main treaty, Panama will gradually recover all the territory that is now the U.S.-administered Canal Zone. On December 31, 1999, full ownership of the canal will pass to Panama. The second treaty gives the United States the right to intervene militarily if there is any threat to the neutrality or operation of the canal until the canal is transferred to Panama. (Panamanians approved both treaties in a referendum on October 23. The treaties must be approved by two thirds of the U.S. Senate before they can go into effect.)

Zero Mostel as Tevye in a scene from *Fiddler on the Roof*. Mostel died in September, at the age of 62.

Canadian and U.S. officials in Ottawa to sign an agreement to build a natural gas pipeline through Canada from Alaska. Prime Minister Pierre Elliott Trudeau is on right.

8   Zero Mostel, 62, American actor, died. A star of movies and Broadway shows, Mostel was especially admired for his portrayal of Tevye in *Fiddler on the Roof*.

13   Leopold Stokowski, 95, American symphonic conductor, died. In a career of 70 years, Stokowski conducted many orchestras, notably the Philadelphia Orchestra. He encouraged many young musical performers and was a great promoter of modern music.

20   The 32nd regular session of the United Nations General Assembly opened at UN headquarters in New York City. Lazar Mojsov of Yugoslavia was elected to serve as Assembly president for one year.

20   Two countries were admitted to the United Nations. The newly independent republic of Djibouti became the 148th member, and Vietnam became the 149th member.

20   The United States and Canada signed an agreement to build a pipeline that will carry natural gas from Alaska through Canada to American users. It will be built by U.S. and Canadian companies. The pipeline may be extended to carry Canadian gas to consumers in southern Canada.

9 A Soyuz spacecraft with two cosmonauts aboard was launched from the Soviet Union. The Soyuz was to have docked with the orbiting space station Salyut 6. The linkup was planned as part of the celebration commemorating the 60th anniversary of the Russian Revolution. However, because of a malfunction, the cosmonauts failed to dock with the space station. They abandoned their mission and returned to earth two days later.

12 Sweden announced that it was canceling $220,000,000 in debts that were owed by eight developing, or third-world, nations. (Canada had set the example in September, when it announced that it was canceling $254,000,000 owed by ten developing countries.) Debt cancellation is a major issue on which the poorer, developing countries and the wealthier, industrialized countries generally disagree.

14 Bing (Harry Lillis) Crosby, 73, American singer and motion picture actor, died. A star for 50 years, Crosby delighted several generations of fans. His records sold more than 300,000,000 copies, and his voice was heard all over the world on radio and television and in the movies. Crosby won a 1944 Academy Award for his lead role in *Going My Way*.

Betty Williams and Mairead Corrigan were the winners of the 1976 Nobel peace prize, for their peace movement to end the violence in Northern Ireland.

18   Queen Elizabeth II of Britain opened a new session of the Canadian Parliament in Ottawa, addressing the gathering in both English and French. It was the highlight of her six-day Silver Jubilee visit to Canada.

19   A supersonic Concorde jet landed at Kennedy airport in New York and took off the following day. The British-French airliner had been the subject of many legal battles and had been banned from Kennedy airport for nineteen months. It had been feared that the plane would exceed the legal noise limit.

20   In Thailand, the year-old civilian government of Premier Thanin Kraivichien was dismissed by the military. (In November, General Kriangsak Chamanad was appointed premier.)

THE 1977 NOBEL PRIZES

Chemistry: Ilya Prigogine of Belgium, for his work in thermodynamics (the study of how heat is related to other forms of energy). His work advances the understanding of how living organisms and societies use energy in order to grow.

Economics: Bertil Ohlin of Sweden and James E. Meade of Britain, for their independent studies of the theory of international trade.

Literature: Vicente Aleixandre of Spain, for his poetry, which tells of "man's condition in the cosmos and in present-day society."

Peace: Amnesty International, the world's largest human rights organization, which works for the release of nonviolent people who have been imprisoned for their political or religious beliefs.

Peace: The 1976 peace prize was awarded to Betty Williams and Mairead Corrigan of Northern Ireland, for their peace movement (begun in 1976) to end the violence in Northern Ireland. (Since 1969, about 2,000 people have been killed in fighting between Roman Catholics and Protestants.)

Physics: John H. Van Vleck and Philip W. Anderson of the United States and Sir Nevill F. Mott of Britain, for their independent work in solid-state physics, which has aided in the development of computer memories and other modern electronic devices.

Physiology or Medicine: Rosalyn S. Yalow, Roger C. L. Guillemin, and Andrew V. Schally of the United States, for their independent research involving the role of hormones in the chemistry of the human body.

NOVEMBER

1 President Jimmy Carter signed into law a bill that increases the minimum wage. Under the new law, the minimum wage will rise from the present $2.30 per hour to $2.65 in 1978; to $2.90 in 1979; to $3.10 in 1980; and to $3.35 an hour in 1981.

1 President Jimmy Carter withdrew the United States from the International Labor Organization (I.L.O.) on the grounds that the agency had become too political. The I.L.O. is the oldest specialized agency of the United Nations. It seeks through international action to improve labor conditions, raise living standards, and promote productive employment around the world.

3 The Carter Administration announced that the United States would return the Crown of St. Stephen to Hungary, in a move to improve relations with that country. The crown is a symbol of Hungarian nationalism. It was given to the first King of Hungary by Pope Sylvester II in the year 1000. The crown has been in American custody since the end of World War II, when the Hungarians gave it over to the United States to keep it out of the hands of Soviet troops who were advancing on them.

Princess Anne and her husband, Captain Mark Phillips, leave the hospital with their newborn son.

The United States announced that it would return the Crown of St. Stephen to Hungary. The crown is a symbol of Hungarian nationalism.

8 It was announced that astronomers had discovered an object between Saturn and Uranus that is orbiting the sun. The object could be part of an undiscovered belt of asteroids, or it could be the solar system's tenth and smallest planet. Because the object is so small—about one-tenth the size of Mercury—it is temporarily being described as a "mini-planet."

15 A son was born to Britain's Princess Anne and her husband, Captain Mark Phillips. The child is the first grandchild of Queen Elizabeth II, and is fifth in line to the British throne. In a departure from tradition, the child will not be given a royal title.

19 A cyclone hit the southeastern coast of India and battered the state of Andhra Pradesh. Tidal waves as high as 18 feet (5.5 meters) engulfed whole villages in the worst natural disaster in India since 1864. The death toll was estimated at 20,000. More than 2,000,000 people were left homeless and crop damage was enormous.

19– 21 President Anwar el-Sadat of Egypt made a three-day trip to Israel. It was the first time that an Arab leader had visited Israel since its founding in 1948. (Israel and Egypt have fought four wars against each other.) President Sadat addressed the Knesset, Israel's parliament, and stated the Arab case for peace. Later, Israeli Prime Minister Menahem Begin and Sadat held private talks. In a joint interview at the end of the historic visit, Begin and Sadat pledged that there would be "no more war."

5 Bophuthatswana became the second of South Africa's nine black homelands to be given independence. All of South Africa's 2,500,000 Tswanas were made citizens of this homeland, and were thus forced to give up their citizenship and the few political rights they had in South Africa. Almost every foreign nation views the homeland plan as South Africa's way of maintaining its racial policy of apartheid (separation of the races).

5 Egyptian President Anwar el-Sadat broke off diplomatic relations with five other Arab nations—Syria, Iraq, Algeria, Libya, and Southern Yemen. Sadat's action came as a result of those countries' strong opposition to his recent peace moves toward Israel.

11 Soyuz 26, a Soviet spacecraft with two cosmonauts aboard, docked successfully with the earth-orbiting Salyut 6 space station. The cosmonauts began a program of scientific experiments aboard the Salyut.

Charlie Chaplin in a scene from the silent movie *A Dog's Life*. Chaplin (the Little Tramp) died in December, at the age of 88.

Israeli prime minister Menahem Begin in Egypt: Another historic visit in the search for peace in the Middle East.

19 Queen Juliana of the Netherlands swore in a new cabinet headed by Prime Minister Andreas A. M. van Agt. The Netherlands had been without a formal government since March, the longest cabinet crisis in Dutch history.

25 Charlie Chaplin, 88, British actor, producer, and director, died. He was known and loved throughout the world for his many films—especially his silent movies, which brought laughter and tears to millions of people who did not need language to understand his pantomime. Because he often appeared with floppy shoes, battered derby, and twirling cane, Chaplin became known as the Little Tramp. Charlie Chaplin was knighted by Queen Elizabeth in 1975.

26 Prime Minister Menahem Begin of Israel and Egyptian President Anwar el-Sadat ended a two-day conference in Ismailia, Egypt. It was the first time that an Israeli head of state had ever visited an Arab country officially. Although the meeting ended without agreement on the main issues that stand in the way of peace, both leaders vowed to continue their peace efforts through further negotiations.

31 Cambodia broke off diplomatic relations with Vietnam, the result of a border dispute between the two neighboring countries in Southeast Asia. It was the first time that a formal diplomatic break had ever occurred between Communist nations.

TOP OF THE NEWS

American tourists in Havana. In 1977 the United States ended its 17-year ban on travel to Cuba, as relations between the two countries began to improve.

U.S.–CUBAN RELATIONS

Cuba, an island nation in the Caribbean, lies just 92 miles (148 kilometers) off Key West, Florida. The country was granted independence from Spain in 1902 after the Spanish-American War. For more than 50 years the United States had strong political and economic influence in Cuba, and there was a close friendship between the two countries, as well.

But in 1956 a change took place. A young revolutionary named Fidel Castro organized a small band of guerrillas and began a war against the government. In a little over two years, Castro was in power. He changed almost everything in Cuba. His most significant move was to ally his government with the Communist world. By 1961, after Castro had nationalized all U.S. property in Cuba, the United States ended trade with the country and broke off diplomatic relations. And that's how it remained for sixteen years.

Then in 1977 there were signs that the "cold war" between the United States and Cuba was coming to an end. Shortly after President Jimmy Carter took office in January, he began to take steps to improve relations between the two countries. In April the first direct talks between U.S. and Cuban officials since 1961 took place. As a result of the negotiations, a fishing agreement was signed permitting Cuban vessels to fish in U.S. waters.

Perhaps the most important breakthrough in re-establishing ties came in September when Cuba opened a mission in Washington, D.C., and the United States opened a similar mission in Cuba. This did not establish full diplomatic recognition, but it did form a direct communication link between the two countries.

There was great optimism about improved relations. Then, in the summer and fall of 1977, the optimism began to fade. The United States became concerned about the Cuban military buildup in Angola and Ethiopia. It was believed that about 26,000 Cuban soldiers and military advisers were involved in the internal affairs of at least sixteen African countries. President Carter called the Cuban military presence a threat to the peace of Africa. He also said it would hurt the growing improvement in U.S.–Cuban relations.

At the end of the year, full diplomatic relations were still not re-established. But hope remained that the problems existing between the two nations could be worked out.

AFRICA: A CONTINENT IN TURMOIL

Africa remained a continent in turmoil throughout 1977. Two especially bad trouble spots were Zaïre and the Horn of Africa.

▶ZAÏRE

In March, about 3,000 soldiers invaded Zaïre. They had crossed the border from Angola and marched into Zaïre's Shaba province (formerly known as Katanga). President Mobutu Sese Seko of Zaïre claimed that the invaders were Katangan soldiers who had been in exile from Zaïre for over ten years. He said they were being supported by Angola, Cuba, and the Soviet Union.

As in most wars, the involvement spread far beyond the borders of the actual fighting. Many world leaders viewed the invasion as a serious threat to Mobutu's government. The United States, Belgium, France, and China shipped military supplies to Zaïre; French transport planes airlifted 1,500 Moroccan soldiers into the country; and Egypt sent in pilots. Mobutu convinced most African governments that this challenge from rebel forces was really a challenge for the whole continent.

The fighting continued for two months, with each side claiming the capture and recapture of towns and villages. In May, Zaïrian troops recaptured the last towns held by the rebel invaders and it appeared that the invasion of Shaba province had been crushed.

▶THE HORN OF AFRICA

Ethiopia, in the Horn of Africa, has been involved in a war on two fronts. For many years, the Eritrean Liberation Front (ELP) has been fighting for the independence of Ethiopia's seacoast province, Eritrea. It made major gains against the Ethiopian government in 1977, and though the government held the major cities, the separatists controlled most of the countryside. The rebel forces appear to have turned back all attempts by government forces to retake the territory.

But the Eritrean war is not Ethiopia's biggest problem. Ethiopia's conflict with neighboring Somalia has become the world's bloodiest war being fought today. Hostilities erupted between the two countries in July when the Somalis tried to gain control of Ethiopia's Ogaden region. (Ethiopia had conquered the Ogaden region from Somalia in the late 19th century. The land is particularly important to the Somalis because their camels, sheep, and goats must cross the Ogaden during certain times of the year to reach their pastureland.)

Somalia claimed that guerrillas were doing the fighting. But the Ethiopians said that the soldiers were actually regular Somali troops and that the government was actively involved in the conflict.

As the fighting continued, Somali forces made great advances into the Ogaden region.

Members of Ethiopia's new peasant army wear North Korean camouflage uniforms and carry Soviet-made weapons.

By the end of the year, they controlled all but two of the major towns and most of the countryside. Ethiopia continued to fight the invaders with devastating air strikes, but was unsuccessful in recapturing any territory.

The Soviet Union found itself in the middle of the Ethiopia-Somalia conflict. For several years Somalia had been the most important Soviet ally in the African Horn. In return for Soviet economic aid, the Somalis allowed the Soviets to build naval facilities at the port of Berbera, which is in a strategic spot near the entrance to the Red Sea.

Early in 1977, however, the Soviet Union turned its attention to Ethiopia. The Soviets hoped that they might gain friendship with Ethiopia without weakening their alliance with Somalia. This angered the Somalis, and in November Somalia broke its treaty of friendship with the Soviet Union, expelled Soviet military and civilian advisers, and closed the naval bases at Berbera. Within a month, the Russians had mounted an airlift of arms and military equipment to the Ethiopians.

And the war between Somalia and Ethiopia continued to rage.

▶RHODESIA

Black majority rule in Rhodesia continued to be the important issue in this conflict-torn country. Guerrilla activity increased as talks continued between black and white leaders. In December, Prime Minister Ian D. Smith met with black leaders to seek a settlement based on majority rule by the blacks, with safeguards for the white minority.

▶CONGO

On March 18, Marien Ngouabi, president of Congo since 1968, was assassinated. Colonel Joachim Yombi Opango was named to succeed him.

▶SOUTH AFRICA

Demonstrations demanding civil rights for blacks continued throughout South Africa. A devastating blow to the black cause came with the death of Steven Biko, one of the foremost young leaders of the black movement. Biko died while being held in prison.

In the general elections, held on November 30, Prime Minister John Vorster won an overwhelming vote of support from the white minority. The country's 18,600,000 blacks had not been allowed to vote. This victory strengthened Vorster's power and his opposition to social reform for the blacks.

In November the United Nations Security Council took a major step against the racial policies of the South African government. This was the first time in the history of the United Nations that severe action was taken to punish a member state. The Security Council ordered a worldwide embargo of military supplies against South Africa. But since the U.N. has no real way to enforce its resolutions, the success of the embargo depends on the willingness of the member nations to observe it.

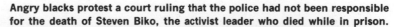

Angry blacks protest a court ruling that the police had not been responsible for the death of Steven Biko, the activist leader who died while in prison.

BLACKOUT!

Sometimes it can be very exciting if the electricity goes off and you have to use candles and flashlights to see—as if you were camping out. But it was not much fun at all for the people of New York City and nearby areas when a power failure caused a massive blackout in the summer of 1977. For one thing, the electricity stayed off for more than a day. And it was not just one house or one neighborhood that was without power. It was a whole city.

The trouble was started by lightning. At about 8:30 on the evening of July 13, a violent storm struck north of New York City. For the next hour, bolts of lightning crashed down on earth. Some of them struck large transmission wires that carry electricity to the city from out-of-town power plants. By 9:35 P.M., so many wires were damaged that 9,000,000 people were without power.

It was as if a giant had flicked a switch and turned off all the lights. Homes, buildings, and streets were in darkness. That's why the power failure was called a blackout.

People sat glued to their transistor radios, in rooms dimly lit by whatever candles they could find. But it was not just the lights that did not work. Elevators couldn't run, leaving many people stranded high up in buildings. Traffic signals couldn't work, causing long lines of cars that didn't know whether to stop or go. Subway trains stalled, some in the middle of long, dark tunnels. A Ferris wheel at an amusement park stopped, leaving passengers hanging in mid-air. Police and volunteers had to crank the wheel by hand to rescue them.

With New York in darkness, life in the city was different from usual, and some people did things they would not normally do. Stores were robbed, and buildings were set on fire. While most of the people obeyed the laws during the emergency, those who did not kept police and firemen very busy.

The power stayed off throughout the night and into the next day. Refrigerators weren't working and food began to spoil. Electric pumps that help supply water to many apartment buildings went off and people had to carry pails from the street—or go without. Air conditioners couldn't operate, and it was one of the hottest days of the summer. Many businesses closed because their employees could not get to work, or because employees needed electric power to do their jobs.

Electricity in a few parts of the city was turned back on within four hours after the

The usually bright New York City skyline became a crooked line of darkness during the blackout.

blackout began. But most of the city had no power for almost a full day. The last neighborhood to be switched back on had gone without power for 25 hours.

Once full power was restored, the job was to find out exactly what had gone wrong, and to figure out ways of solving the problem in the future. Lightning storms happen often. If they could occasionally knock out a city's power so easily, the country might be in for a lot of trouble.

Part of the problem is that so much electricity is needed. Many power plants, transmission lines, and distribution stations are necessary to produce and deliver a large enough supply. The plants, wires, and stations are connected in large, complicated systems. If one part of a system fails and is shut down, the other parts are supposed to take over its share of the load. But if the failure is very large, the extra load may be too much for the remaining parts to handle. When that happens, one shutdown leads to another, which leads to another, and so on. It's like a row of falling dominoes.

That's just what happened in the blackout of 1977, but it was not the first time the problem had occurred. In 1965 a power failure spread across much of the northeastern United States and parts of eastern Canada. After that black-out, the government ordered electric companies to install safeguards to keep power failures from spreading. The safeguards were to shut off power to small areas when part of a system failed. That way, the rest of the system would not be overworked by taking up the slack.

The safeguards did keep the 1977 blackout from spreading outside of New York City and a few of its suburbs. But they should have stopped the problem from going as far as it did. The government and Consolidated Edison, the electric company that serves New York City, conducted investigations of what went wrong on the night of July 13. However, even after the reports came out, many questions were still left unanswered.

The answers are important because the blackout of 1977 showed how easily a large electric system can be shut down—and how damaging such a failure can be. If more proof of that fact were necessary, it came only two months later when a power station in northern Canada broke down. The failure, which lasted several hours, spread throughout Quebec Province, including Quebec City and Montreal, and affected 6,000,000 people.

The question remains: How can future blackouts be prevented?

Sadat in Israel: treated as a friend, not an enemy.

A happy Israeli soldier carries the flags of Israel and Egypt.

EGYPT AND ISRAEL: HISTORIC PEACE MOVES

"He's a brave man, a man of peace!" shouted the supporters of the historic journey.

"He's a traitor!" cried those who disapproved.

The man at the center of this controversy is Anwar el-Sadat, the president of Egypt. On November 19, 1977, Sadat went to Israel, a country with which Egypt is technically at war. It was the first time ever that an Arab leader had visited the Jewish nation.

Israel was founded in 1948. It is surrounded by Egypt and other Arab nations that have long refused to accept Israel's right to exist. Ever since it was founded, Israel and its neighbors have been fighting with each other. Four major wars have been fought, in 1948, 1956, 1967, and 1973.

The cost of the fighting has been great for both sides. Many lives have been lost. Money needed for housing, education, and other social needs has been spent on guns and tanks.

Attempts to negotiate a peace have met with little success. It was hoped that the warring nations would get together at a conference in Geneva, Switzerland, but progress was slow. And so in early November, Sadat said he would go anywhere, even to Israel, to discuss peace. Few people thought he meant it. But the prime minister of Israel, Menahem Begin, invited Sadat to Jerusalem, saying he was ready to meet with Sadat "any time, any day."

When Sadat accepted the invitation, the other Arab nations were furious. They believed it would weaken their cause and they feared Egypt would seek a separate peace with Israel. They even called for the overthrow of Sadat. But the Egyptians were strongly behind their leader. Most of the rest of the world also applauded the surprise move.

On November 19, Sadat flew to the country with which he was at war. Shortly after 8 P.M., he stepped off the plane and stood on Israeli soil. He was greeted by Begin, who said, "It's wonderful to have you. Thank you for coming."

Sadat was treated as a friend, not an enemy. He was immediately honored with a 21-gun salute, a red carpet, and a receiving line of Israel's most important leaders. And throughout his three-day visit, he was shown great warmth by Israeli citizens.

On November 20, Sadat worshiped in Al Aksa Mosque in Jerusalem, one of the holiest places in the Muslim world. He also visited Yad Vashem, the memorial to the 6,000,000 Jews killed by the Nazis. He then went to the Knesset, the Israeli Parliament. In a speech that was televised around the world, Sadat made a dramatic appeal for peace:

"Any life that is lost in war is a human life, be it that of an Arab or an Israeli. A wife who becomes a widow is a human being entitled to a happy family life, whether she be an Arab or an Israeli. Innocent children who are deprived of the care ... of their parents are ours ... be they living on Arab or Israeli land. They command our full responsibility to afford them a comfortable life today and tomorrow."

He accepted Israel's right to exist, saying, "We welcome you among us with full security and safety." But he also stated his support of the major Arab demands: that Israel has to recognize the rights of the Palestinians, the people who were displaced when Israel was founded in 1948; and that Israel must withdraw from the Arab lands it has occupied since the 1967 war.

Sadat's speech was followed with a speech by Begin, who praised Sadat's courage in visiting Israel, and said, "There are no eternal enemies. After every war comes the peace."

Private talks between the two leaders followed. Sadat and Begin conceded that important differences existed between their nations. But they pledged to seek a solution, and that there would be "no more war."

Events moved quickly. Within a week of his return to Egypt, Sadat invited the other Arab nations and Israel to Cairo. The United States, the Soviet Union, and the United Nations were also invited. The purpose: To discuss preparations for a Geneva conference. The Arab nations and the Soviet Union refused to go. Some of the Arabs were so hostile that Sadat broke diplomatic relations with them.

On December 25, Christmas Day, another historic event took place. Begin met with Sadat on Egyptian soil, the first time an Israeli leader had visited an Arab country officially.

And so the search for peace in the Middle East continues.

THE DEATH PENALTY: YES OR NO?

There is a common saying: "The punishment should fit the crime." But what punishment fits what crime?

Here is a list of possible crimes. What punishment do you think would be proper for each crime?

1) Stealing grapes
2) Practicing witchcraft
3) Hijacking an aircraft
4) Killing farm and household animals without permission
5) Cursing one's parents
6) Committing treason
7) Murdering a police officer

Now look over your list. How many different kinds of punishment did you choose? Believe it or not, all seven "crimes" have been subject—at one time or another in the United States—to the same punishment: death.

But opinions do change. As the years have passed the number of crimes for which the death penalty can be imposed has shrunk. In recent years it has been mainly limited to the crimes of murder, rape, airplane hijacking, and treason.

In 1967 a man was put to death in the Colorado gas chamber. His crime: murdering his wife and three of their seven children. In the following nine years, however, no executions took place in the United States.

The executions were halted by a series of important legal battles. Many people on death row (those sentenced to death) had appealed their cases to the courts. They argued that the death penalty was unconstitutional. In 1972 the United States Supreme Court agreed—but only in part.

In the 1972 ruling, the Supreme Court upset all death penalty laws then in effect in the United States. The Supreme Court said that the laws set no clear standards for a judge or jury to follow. One judge might give a convicted murderer a light sentence. Another judge might order the death penalty—in the very same circumstances. According to the Supreme Court, this was "cruel and unusual punishment." The Eighth Amendment to the U.S. Constitution specifically prohibits cruel and unusual punishments.

The Court did not say, however, that the death penalty itself was "cruel and unusual." But the rules for applying it, said the Court, were "cruel and unusual," and therefore unconstitutional.

Many states began to draw up new laws that would meet the standards set by the Supreme Court. And in July, 1976, the Court upheld the capital punishment laws of Florida, Texas, and Georgia.

When is the death penalty constitutional and when isn't it? The Court set down two guidelines:

1) It is constitutional—at least for the crime of murder—when there are clear rules to guide the judge or jury in deciding the sentence. The circumstances in which the crime took place should be considered. (For example, was the murder planned in advance, or was the murder committed on the spur of the moment in anger?) The character of the defendant must also be considered.
2) It is not constitutional to keep people who oppose the death penalty off juries.

With the 1976 Supreme Court ruling, 418 men and five women then on death row across the United States were suddenly in real danger of losing their lives.

One case made headlines. Gary Gilmore—convicted of murdering two men in Utah—pleaded with the courts to let him be executed. The courts postponed the date to reconsider his case—but finally set another date. And on January 17, 1977, Gilmore was executed by a firing squad. It was the first time a prisoner had been executed in the United States since 1967.

Many countries have abolished capital punishment—Venezuela, the Netherlands, Sweden, West Germany, and Britain, to name just a few. Most recently, in 1976, Canada abolished it except for military personnel convicted of traitorous acts. But in the United States the controversy continues. People are arguing as to whether or not the death penalty is really needed. Read the arguments—pro and con—and then decide for yourself.

PRO

CON

1) The death penalty is needed to help stop violent crime. Without a death penalty, criminals have little to fear. They know that if they get caught, the worst that can happen is that they will go to jail. And then there is almost always a chance for parole.

The death penalty, on the other hand, is final. It is the ultimate penalty. Where the death penalty exists for the crime of murder, people will think twice before killing someone. Lives will be saved.

One scientific study estimates that each execution may save seven or eight lives—the lives of people who might have been murdered if the death penalty did not exist.

2) The death penalty upholds the value of human life. It shows that society cares about innocent lives. There is something wrong with a society that won't defend its members.

Some people cry: "Save the murderer." What about his victim? We should be more concerned for the innocent than for the guilty. The way to show that concern is to make murderers pay with their lives.

3) Some crimes are too hideous to be punished with mere jail sentences. What about a man who stabs, strangles, and mutilates eight student nurses? Or a gang that invades a home and stabs to death a pregnant woman and her guests?

1) The death penalty doesn't stop violent crime at all. Scientific studies show it makes little difference in murder rates. Most murderers are not rational people. They don't stop to consider the possible penalty. They kill on a sudden impulse—during a fight in a bar, or in an argument at home, or when cornered by police.

Here's what a former prison warden says: "I have yet to meet the man who let the thought of the gas chamber stop him from committing murder."

2) The death penalty is cruel and unusual punishment. It should be banned under the Constitution. A man who steals bread is no longer punished by having his hand cut off. Society now recognizes such punishment as cruel. We must also recognize that putting people in gas chambers or electric chairs is barbarous.

3) The death penalty is imposed unfairly. Blacks and poor people are much more likely to be executed than whites and rich people—even if they are found guilty of similar crimes.

The U.S. Supreme Court has tried to set standards to guard against unfair sentences. But judges and juries will always have prejudices that no rules can wipe out.

The death penalty is an awesome thing. Once done, it cannot be undone. And mistakes do happen. People have been executed and later proved innocent.

INDIA AND SRI LANKA: CHANGES IN LEADERSHIP

At the beginning of 1977, women headed the governments of only two nations in the world. By coincidence the two were neighboring countries in southern Asia. Indira Gandhi was prime minister of India, the second most populous nation in the world. Sirimavo Bandaranaike was premier of the much smaller Republic of Sri Lanka, located on a teardrop-shaped island across the Palk Strait from India. By the end of the year, both women had been toppled from power in free elections held in their countries. But neither of these powerful leaders had lost her position because she was a woman.

▶ INDIRA GANDHI

In India the major campaign issue was whether the nation would continue to be a democracy. Until recently India had been the world's largest democracy. But India has always been one of the world's poorest nations, a country with deep problems and conflicts. Some people wondered whether a nation with such deep problems could afford to be a democracy. In a democracy, people are free to argue and disagree. Perhaps India would be stronger if there weren't so many arguments and disagreements.

When Mrs. Gandhi became prime minister of India in 1966, few people would have thought that she would ever be a threat to the nation's democratic system. She is the daughter of the late Jawaharlal Nehru, India's prime minister from the time of national independence in 1947 until his death in 1964. While other newly independent nations were turning into dictatorships, India under Jawaharlal Nehru remained firmly a democracy.

And during the first nine years in which Mrs. Gandhi headed the Indian government, the country continued to remain a democracy. By 1975, however, the nation's problems were deeper than ever. Industries were paralyzed by strikes. There were severe food shortages. Government corruption was widespread. An Indian court judged Mrs. Gandhi herself guilty of breaking election laws during a campaign. Before the nation's supreme court could hand down a decision on the issue, Mrs. Gandhi declared a state of emergency.

During the next year and a half, her rule in India was like a dictatorship. Freedom of the press was sharply curtailed, with newspapers free to print only news favorable to the government. Political opponents were jailed by the thousands.

Then in January, 1977, there came another sudden change. Mrs. Gandhi announced that

Indira Gandhi, the former prime minister of India.

Sirimavo Bandaranaike, the former premier of Sri Lanka.

free elections for India's legislature would be held in March. Political prisoners were released from jail so they could campaign in the election.

The campaign lasted six weeks. Mrs. Gandhi's opponents argued that India would become a dictatorship for good unless she were defeated. They attacked not only Mrs. Gandhi but her 30-year-old son, Sanjay, who was running for the legislature for the first time. Many people resented Sanjay. He had never been elected to office yet he had a lot of power. It was widely felt that Mrs. Gandhi showed him far too much favoritism.

Mrs. Gandhi denied that she would be a dictator. If she wanted to be a dictator, she asked, why had she allowed free elections? The emergency measures that she had put into effect had been for the good of the nation. As a result of the harsh measures, crime and corruption had been greatly reduced, she claimed.

When the ballots were finally counted, the results showed that the voters had turned against Mrs. Gandhi. She lost her own seat in the Indian legislature, and the Congress Party that she headed was soundly defeated. For the first time since India had become an independent nation, the Congress Party did not control the government. Morarji Desai, the 81-year-old leader of the Janata People's Party, succeeded Mrs. Gandhi as prime minister.

▶ SIRIMAVO BANDARANAIKE

Very similar events occurred several months later in neighboring Sri Lanka. Premier Sirimavo Bandaranaike was defeated, also after a long period of rule. In 1960, Mrs. Bandaranaike had become the first woman ever to be elected as head of a government. She ruled Sri Lanka at various times for twelve of the next seventeen years.

By 1977, Sri Lanka, like India, was in deep economic trouble. Many people were out of work, and the cost of living was rising rapidly. Like Mrs. Gandhi, Mrs. Bandaranaike had used emergency powers to repress free speech and censor the press. And she, too, had a young son, 28 years old, whom many people resented.

When the election was held in July, Mrs. Bandaranaike kept her seat in the legislature. But the party she headed was overwhelmingly defeated, winning only 8 seats out of a total of 168 seats in the legislature. Mrs. Bandaranaike lost the premiership, bringing to power 70-year-old Junius R. Jayewardene. "If the people of India can do it," Mr. Jayewardene had said during the campaign, "we can too."

CONTROLLING THE OCEAN

How vast the ocean seems when we stand on the beach and gaze out at the far horizon. Those shimmering, swirling waters—the world's seas—cover about three quarters of the earth's surface. The oceans seem a mighty kingdom that nobody can ever conquer or own. And yet in 1977 many coastal nations began reaching out to control large stretches of the ocean off their shores.

It was not the first time nations had tried to control the earth's waters. Such actions began in the late 1400's, when explorers were first learning the sizes and locations of the oceans. At this time Spain and Portugal, the chief seafaring and colonizing nations, divided the whole world—including its seas—between them.

As other nations gained power on the seas, they defied or ignored the claims of Spain and Portugal. Holland and England in particular wanted to trade and colonize freely the world over. So they got a legal scholar named Hugo Grotius to defend their rights. In the early 1600's Grotius pleaded their case for "complete freedom of the high seas for the innocent use and mutual benefit of all." His ideas were approved by most nations, and the principle of the freedom of the high seas was upheld for 300 years.

▶THE CONTINENTAL SHELVES

But in the mid 1900's some world conditions changed. Oil became an important fuel, and large deposits of it were found in parts of the ocean floor known as the "continental shelves." These deposits were often out beyond the 3-mile (4.8-kilometer) limit (the stretch of coastal waters then considered to be part of a nation's territory, or a "territorial sea").

The continental shelves are offshore regions around each continent where the ocean is relatively shallow. The shelves were once part of the nearby continent; but long ago, when the oceans rose, they were submerged. Most continental shelves stretch about 200 miles (320 kilometers) out from the shoreline before falling off sharply toward the deep seabed. The continental shelves are rich in minerals besides oil and often underlie rich fishing grounds.

In 1945, following World War II, the United States declared the minerals of the continental shelves off the United States to be under U.S. control. But it did not try to control fishing or to make the shelves a territorial sea. Other nations followed the United States in claiming rights to resources in the continental shelves.

Then, in the 1950's and 1960's, conditions changed again. Japan and the Soviet Union built giant fishing trawlers, with nets so huge that they could scoop up all the fish from vast sections of the ocean in a single night. These ships fished near the shores of North America, scraping the ocean bottom nearly clean and greatly reducing the number of fish caught by North American fishermen. And some species of fish were overfished so ruthlessly they almost disappeared.

In 1977, in the face of such dangers (both to the fishing industry and to the fish), the United States claimed control of its coastal waters for 200 miles (320 kilometers) out to sea. This new claim, which is known technically as an *exclusive economic zone,* far exceeds the old, traditional 3-mile (4.8-kilometer) limit. Although ordinary ship traffic is not interrupted, all fishing vessels must obtain licenses from the U.S. Coast Guard in order to fish.

The licenses regulate both the species and the amount of fish that can be taken by any foreign vessel. The Soviet Union tested the new U.S. law soon after it was put into effect. The U.S. Coast Guard seized the offending Soviet trawler (which was carrying more than the legal amount of a regulated species), and held it in Boston Harbor until the Soviet government agreed to pay a fine and to obey U.S. fishing laws in the future.

As soon as the United States claimed a larger economic zone, other nations followed suit. Canada, the European Community, Japan, and the Soviet Union all extended their control over 200 miles (320 kilometers) of coastal seas. Some nations, such as Iceland and Mexico, had already made such claims, and their actions now seemed justified.

▶MINING THE DEEP SEABED

Not all the minerals in the ocean floor are on the continental shelves. Far out in the middle of the oceans, in the deep seabed, is a

The Soviet Union tested the new U.S. fishing law. The result: A Soviet trawler, carrying an illegal catch, was seized and held in Boston Harbor for a few days.

special kind of mineral treasure. It is manganese, which occurs in potato-shaped nodules resting on the ocean floor. Copper, nickel, and cobalt are often found in these nodules along with the manganese. The supply is plentiful, and will be of great importance in the future. But right now, this mineral treasure is a subject of intense controversy.

The disagreement is about what rules should govern the mining and distribution of the deep-seabed minerals. At the United Nations the dispute has stalled the Law of the Sea Conference, which has been meeting yearly since 1973. The Conference had hoped to get a general agreement among nations on all issues affecting the oceans, including what offshore territorial limits should be. But because of the disagreement over deep-ocean mining, the Law of the Sea Conference has as yet reached no final agreements.

Mining the deep-ocean floor will cost about $300,000,000 when it is first undertaken. Only a few nations have the money to start the mining, and only the United States has both the money and the know-how. But the minerals are under a part of the ocean that does not belong to any one country, even with the new, larger coastal economic zones. Many nations believe that this part of the seabed is owned in common by all mankind. Therefore, they say, any profit reaped from a mining operation here should be distributed among all the world's nations. And this is the stumbling block—for so far, the nations who would finance the mining cannot promise that the companies carrying out the job would be willing to share the wealth.

Probably the principle of the 200-mile (320-kilometer) offshore economic zones will soon be recognized in international law, since most nations have already put it into practice. And when mutually acceptable rules for deep-sea mining are arrived at too, then a fair and just Law of the Sea should be close at hand.

THE PANAMA CANAL

The Panama Canal is one of the most important waterways in the world. The United States has controlled the Panama Canal Zone and the operating of the canal since the original treaty was signed with Panama in 1903. But for many years, the canal has been an issue of great controversy to both Panamanians and Americans.

In 1977 two new treaties were signed by U.S. President Jimmy Carter and Panamanian leader General Omar Torrijos. Under the terms of the treaties, Panama will run the canal and have complete control of the Canal Zone by the year 2000.

▶ THE ORIGINAL TREATY

Until the Panama Canal was built, a ship traveling between the Atlantic and Pacific oceans had to make a long, costly, and dangerous voyage around the southern tip of South America. In 1903 the United States and the newly independent country of Panama signed a treaty allowing the United States to build a canal across Panama connecting the two great oceans. Under that treaty, the United States got complete control of the Canal Zone "in perpetuity," that is, forever. In return, the United States agreed to pay Panama a certain amount of money each year. (Since the canal was officially opened in 1914, the United States has paid Panama a total of about $70,000,000.)

The Panama Canal Zone is the canal itself and the lands on either side of it. The canal is about 50 miles (80 kilometers) long, and the Canal Zone is some 10 miles (16 kilometers) wide. The zone cuts across the center of Panama. In the zone live about 35,000 Americans —canal employees, military personnel, and their families.

Many Panamanians, however, have been unhappy about the American presence in their country. In 1964 angry confrontations broke out between Panamanians and Americans in the Canal Zone. Rioting followed, in which both Americans and Panamanians were killed. Because peace and stability are necessary for the successful operation of the canal, the United States and Panama began a long, slow process to negotiate new treaties.

In August, 1977, the two countries finally reached agreement. It was hoped that the new treaties would put an end to Panamanian resentment.

▶ THE NEW TREATIES

These are some of the important terms of the new treaties:
• The operation and control of the waterway will gradually change from American to Panamanian hands. In the year 2000, Panama will have full control of the canal.
• American citizens working for the canal will not lose their jobs.
• Panama will receive much higher yearly payments than it has in the past, most of the money coming from tolls collected from ships passing through the canal.
• The United States will give Panama loans for economic development and military assistance if necessary.
• The two countries will be responsible for defending the canal in case of war. Before the new treaties, the defense of the canal had been the responsibility of the United States alone.
• The canal will be open to ships of all nations. In case of international hostilities, the canal will remain neutral, unless the canal itself is attacked.

▶ THE PRESENT SITUATION

After the negotiators for both countries agreed on the terms of the treaties, President Carter and General Torrijos presented the treaties to the people of their countries.

On October 23, the people of Panama voted by a margin of two to one to accept the treaties. General Torrijos saw this vote as a great victory for his government. He had been receiving criticism from some Panamanian citizens who feared that the treaties give the United States too much right to interfere in their military affairs.

In the United States, President Carter also faced opposition. In order for a treaty to be ratified, it must be approved by a two-thirds vote of the Senate. That means that at least 67 of the 100 U.S. senators would have to vote "yes" on the new treaties. But by the end of 1977, the vote in the Senate had still not taken place, and President Carter was unsure whether or not he could line up 67 senators on his side.

By the year 2000, total control of the Panama Canal will have passed from the United States to Panama.

The opponents believe that the treaties are a giveaway of U.S. property. These Americans fear that the United States will lose prestige in the world by giving up control of the canal. Also, many Americans do not trust General Torrijos. They believe he is a dictator who has little regard for human rights. To sign treaties with him, they say, would be to give support to an anti-democratic regime.

In order to win ratification in the Senate, President Carter's administration has tried to answer these arguments.

First, administration spokespersons say, the Canal Zone is not U.S. property. The United States merely controls it. The original treaty of 1903 makes that clear.

Next, U.S. prestige would increase, not decrease, if the treaties are approved. The United States would be showing the nations of the world that it could act with fairness in its dealings with small nations. Besides, 200 years ago America fought to remove a foreign power from its land. How can the United States now object to Panama's desire to do the same thing?

On November 12, General Torrijos promised to halt all human-rights violations in Panama. He even said that he would resign, if necessary, in order to get the U.S. Senate to ratify the treaties. "The interests of the country [Panama] are ahead of the interests of General Torrijos," he said.

Some U.S. senators were impressed with his statements. But the question of whether or not the Senate is impressed enough to ratify the treaties will have to wait until 1978 for an answer.

THE ANIMAL WORLD

There are many unusual creatures in the world of animals. This is a blue-legged strawberry frog.

THE MYSTERY OF THE MONARCHS

For almost forty years, Fred Urquhart tried to solve a mystery. He wasn't alone. Thousands of people helped him track his subject. Reports from the field poured in—the subject was seen in Florida, in Tennessee, in Texas.

Fred Urquhart is a professor of zoology at Scarborough College in Toronto, Canada. His subject is the monarch butterfly.

The delicate black and orange monarch is a common summer sight where Urquhart lives. It is familiar to most people who live in Canada and the northern United States. Go into a garden or a field and you are almost certain to see a monarch or two enjoying the flowers and the warm sun.

Monarch butterflies gather in dense, hanging clusters on the branches of trees.

But as the night grows longer and cooler, and autumn comes, the monarchs leave their summer homes. Like many birds and other animals, but unlike most butterflies, they migrate to a warmer place for the winter.

Those that summer in western parts of Canada and the United States fly to central and southern California. There, they gather in dense, hanging clusters on the branches of pine, oak, cypress, and eucalyptus trees.

And those that summer in the eastern parts —well, no one could discover where they went. Urquhart worked hard to solve this mystery. But the trail always seemed to disappear in Texas, on the Mexican border.

Urquhart's wife wrote to Mexican newspapers, asking people to write if they saw monarchs. This eventually led to a phone call in January, 1975, from a resident of Mexico City, who believed the colony of monarchs had been found.

Urquhart and his wife journeyed to the Sierra Madre mountains in south central Mexico. And there, on a remote mountainside, they saw millions and millions of monarch butterflies hanging from the trees.

"I gazed in amazement at the sight," wrote Urquhart. "They clung in tightly packed masses to every branch and trunk.... They swirled through the air like autumn leaves and carpeted the ground.... Unbelievable! What a glorious, incredible sight!"

Scientists would like to keep the location of the Mexican mountainside a secret. They don't want it turned into a tourist attraction. They also want to prevent local farmers from collecting the butterflies, which are a rich source of protein, to use as cattle food.

And so, a mystery has been solved. But another, perhaps more interesting mystery remains unsolved. How do the monarchs know where to go? Monarch butterflies live less than a year. Those that flew south last fall will die this spring or summer. A new generation of monarchs, hatched from eggs laid this year, will head south in the fall. How do these monarchs—who have never before flown south—know where to go? How do they know about that remote mountainside in Mexico, some 3,000 miles (5,000 kilometers) away?

IT'S A DOG'S LIFE

It's a dog's life. And what a life it is! From a Connecticut dog pound, Sandy went to instant fame as one of the major characters in the hit Broadway musical *Annie*. Annie is Little Orphan Annie, and Sandy is her faithful dog.

Ah, but life for the lovable pooch wasn't always bright lights, expensive dog biscuits, and applause. There were tough times too. No one knows where life began for Sandy. And no one knows his parentage, although there are hints of Irish wolfhound and Airedale in his background. But, whatever his parentage, Sandy turned into a shaggy, sad-eyed, huggable mutt. His days must have been lonely after he left whatever home he had. His travels finally took him to the Connecticut Humane Society pound in Newington. This was probably not Sandy's idea of the perfect home.

But one day fate stepped into the picture. A young man walked into the Connecticut pound looking for the perfect pooch to play the role of Sandy in a new musical called *Annie*. The man noticed a scruffy dog with big sad eyes sitting nervously in the back of the cage at the pound.

The sad eyes did the trick. The perfect dog had been found—and not a moment too soon. The mongrel would have been put to sleep the very next day.

And the rest of the story is show biz history. The dog was given the name Sandy and taught his onstage role. There were a few "arfs" to be memorized, plus some tricks like rolling over and playing dead, and stalking across an empty stage. Sandy learned his part in no time at all. He went on to charm audiences in Connecticut and Washington, D.C., where *Annie* had its pre-Broadway tryouts.

In Washington, Sandy really hit the big time. He—along with the rest of the cast—was invited to the White House. Sandy rose to the grand occasion and, with his best paw forward, shook hands with President Carter.

What could possibly equal that honor for a former homeless mongrel? Only Broadway, and that was the next stop. *Annie* opened in April, 1977, to rave reviews, which means that Sandy will be dining on choice bits of meat and tasty dog biscuits for quite some time.

ANIMALS IN THE NEWS

It seems as if everybody is playing Frisbee—even dogs! This is Ashley Whippet, who set a world record by dashing 106 yards (97 meters) to catch a flying Frisbee with his teeth.

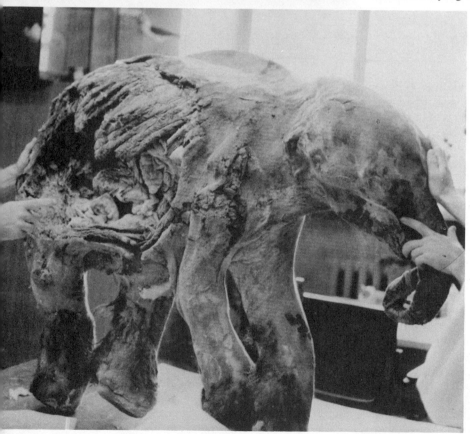

Mammoths are prehistoric relatives of the elephant. In 1977 the frozen remains of a baby mammoth were found at an excavation site in northeastern Siberia. Scientists believe that it died about 10,000 years ago. After it has been examined and studied, the mammoth will be stuffed and put on display in a museum in the Soviet Union.

A puffin is a little seabird that looks something like a penguin. It has sad eyes and a large red, brown, and yellow beak. Puffins were once a common sight on the islands off Maine. But in the early 1900's they moved on to a new home in Newfoundland and were not seen again in Maine for more than 70 years. A few years ago an experiment was begun to get the puffin back to Maine—and it seems to have worked. In the summer of 1977 there were twenty reported sightings of them off the coast of Maine— happy news for bird lovers.

To win the Triple Crown of horse racing, a horse must win the Kentucky Derby, the Preakness, and the Belmont Stakes—all in the same year. Only ten horses have ever done it. This is Seattle Slew, who did it in 1977. Seattle Slew also set a record—he won the Triple Crown without having lost any race prior to winning the "Big Three."

In 1977, Dersade Bobby's Girl became the new reigning queen of dogdom: the Sealyham terrier was chosen best in show at the Westminster Kennel Club show—the most important dog event in the United States.

YOUR OWN VIVARIUM

A vivarium is any container in which an animal is kept, and which provides conditions that are similar to the animal's natural environment. A vivarium can be as simple as a cheesecloth-covered jar containing a lettuce leaf, which will maintain enough moisture for a pet snail. Or it can be as complicated as a glass tank that maintains a desert environment, complete with artificial sun, for a desert lizard.

▶ FIND OUT YOUR ANIMAL'S NEEDS

An animal's "environment" is not necessarily the same as the climate in which the animal naturally lives. In planning a vivarium in which an animal can stay healthy, you have to learn about the animal's immediate environment and how it uses that environment.

For example, a particular lizard may come from an area where the temperature climbs to 120° F (49° C) at noon and drops to 60° F (16° C) at night. But the lizard seeks shade and burrows under a rock to keep cool in the highest temperatures, and then uses the stored heat of the same burrow to keep warm at the coolest temperatures. The actual temperature range within which the lizard can eat and digest may only be from 90° F to 110° F (32° C to 43° C). This same lizard spends hours basking in the sun. Without the ultraviolet rays in sunlight, these animals cannot produce the vitamin D they need to stay alive. Thus a vivarium for such a desert animal should include a source of heat; sand and rocks for shade; and an artificial source of ultraviolet light.

You must also consider the animal's drinking habits when planning your vivarium. Some lizards will drink only from droplets of water sprayed onto the tank walls or onto the leaves of a plant in the tank. A tortoise leans down and sucks up water, so it requires a dish that is sunk into the sand—large enough to dip its snout into, but small enough so it can't fall in. There are lizards that don't drink at all. Most of their water comes from the food they eat. But they also absorb water through their skins, and in captivity they may need a shallow dish to soak in.

Before you build your vivarium, you should find out all the needs of the animal that you plan to keep in it. You'll have to do some careful research at the library, and perhaps write to a zoo as well.

▶ BUILDING YOUR VIVARIUM

• The basic container for most vivariums is a glass tank, and it's usually best to buy a new one. The size of the tank will depend on how big and how active the animal is. Usually a 10-gallon (38-liter) tank is the smallest practical vivarium. Even an 18-inch (46-centimeter) baby boa or common iguana would need an 18-gallon (68-liter) "tall" tank.

• You will need a top on your vivarium for every animal except a turtle, which cannot climb well.

Use a screen top if you want to provide good air circulation. Screen tops are available at pet stores, or you can make your own by using ½-inch (1.3-centimeter) mesh hardware cloth, which is sold in hardware stores.

To keep the humidity very high for such animals as salamanders and tree frogs, use either a glass top cut to size by a glazier or a pre-cut one from a pet store.

• A vivarium may or may not need a source of heat, depending on the animal you are housing. But there are some things you should never do. Never put the tank in sunlight. The glass walls act like a greenhouse, and the rapid climb in temperature can quickly kill many pets. Also avoid rooms where there are sudden temperature changes.

Tape a thermometer inside the tank, halfway up one wall, to check the temperature variations at different times of the day. If the temperature drops below the level your pet requires, you will have to provide artificial heat. One way to supply extra heat is with an incandescent (heat-producing) light bulb. The fixture, which is sold in pet stores, rests on top of the tank or the tank lid. A clear, tube-shaped incandescent bulb screws into one end of the fixture. To control the temperature inside your vivarium, check the thermometer frequently and turn the light on and off as needed.

Some animals will need heat on all the time in cool weather; others can tolerate and may even need the coolness and darkness of night. Some desert pets need a period of "pre-heating" before they become active enough to eat.

• Ultraviolet light is just as important as heat to many animals. You can provide ultraviolet light only with a fluorescent tube called a Vita-

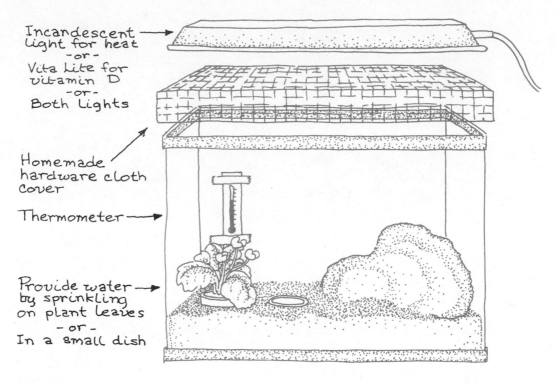

Incandescent
Light for heat
-or-
Vita Lite for
vitamin D
-or-
Both Lights

Homemade
hardware cloth
cover

Thermometer

Provide water
by sprinkling
on plant leaves
-or-
In a small dish

Set-up for hot, dry desert environment

Lite, specially developed for basking reptiles. Ordinary fluorescent lights do not provide the correct ultraviolet light for producing vitamin D. Pet stores sell an aquarium fixture that looks like the incandescent one but can hold the Vita-Lite fluorescent tube.

Fluorescent light can't be depended upon to provide much warmth. It will usually have to be used along with an incandescent fixture. Keep the Vita-Lite on for about eight hours a day.

▶ KINDS OF VIVARIUMS

• A desert vivarium provides a hot, dry environment. Sand, which is used for the floor, makes an excellent burrowing place for animals that like dryness. Animals that would do well in a desert vivarium include land tortoises and lizards. Use cacti and succulents in a vivarium for lizards. However, don't use plants with tortoises; they knock plants over.

• A woodland environment is necessary for a moisture-loving animal. The floor of this vivarium is built up in layers. Start with 2 inches (5 centimeters) of bone carbon charcoal, avail-

able in pet stores. This special product helps prevent decay and keeps the vivarium from getting smelly. Cover the charcoal with a thin layer of well-rinsed pebbles. Put about 3 inches (7.5 centimeters) of soil on top of the pebbles.

Collect small woodland plants such as ferns, partridge berry, or ground pine for your vivarium. Use soil from the same area. Dig the plants up carefully so that plenty of soil clings to their roots. Keep them in plastic bags until you are ready to plant. If you are buying plants—for example, baby's tears or African violets—use packaged soil.

When planting, set plants in the soil as deep as their root systems will go. Water liberally right away. The surface of the soil can be covered with moss, bark, and rocks.

If the vivarium is covered with glass to maintain the highest humidity, spray once a week with a plant mister. If the vivarium is covered with screening to increase the air circulation, water more often.

Animals that would do well in a woodland vivarium include small salamanders, tree frogs, and land snails. But a woodland vivar-

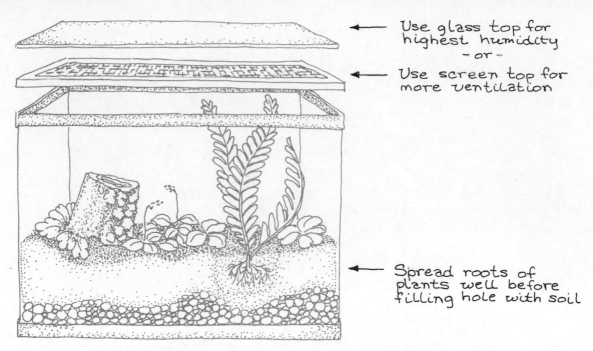

Use glass top for
highest humidity
– or –

Use screen top for
more ventilation

Spread roots of
plants well before
filling hole with soil

Set-up for a moist woodland environment

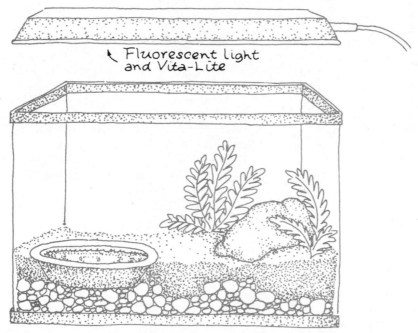

Fluorescent light
and Vita-Lite

Sunken dish semi-aquatic vivarium
can be planted in any way you wish.

Use a shallow dish with sloping
sides. Lift it out to clean it.

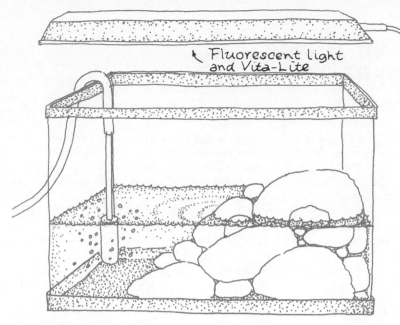

Sloped incline semi-aquatic vivarium is made by building a gradual hill of smooth stones, or by leaning a log or piece of bark against one end of the tank.

ium is very hard to clean and should be used only for small animals that do not need cleaning up after.

• To make a semi-aquatic vivarium for animals who bathe or eat underwater, you have to be sure that the tank does not leak. Here are two types of semi-aquatic vivariums.

One type uses a dish of water sunken into the soil of a woodland-type vivarium to form a pool. The sunken dish must be shallow or have sloping sides so the animal—usually a salamander, small frog, or very small water turtle —can climb in and out. The dish can be removed for daily cleaning.

The other semi-aquatic vivarium has much more water, and would be suitable for a water turtle or a water snake. This vivarium is made by using smooth stones to build a gradual "hill" at one end of the tank. The stones should slope gently into the water so the animal can climb in and out easily. You can also use a large piece of thick bark as the slope. The slope must be high enough above the water so that your pet can thoroughly dry off from time to time. This is especially important for reptiles, which are likely to get fungus infections if they can't dry themselves off completely.

The water in a deep-water vivarium must be

kept fresh. This can be done with an aerator. An aerator is an inexpensive machine that bubbles oxygen through the water, slowing the decay of food particles that would otherwise foul the tank in a matter of days. Even with the aerator, you have to change the water at least every two weeks and clean the tank walls with a plastic scrubbing pad.

▶ SPECIAL NEEDS

As you learn about the animal you are building your vivarium for, take note of any of its habits that may require special luxuries. Land hermit crabs, for instance, do a lot of climbing and should have rough bark or coarse screening to clamber upon. Snakes may lie along branches to bask under their bulbs. They may also appreciate a box or other hiding place in which they can escape the heat or simply feel protected. And all snakes need large water dishes in which they can comfortably soak before they shed their skins. Such small details of a well-planned vivarium may make the difference between a depressed, weakened, and boring pet and an active, interesting, and healthy one.

SARA BONNETT STEIN
Author, *Great Pets!*

AND THEN THERE WERE SOME

The snail darter is a fish belonging to the perch family. It is only about 3 inches (8 centimeters) long. But in 1977 this tiny fish stopped the construction of a big dam in Tennessee.

The snail darter did not stop the construction of the dam by itself. It had plenty of help from conservationists, people who try to protect wildlife. They said that building the dam would endanger the existence of the snail darter. They claimed that this was against a U.S. law, the Endangered Species Act, passed by Congress in 1973.

The snail darter lives in the lower few miles of the Little Tennessee River. The water there is shallow and cool, and there are plenty of snails to eat. As far as is known, all the snail darters in the world live in those few miles of the Little Tennessee River. If the dam were completed, the water would get very deep, and the snail darter could not survive.

But more than $100,000,000 had already been spent on the dam. Wasn't it foolish to stop work on a dam for a little fish that most people had never even heard of? The judge who ruled on this case did not think so. He ordered construction of the dam halted. But many darters had already died, and the dam was preventing others from getting upstream to spawn. Scientists are now trying to move the few hundred remaining fish upstream.

The snail darter is just one of many kinds of animals that are endangered. This means that they are in danger of becoming extinct, or dying out. In the 1970's people have become very concerned about endangered wildlife.

▶ HOW WILDLIFE BECOMES ENDANGERED

Endangered wildlife is found on every continent. It includes species of such familiar animals as tigers, leopards, monkeys and apes, rhinoceroses, bears, and whales. About 275 species of mammals, 345 of birds, 186 of reptiles and amphibians, plus many other forms of animal life are in danger of extinction.

Actually, it is nothing new for animal species to become extinct. Most species that have lived on earth are now extinct. This is not surprising, considering that animal life has been on earth for hundreds of millions of years. (You have read about dinosaurs and other great reptiles that disappeared from the earth millions of years ago.) But if it is normal for animal species to become extinct, why are conservationists so worried about it today?

They are worried because the extinction of wildlife is now going on at a greatly increasing rate. In the 1600's and 1700's, one animal species became extinct every 15 or 20 years. But in the 1900's, one species has become extinct every year.

The basic cause of this growing threat to wildlife is the spread of human settlement into every corner of the earth. As the human population grows and grows, the face of the earth changes rapidly. Wilderness gives way to towns and cities; jungles and forests are cleared for agriculture and cut for timber. Most animals cannot adjust to the new conditions and are forced into smaller and smaller areas. Animals that get in the way of human progress are killed. And environmental pollution caused by man kills many animals too. Water pollution has killed many fish and birds; the use of chemicals to kill crop-eating insects has interfered with the breeding of some species of birds.

Other animals are killed because they provide a product that can be sold. Many cheetahs, leopards, and other cats have been killed for their furs. And many species of whales—including the largest creature ever to have lived on earth, the blue whale—have been slaughtered almost to the point of extinction by whalers for the oil and other products.

▶ STOPPING THE KILLING

Many governments have passed laws that prohibit the killing of endangered animals. Endangered wildlife acts were passed by the United States and Canadian governments in 1973. And in 1977 the East African nation of Kenya, famous for its abundance of game, banned all hunting within its borders.

Nations have also co-operated to stop the killing of endangered wildlife. About 25 nations, including the United States, have agreed to stop importing products made from endangered animals—for example, furs of cheetahs or leopards. And whaling nations are working on agreements that would more strictly limit the killing of whales.

Bengal tiger.

PROVIDING A HOME FOR WILDLIFE

Besides stopping the killing, nations are trying to provide environments in which endangered wildlife can survive. One way to do this is to pass laws against pollution—these benefit both people and animals.

Governments have also set aside large wilderness areas where wildlife can live without being harmed by people. These areas are called animal reserves. In recent years, the number of animal reserves in the world has grown rapidly. There are now more than 1,300.

Still, some species have been reduced to such small numbers that it is uncertain whether they would survive even in an animal reserve. So other ways are being tried to save these endangered species. One way is to establish a mini-reserve of only a few thousand acres where a particular species or several species can flourish. A mini-reserve gives animals more freedom than they would have in a zoo. It also enables conservationists to protect the animals from enemies, furnish them with water during a drought, and look after them in

other ways. One new mini-reserve is the Hai Bar Reserve in Israel. There, conservationists are trying to build up herds of animals that lived in Israel in biblical times.

Zoos help too. Animals that are becoming extinct in the wild may be able to survive and breed in zoos. Still another way to save endangered species is to relocate them, as was done with the snail darter.

So, for at least some endangered animals, the outlook is much brighter than it was only a few years ago.

BENGAL TIGER

Anyone who has ever read the adventures of Mowgli in Rudyard Kipling's *Jungle Books* remembers Mowgli's death battle with the tiger. If the *Jungle Books* were written today instead of having been written in the 1890's, Mowgli might have a hard time finding a tiger to fight. In the days of the *Jungle Books,* there were about 40,000 tigers in India. By the early 1970's the number had been reduced to about 2,000, as more and more of the tiger's jungle home became populated by people.

Recently this decline has been reversed. The Indian government began Project Tiger in 1973, and since then nine tiger reserves have been established. Not only is the tiger population on the increase, but still more land is being returned to its natural jungle state.

▶ VICUÑA

The vicuña is a member of the camel family. It is smaller than another South American member of the family, the llama. Unlike the llama, the vicuña has never been domesticated. It has freely roamed the Andes since prehistoric times. From the days of the Incas, the vicuña has been prized for its extremely fine fleece. Among the Incas, vicuña garments were worn only by royalty.

The Incas hunted the vicuña by forming huge circles, closing in on the herd, then capturing them. After the vicuñas were sheared, they were set free. Modern hunters, however, have simply killed the vicuña. Helicopters, jeeps, high-powered rifles, and even machine guns have been used in killing them for the fleece. As a result, the vicuña population fell from 1,000,000 in 1900 to 5,000 in 1970.

Conservationists and government officials have been working to save the vicuña. Peru set up a reserve for the animals, and this herd has grown from about 650 in 1965 to more than 20,000 today. In addition, the United States and other countries have banned the importing of vicuña skins. And Peru, Bolivia, Argentina, and Chile prohibit killing vicuñas or selling the skins.

The number of vicuñas in South America has risen to about 40,000. It is possible to save many more if people try to make coats from the vicuña's fine fleece without killing this little animal.

▶ WOOD BISON

The wood bison is larger, darker, and woollier than the bison of the plains. Tens of thousands of wood bison once ranged through the forests of western Canada. In the late 19th century its numbers were greatly reduced by hunters and by settlement. More recently its numbers have dwindled because of disease, and mixed breeding with the plains bison. Only some 300 wood bison remain. Most of them are in the Mackenzie Bison Range in Canada's Northwest Territories.

The Canadian Government has begun to reestablish wood bison in British Columbia, Alberta, Manitoba, Saskatchewan, and the Northwest Territories. The outcome of the project is not yet certain, but it is believed that the wood bison has a bright future.

▶ WHOOPING CRANE

At one time this large bird with its great trumpeting hoot ranged across America's marshes and prairies. But as people settled on this land, the whooping crane lost most of its nesting areas. Finally, only one small flock was left in the wild. With only one wild flock in existence, a single catastrophe, such as a hurricane, could wipe out all the wild whooping cranes.

In 1975 conservationists began trying to

Vicuñas.

Wood bison.

65

Whooping crane.

Southern bald eagle.

start a second flock of whoopers. Eggs were removed from whooping crane nests and placed in the nests of its numerous cousin, the sandhill crane. The experiment has worked. A number of whoopers have been raised by sandhills, and have started a new flock of their own.

Today there are about 125 whooping cranes in the wild and in captivity. There were only about 40 whoopers thirty-five years ago. The outlook is now so favorable that the U.S. Fish and Wildlife Service declared 1977 to be a "spectacular year" for the whooping crane.

▶**SOUTHERN BALD EAGLE**

In 1782 the U.S. Continental Congress chose the southern bald eagle as the national bird. At that time, this great eagle was a common sight throughout the nation. In the years since then, the southern bald eagle has been crowded out of most of its nesting areas. Recently, too, it fell victim to a new enemy called DDT. This chemical was widely used to kill crop-eating insects. As DDT spread through the environment, it found its way into the bodies of many animals and humans, often with harmful effects. DDT caused the eggs of some birds, including the southern bald eagle, to become thin-shelled. The eggs broke before the chicks could hatch.

Then, about five years age, the use of DDT was banned in the United States. Today most eagle eggs no longer break before the eaglet hatches. Moreover, thousands of acres of land have been set aside as eagle preserves, so that these birds will have places where they can lay their eggs. As a result, the number of southern bald eagles is rapidly on the rise.

▶**AMERICAN ALLIGATOR**

Alligators were once very common in swampy areas of the southern United States. But hunters have killed large numbers of alligators. Alligator skins bring high prices because they make handsome wallets, belts, shoes, and handbags.

Also, many swamps have been drained to make way for homes or factories. Alligators had fewer and fewer swamps in which to live, so their numbers greatly declined. Unless something were done soon, there would be no American alligators except in zoos.

In 1967 a federal law was passed, prohibiting the killing of alligators. And conserva-

American alligator.

Eastern timber wolf.

tionists worked hard to limit the draining of wetlands. As a result, the number of alligators has increased from 50,000 to about 650,000. In fact, they are so numerous in some places that the federal government now lets each state decide whether to permit the hunting of alligators.

▶EASTERN TIMBER WOLF

The eastern timber wolf once inhabited most of the United States east of the Mississippi River. With the spread of settlements, wolves were hunted out of more and more areas. In 1973 there were only about 1,000 of these wolves. Almost all were in wilderness areas of Minnesota.

To help protect the wolf, the U.S. Government set up the Eastern Timber Wolf Recovery Team. Now there are more wolves than there have been for decades. In fact, the Recovery Team has recommended that some killing of wolves be permitted.

Most of the Eastern Timber Wolves still live in Minnesota. The Team wants to re-introduce this wolf into wilderness areas in other states. It is trying to convince people that wolves are no threat to man. Experts claim that there is no known instance in North America of a wolf in the wild attacking a human.

BENJAMIN HAIMOWITZ
Science Writer

THE RIVERBANKS BIRDHOUSE

A brightly colored turaco flies through the rain forest. She reaches her nest and begins to feed her young. Suddenly a boom of thunder shatters the quiet. Rain begins to pour down. And then you see a most unusual sight: As the rain wets the turaco, the red color washes out of her feathers—just as the color might wash out of a red T-shirt.

Turacos, which are about the size of pigeons, live in Africa. But you don't have to go that far to see the beautiful turaco, and maybe even witness this extraordinary phenomenon. Just head for the birdhouse at the Riverbanks Zoological Park in Columbia, South Carolina.

This zoo, which opened in 1974, has some of the most interesting bird exhibits to be found anywhere in the world. Instead of being kept in small cages, many of the birds live in large communal areas that are like their native habitats. These areas, which are set up as exhibits, are called ecosystems.

An ecosystem exhibit lets you see how a bird really lives. You can see how the bird runs or flies. You can watch it catch an insect or pick a ripe berry. You can see what kind of weather it is exposed to. For example, the rain-forest exhibit at Riverbanks has a storm twice a day —storms are common occurrences in a "real" rain forest. Water falls from sprinklers in the ceiling. A tape recorder provides the sounds of thunder, and strobe lights produce flashes of lightning.

Because the birds feel at home, they behave more naturally than they would in small, empty cages. You can tell just how "at home" they feel by the rate at which they reproduce. At Riverbanks, more than 40 percent of the birds have hatched young—an exceptionally high percentage for zoo birds.

Reproduction is very important to zoos. Not too long ago, many people believed there would always be lots of birds to be captured in the wild. If a zoo's only turaco died, it was not too difficult to buy another turaco. Now, however, many birds are scarce and are considered to be endangered species. Zoos, therefore, are trying to keep their birds happy. Happy birds live longer —and produce more young.

KINDS OF ECOSYSTEMS

There are nine bird ecosystems at Riverbanks. Here is a description of them, and some of the birds and other animals in each one.

The *Rain Forest* is a tropical environment, with palm trees and other green, abundantly growing plants. In addition to Schalow's turacos, there are Nicobar pigeons and bare-throated bellbirds.

The *Desert* is a dry, sandy place. The birds include tinamous and roadrunners.

The *Plains* are grasslands. Here you'll see glossy starlings and red-crested cardinals.

The *Swamp* is a wet place. There are lots of plants. Spanish moss hangs from the trees. Here are black rails, ringed teal, and aquatic turtles.

The *Seashore* has a narrow beach in front of steep, rugged cliffs. Here are guanay cormorants, killdeer, and black-headed gulls.

The *Canyon* is a dry, rocky place. The only birds you'll see are a pair of king vultures.

The *Canopy* is the world of the treetops. Here are two-toed sloths, Pekin robins, and black-necked aracaris.

The *Arctic Tundra* is a cold, barren place. The only birds are a pair of snow owls.

The *Antarctic* is a land of ice. The Riverbanks ecosystem consists of an "ice shelf" made of fiberglass. There is also a deep pool. The birds you'll see here are penguins. And a sound system allows you to hear the penguins as they sit on their nests, waddle across the ice, and swim in the water.

A WALL OF DARKNESS

Except for the penguin ecosystem, there are no glass walls, fences, or other barriers between you and the ecosystem exhibits at Riverbanks. But you needn't worry that a vulture will fly over and sit on your shoulder. You will be standing in a dark corridor, and the bird exhibits are lighted. Birds will generally not fly from a well-lit, natural environment to a dark area such as a corridor filled with people.

And if you were lucky enough to have seen the turaco lose its color, you do not have to worry about that either. Once a year turacos molt, losing their old washed-out feathers and growing new, bright red ones.

ROBERT E. SEIBELS
Curator of Birds
Riverbanks Zoological Park

The Rain Forest ecosystem.

The Desert ecosystem.

There are few walls or other barriers separating the ecosystems from the visitors. But there is a "wall of darkness": the birds will not fly from their well-lit environments into the dark corridors of Riverbanks.

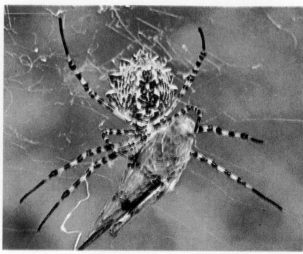

It may seem cruel for a spider to kill its prey, but it's an important part of nature.

Predators are found everywhere in the world. Here the bear is the predator, and the fish is its prey.

Many predators, like the wolf, must kill other animals to get food to feed their young.

PREDATORS ARE IMPORTANT TOO

The mother lion crept silently through the tall grass of the African plain. She was hungry, and ahead of her she saw what might be her next meal. Slowly she sneaked nearer as her prey, a lone gazelle, continued feeding intently on a tender young plant. Suddenly the mother lion took three big running leaps and landed on the surprised gazelle before it had time to flee more than a few steps. With one big, powerful bite she crushed its neck, killing it quickly. The mother lion now had food for herself and her cubs.

The lion is called a predator because it kills other animals for food. The animals that are eaten are called prey. Predation is the act of catching prey. It may seem cruel, but it is a necessary part of nature and has existed almost since the beginning of life on earth. Predation affects all kinds of life, from the one-celled animals to the insects, worms, fishes, reptiles, birds, and mammals.

Predators are important everywhere around the world. In Alaska the polar bear preys on seals, and the black bear preys on salmon. In Yellowstone National Park, grizzly bears sometimes prey on elk. Mountain lions prey on deer. Coyotes and wildcats prey on small mammals.

"Why," you ask, "is nature so cruel? Why should predators be allowed to live?"

It is easy for us to be shocked when we see one mammal kill another, but few of us think twice when a bird eats a worm. The wolf kills a moose, and everyone thinks, "Oh, the poor moose!" But does anyone think about the poor wolf if it doesn't get anything to eat?

Most of the animals in nature are plant eaters (herbivores). Fewer animals are meat eaters (carnivores). Both kinds of animals have been adapting slowly over millions of years. In nature, as we see it today, both kinds are in balance with each other and with their environment. The less-fit species become extinct. Those species that adapt to the conditions around them are able to survive. Some of the conditions to which species must adapt are climate, food supply, water supply, living space, and predation.

Predators help to keep animal populations healthy and fit by removing the sick, slow, or careless individuals. In the national parks of Africa, predators are protected because their importance is recognized. Lions, hyenas, leopards, cheetahs, wild dogs, and jackals are known to kill the sick, slow, or careless animals.

You may wonder why predators don't catch and kill every single prey animal for food. The answer is that a predator simply can't catch just any animal. A spotted hyena, for example, may chase a wildebeest for a hundred yards or so to "test" it. If the wildebeest successfully runs away, the hyena abandons the chase. But if the wildebeest is slow and the hyena finds it can easily chase the wildebeest, the hyena continues after it. It is by testing their prey in this way that the predators are able to pick out the weak and less fit. The most alert and most healthy animals escape.

Predators help to limit the numbers of some animals. This is important because if there are too many plant-eating animals in one area, they may eat all the food, and then later starve to death. In the United States, where many wolves have been killed, deer sometimes become so abundant that they starve to death by the thousands during the snowy winter when their food is scarce. And where coyotes have been eliminated, rabbits and rodents often become a problem.

Many predators are also scavengers (cleaner-uppers). Once a predator has caught its prey, it must be alert that other meat eaters don't try to take the prey away. The Arctic fox steals scraps of food from the polar bear. Lions sometimes steal food killed by wild dogs or cheetahs. Jackals steal food from lions and hyenas. Vultures try to steal food from all the predators. Leopards try to avoid this competition by carrying their food high into the treetops. But all these meat eaters do a good service by cleaning up every last bit of the animals that are killed or that die from sickness or old age. In nature nothing is wasted.

The next time you see a spider kill a fly or a cat kill a bird, you will understand that you are watching an important part of life. Before you think bad things about the predator, or feel sorry for the prey, remember that all animals need to eat. Wild animals normally do not kill for fun, nor do they waste food. Predation is part of nature.

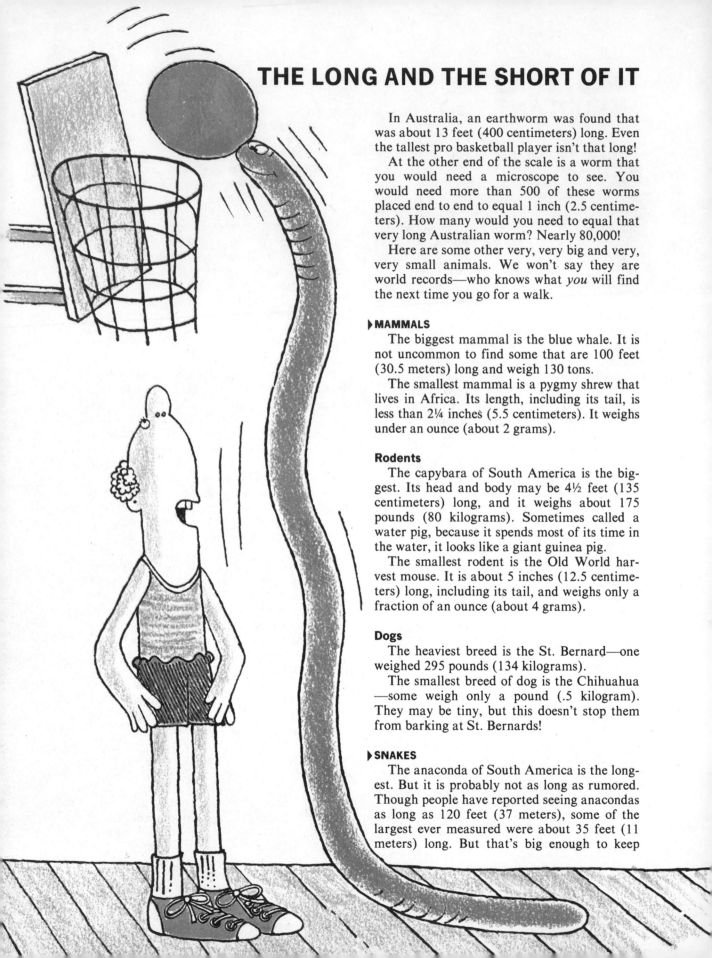

THE LONG AND THE SHORT OF IT

In Australia, an earthworm was found that was about 13 feet (400 centimeters) long. Even the tallest pro basketball player isn't that long!

At the other end of the scale is a worm that you would need a microscope to see. You would need more than 500 of these worms placed end to end to equal 1 inch (2.5 centimeters). How many would you need to equal that very long Australian worm? Nearly 80,000!

Here are some other very, very big and very, very small animals. We won't say they are world records—who knows what *you* will find the next time you go for a walk.

▶ MAMMALS

The biggest mammal is the blue whale. It is not uncommon to find some that are 100 feet (30.5 meters) long and weigh 130 tons.

The smallest mammal is a pygmy shrew that lives in Africa. Its length, including its tail, is less than 2¼ inches (5.5 centimeters). It weighs under an ounce (about 2 grams).

Rodents

The capybara of South America is the biggest. Its head and body may be 4½ feet (135 centimeters) long, and it weighs about 175 pounds (80 kilograms). Sometimes called a water pig, because it spends most of its time in the water, it looks like a giant guinea pig.

The smallest rodent is the Old World harvest mouse. It is about 5 inches (12.5 centimeters) long, including its tail, and weighs only a fraction of an ounce (about 4 grams).

Dogs

The heaviest breed is the St. Bernard—one weighed 295 pounds (134 kilograms).

The smallest breed of dog is the Chihuahua —some weigh only a pound (.5 kilogram). They may be tiny, but this doesn't stop them from barking at St. Bernards!

▶ SNAKES

The anaconda of South America is the longest. But it is probably not as long as rumored. Though people have reported seeing anacondas as long as 120 feet (37 meters), some of the largest ever measured were about 35 feet (11 meters) long. But that's big enough to keep most of us from taking late evening walks along the Amazon River.

The smallest snake is found on the Caribbean islands of Martinique, Barbados, and St. Lucia. It is a thread snake that is only about 4½ inches (11.5 centimeters) long.

▶BIRDS

The ostrich of North Africa is the biggest. Males average 8 feet (245 centimeters) in height and 275 pounds (125 kilograms) in weight. One fellow tipped the scales at 345 pounds (156 kilograms). No wonder they can't fly!

The smallest bird is the bee hummingbird, found in Cuba and on the Isle of Pines. The males have body lengths of about 2½ inches (6.5 centimeters). They weigh a fraction of an ounce (about 2 grams).

▶AMPHIBIANS

The Chinese giant salamander is the biggest. One huge individual measured about 5 feet (150 centimeters) from the tip of its snout to the end of its tail. It weighed almost 100 pounds (45 kilograms).

The smallest amphibian is an arrow-poison frog of Cuba, which is less than ½ inch (1.25 centimeters) long.

▶FISH

The whale shark is the largest, and it lives in the warmer parts of the Atlantic, Pacific, and Indian oceans. One whale shark was 59 feet (18 meters) long and weighed 90,000 pounds (41,000 kilograms). However, these creatures won't star in a remake of *Jaws*—they feed on tiny ocean plants and animals, not on people.

The smallest fish is the dwarf pygmy goby, found in freshwater streams and lakes in the Philippines. It is about ¼ inch (.5 centimeters) long—the smallest animal with a backbone.

Learn almost everything you want to know about insects at this special zoo.

THE SMITHSONIAN'S INSECT ZOO

On a sidewalk near the Smithsonian Institution in Washington, D.C., a honeybee finds treasure—melting ice cream dropped by a careless child. Follow that bee! It will lead you to a fascinating place—the Insect Zoo.

This new zoo is actually a very large room in the Smithsonian's National Museum of Natural History. And the honeybee lives there. The bee has its own special entrance to the building, and to its hive. You must use another entrance to go in. But once you're in the zoo, you can wander over and look inside the four-level hive where the honeybee and all its relatives live. And there are lots of other things to see too.

There are more than 1,000,000 kinds of insects in the world. They vary greatly in shape, color, size, life-style, and movement. They make different sounds and eat in different ways. At the Insect Zoo you will see thousands of insects, various types leading their lives in various ways. You may see a large rhinoceros beetle feeding on a banana; a tomato hornworm eating a tomato plant; a lubber grasshopper chewing on a head of lettuce; an ant

falling into a pit that was dug by a doodlebug; water beetles swimming in a pond; the hatching of a beautiful butterfly.

The zoo also has some relatives of insects, such as spiders, centipedes, and millipedes. One of the most popular attractions is the tarantula—especially at dinnertime. Its dinner is a cricket, and you can watch the tarantula capture and eat it. Because tarantulas may eat only once a week, the zoo has seven of them. A different tarantula is on display—and being fed—each day of the week.

Another interesting exhibit in the zoo shows insects that sometimes live in people's homes and gardens. There are termites, eating wood that could be part of a house. There are cockroaches under a sink. And there are Colorado potato beetles, causing the same kind of damage as they do in a farmer's field.

Insects and their relatives have been around for over 400,000,000 years. They live in every part of the world. At the Insect Zoo you will learn many fascinating things about these tiny neighbors of yours.

Would you like to hold the hickory horned devil? (This insect larva will eventually become a moth.)

The honeybees have their own special passageway between their hive and the outside world.

The male scarab beetle fascinates these youngsters.

Pampered pets at a dog show: being squirted with hair spray . . .

. . . keeping clean in a playpen . . .

PAMPERED PETS

Have you ever seen a dog getting its eyelashes trimmed or its toenails cut? Or a dog with its head protected by a bonnet? Just go to a dog show. There, everything is done to take special care of dogs when they are competing for ribbons and top honors.

Dog shows are held all over the world. In some places, there are shows every weekend. Not all the shows are as fancy or as famous as the Westminster Kennel Club show, which has been held every year in New York City for the past 100 years. But wherever the show is held, you'll see plenty of pampered pets.

Because they are judged on the beauty of their coats, the dogs are carefully washed and groomed before they arrive for the show. To keep them clean, the dogs' owners sometimes carry them or wheel them around in cages so their paws won't get dirty. Other dogs wear little bootees on their feet. Even playpens are used to keep the dogs off the ground while they wait their turn to be exhibited.

You'll see dogs wearing bibs so that food won't spill on their shiny coats. After being combed and brushed, some dogs get a squirt of hair spray to keep everything in place. And scissors are always kept handy for a last-minute trim.

After long hours of training and grooming, the dogs are ready for the show, which is a big elimination contest. First the judges look for the dog that best represents the standard for its breed. Then there are still more eliminations, until that one outstanding animal is selected Best in Show—the greatest honor. For that lucky dog and its owner, all the training and pampering have paid off.

MICHELE AND TOM GRIMM
Authors, *What Is a Seal?*

. . . its head protected with a bonnet.

WILD ASIA

Hop onto the Bengali Express and get ready for an exciting ride. You will be traveling on a monorail train through lovely hilly country. And soon you will see elephants, tigers, deer, rhinos, Indian peafowl, and ten other species of Asian mammals and birds.

Where are we? On the grasslands of India? No. We—and the animals—are in New York City, at the new Wild Asia exhibit at the Bronx Zoo. In Wild Asia, animals live in environments like those enjoyed by their relatives in the wild. Before the exhibit opened, the rhinos lived in a small stone-walled pen. Now they live on a large area of land called Chitawan Valley. This is very much like the distant Asian lands where their wild brothers and sis-

ters live. In such an environment the rhinos behave more naturally, and it is hoped that they will breed, which is something that is rare among zoo rhinos.

Nearby, on land called the South China Hills, is a herd of more than 50 sika deer. This animal breeds readily in zoos. In fact, the species is extinct in the wild; the only remaining sika deer are those in the zoos.

The Wild Asia exhibit covers about 38 acres (15.4 hectares) of land. About 200 mammals and birds live there, in eight habitats. The habitats are separated from each other—and from the city beyond—by fences that are hidden in bushes. So there is no chance that the tigers will attack an elephant or a person.

The next time you're in the mood to see wild animals of Asia, go to New York City and take a trip on the Bengali Express.

If you take the Bengali Express, you are sure to see these great Indian rhinos.

The Siberian tigers at Wild Asia come from China, Korea, and Siberia. Fewer than 300 of them remain in the wild.

A group of Barasingha deer peek through the trees of their new wooded home in Wild Asia.

WORLD OF SCIENCE

The Alaska pipeline, completed in 1977, is one of the greatest construction projects of all time.

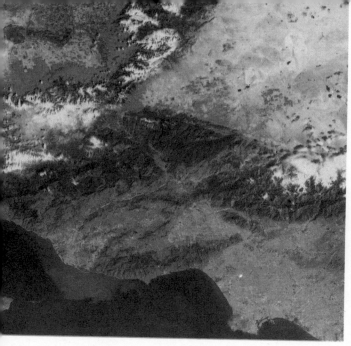

Question: The blue-gray area in the lower right corner shows the metropolitan area of the largest city on the west coast of the United States. What city is it?

Answer: Los Angeles. The triangular area in the upper right corner is the Mojave Desert. Red squares in the desert are irrigated farmland areas.

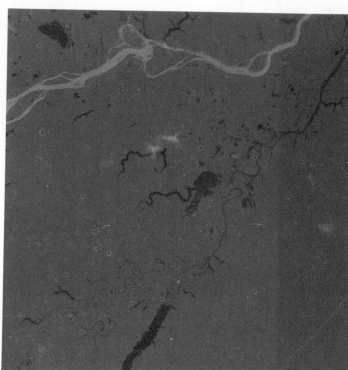

Question: The twisting, braided object at the top of the picture is a part of the longest river in South America. The red background is the tropical rain forest through which it flows. What is the name of the river?

Answer: The Amazon River. The river flowing from lower left to upper right is the Purus, a tributary of the Amazon. The white line in the lower right corner is a road cut through the rain forest.

Question: The blue-gray area shows the largest city in the United States, with neighboring cities and suburbs. What is the name of this largest city?

Answer: New York City. The red areas within the city are trees and grass in the city parks.

WHAT ON EARTH. . .?

Two United States satellites, Landsat 1 and 2, are following a nearly circular orbit around the earth. From a height of 570 miles (917 kilometers) they send information that enables earth-based computers to assemble amazingly detailed pictures of the earth, like those you see here. These pictures are being used by many countries around the world to make accurate maps, plan transportation routes, check on floods, trace sea ice, monitor air pollution, and do many other jobs in surveying the earth and its resources.

Because of the way the pictures are produced, they usually have false colors—the colors are not "actual" colors of the earth as seen from a spacecraft. So remember as you look at the pictures on these pages: grass and trees are seen as red; clear deep water is black; shallow water is blue; and cities are blue-gray. Now, can you tell what on earth you are seeing in these pictures?

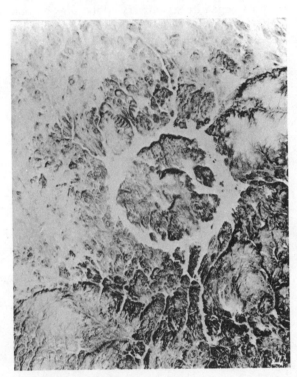

Question: Imagine a line passing between the two small islands near the center of the picture. That line forms the boundary between two great countries on two continents. The line also separates Monday from Tuesday. What is the line called? Which countries and which continents does it separate?

Answer: The line is the International Date Line, which is also the boundary between Siberia in the Soviet Union (*left*) and Alaska in the United States (*right*). The continents are Asia and North America.

Question: The circular object is in east central Quebec, in Canada. It is 41 miles (66 kilometers) in diameter. What is the object? What are the branchlike structures around it?

Answer: This is Lake Manicouagan, partly frozen over. The branching objects are frozen streams. The lake fills a depression that may have resulted from the explosion of a gigantic meteor, or it may be the remains of an ancient volcanic cone.

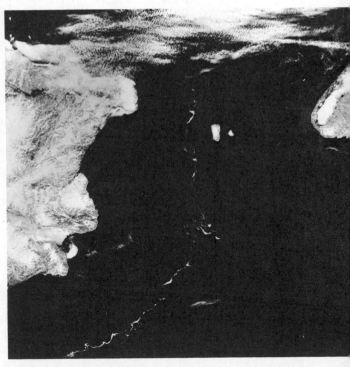

PREDICTING EARTHQUAKES

It was a lovely, quiet morning in Southern California's San Fernando Valley. A bright, sunny day was predicted. The date: February 9, 1971. The time: 6 A.M.

Seconds later, powerful shock waves tossed people out of bed, toppled buildings, and knocked down concrete highway bridges. It was an earthquake—the area's worst since 1933. The tremor lasted less than a minute, but it killed 64 people and injured 1,000 others.

Every year earthquakes kill people and destroy their homes. They cause billions of dollars worth of damage. There is no known way to stop earthquakes. But scientists are learning how to predict them. If people could be told when and where an earthquake will occur, they could leave the area before the quake hits. Ambulances, fire trucks, helicopters, and other emergency forces could be ready to rush to the quake area.

It is even possible that scientists will be able to predict quakes several years in advance. This would enable a community to check buildings to make sure that they are sound. Buildings not strong enough to withstand a quake could be fixed or torn down.

In recent years scientists have correctly predicted more than twenty quakes. The first quake to be correctly predicted in the United States was a small one in the Adirondack Mountains of New York. The second was a slightly bigger quake in California.

Let's look at the clues scientists are studying in their efforts to predict earthquakes.

▶CAN ANIMALS WARN OF EARTHQUAKES?

In ancient times the Chinese believed that animals acted strangely before an earthquake. Chinese scientists still believe this—and they are slowly convincing other people that animals make excellent earthquake predictors.

At Stanford University in California, some people were studying chimpanzees. On two occasions they noticed that the chimps were very, very restless. Both times the animals' unusual activity occurred just one day before a quake.

A scientist studying cockroaches found that these little insects also became exceptionally active right before a quake. And Japanese scientists have evidence that fish move into different waters a day or two before a quake.

No one knows why animals act strangely before a quake. And this behavior would be of value only if it occurred long enough before the quake for people to take action. Once, hundreds of rats started running through the streets of Cape Town, South Africa. (What a frightening sight that must have been!) A few minutes later an earthquake hit the city. The few minutes warning given by the rats was not enough time for people to flee the quake.

In early 1975 many animals in northeastern China began behaving very oddly. Pigs bit one another. Cows fought. Turtles cried. Snakes stopped hibernating and came out of their winter dens. Chickens flew to the tops of trees. Prompted largely by this unusual animal behavior, scientists warned people in the area that an earthquake would occur. Buildings were evacuated. People left cities for the countryside. On February 4 a very strong quake struck, within a few hours of the predicted time. Damage was severe, but Chinese officials believe that many thousands of lives were saved by the warning.

▶PRESSURE WAVES

Just as unusual animal behavior seems to signal a coming earthquake, an unusual pressure wave pattern on a seismograph is now believed to be a warning signal too. (A seismograph is an instrument that measures the pressure waves in the earth's crust.) Scientists have recently noticed that seismographs sometimes record a sudden slowing of the speed of pressure waves passing through certain underground rocks. The pressure waves then return to their normal speed. And shortly after their return to normal, an earthquake occurs.

Here is what scientists believe this unusual pattern on the seismograph is recording. Rocks under pressure are laced with many tiny cracks. These cracks are filled with underground water. Pressure waves travel through these water-filled cracks at a certain regular rate of speed.

If stress on the rocks increases greatly, the cracks inside the rocks suddenly spread and widen. Because the cracks have grown larger so suddenly, they are no longer completely filled with water. Pressure waves always travel

Can strange animal behavior be an earthquake warning signal? This is what happened prior to an earthquake in China: pigs bit one another, cows fought, turtles cried, and chickens flew into trees.

more slowly through dry space than through water-filled space; so the seismograph is recording that the pressure waves have slowed down. But later, when underground water seeps in and completely fills up the enlarged cracks, the pressure waves return to normal. And very soon after this, the rocks, which have been terribly weakened by the wide cracking and the increased water pressure, break apart in an earthquake.

Something else that happens when the rocks in the earth's crust come under tremendously increased stress is a swelling, or bulging, of the earth's surface. Along the San Andreas Fault in California, the earth has bulged as much as 10 inches (25 centimeters). Sometimes such

bulging has been followed by a quake. There was, for example, such a bulge in the San Fernando Valley shortly before the 1971 quake.

Not all earthquakes have been preceded by bulges. And sometimes bulges have formed but no big earthquake has followed. Still, scientists want to know what's happening underneath any bulges.

In the past decade, scientists have learned a great deal more about earthquakes. Many of them believe that accurate earthquake prediction will soon be a reality. Once scientists reach this goal, they will turn their attention to learning to prevent and control earthquakes.

JENNY TESAR
Consultant, Curriculum Concepts, Inc.

1. Crayons are made of wax and colored powders called pigments.

2. The liquid wax and the pigment of one color are mixed together in a huge vat.

3. After wax and pigment are blended, the liquid is poured into crayon molds.

4. After wax has hardened, the crayons are removed from the molds and inspected.

5. The crayons are labeled, and then an assortment of colors is put into boxes.

6. After lids are put on, these boxes of crayons are ready to be shipped.

RAINBOW IN A BOX

Name any color you can think of and it is probably in a box of crayons. Red, yellow, purple, black, green, blue, white. Then there are some surprising colors, too, ones you never even thought of. Apricot, thistle, mulberry, and salmon might also be found in a crayon box. Some boxes have as many as 72 different shades of crayons. And they're all there waiting to be used in your coloring book, on your party decorations, or for a special school assignment.

Did you ever wonder when crayons were invented? Or how they are made? Crayons certainly aren't something new. As far back as the Stone Age, people were using a kind of coloring stick to decorate the walls of their caves. They often drew pictures of the wild animals that roamed the land. It must have taken a lot of color sticks to draw a huge mammoth.

Thousands of years later, artists drew pictures with colored sticks of chalk. These sticks were called crayons and they are the ancestors of our modern crayons. The wax crayons that we use today were first invented about 100 years ago. At that time they came in just one color—black. It was not until 1903 that the first assortment of 16 colors was produced. Since that time more and more colors have been added to the selection, and today the crayon box is a rainbow of colors.

Let's take a tour through one of the most colorful places in the world—a crayon factory. Here we can see how today's crayons are made. It's a fairly easy process, but a lot of care has to be taken so that the color and texture of each one is perfect. Crayons have to be soft enough to leave a mark when you draw a picture or make a decoration, but at the same time sturdy and long-lasting.

Just follow the numbers and you'll see how a "rainbow in a box" is made.

SPACE BRIEFS

Two U.S. spacecraft, Voyagers 1 and 2, set out in 1977 to explore the outer reaches of the solar system. The unmanned vehicles will visit Jupiter and Saturn and their moons, and one spacecraft may even reach Uranus and Neptune. The Voyagers will travel for so long, to so many unexplored worlds, that children in 1977 will be adults before the mission is over.

Voyager 1 will approach Jupiter in March, 1979. Its twin sister ship, Voyager 2, will be about four months behind. If all goes well, the spacecraft will send television pictures back to earth as they pass the giant planet. The cameras will focus on a large red spot on Jupiter's gassy surface. The spot has puzzled scientists, who so far have been able to see it only through telescopes. The cameras will also scan the four largest of Jupiter's thirteen known moons, and may even discover a suspected fourteenth moon. Other instruments will study the chemical makeup of the planet and chart its magnetic fields.

Jupiter itself will give the Voyagers a boost on their way to the other planets. As Jupiter speeds along its orbit of the sun, its gravitational force will pull the Voyagers along, and then fling them out toward Saturn. If it were not for this "slingshot effect," the spacecraft would not be able to reach the ringed planet.

Experiments near Saturn will include a study of its rings, and of Titan, its largest moon. Titan is the only moon in the solar system known to have an atmosphere. In some ways the atmosphere is similar to Earth's.

If Voyager 1's mission near Saturn is successful, Voyager 2 will not have to pass so close to that planet. Then scientists will be able to aim the second ship so that it can take advantage of Saturn's "slingshot effect." Voyager 2 will then be headed out to explore Uranus and Neptune. It would reach Uranus in 1986, and Neptune in 1989, twelve years after having been launched.

Both Voyagers will eventually leave the solar system and wander forever through the universe. Each ship carries a message—just in case there are living beings out there to find it billions of years from now. The messages are on records telling what life is like on Earth. They also give examples of music (even rock-and-roll) and they carry greetings in many languages. One is from President Jimmy Carter. Part of it says, "This record represents our hope and our determination, and our goodwill in a vast and awesome universe."

The Voyager missions represent our attempt to better understand that universe.

An artist's conception of the Voyagers' journey to Jupiter and Saturn.

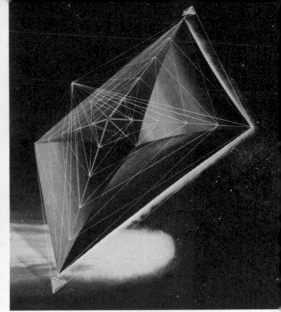

The first close look at Phobos, a Martian moon.

An artist's conception of a giant square solar sail.

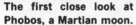 **PHOBOS: A MARTIAN MOON**

Phobos is not the most beautiful place ever seen. It is jagged, barren, dark, and covered with craters. Still, in 1977 scientists were very happy to get their first close look at it. Phobos is the larger of the two moons of Mars, and pictures of it were sent back to Earth by the Viking I spacecraft.

The pictures have given us the best look yet at another planet's moon. Scientists are excited about the pictures because they may be able to find out what Phobos is made of. And if scientists know that, they may also be able to learn how Phobos originated and where it came from.

Some scientists believe that Phobos is an asteroid—a small, planetlike body—that wandered too close to Mars and was captured by its gravity. Others think it was made from leftover material when Mars was first formed.

From the photographs, Phobos appears to be very much like an asteroid. As scientists examine them more closely, we will learn more about this Martian moon—and about the history of the solar system.

CLIPPER SHIPS

There are no breezes in space because there is no air. Why, then, is the National Aeronautics and Space Administration (NASA) building a sail-powered spacecraft? What will fill its sails and push it along? The answer may seem strange. It's sunlight.

Light rays are made up of little bundles of energy called photons. When light bounces off a surface, the photons give a small push—so small that people can't feel it. But when a lot of sunlight reflects off a huge, shiny sail, the many little pushes add up to a great force.

NASA is trying to build such a solar sail. It would be used to maneuver a spacecraft that contained cameras and scientific instruments. Solar clipper ships would be able to explore throughout the solar system, reaching speeds of 135,000 miles per hour (217,000 kilometers per hour), without needing any fuel.

Two kinds of solar sails are now under development. One kind is a giant square about a half mile (800 meters) long on each side, with a rigid frame to hold the sails. The spacecraft would sail along in outer space the way a wind-driven sailboat does in the water. The other kind of sail is a giant pinwheel called a heliogyro. It would have twelve sailcloth "blades," much like helicopter blades. Each would be 3½ miles (5,600 meters) long, and extremely narrow. Centrifugal force would keep the blades rigid. The entire spacecraft would spin through space. The sails for both designs would be made of a film of extremely thin plastic, coated with reflective aluminum.

In 1981, NASA plans to use a space shuttle to put the first clipper into orbit. The sail will be unfolded in space and the ship will be sent sailing for a rendezvous with Halley's comet, in 1986.

MOPEDS

Michael Patterson drives a special kind of vehicle—it goes 180 miles on one gallon of gas (77 kilometers on one liter)! He's saving money on gas, he's saving energy, and he's saving our environment by polluting it less. Michael is one of the many people who have discovered mopeds (pronounced MO-ped). The moped—short for "motor plus pedals"—is a motorized bicycle.

For many years, millions of Europeans and Asians have been using mopeds as their basic form of transportation. But these vehicles have only recently become popular in North America. Now, executives are riding them to work. Housewives are using them to go shopping. Students are using them to get to school. (Anyone who is at least 16 years old—14 in some areas—may ride one.) And besides being an energy-saving form of transportation, mopeds are fun to ride.

Most mopeds weigh about 90 to 100 pounds (40 to 50 kilograms). The engine runs on gasoline mixed with a little motor oil. They have automatic transmission, which means the rider doesn't have to shift gears. A moped, which costs about $300 to $600, comes with headlight and taillight, as well as other safety equipment. All kinds of accessories can also be bought: rearview mirrors, baskets and saddlebags, even a carrier that attaches the moped to the rear bumper of a car.

It takes just a few minutes to learn to operate a moped. You start the engine by pedaling. Once it is running, you don't do any more pedaling—unless you want to. (On a steep hill, you may have to pedal to help the engine.) To stop, you use the hand brakes.

Mopeds are designed for short-distance trips. You can ride them at speeds of about 17 to 25 miles per hour (27 to 40 kilometers per hour), depending on the laws in your area. But you cannot ride them on limited-access highways, such as freeways and thruways.

Some Moped Tips. Before buying one, find out about the laws that apply to mopeds in your area. In some states and Canadian provinces, your moped must be licensed, registered, or insured, and you must wear a helmet; in other areas, a moped is considered a kind of bicycle, and there are few laws. When you ride a moped, follow the same safety rules that you would if riding a bicycle. Ride on the right side of the road, single file. Use hand signals when turning. At night, use lights. Don't ride your moped on the sidewalk. Park your moped as you would a bike, and use a high-security lock.

Happy mopeding!

BATILLUS

Batillus, a new seagoing oil tanker built for Société Maritime Shell, is the largest moving object ever built. The tanker, which can carry 550,000 tons of cargo, measures about 1,358 feet (414 meters) in length and 241 feet (73 meters) in height. These measurements make it slightly taller than, and twice as long as, the Houston Astrodome. *Batillus* is fitted with just about every piece of sophisticated technical equipment ever designed by marine engineers. If the ship runs into trouble and breaks down at sea, it may have to be towed to one of only six dry docks in the world that can repair a ship of this size.

The winter of 1976–77 was one of the worst ever recorded. Most of the United States experienced severe cold and abundant snow. And for the first time ever, it snowed in Miami, Florida!

THE CRUELEST WINTER

People in the United States will remember the winter of 1976–77 for a long time. Some of the memories will be happy ones. There was plenty of snow for sledding and skiing and plenty of ice for skating. But this winter will be remembered mostly for the pain and hardship it caused. There was just too much snow and too much cold.

It all began in October, 1976, when the eastern part of the country had lower temperatures than normal. The unusual cold continued into November and December, and became still worse in January and February. The lowest temperatures in history were recorded in many states—from Texas to Minnesota and from Maine to Florida. And the East was hit by one snowstorm after another. Some snow even fell on Miami, Florida, and that had never happened before. (Strangely enough, the West got so little snow that the long drought in California and other western states became worse.)

Every winter brings cold weather and storms to some places. But this winter was different: it brought very bad weather to a large area for a long time. The results were disastrous. In Alexandria, Virginia, hundreds of people were injured in falls on slippery streets. In Detroit, Michigan, eleven people died from heart attacks while shoveling snow. In Ohio five men died from carbon monoxide poisoning after their car became stranded in a storm. In Buffalo, New York, a severe blizzard blew snowdrifts up to 20 feet (6 meters) high and killed at least fourteen people in one week. Driving was often dangerous, especially in the South, where people are not used to icy roads. On one stormy night there were 600 automobile accidents in Birmingham, Alabama.

The cruel winter brought other suffering and destruction, too. Many homes were left without water when pipes burst because of ice expanding within them. Houses burned to the ground because fire trucks could not get through snow-clogged roads. Thousands of people were forced from their apartments when furnaces could not provide enough heat. Other people were stranded in their homes for days while snowplows struggled to rescue them. And the frigid weather that brought snow to Florida also brought frost that killed millions of dollars worth of fruit and vegetables.

Another major problem was that the country almost ran out of fuel for heating. About

An eerie scene in Minneapolis, Minnesota: Firemen fought a blaze in below zero weather; the gutted warehouse was transformed into an "ice palace" as the water from the firehoses turned to icicles.

50 percent of U.S. homes and businesses are heated by natural gas. Natural gas is pumped from underground deposits, stored in large tanks, and distributed around the country through pipelines. By January there wasn't nearly enough of it to go around.

The gas shortage caused a national crisis. Thousands of schools and factories were closed so the fuel could be used to warm homes. More than 2,000,000 people were put out of work by the closings. President Carter asked people to save energy by turning their thermostats down to 65° F (18° C).

Why was there a shortage of natural gas? The federal government blamed the companies that supply natural gas, saying that there should have been enough gas to meet any need. But the companies argued that they did not have enough money to search for and develop new supplies of natural gas. And they did not have enough money, so they said, because the government was regulating the prices the companies charged. The government and the companies are trying to work out the problem so that there will never be another gas shortage.

Everyone hopes that such a terrible winter will not happen again. But meteorologists (people who study weather and climate) aren't sure what to expect. They just don't know enough about how the weather works. The winter of 1976–77 was different, the meteorologists say, because of a strange action of a basic weather pattern called the westerlies. The westerlies are winds that blow in a continuous stream across Canada, from west to east, about 7 miles (11 kilometers) above the ground. Sometimes in winter the path of the westerlies dips south for a while, carrying cold air from the Arctic into the United States. When that happens, the northern part of the United States has its most frigid days of the year. Usually these cold spells last only a few days—until the westerlies return to their normal course. But in 1976–77 the westerlies did something unusual: they dipped south in October, farther south than they had ever been known to go before, and they stayed there for most of the winter.

That's what happened, but the meteorologists aren't sure why it happened. Most believe that the change took place because of unusual weather conditions in other parts of the world. These conditions are not likely to happen again in the same way. If this view is correct, the cruelest winter will be just a bad memory—and not the beginning of a continuing disaster.

DAVID KULL
Science Writer

A TOUCH OF BEAUTY

Heavy snowfalls can be cruel acts of nature. They often cause great hardships for people and severe damage to property. But some people welcome snowstorms because of the beauty they bring to the cold, barren winter landscape.

What do you feel when you see snowflakes falling? Perhaps you think about building snowmen, sledding with friends, skiing, and snowball fights. Or perhaps you think about how lovely and fragile the snowflakes are.

But did you ever wonder where those snowflakes come from? Or what they are made of?

A snowflake is actually a clump of ice crystals. Each crystal is a tiny six-sided figure. A snowflake begins its life in a cloud, as a microscopic speck of matter such as a grain of dust or a tiny splinter of another ice crystal. Molecules of water freeze onto this speck, and the crystal grows and grows until it finally falls to earth as a snowflake.

Perhaps you've heard that no two snowflakes are the same. It's true—but you'd have to look at the flakes through a microscope to see this for yourself. The snowflakes you see here have been greatly enlarged so that you can enjoy the beauty of their designs.

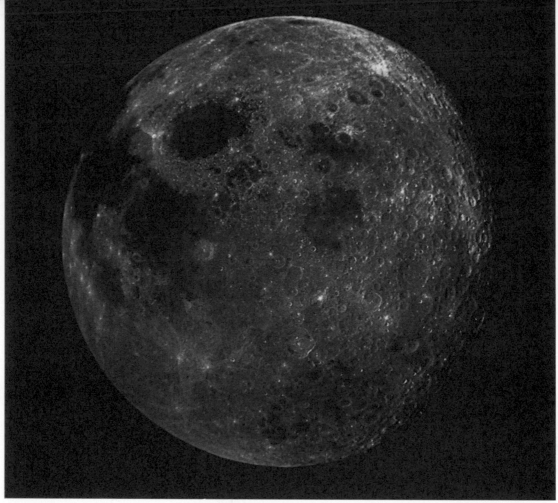

This photograph of the moon was snapped by the Apollo 17 crew in 1972.

WHAT'S NEW ON THE MOON?

In 1969, more than 500,000,000 people witnessed the "impossible" coming true as the first men walked on the surface of the moon. For the next three years, people watched as one of the great explorations in human history was displayed on their television screens.

Between 1969 and 1972, supported by thousands of scientists and engineers back on earth, 12 astronauts explored the surface of the moon. In their space suits, the astronauts were protected against the airlessness and the killing heat of the lunar environment. They stayed on the moon for days, and some of them traveled for miles across its surface in Lunar Rovers. They made scientific observations and set up instruments to probe the interior of the moon. They collected hundreds of pounds of lunar rock and soil, thus beginning the first attempt to discover the origin and geological history of another world from actual samples of its crust.

The initial excitement of success and discovery has passed. TV sets no longer show astronauts moving across the sunlit lunar landscape. But here on earth, scientists are only now beginning to understand the immense treasure of new knowledge returned by the Apollo astronauts.

The Apollo Program has left us a large and priceless legacy of lunar materials and data. We now have moon rocks that were collected from nine different places on the moon. The six Apollo landings returned a collection weighing 843 pounds (382 kilograms). And three automated Soviet spacecraft, Luna 16, Luna 20, and Luna 24, returned small but important samples.

Instruments that were placed on the moon by the Apollo astronauts as long ago as 1969 detected moonquakes and meteorite impacts, measured the moon's motions, and recorded the heat flowing out from the inside of the moon. Cameras on the Apollo spacecraft obtained so many accurate photographs that we now have better maps of parts of the moon than we do for some areas on earth. Special detectors near the cameras measured the weak X rays and radioactivity given off by the lunar surface. From these measurements, we have been able to determine the chemical composition of about one quarter of the moon's surface, an area the size of the United States and Mexico combined. By comparing the flight data with analyses of collected moon rocks, we can draw conclusions about the chemical composition of the entire moon.

Thus, in less than ten years, science and the Apollo Program have changed our moon from an unknown and unreachable object into a familiar world.

▶ **WHAT HAVE WE LEARNED ABOUT THE MOON?**

Before the Apollo Program, the nature and origin of the moon were still mysteries. Now we can answer questions that remained unsolved during centuries of speculation and scientific study.

Is there life on the moon? Despite careful searching, no living organisms or fossil life has been found in any lunar samples. The lunar rocks were so barren of life that the quarantine period for returned astronauts was dropped after the third Apollo landing.

The moon has no water of any kind. Water is necessary for life, and it is therefore unlikely that life could ever have originated on the moon. Furthermore, lunar rocks contain only tiny amounts of the carbon and carbon compounds out of which life is built. And most of this carbon is not native to the moon, but is brought to the lunar surface in meteorites and as atoms blasted out of the sun.

What is the moon made of? Before the first moon rocks were collected, we could analyze only two types of bodies in our solar system: our own planet earth and the meteorites that occasionally fall to earth from outer space. Now we have learned that the moon is chemically different from both of these, but it is more like the earth.

The moon is made of rocks. The moon rocks are so much like earth rocks in their appearance that we can use the same terms to describe both. The moon rocks are all igneous, which means that they formed by the cooling of molten lava. (No sedimentary rocks—such as limestone or shale, which are deposited in water—have been found on the moon.)

The dark regions are called maria and they form the features of "the man in the moon." These regions are low, level areas covered with layers of basalt lava, a rock that is similar to the lavas that erupt from volcanoes in Hawaii and Iceland, and elsewhere. The light-colored parts of the moon are called highlands. They are higher, more rugged regions that are older than the maria. These areas are made up of several different types of rocks that cooled slowly deep within the moon. We call these rocks gabbro, norite, and anorthosite.

However, despite similarities, moon rocks and earth rocks are basically different. It is easy to tell them apart by analyzing their chemistry or by examining them under a microscope. The most obvious difference is that moon rocks have no water at all, while almost all earth rocks contain at least a tiny amount of water. The moon rocks are therefore very well-preserved, because they never reacted with water to form clay minerals or rust.

Another important difference is that the moon rocks formed where there was almost no free oxygen. As a result, some of the iron in lunar rocks was not oxidized when the lunar lavas formed and still occurs as small crystals of metallic iron.

Because moon rocks have never been exposed to water or oxygen, any contact with the earth's atmosphere could "rust" them badly. For this reason, the collected Apollo samples are stored in an atmosphere of dry nitrogen.

The moon rocks are made of the same chemical elements that make up earth rocks, although the proportions are different. Moon rocks contain more of the common elements calcium, aluminum, and titanium than do most earth rocks. Rarer elements like hafnium and zirconium, which have high melting points, are also more plentiful in lunar rocks. However, other elements, like sodium and potassium, which have low melting points, are scarce in lunar material. Because moon rocks are richer in high-temperature elements and contain less

This white, feldspar-rich rock is a sample of the material that covers the light-colored regions, called highlands, of the moon. The rock, a "breccia," is made of many different kinds of rocks pressed together.

This chunk of basalt lava is a sample of the material that covers the dark regions, called maria, of the moon. The hollows were formed by bubbles of gas in the molten rock.

low-temperature elements, scientists believe that the material that formed the moon was once heated to much higher temperatures than material that formed the earth.

The chemical composition of the moon is different in different places. Soon after the moon formed, various elements sorted themselves out to form different kinds of rock. The light-colored highlands are rich in calcium and aluminum, while the dark-colored maria contain less of those elements and more titanium, iron, and magnesium.

What is the inside of the moon like? Sensitive instruments placed on the lunar surface by the Apollo astronauts recorded the tiny vibrations caused by the meteorite impacts on the surface of the moon and by small "moonquakes" deep within it. These vibrations provide the data from which scientists determine what the inside of the moon is like.

About 3,000 moonquakes are detected each year. All of them are very weak by earth standards. The average moonquake releases about as much energy as a firecracker. The moonquakes occur about 370 to 500 miles (600 to 800 kilometers) deep inside the moon, much deeper than almost all the quakes on our own planet. Certain kinds of moonquakes occur at about the same time every month. This suggests that they are triggered by repeated tidal strains as the moon moves in its orbit around the earth.

A picture of the inside of the moon has slowly been put together. It shows that the moon is not uniform inside. It is divided into a series of layers, just as the earth is, although the layers of the earth and moon are different. The outermost part of the moon is a crust about 37 miles (60 kilometers) thick. It is probably composed of calcium- and aluminum-rich rocks like those found in the highlands. Beneath this crust is a thick layer of denser rock, the mantle, which extends down to more than 500 miles (800 kilometers).

The deep interior of the moon is still unknown. The moon may contain a small iron core at its center; and there is some evidence that the moon may be hot and even partly molten inside.

The moon does not now have a magnetic field like the earth's, and so the most baffling and unexpected result of the Apollo Program was the discovery of preserved magnetism in many of the old lunar rocks. One explanation is that the moon had an ancient magnetic field that somehow disappeared after the old lunar rocks had formed.

The Apollo instruments have also provided information about the space environment near the moon. For example, the sensitive devices used to detect moonquakes have also recorded the vibrations caused by the impacts of small meteorites onto the lunar surface. We now have records of how often meteorites strike the moon, and we have learned that these impacts do not always occur at random. Some small meteorites seem to travel in groups. Several such swarms, composed of meteorites weighing a few pounds each, struck the moon in 1975. The detection of such events is giving scientists new ideas about the distribution of meteorites and cosmic dust in the solar system.

What is the moon's surface like? Long before the Apollo Program, scientists could see that the moon's surface was complex. Earth-based telescopes could distinguish the level maria and the rugged highlands. We could recognize countless circular craters, rugged mountain ranges, and deep winding canyons, or rilles.

Because of the Apollo explorations, we have now learned that all these lunar landscapes are covered by a layer of fine, broken-up powder and rubble about 3 to 60 feet (1 to 20 meters) deep. This layer is usually called the "lunar soil"; but it contains no water or organic material, and it is totally different from soils formed on earth by the action of wind, water, and life.

The lunar soil is something entirely new to scientists, for it could only have been formed on the surface of an airless body like the moon. The soil has been built up over billions of years by the continuous bombardment of the unprotected moon by large and small meteorites. Most of these meteorites would have burned up if they had entered the earth's atmosphere.

These meteorites form craters when they hit the moon. Tiny particles of cosmic dust produce microscopic craters, while the rare impact of a large body may blast out a vastly larger crater. Each of these impacts shatters the solid lunar rock, scatters material around the crater, and stirs and mixes the soil. As a result, the lunar soil at any location is a well-mixed sample of a large area of the moon.

However, the lunar soil is more than ground-up and reworked lunar rock. It is the boundary layer between the moon and outer space. It absorbs the matter and energy that strike the moon from the sun and the rest of the universe. Tiny bits of cosmic dust and high-energy atomic particles, which would be stopped high in the earth's protective atmosphere, rain continuously onto the surface of the moon.

How old is the moon? Scientists now think that the solar system first came into being as a huge, whirling, disk-shaped cloud of gas and dust. Gradually the cloud collapsed inward. The central part became massive and hot, forming the sun. Around the sun, the dust formed small objects that rapidly collected together to form the large planets and satellites that we see today.

By carefully measuring the radioactive elements found in rocks, scientists can determine how old the rocks are. Measurements on meteorites indicate that the formation of the solar system occurred 4,600,000,000 (billion) years ago. There is chemical evidence in both moon and earth rocks that the earth and moon also formed at that time. However, the oldest known rocks on earth are only 3,800,000,000 (billion) years old; scientists think that the older rocks were destroyed by the earth's continuing volcanism, mountain-building, and erosion.

The moon rocks fill in some of this gap in time between the earth's oldest preserved rocks and the formation of the solar system. The lavas from the dark maria are the moon's youngest rocks, but they are as old as the oldest rocks found on earth. Rocks from the lunar highlands are even older. Most highland samples are about 4,000,000,000 (billion) years old. Some moon rocks preserve traces of even older lunar events. Studies of these rocks indicate that widespread melting and chemical separation were going on within the moon about 4,400,000,000 (billion) years ago, or not long after the moon had formed.

Even more exciting is the discovery that a few lunar rocks seem to record the actual formation of the moon. Some tiny green rock fragments have yielded an apparent age of 4,600,000,000 (billion) years, the time at which scientists think that the moon and the solar system formed. Early in 1976, scientists identified another crystalline rock with the same ancient age. These pieces may be some of the first material that solidified from the once-molten moon.

What is the history of the moon? The first few hundred million years of the moon's lifetime were so violent that few traces of this time remain. Almost immediately after the moon formed, its outer part was completely melted to a very great depth. While this molten layer gradually cooled and solidified into different kinds of rocks, the moon was bombarded by huge asteroids and smaller bodies. Some of these asteroids were the size of small states, like Rhode Island or Delaware, and their collisions with the moon created enormously wide basins.

This catastrophic bombardment died away about 4,000,000,000 (billion) years ago, leaving the lunar highlands covered with huge overlapping craters and a deep layer of shattered and broken rock. As the bombardment subsided, heat produced by the decay of radioactive elements began to melt the inside of the moon at depths of about 125 miles (200 kilometers) below its surface. Then for the next half billion years great floods of lava rose from

inside the moon and poured out over its surface, filling in the large impact basins to form the dark parts of the moon that we see from earth today.

As far as we now know, the moon has been quiet since the last lavas erupted more than 3,000,000,000 (billion) years ago. Since then, the moon's surface has been altered only by rare large meteorite impacts and by atomic particles from the sun and the stars. The moon has preserved features that were formed 4,000,000,000 (billion) years ago. If people had landed on the moon a billion years ago, it would have looked to them very much as it does to us now. The surface of the moon now changes so slowly that the footprints left by the Apollo astronauts may remain clear and sharp for millions of years.

This preserved ancient history of the moon is in sharp contrast to the changing earth. The earth still behaves like a young planet. Its internal heat is active, and volcanic eruptions and mountain-building have been going on continuously as far back as we can decipher the rocks.

Where did the moon come from? Before we explored the moon, there were three main suggestions to explain its existence: that it had formed near the earth as a separate body; that it had separated from the earth; and that it had formed somewhere else and been captured by the earth.

Scientists still cannot decide between these three theories. However, we have learned that the moon formed as a part of our solar system and that it has existed as an individual body for 4,600,000,000 (billion) years. Separation from the earth is now considered less likely, because there are many basic differences in chemical composition between the two bodies, such as the absence of water on the moon. But the other two theories are still evenly matched in their strengths and weaknesses. We will need more data and perhaps some new theories before the origin of the moon is settled.

▶**WHAT HAS THE MOON TOLD US ABOUT THE EARTH?**

It might seem that the active, inhabited earth has nothing in common with the quiet, lifeless moon. Nevertheless, the scientific discoveries of the Apollo Program have provided a new and unexpected look into the early history of our own planet.

THE EVOLUTION OF THE MOON

THE MOON 3.9 BILLION YEARS AGO. Shortly after its formation, the moon solidified and its surface began to record collisions by huge asteroids and smaller bodies. By the time the catastrophic bombardment had died away, the lunar highlands were covered with huge overlapping craters. The largest of them was the multiringed basin seen at the upper left.

THE MOON 3.1 BILLION YEARS AGO. Soon after the bombardment ended, deeply shattered rock beneath the impact sites allowed molten lava within the moon to reach the surface and flood across the basin floors, forming most of the maria. Maria appear dark because they contain more of such elements as iron and magnesium than other surface rocks.

THE MOON TODAY. Many bright, rayed craters, such as Copernicus and Tycho, have appeared since the formation of the maria. Rays of other craters now lie buried under lava. Unless some unforeseen disaster were to occur, the moon will retain this appearance for many millions of years to come.

The moon's rocks contain the traces of the process of planetary creation which occurred about 4,600,000,000 (billion) years ago. The same catastrophic impacts and widespread melting that we recognize on the moon must also have dominated the earth during its early years. About 4,000,000,000 (billion) years ago the earth may have looked much the same as the moon does now.

The two worlds then took different paths. The moon became quiet while the earth continued to generate mountains, volcanoes, oceans, an atmosphere, and life. The moon preserved its ancient rocks while the earth's older rocks were continually destroyed and re-created as younger ones.

The earth's oldest preserved rocks occur as small remnants in Greenland, Minnesota, and Africa. These rocks are not like the lunar lava flows of the same age. The earth's most ancient rocks are granites and sediments. They tell us that the earth already had mountain-building, running water, oceans, and life at a time when the last lava flows were pouring out across the moon.

In the same way, all traces of any intense early bombardment of the earth have been destroyed. The record of later impacts remains, however, in nearly 100 ancient impact structures that have been recognized on the earth in recent years. Some of these structures are the deeply eroded remnants of craters as large as those of the moon; they give us a way to study on earth the process that once dominated both the earth and moon.

Lunar science is also making other contributions to the study of the earth. The new techniques developed to analyze moon samples are now being applied to earth rocks, and their ages can now be measured far more accurately than before Apollo.

▶ WHAT HAS THE MOON TOLD US ABOUT THE SUN?

One of the most exciting results of the Apollo Program is that, by going to the moon, we have also been able to collect samples of the sun.

The surface of the moon is continually exposed to the solar wind, a stream of atoms boiled into space from the sun's atmosphere. Since the moon formed, the lunar soil has trapped billions of tons of these atoms ejected from the sun. These high-energy atoms leave permanent tracks when they strike particles in the lunar soil.

By analyzing the soil samples returned from the moon, we have been able to determine the chemical composition of the matter ejected by the sun, and thus learn more about how the sun operates. A major surprise was the discovery that the material in the solar wind is not the same as that in the sun itself. The ratio of hydrogen to helium atoms in the solar wind that reaches the moon is about 20 to 1. But the ratio of these atoms in the sun, as measured with earth-based instruments, is only 10 to 1. Some unexplained process in the sun's outer atmosphere apparently operates to eject the lighter hydrogen atoms in preference to the heavier helium atoms.

Even more important is the fact that the lunar soil still preserves material ejected by the sun in the past. We now have a unique opportunity to study the past behavior of the sun. Our very existence depends on the sun's activity. And by understanding the sun's past history, we can hope to predict better its future behavior.

These studies of the lunar soil are only beginning, but what we have learned about the sun so far is reassuring. Chemical features of the sun show no change for at least the past few hundred thousand years. The lunar samples are telling us that the sun, in the recent past, has behaved very much as it does today. This makes us optimistic that the sun will remain the same for the foreseeable future.

▶ WHAT ELSE CAN THE MOON TELL US?

Although the Apollo Program officially ended in 1972, the active study of the moon goes on. More than 125 teams of scientists are studying the returned lunar samples and analyzing the information that was recorded by the various instruments on the moon. Less than 10 percent of the lunar sample material has been studied in detail, and more results will emerge as new rocks and soil samples are examined.

The scientific results of the Apollo Program have spread far beyond the moon itself. By studying the moon, we have learned how to go about the business of exploring other planets. The knowledge gained from the moon is being used with the photographs returned by Mariners 9 and 10 to understand the histories of

Mercury and Mars, and to interpret the data returned by the Viking mission to Mars.

WHAT MYSTERIES REMAIN ABOUT THE MOON?

Despite the great scientific return from the Apollo Program, there are still many unanswered questions about the moon.

What is the chemical composition of the whole moon? We have sampled only nine places on the moon. The chemical analyses cover about a quarter of the moon's surface. We still know little about the far side of the moon and nothing whatever about the moon's polar regions.

Why is the moon uneven? Orbiting Apollo spacecraft used a laser device to measure accurately the heights of peaks and valleys over much of the lunar surface. From these careful measurements, scientists have learned that the moon is not a perfect sphere. It is slightly egg-shaped, with the small end of the egg pointing toward the earth and the larger end facing away from it.

There are other major differences between the two sides of the moon. The front (earth-facing side), which is the small end of the egg, is covered with large dark areas which were produced long ago by great eruptions of basalt lava. However, the far side of the moon is almost entirely composed of light-colored, rugged, and heavily cratered terrain identical to the highland regions on the front side, and there are only a few patches of dark, lava-like material. Furthermore, the moon's upper layer (the crust) is also uneven. On the front side, where the maria are, the lunar crust is about 37 miles (60 kilometers) thick. On the back side, it is over 62 miles (100 kilometers) thick.

We still do not know enough to explain these different observations. Perhaps the moon points its small end toward the earth because of tidal forces that have kept it trapped in that position for billions of years. Perhaps lava erupted only on the front side because the crust was thinner there. These differences could tell us much about the early years of the moon, if we could understand them.

Is the moon now molten inside? We know that there were great volcanic eruptions on the moon billions of years ago, but we do not know how long they continued. To understand the moon's history completely, we need to find out if the inside of the moon is still hot and partly molten.

Does the moon have an iron core like the earth's? This question is critical to solving the puzzle of ancient lunar magnetism. At the moment, we have so little data that we can neither rule out the possible existence of a small iron core nor prove that one is present.

How old are the youngest lunar rocks? The youngest rocks collected from the moon were formed 3,100,000,000 (billion) years ago. We cannot determine how the moon heated up and then cooled again until we know whether these eruptions were the last, or whether volcanic activity continued on the moon for a longer time.

Is the moon now really "dead"? Unexplained occurrences of reddish glows, clouds, and mists have been reported on the moon's surface for over 300 years. These "lunar transient events," as they are called, are still not explained. It is important to determine what they are, because they may indicate regions where gases and other materials are still coming to the surface from inside the moon.

WHAT DO WE DO NOW?

For all we have learned about the moon, the exploration of our nearest neighbor world has only just begun.

To further explore the moon, we can send machines in place of men. An unmanned spacecraft could circle the moon from pole to pole, measuring its chemical composition, radioactivity, gravity, and magnetism. This mission would carry on the tasks begun by the Apollo Program and would produce physical and chemical maps of the whole moon.

Other spacecraft, like the Soviet's Luna 16 and Luna 20 landers, could return small samples from locations never before visited: the far side, the poles, or the sites of the puzzling transient events. Because of the Apollo Program, we now know how to analyze such small samples and how to interpret correctly the data we obtain.

Finally, we may see men and women return to the moon, not as passing visitors but as long-term residents. There, they could build bases from which to explore the moon, and erect astronomical instruments that would use the moon as a platform from which to see deeper into the mysterious universe that surrounds us.

DR. BEVAN M. FRENCH
Program Chief, NASA Extraterrestrial
Materials Research Program

THE ALASKA PIPELINE

One of the greatest construction projects of all time was completed in 1977. It is the world's longest oil pipeline, the Trans-Alaska Pipeline system. Built across one of the coldest stretches of land on earth, the 800-mile-long (1,290-kilometer-long) pipeline carries oil from Prudhoe Bay on the northern coast of Alaska to the port of Valdez on the southern coast. From Valdez the oil is transported by ship to American refineries, where it is made into gasoline, heating oil, and other petroleum products.

The oil field at Prudhoe Bay was first discovered in 1968, and it is the largest ever found in the United States. But the oil is only of value if it can be transported to the "lower 48 states," where it is needed. Since Prudhoe Bay is hemmed in by ice most of the year, the oil cannot be taken out by ship. Instead it must be pumped overland through a pipeline. The pipeline solves the problem of getting the precious oil out of the far north and to the "lower 48."

Today the Alaska pipeline is helping to meet the great demand in the United States for gasoline and other oil products. Yet many people tried to stop the pipeline from being built. They claimed that the pipeline would spoil the ecology of one of the world's last great wilderness areas. These environmentalists felt that a great natural wilderness area unspoiled by man was even more precious than oil.

Can people continue to use the earth's natural resources, such as oil, without ruining the earth's natural environment? This is the major question that the building of the Trans-Alaska Pipeline has raised.

▶ OIL IS DISCOVERED

Until the discovery of oil there, the great coastal plain that makes up northern Alaska belonged to caribou, bear, and a scattering of Eskimos. The belief that large deposits of oil were to be found there, however, was not new. As long ago as the 19th century, Eskimos told American and Russian whalers about mysterious black lakes that seemed to ooze out of the ground and that burned.

In 1968 the great discovery was made, and it was found that the oil field around Prudhoe Bay did indeed contain immense amounts of petroleum. Today experts agree that the oil field, covering an area of some 200 square miles (518 square kilometers), will eventually yield about 10,000,000,000 (billion) barrels of crude oil. This amount is equal to about one fourth of all the other petroleum known to be underground throughout the rest of the United States. With so much oil to be sold, oil companies quickly began making plans to build an oil pipeline.

▶ SPECIAL PROBLEMS

Four major problems had to be dealt with before the Alaska Pipeline could be built.

Terrain and climate. From the beginning it was clear that building the pipeline would not be easy. It had to be constructed across a very difficult terrain, across no fewer than three mountain ranges and seventy rivers. The builders also had to contend with the extreme cold and endless darkness of the Arctic winters. The work habits learned in warmer climates are not suited to a place where the temperature drops to -60° F (–51° C), as is common during an Alaskan winter. A hand that touches metal at such temperatures will immediately freeze to it. One carpenter put some nails into his mouth, forgetting about the extreme cold. He had to go to a clinic and wait for the nails to warm up, so they could be removed without tearing out the inside of his mouth.

Helicopters were used to ferry men and supplies across the icy terrain, and the crews faced special dangers. One hazard was called "whiteout." This sometimes happens when the sky is overcast, and the snow-covered ground and the sky blend into a single blur. The pilot cannot tell where the sky ends and the ground begins. The only solution is to land the helicopter immediately and wait until weather conditions change. Because of the danger of whiteouts, helicopter crews carried survival kits at all times, no matter how short the trip.

Even the Alaskan summer presented special problems. In summer the snow and ice on the surface of the land melt and the land becomes a great marsh. When oil was first discovered, there was no road at all to northern Alaska. A road that was hurriedly built in late 1968 turned out to be a disaster; parts of it turned into small lakes in which trucks were stranded for days on end. The highway had to be rebuilt more carefully, at considerable expense.

As difficult as they were, terrain and climate were not the most important obstacles to be overcome before the pipeline could be built. If they had been, the pipeline could have been completed in the early 1970's. But there were other problems too.

The Alaskans' claims. The native peoples of Alaska are the Eskimo, Aleut, and Indian descendants of the people who inhabited that great land before the first Europeans arrived there. At the time oil was discovered at Prud-hoe Bay, these native Alaskans had claims to 90 percent of the land in the state. The claims dated back more than 100 years, to the time when Russia sold Alaska to the United States. These long-pending claims had to be settled before the pipeline could proceed. The result was the Alaska Native Claims Settlement Act of 1971, which gave $962,500,000 and 40,000,000 acres (16,000,000 hectares) to village corporations that represented Alaska's 80,000 natives.

The environmental question. Would an oil pipeline harm Alaska's wilderness environment? This was a major concern of environmentalists. They thought that the construction of the pipeline could cause widespread soil erosion. And if the pipeline ever broke, oil would be spilled over the Alaskan wilderness.

About 85 percent of Alaska's land surface is underlain by *permafrost,* which is ground that is permanently frozen to depths of as great as 2,000 feet (610 meters). In summer, when temperatures rise well above freezing and the sun shines almost all the time, the only thing that keeps the permafrost from melting is a layer of vegetation called tundra. Although only a few inches thick, the tundra insulates the permafrost from the summer's heat. If the tundra is disturbed or cut away (for example by heavy construction vehicles, which make deep ruts) the permafrost melts. In places where the land slopes, the melting waters carry away sub-surface soil. Within a few years even small ruts can develop into wide chasms.

Environmentalists also worried about what the hot oil going through an underground pipeline would do to the permafrost. Petroleum coming out of the ground from an oil well is very hot. And the oil must be kept fairly hot on its entire trip through the pipeline, or it will cease to flow. What would happen as this hot oil coursed through the pipeline? The heat would cause the permafrost to melt. This in turn would cause soil erosion. As the erosion continued, the ground supporting the pipeline would be swept away. With the oil in the pipeline weighing about 1,000 pounds (454 kilograms) per foot, the pipeline would sag and finally break, spilling the oil out and causing a mess that might never be cleaned up.

In addition, environmentalists pointed out that the pipeline was to be built across an area that was prone to earth tremors. A major

Environmentalists were concerned that the Alaska Pipeline would spoil one of the last great natural wilderness areas.

Each section of pipe, 4 feet (1.2 meters) in diameter, was carefully welded to the next section. About half the 800-mile (1,290-kilometer) pipeline was buried underground.

About 10 percent of the construction workers were women. Both the men and the women worked long, hard hours, but made a lot of money.

June 20, 1977—the first oil is pumped into the pipeline. Workers listen for the sounds that mean everything is working.

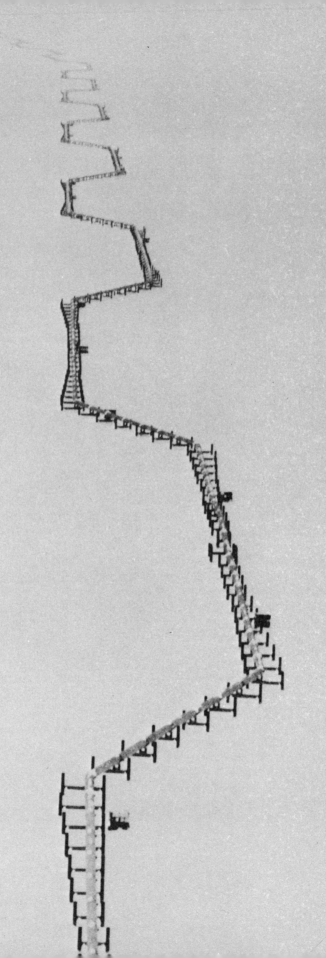

earthquake had struck Alaska in 1964, causing severe damage. The pipeline could easily be ruptured if tremors like that occurred.

CONSTRUCTION BEGINS

For five years following the discovery of oil, construction of the pipeline was held up while the effects it might have on the environment were considered. Then in 1973 political developments in another part of the world helped to speed up the decision. The Arab nations of the Middle East, who sell a great amount of oil to the United States, cut off oil shipments for a few months. The severe shortage of gasoline and petroleum products that resulted made Alaska's oil seem more important than ever, and the U.S. Congress finally approved construction of the pipeline.

Construction then began in earnest. Long sections of pipe were hauled north from Valdez and Fairbanks on a newly built road. The sections of pipe, 4 feet (1.2 meters) in diameter, were to be welded together by skilled workers. Tens of thousands of welds would be required to stitch the 800 miles (1,290 kilometers) of pipe together.

By the middle of 1975 more than 20,000 construction workers were involved in building the pipeline. They worked twelve hours a day and thirteen weeks in a row before taking a vacation. Why did they work so hard? Because a lot of money was to be made. An unskilled laborer could make as much as $1,000 a week, and a skilled craftsmen—for example, a welder—could make $1,600 a week. But prices rose sky-high. In some towns near the pipeline a loaf of bread cost $1.13. Despite the high prices, many of the men and women who worked on the pipeline (about 10 percent of the construction workers were women) managed to save a lot of money, even if they had to work hard for it.

Finally, in 1977, the big project was completed. The first oil from Prudhoe Bay was pumped into the pipeline on June 20. And 38½ days later, that same oil reached Valdez. But it took more than a month longer to get there than it should have taken. That first trip was plagued by a number of mishaps, including an explosion at one of twelve pumping stations that keep the oil moving. Despite such accidents, officials of the pipeline company expressed satisfaction that the process of moving the oil across Alaska had begun. It is estimated that it will be 25 years before all the Prudhoe Bay oil is used up. Until then, the pipeline seems here to stay.

GUARDING THE ENVIRONMENT

In the end, the environmentalists failed to stop the pipeline from being built. But they did cause major changes in the way the pipeline was constructed.

For one thing, the pipeline was *not* built almost entirely underground, as had originally been planned. To keep the hot oil from the permafrost, more than half the pipeline was built above ground, supported by tall support columns. Even with these safety measures, there was concern that the heat might travel down the steel columns into the permafrost. To prevent this, the supports were provided with cooling systems. A special chemical flows up and down inside the columns; it carries any heat that gets to the ground back to the top of the column, where it is then dissipated into the air.

A number of precautions have also been taken to guard against a pipeline break. Each pair of columns is connected by a crossbar on which the pipeline can slide from side to side. This will prevent the pipe from splitting if there is any shifting of the permafrost or even a mild earth tremor. The pipe is also laid out in a zigzag pattern, so the pipe can expand and contract as the weather gets hot and cold. As the metal shrinks in extreme cold, the pipe will stretch out straight. As it expands in warmer weather, the pipe will go into the Z-shape.

In the end, both the oil companies and the environmentalists seem to have done each other some good. By calling attention to the special qualities of the Arctic environment, the environmentalists contributed to the construction of a better pipeline. The oil companies, on the other hand, made a great effort to lessen environmental damage. Perhaps this will be one case in which man can use precious natural resources without destroying a precious natural environment. Only time will tell.

BENJAMIN HAIMOWITZ
Science Writer

The pipeline zigzags across the barren, snow-covered wilderness. Half of it was built above ground to preserve the permafrost.

A MEDICAL MYSTERY

In July, 1976, about 10,000 members of the American Legion attended a three-day meeting in Philadelphia, Pennsylvania. After the legionnaires returned home, some of them began to get sick. First they got headaches and felt dizzy. Then they developed bad coughs, chest pains, and high fevers. Their illness was like pneumonia, but the medicines that cure pneumonia did not help them. More and more people became ill. But no treatment seemed to cure this mysterious illness—which soon became known as the legionnaires' disease.

▶TRACKING DOWN THE CLUES

Like detectives in a mystery story, doctors and scientists began to put together all the clues to find the solution—in this case, the cause of the disease and how to cure it. At first, the clues seemed to indicate that the strange illness might be a form of influenza known as swine flu. If the legionnaires' disease turned out to be swine flu, many people might die. (During an epidemic of swine flu in the winter of 1918–19, more than 20,000,000 people around the world had died.)

To see if legionnaires' disease was swine flu, doctors took blood samples and throat swabbings from the victims. They tested these samples to see if they could detect the virus that causes swine flu. But no viruses were found. The scientists also tested for viruses that cause other kinds of flu. Again, the same result: negative, no virus. Then they tested for other kinds of micro-organisms that cause illness, such as bacteria and fungi. All the tests had the same result: negative.

Scientists began to wonder if legionnaires' disease was caused by some unusual kind of micro-organism. At the same time, they began to look for other substances in the environment, such as a poisonous chemical. They thought the cause might be a chemical because the disease did not spread from one person to another. When members of the Legion became sick, the disease did not spread to members of their families. However, no chemical could be found that might have caused the illness.

By the end of summer, 181 people, most of whom had been at the convention, had gotten sick, and 29 of them had died. Sometimes doctors find it hard to tell what is making one person sick. But it is very unusual when doctors cannot find the cause of an illness that is making many people sick. Some began to think that legionnaires' disease might remain a mystery forever.

▶THE SOLUTION AT LAST

Scientists kept on looking for the cause of the illness. One of these scientists was Joseph E. McDade of the Center for Disease Control,

Tissue samples from victims of legionnaires' disease were frozen and kept for further tests.

an agency of the U.S. Public Health Service. McDade saw certain things under the microscope that led him to believe that the culprit everyone was looking for might be a rickettsia. Rickettsias—a family of micro-organisms that are smaller than bacteria—cause typhus, spotted fever, and other diseases.

Rickettsia can grow and reproduce only inside living cells. McDade and the people he worked with injected lung-tissue samples that had beeen taken from sick legionnaires into guinea pigs. Within a day or two the guinea pigs became ill. Tissue from the guinea pigs was then injected into the yolks of chicken eggs, a standard way to grow rickettsia. The chick embryos in the eggs died. But when McDade examined the yolks under a microscope, he found clusters of rod-shaped micro-organisms that were too large to be rickettsia. The scientists decided that the micro-organisms were some kind of unidentified bacteria that they had not tested for.

Now they had to find out whether these tiny organisms were, indeed, the cause of legionnaires' disease. To do this, they checked blood samples that had been taken from some of the disease victims. The blood samples proved to contain antibodies that reacted with the newly found bacterium. Antibodies are manufactured by the body to fight off foreign organisms. The antibodies had been formed in the cells of the sick legionnaires to fight off the bacteria. And so it was finally determined that this bacterium is the cause of legionnaires' disease. In 1977, new cases of illness caused by the same bacterium were reported in many parts of the country. It was also found that the bacterium had caused several outbreaks of unexplained illness in the past. Eventually, it was discovered that the bacterium had been active since at least 1965. But it is still not known how the disease is spread.

▶ THE DANGERS REMAIN

In the past 100 years scientists have identified most of the micro-organisms that cause disease in people. But as the legionnaires' disease shows, some dangerous micro-organisms are either very rare or remain unknown. In 1976, not long after the outbreak of legionnaires' disease, more than 335 people in the African nations of Zaire and Sudan died of Marburg disease, or green monkey disease. It is caused by a virus that was first discovered as recently as 1967.

Are legionnaires' disease and green monkey disease relatively new diseases, or are they old ones that occur rarely and are difficult to recognize? No one can say for sure. But it is important for scientists to learn how to prevent these diseases, and how to cure them if they do occur.

BENJAMIN HAIMOWITZ
Science Writer

Microscopic view of the bacterium that causes legionnaires' disease.

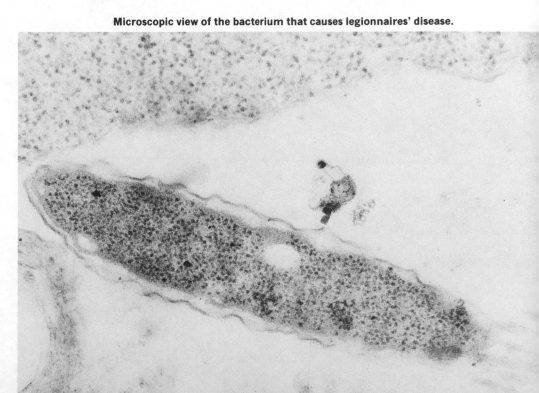

THE WATER CRISIS

Water, water, everywhere
Nor any drop to drink.

The Rime of the Ancient Mariner
Samuel Taylor Coleridge

Suppose you turned on a water faucet and no water came out. And then suppose you were told that the only water you would ever get would be a small bucketful each day. You may think this would be fun. You wouldn't have to wash your hands or take so many baths. But not having plenty of water isn't really fun. Being dirty all the time isn't pleasant. Being thirsty is even worse. Anyone who doesn't have enough water can tell you that.

But you don't have to worry. You do have lots of water. Or do you? Today scientists are saying that we are on the brink of a water crisis, that the world may actually run out of water in the future.

This may seem hard to believe. You know that there is plenty of water on our planet. Oceans and seas cover more than three quarters of the earth's surface. There is still more water in rivers, lakes, and streams. Even the air is full of vaporized water. There is, in fact, a lot of water. The problem is that we can't use most of it. About 97 percent of the world's water is salty and undrinkable. Less than three percent is fresh water. And most of this fresh water is locked away in polar ice caps or buried very deep under the earth. So there really isn't such a very great deal of water that we can get to and use.

All living things except those that live in the oceans must have fresh water to stay alive. But our freshwater supply is beginning to run low. Not just in deserts and other dry areas, but everywhere.

▶ WHY IS THERE A WATER SHORTAGE?

There are a number of reasons for the water crisis. Both nature and people are causing it.

Not enough rain. Most of the world's fresh water comes from precipitation—rain, snow, sleet, and hail. Today scientists and weather experts are very concerned about changing weather patterns that are affecting precipitation. Parts of the earth have been getting less rain than usual. In recent years many areas of the world have had severe droughts—northern Africa, China, southeast Asia, western Europe, and the western United States. This weather pattern may not last long—or it may be the beginning of a major climate change. And if the lack of rain continues, it will only add to the growing water shortage.

We use too much. Too many people are using too much water, especially people who live in industrialized nations. They bathe often and use a lot of water for cooking. They wash cars, water lawns, flush toilets, and fill swimming pools. And they carelessly waste water too. Millions of gallons of fresh water go down the drain every year from open hydrants, half-filled washing machines, and water faucets that people forget to turn off.

Modern industry has also added to the water crisis. Industries provide us with many of the things we need. But they also use vast amounts of fresh water. For example, it takes 150 tons of fresh water to make one ton of steel, 180 tons of water to refine one ton of oil, 250 tons of water to make one ton of paper. And as industry continues to grow, its demand for fresh water grows too.

Water pollution. Industry not only uses vast amounts of water, it also pollutes. When rivers, lakes, and streams become polluted, we lose valuable supplies of fresh water. Many factories return water that contains chemicals and other industrial wastes to rivers and other natural waterways. Nature by itself cannot remove or destroy these chemicals to make the river water pure again. If the impurities cannot be removed, this polluted water can never be used for drinking or cooking or irrigating crops. It is poisoned. Think of what would happen if you poured a cup of dirty water into a pot of clean water. The whole pot of water would become dirty and impossible to use.

Population growth. The more people there are in the world, the more water they will need. Right now there are over 4,000,000,000 (billion) people in the world. That's many, many more than there were 50 years ago. By the year 2,000 there may very well be more than 7,000,000,000 (billion) people on earth. They will need more water to drink, more water to cook with, more water to wash with, and more water to grow crops for food. If there is barely enough fresh water today, where will all these people in the year 2,000 get it?

Nature is one cause of the water shortage: in recent years it has been raining less.

TOTAL WORLD WATER

FRESH
WATER
2.7%

OCEAN
WATER

97.3%

SOURCES OF FRESH WATER

FROZEN
WATER
76.0%

WATER
VAPOR
.04%

GROUNDWATER
1/2 MILE DEEP
11.7%

GROUNDWATER
BELOW 1/2 MILE
11.7%

SOIL
MOISTURE
.2%

LAKES,
RIVERS,   .36%
STREAMS

About 97 percent of the world's water is undrinkable. Less than 3 percent is fresh water. And most of this fresh water is locked away in polar ice caps. Some countries are now planning to tow icebergs to areas that need fresh water.

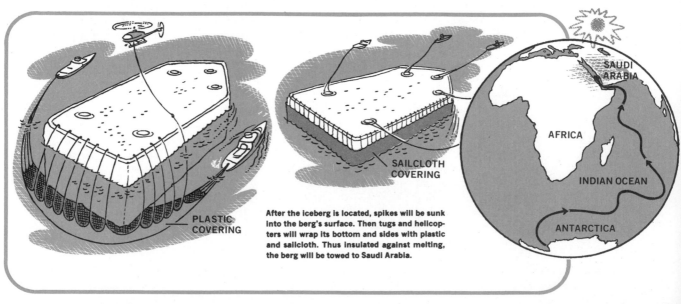

PLASTIC
COVERING

SAILCLOTH
COVERING

After the iceberg is located, spikes will be sunk into the berg's surface. Then tugs and helicopters will wrap its bottom and sides with plastic and sailcloth. Thus insulated against melting, the berg will be towed to Saudi Arabia.

SAUDI
ARABIA

AFRICA

INDIAN OCEAN

ANTARCTICA

People are another cause of the water shortage: we use a lot, especially if we live in an industrialized country. With a flush of the toilet, a great deal of fresh water goes down the drain.

THE UN WATER CONFERENCE

In March, 1977, the United Nations held a two-week conference on the water crisis. Politicians and technical experts from more than 100 countries met at Mar del Plata in Argentina. They talked about water: the lack of pure drinking water in many parts of the world; the droughts in Europe, Asia, Africa, and North America; hydroelectric power; flood control. One thing they all agreed on was that nature alone can no longer take care of the world's water needs. Nature needs help.

NEW SOURCES OF FRESH WATER

Towing icebergs. Two thirds of the world's fresh water is in icebergs found at the north and south poles. In other words, icebergs are frozen fresh water. Icebergs often break away and drift toward warmer parts of the world. But they move slowly and usually melt back into the sea before they get very far.

Recently a number of countries have become interested in an unusual idea—towing icebergs from the polar regions to areas that need fresh water. The oil-rich country of Saudi Arabia hired a French company to study the idea. The company said it could wrap a 100,000,000-ton iceberg in a thick plastic sheet. Then several powerful tugboats would tow it 7,500 miles (12,000 kilometers), from Antarctica to Saudi Arabia. About one fifth of each iceberg would

be lost during the long journey, but the remaining ice would be melted for drinking water and irrigation. The project would cost less than it does for Saudi Arabia to make the same amount of water by desalting seawater.

Fossil water. Another source of new fresh water is fossil water—water that is buried deep under the earth, especially under deserts. People have been digging wells for centuries, but these wells do not reach this deep fossil water. Until a short time ago there was no way to get at fossil water in most places. But modern scientific prospecting and drilling methods may be able to bring it to the surface.

Special crops. Scientists say we should develop food plants that can be irrigated with seawater—which is salty. About 80 percent of the fresh water that is available to us is now used for agriculture, especially for irrigation. If land could be irrigated with seawater, huge amounts of fresh water would be freed for other uses. One country that has started to do this is Tunisia: it is successfully growing date palms with salty water.

Until then. . . . Getting new supplies of fresh water is important, but it will take time. Until new supplies are available, we must use what we have more carefully. We must stop wasting water and we must stop polluting water.

JOSEPH MORSCHAUER
Science Writer

115

IS ANYBODY OUT THERE?

A great whirlwind surrounded by fire came out of the north. From its midst came four creatures. They looked somewhat like people, but each had four faces, those of a man, a lion, an ox, and an eagle. Each creature had four wings and brass-colored feet that resembled a calf's.

These awe-inspiring creatures were described by the Prophet Ezekiel thousands of years ago. But throughout the ages, writers and artists have described their visions of fan-

tastical creatures. When presented as being scientifically possible, these descriptions are called science fiction. And yet, is it really fiction? Maybe there are such creatures—living, intelligent beings in outer space, with whom people on Earth can communicate.

Many scientists think this is possible. They believe that ours isn't the only advanced civilization in the universe. The scientists point out that there are probably millions and millions of other planets in the universe, revolving around suns, or stars, much like our own sun. Many of these planets probably have environmental conditions that would support some sort of life, resembling bacteria perhaps. But on some planets, there might be intelligent creatures much more advanced than Earth's human beings.

How can we find these intelligent beings? Scientists are using three methods in their search: sending unmanned spacecraft, sending messages, and listening for messages.

In 1972 the United States launched a spacecraft called Pioneer 10. It traveled toward Jupiter, which it passed in 1973, sending back a lot of valuable information about the giant planet. Pioneer 10 continued on its path away from Earth. A few years from now it will leave our solar system, on an endless journey toward other stars and planets. Maybe a strange civilization will see and capture it. In case that happens, scientists have put a message on board the spacecraft. The message, engraved on an aluminum plaque, includes pictures of a woman and a man and diagrams of facts about Earth, the rest of our solar system, and the hydrogen atom. This was the first attempt to send a written message into outer space.

Another kind of message was placed aboard a Voyager spacecraft that was launched in 1977. The Voyager is expected to pass by Jupiter, Saturn, and Uranus. After twelve years in our solar system, it too will pass into outer space. The Voyager carries a record player and a copper record. The recorded message includes greetings in 60 different languages, and even from some whales. Also on the record are coded signals that can be turned into 116 photos of people, things, and places on Earth. Then there is a sequence of Earth sounds, such as earthquakes, rain, wind, a baby's cry, cars, planes. Most of the record is music—a variety that includes Bach, Beethoven, Chuck Berry, and a Peruvian wedding song.

Don't expect to hear next year—or even in your lifetime—that another civilization has received these messages. Our solar system's *nearest* neighbor is the star Alpha Centauri. It will take the Voyager 40,000 years to reach this star, and perhaps millions of years before it nears a place inhabited by intelligent beings.

Since messages in spacecraft take so very long to reach another part of the universe, some scientists believe this isn't the best way to contact other beings. They believe we should listen for, and send, signals, which travel much faster than spacecraft.

About 1960, scientists decided that the best signals to use were radio signals. Radio signals, or radio waves, travel at the speed of light—186,282 miles (300,000 kilometers) per second. In addition to traveling very fast, radio waves are not usually lost or weakened as they move through the atmosphere or outer space.

The United States space agency (NASA) has recommended a project called SETI—*S*earch for *E*xtra*t*errestrial *I*ntelligence. The project would be carried out over a period of six years by two research teams.

The researchers would use radiotelescopes to "listen" for radio waves coming from space. One team would map the part of the sky that is visible over the southwestern United States. The second team would listen to stars that lie within 100 light years of Earth. (A light year is the distance that light travels in a year—which is about 6 trillion miles, or 9.5 trillion kilometers.)

As you may know, radio waves have many different frequencies. Think what problems you would have if a friend told you to listen to a special radio program tonight, but didn't tell you what station, or frequency, to tune to. Like your radio, a telescope can be tuned to only one frequency at a time. The SETI scientists would listen to either of two radio frequencies. One is the frequency of the radio waves given off by hydrogen atoms. The other is the frequency of the combination of one hydrogen atom and one oxygen atom, called the hydroxyl radical. Scientists reason that if there are scientists on other planets, they might guess that these radio frequencies are the best "channels" of interplanetary communication.

Other projects have already listened for radio waves from outer space. So far, all they have heard have been hissing and crackling

sounds. These are the constant noises that radio telescopes pick up from anywhere in space.

Sending messages with radio signals is faster than sending them in spacecraft, but it still takes a long, long time—if it works at all. Even a message from a planet in a fairly nearby solar system would take 200 years to reach us. As one scientist commented, "They say 'Hello, how are you?' and 200 years later they hear us say, 'Fine!' It's not what you would call a snappy dialogue!"

Of course there's always the chance that creatures from outer space may come to visit us. Some people think this has already happened. But most scientists put more faith in spacecraft and radiotelescopes than in reports of encounters with flying saucers and whirlwinds surrounded by fire.

ENERGY-CONSERVATION PATENTS

Energy crunch! Energy crisis! Energy conservation! These are the cries we hear every day from scientists, public officials, and statesmen as they try to design a program to solve the world's growing energy shortage.

We need petroleum for making gasoline to drive our cars, diesel fuel to run our trains and trucks, oil to heat our homes, and many useful chemicals. But the supply of petroleum is becoming scarce and the same is true of natural gas. At the same time, the need for energy is continually increasing as the world's population grows and as more countries become industrialized.

Other sources of energy, such as solar, nuclear, wind, and geothermal energy, are now being developed and expanded. But until they are fully developed, we are all urged to use less energy and to use it more efficiently. We should drive our cars less, ride in car pools, use public transportation, insulate our homes, and keep the thermostat down in home, office, and factory.

These are just some of the ways that people are trying to conserve energy today. But long before today's energy crisis struck, ingenious inventors were coming up with imaginative ideas to accomplish the same purpose. Some of them thought of ways to travel without using a single drop of gasoline or a single watt of electricity. We find their ideas embodied in inventions for which they obtained patents as long as 100 years ago.

A patent is a document granted to an inventor by the government. Even a child can get one. The patent gives the inventor the exclusive rights to his or her invention for a fixed number of years. This means that no one else can make, use, or sell the invention without the inventor's permission.

Many patents have been granted for inventions intended to conserve energy. Here are some early ones that are quite ingenious and amusing.

HARRY GOLDSMITH
Former Patent Counsel

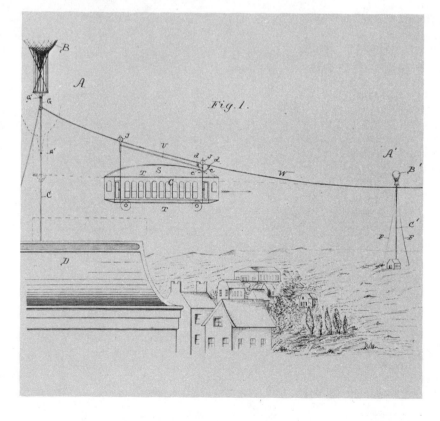

Fig. 1.

The Aerial Railway and Car was patented in 1885. Balloons, soaring high above the earth, are anchored to the ground along the route you want to travel. A cable connects the balloons. Suspended from the cable is a cable car carrying passengers. To make the car move along the cable, the ballons are raised or lowered to incline the cable properly. By the energy of its own weight—that is, by gravity—the car will travel down the cable from one station to the next, somewhat like a child zooming down a slide.

The Dogmobile was patented in 1870. It has a cylinder-shaped cage for a front wheel. Inside the cage are two dogs. When the dogs run, they turn the wheel, making the car move. The dogs get exercise and the driver gets to his destination and back at dog speed.

An Aerial Auto was patented in 1887, in which living motors replace mechanical ones. In this invention eagles, vultures, or condors are connected to the vehicle by a special harness. When the giant birds flap their wings, they are able to drive the auto in any direction.

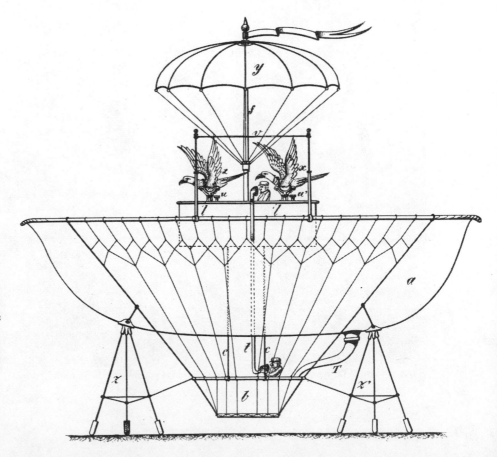

A trip on Lunar Odyssey will give you an idea of what space flight may be like 50 years from now.

THE LARGEST SPACE MUSEUM IN THE WORLD

Would you like to fire a real rocket engine, handle the controls on a make-believe space mission, and get a closeup look at a spaceship that took astronauts to the moon? You can do all this and more at the Alabama Space and Rocket Center, the largest space museum in the world.

The Center is in Huntsville, Alabama, and it has an exciting story to tell. It's the story of our journey into space—from the earliest missions, to moon landings, and beyond.

The first lady of space. One of the world's first space explorers lives at the Space and Rocket Center. She isn't a person—she's a monkey named Miss Baker. Miss Baker was one of the first two monkeys to travel successfully in space, in 1959. Wearing a special space suit and helmet, she was carried in a Jupiter rocket on a 15-minute trip, at speeds up to 10,000 miles per hour (16,000 kilometers per hour). During the voyage, electronic instruments recorded her heartbeat, her rate of breathing, and other information about how her body was working in space. This information gave scientists a very good idea of what space travel would be like for humans.

Miss Baker now lives in a special "monkeynaut" house at the Center. If you don't get a chance to visit her there, you might write her a letter. Her address is: Miss Baker, Alabama Space and Rocket Center, Huntsville, Alabama 35807.

Space Hall and Rocket Park. After space flights using Miss Baker and other animals, scientists were ready for manned missions. The Center's collection of space hardware includes many of the actual vehicles (or similar ones) that were used on those trips. In Space Hall, you can see a Soviet Vostok capsule like the one flown by the first man in space. There's also a lunar buggy like the one driven on the moon by American astronauts. And you can inspect the actual Mercury capsule that was flown by the first American to orbit earth.

In Rocket Park, there are 32 full-size rockets and missiles, including an Apollo Saturn V. The Apollo Saturn V is the largest rocket ever built. It is longer than a football field—and these rockets were used to send astronauts to the moon.

Lunar Odyssey. Only specially trained people have flown in space so far. But scientists believe that within 50 years people will fly to the moon as easily as they ride on jet planes today. A ride on the Center's Lunar Odyssey—a make-believe spaceship—gives you an idea of what that trip will be like.

You begin by walking through a hatch into a huge, circular, dome-covered room. You strap yourself into one of the 46 passenger couches. The pilot takes his place at the controls, begins the countdown, and you blast off—on a simulated journey to the moon.

The rocket engines roar and you are pushed back against the couch by a force that is similar to what astronauts feel when their ships speed up very quickly. As Odyssey enters space, the force stops and your couch lifts off the floor, free-floating in the spaceship. It's as if you are weightless. The ceiling becomes an enormous viewing window, and you can watch the earth falling away as you speed toward the moon. Soon the pilot enters lunar orbit, and you can see the crater-covered surface of the moon. Then you land at Lunar Base One, and your fantastic journey is over. You won't really have traveled to the moon, but you will have gotten a preview of what the trip may be like in the future.

Marshall Space Flight Center. The spacecraft of tomorrow are being developed at the nearby Marshall Space Flight Center. There, you can inspect a Space Shuttle, and you can even go inside a model of a Skylab space station. Astronauts lived and worked in such a space station for nearly three months. You will see how they cooked, washed, and slept in space.

You can also visit a "Solar House," which gets all its energy—for heating and cooking—from the sun. Scientists built the "Solar House" using knowledge and materials developed in the space program. It is an example of how we can use on earth the things we learn in our exploration of space.

These exhibits are only part of the story of space exploration. A trip to the Alabama Space and Rocket Center is an exciting way to learn the rest of the story.

DAVID KULL
Science Writer

The topiary garden in Portsmouth, Rhode Island.

GREEN ANIMALS

A giraffe that can't bend its neck. A bear that won't chase you. A rooster that doesn't crow. A swan that can't swim.

Is this an animal hospital? No, it's a garden where all these animals are green. Though they look like animals, they are really green plants that have been given animal forms.

The art of shaping plants into special forms is called topiary gardening. It is a very ancient art, begun by the Romans. It reached its greatest popularity in England, about 300 years ago. Today, many fine topiary forms can still be seen in English gardens.

One excellent topiary garden in the United States is in Portsmouth, Rhode Island. It is named Green Animals, and it has 85 topiary plants. Some are geometrical shapes—spirals, cones, balls, columns, and arches. But the most popular shapes are the animals, such as the elephant, mountain goat, dogs, and ostrich. There's even a man riding a horse.

Not every plant can be trained into a topiary form. The best plants to use are trees and bushes with small, closely packed leaves or needles. Boxwood, privet, yew, and hemlock are plants that are often used.

Some topiary shapes are fairly simple to create, such as a tree in the shape of a ball or pyramid. Other shapes, such as animals, are more difficult to achieve. It may take five or six years to create a large animal.

To keep its shape, topiary sculpture must be pruned—the branches, twigs, and leaves that aren't needed must be cut off. Pruning has to be done several times a year. If it isn't, that giraffe will grow a beard, and the elephant's trunk will get very, very long.

But you don't need a large garden or big bushes to practice topiary gardening. Plant a small boxwood in a pot and keep it indoors or on a patio. By carefully pruning it and using wires to train it, you can slowly create an unusual shape. It will take lots of time and patience, but you might be the first person in your neighborhood to have a green animal as a pet.

JENNY TESAR
Consultant, Curriculum Concepts, Inc.

A chicken.

A giraffe.

A bear.

A camel.

FUN TO MAKE AND DO

A group of high school students in Nyack, New York, came up with an exciting project in 1977. In an effort to beautify their Main Street, they created a mural on the outside wall of a store. The mural shows what two Nyack streets looked like at the turn of the century. Maybe the residents of the town or city where you live would like to have a mural too.

START A KIDS-ONLY CLUB

A club brings together, on a regular basis, friends or people who have similar ideas or interests. It brings them together to do something. The something that they decide to do is what the club is all about.

So why don't you start a kids-only club? It's great fun, mainly because *you* are the ones in charge. A kids-only club doesn't have adults around to tell members how everything should be done. The members themselves decide what the club is going to do.

▶ YOUR FIRST CLUB MEETING

One of the reasons why many adult clubs last and most kids-only clubs do not is that grown-ups have learned that there must be somebody who takes charge. Every group needs a leader. So, first thing, vote on who's to be in charge.

Pick a temporary chairperson. Even at this first get-together, you'll need somebody who will lead and keep things in order.

You'll also need a temporary secretary to write things down.

Also at the first meeting, you have to set up a list of simple ground rules for your club. When people play an organized game, like baseball or football, they follow ground rules. Everybody agrees ahead of time what the rules are to be and promises to follow them. That is the best way to avoid arguments and to keep the game going. It is the best way to organize a club, too.

Mention in the ground rules the main *reason* or *purpose* for your club (to put on shows, to run a carnival, to collect and trade stamps, to help animals, or whatever).

The rules should also tell about the *members* (who they can be). It should tell all about the *officers* (how many the club will have—president or chairperson, secretary, and so on—what these officers' jobs will be, how they are to be elected, how often you will vote for new officers, and so on).

Tell when the club's *meetings* will be held (once a week or once a month, on which days, at what time).

Another ground rule to be decided is how

many members must be present to take a *vote* on any matter to make it stick.

Don't vote on these suggested ground rules during the first meeting. This list is just for everybody to think about. When members come back for the second meeting, vote on them then. And remember, these rules are not forever. If members want to change them later, they can vote in new rules, just like with any law in government.

Another thing you can talk about during the first meeting and vote on during the second is a name for your club. The name tells your members and the world clearly what you do. At the second meeting, with your temporary chairperson in charge, let everyone discuss the names suggested and then vote on them.

VOTING FOR OFFICERS

Once you have your name and your ground rules, the temporary chairperson and secretary have done their jobs. Now regular officers can be elected. These officers can serve for a month or a year or whatever your club decided in the ground rules. Most clubs have a president, a vice president, a secretary, and a treasurer. The president runs the club, the vice president is in charge when the president is absent, the secretary takes notes and answers letters, and the treasurer takes care of the money.

When you vote for club officers, you don't want to hurt anyone's feelings. So keep your votes secret by having members write their choices on pieces of paper rather than by holding up their hands while everybody watches.

CLUB DUES

Many of the things that your club will do won't cost any money. Other things may cost a little to get started, though they may turn out to be money-making in the end. For example, to put on a craft fair you'll need to buy supplies, but by the time the craft fair is over, you'll probably have made more money than you spent.

Start off by deciding on a specific amount (perhaps a dollar) that all members must pay to join. This is an *initiation fee* and will give you something to start with. Then set *dues*, the small amount of money each member will give at each meeting.

The amount of dues can be decided by your group. Don't make your dues too high or some members might have to drop out because they can't afford it.

RUNNING YOUR MEETING

Here's how most people run their club meetings so that everything can be talked about and decisions made without members getting into arguments:

1) The president calls the meeting to order. In other words, he gets everybody quiet.

2) The secretary calls the roll. Members answer "Here" when their names are called.

3) The secretary reads the notes made at the last meeting. These notes (called "minutes") tell what was decided at the last meeting.

4) The treasurer tells how much money the club has and how it is being spent.

5) Dues are collected.

6) Old business (any matters discussed by the members at the last meeting but not decided on by a vote) is taken care of.

7) Plans for things you want to do in the future are talked about and voted on. This is called "new business." Sometimes a vote is not taken, so this "new business" becomes "old business" at the next meeting.

8) Then you do whatever you decided to do at this meeting (make your puppets or posters, write the play or news release, construct the games for your carnival, make the decorations for your party).

9) At the end of every meeting make absolutely sure that you have fully planned what you are going to do at the next get-together and that all the members know when and where the next meeting will be held.

10) Straighten up. Pick up. Clean up. If you leave your meeting room even neater than you found it, you and your friends will always be welcomed back.

▶ WHERE TO MEET

A club member's home will work very well as a meeting place the first few times you get together.

The very best meeting place for a kids-only club will have:

1) Privacy
2) Enough room for all the members
3) A place that you can fix up to suit your particular activity. (This may be hard to find and may be something you have to do without.)

If you can't find these things at a club member's home, try a local church or a community center. All these places have meeting rooms. Or you can try storekeepers and merchants who may have an interest in the purpose of your group. A coin club could check out the local coin dealers; a model-building club, the local hobby shop; a magic club, the nearest magic store.

Other leads for you to follow are schools (call the principal's office and ask if you can meet after hours in a classroom or the auditorium); the YMCA or YWCA; parks and playgrounds (many have buildings where people can get together); and libraries.

▶ A SPECIAL SIGN

You may want everyone to know that you're a member of a special club. If you do, you can try designing a sign for your club and make it your official emblem. Once you have selected your emblem, hang it up on your clubroom wall for all to see. You can also have a rubber stamp made of your club emblem to use on any official papers, notices, or posters.

If you have enough money in your treasury, you can even send a copy of your emblem to a patch maker and have a jacket patch made for each member. This makes a super gift for new members. You'll find patch makers in your city listed under Emblems in the Yellow Pages of the telephone book.

With your ground rules, officers, meeting plans, and emblems, you're on your way to being the most organized and successful club in your neighborhood.

There are many things your club can do, but at the beginning it's best to do them one at a time.

Start by letting everyone pick one activity that he or she would most like to do. Talk about each idea and then take a vote. Most of the members of the club should agree on the project before it is started.

Some activities can be enjoyed with little planning, at the very next meeting (like making puppets or playing some games). Others (like putting on a play) will take a number of meetings to prepare.

Here are some tips on how to plan an event requiring a lot of preparation.

In choosing a date for the event, pick a day that is best for most of your members. It's not always easy to find one day that's perfect for everybody, but if you plan ahead, people will set the day aside so they can be there.

If you would like the public to come, be sure to advertise early enough to let everybody know that you're having a special event and that everyone is invited. Think about the people you want to attract, and choose a day and an hour when they would probably be free to come.

Give your kids-only clubbers plenty of time before that date to work up the project you have all chosen. Preparing for your party or carnival or craft fair can be almost as much fun as giving it, so don't cheat yourselves by having to rush it.

Think about all the different things you have to do. Make a list and figure out how much time each job will take. Two weeks isn't enough time to plan a craft fair but should be plenty for planning a picnic.

One general rule to remember when you're setting the day: everything takes just a little longer than you think it will. Make sure you allow enough time to get everything done.

Once you have picked an event and the date, vote on a member who will be in charge. That person must make sure that everyone is doing the job he or she promised to do, and that everything is in place when it's needed on that day.

Then divide the club members into small groups, or committees. Each committee should be responsible for one part of the project.

Now that you and your friends know how to set up and run a kids-only club and how to go

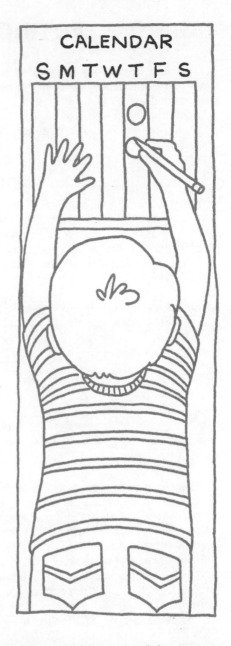

about organizing activities, you might want to plan block parties, a pet-walking or babysitting service, or a neighborhood talent show or swap meet. You might even try starting your own neighborhood newspaper. It's all up to you. You can do it.

Your club can be one of the nicest things you do with your friends. Now go out and have a simply wonderful kids-only club time.

SHARI LEWIS
Puppeteer and Author, *The Kids-Only Club Book*

COIN COLLECTING

The year 1977 brought events of uncommon interest to collectors of coins, paper money, and related items. These events included unusual errors in the printing of paper money in the United States; the Silver Jubilee in Britain; and a new coinage series from the Cocos Islands.

Official medal marking Carter's inauguration.

▶ U.S. ISSUES AND NEWS

From late 1976 through the first quarter of 1977, newly released paper money, in denominations of $1 through $20, provided eagle-eyed collectors with many bonanzas. The bills had been printed with errors on them. These

Upside-down printing on a U.S. $1 bill.

had gone undetected when the bills were processed through new automatic equipment at the Bureau of Engraving and Printing. The errors that made the bills valuable were mainly inverts (upside-down printing) of serial numbers or the seal. Discoverers were enriched by amounts ranging from about $100 to several times that amount, depending on the denominations.

The debate over the future of some U.S. bills and coins continued. The Department of the Treasury suggested that the 1-cent and half-dollar coins be abolished, and the dollar coin be made smaller in size. They argued that the cent, which is rapidly losing purchasing power, is costly to produce and that the two other coins are rarely seen in circulation because of their large size. A new dollar coin slightly larger than the quarter was recommended.

The election of Jimmy Carter to the presidency in 1976 had several effects on the coin-collecting hobby in 1977. The official medal to

mark his inaugural had a profile portrait designed by the Atlanta artist Julian Harris. It was produced by the Franklin Mint. Another presidential medal, this one issued by the U.S. Mint, was designed by the Mint's sculptor and engraver Frank Gasparro.

President Carter appointed Azie Taylor Morton as treasurer of the United States and W. Michael Blumenthal as secretary of the treasury. The signatures of these officials are on the 1977 paper currency series.

Each year proof sets and mint sets of U.S. coins are available to collectors. In 1977 proof sets were offered at $9 a set. Proof sets contain one specially struck coin of each denomination, from the cent through the dollar. Mint sets also contain one coin of each denomination, but they are not specially struck. They consist of coins produced for general circulation.

▶ A POCKETFUL OF NEW COINS

A royal anniversary in Britain—the Silver Jubilee (25th anniversary) of Queen Elizabeth's accession to the throne—brought a flurry of commemorative coins from around the world. Britain issued a 25-pence coin in silver for collectors and a 25-pence coin in nickel for general circulation. Canada offered two coins—a $100 gold piece, with a portrait of the Queen on the face and a graceful bouquet of Canadian provincial flowers on the reverse, and a silver dollar. Other distinctive Jubilee coins included Australia's 50-cent piece; a

COINS COMMEMORATING THE SILVER JUBILEE

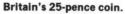

Britain's 25-pence coin.

130

Canada's $100 gold piece.

$100 gold coin from the Cayman Islands.

25-pence coin from Tristan da Cunha.

$100 gold coin from the Cayman Islands; a 25-pence coin from the Tristan da Cunha Islands; and a gold 100-tala issue, along with a 1-tala coin in nickel and silver versions, from Western Samoa.

The most interesting coinage of the year came from the Cocos Islands to celebrate the 150th anniversary of settlement there. The Cocos, also called the Keeling Islands, are a group of islets in the Indian Ocean about mid-

25-rupee silver coin from the Cocos Islands.

way between Australia and Sri Lanka (Ceylon). The islands were first sighted in 1609 by William Keeling of the East India Company. They were later settled by Malays and Britons led by John Clunies Ross, who established a coconut plantation. Today the islands are a protectorate of Australia. The new coins are a 150-rupee gold coin and silver coins of 25 and 10 rupees. They represent the first metal coinage of these islands. Previously, the islands had issued tokens, made at first of ivory or Celluloid and later of plastic.

Mexico issued a large 100-peso silver coin

Mexico's 100-peso silver coin.

with a picture of the patriot and priest José María Morelos y Pavón.

A portrait of former Prime Minister David Ben-Gurion appears on an Israeli 500-pound

Israel's 500-pound note.

note. The note has the highest value in the history of Israel's paper money.

CLIFFORD MISHLER
Publisher, *Numismatics News Weekly*

CALCULATOR TALK

If you have a little pocket calculator, it can be more fun than you think. It will do much more than add 2 and 2. You can make your calculator talk to you! Well, almost. Would you like to get acquainted?

Multiply .3867 by 2. Do this by pressing down on the decimal point (.), then the digits **3, 8, 6,** and **7.** Press the multiply (×) button, then enter the number **2.** Press the equals (=) button. Now turn the calculator so that you are reading the answer upside down. See how friendly your calculator can be?

Here's some more calculator talk:

1. A person who is very messy is sometimes called a _ _ _ _. (**2 × 4000 + 75 =**)

2. If you want to see many different kinds of animals, go to the _ _ _. (**0.06 ÷ 3 =**)

3. A _ _ _ produces honey. (**151 × 2 + 36 =**)

4. When Santa Claus comes down the chimney, he says _ _ _ _ _ _. (**1.21212 ÷ 3 =**)

5. When it is raining and you have galoshes on, it is fun to _ _ _ _ _ around in puddles. (**50,000 − 4925 =**)

6. After a game of Monopoly in which he went bankrupt, Tom said "_ _ _ _ _." (**8775 × 4 − 29 =**)

7. A worm, a snake, and a fish are all _ _ _ _ _ _ _. (**5,000,000 + 500,000 + 37,000 + 937 =**)

8. Many people read the _ _ _ _ _ every day. (**113454 ÷ 3 =**)

9. If you scared a snake, it might rise up and _ _ _ _ at you. (**11 × 500 + 14 =**)

10. When you are making pancakes, the griddle will _ _ _ _ _ _ when it is ready. (**744430 ÷ 2 =**)

11. Children often get an upset stomach if they _ _ _ _ _ _ their food. (**47250 × 8 + 809 =**)

12. In school, the teacher tries to teach us to keep our handwriting very _ _ _ _ _ _ _. (**5 × 756200 + 937 =**)

13. You might very well still find an Eskimo that lives in an _ _ _ _ _ _. (**0.2373 ÷ 3 =**)

14. Before you can eat an _ _ _, you must break the _ _ _ _ _ _ _ _. (**1986 ÷ 2 =**)(**1546900 × 50 + 993 =**)

15. The girl was taking lessons to learn to play the _ _ _ _. (**4555 − 1475 =**)

16. When a person is sad, he or she might cry _ _ _ _ _ _ or just _ _ _. (**0.32064 ÷ 8 =**)(**900 − 95 =**)

132

17. The _ _ _ likes to _ _ _ _ in the _ _ _. $(226 \times 4 =)$ $(18 \times 500 + 75 =)$ $(1000 - 92 =)$

18. During a long rain, _ _ _ _ often turns into a lot of _ _ _ and _ _ _ _. $(5 \times 1421 =)$ $(0.81 \div 9 =)$ $(4821 - 1621 =)$

19. A _ _ _ _ _ is helpful to a student studying geography. $(9 \times 4231 =)$

20. The _ _ _ _ _ _ _ _ _ _ _ _ and _ _ _ _ _ the _ _ _ _ _ _ _ _ _ _. $(2754 \div 3 =)$ $(4 \times 2002 =)$ $(30449 + 1426 + 25832 =)$ $(117048 - 63258 =)$ $(14 \times 1589 + 12761 =)$ $(17776 - 2666 + 19899 =)$

You may have figured out which numbers form which letters:

I	1
Z	2
E	3
H	4
S	5
L	7
B	8
G	9
O	0

Here are some more calculator words. Try to make your own sentence-puzzles with them. And make up some of your own words too. There are lots more!

be	38	hoe	304
beg	938	hole	3704
bell	7738	hose	3504
bless	55378	I	1
bliss	55178	ill	771
bobble	378808	leg	937
boil	7108	less	5537
boss	5508	lie	317
ego	0.93	log	907
else	3573	lose	3507
giggle	379919	obese	35380
glee	3379	oblige	391780
go	0.9	oil	710
goes	5309	sell	7735
gosh	4509	she	345
he	34	shell	77345
heel	7334	sigh	4915
hi	14	size	3215
high	4914	sleigh	491375
hill	7714	so	0.5
his	514	sole	3705
hobo	0.804	SOS	505

A TREE HOUSE MAZE

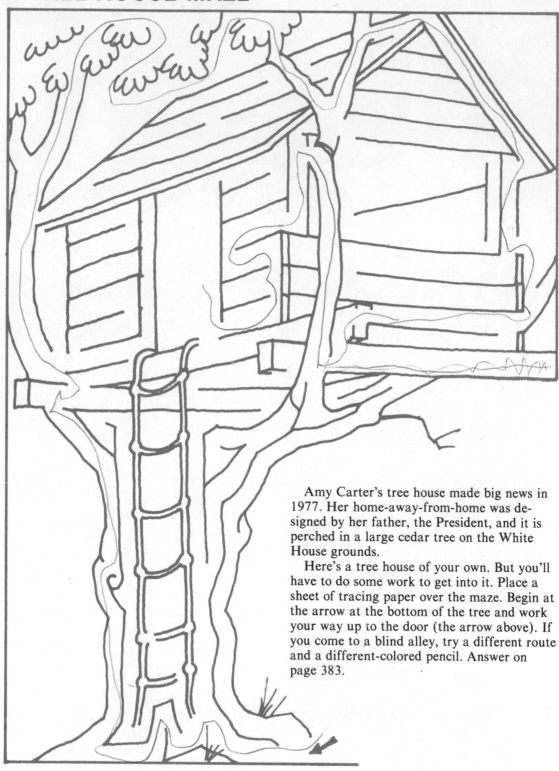

Amy Carter's tree house made big news in 1977. Her home-away-from-home was designed by her father, the President, and it is perched in a large cedar tree on the White House grounds.

Here's a tree house of your own. But you'll have to do some work to get into it. Place a sheet of tracing paper over the maze. Begin at the arrow at the bottom of the tree and work your way up to the door (the arrow above). If you come to a blind alley, try a different route and a different-colored pencil. Answer on page 383.

A HIDDEN PICTURE

In this picture find the key, Halloween cat, ladder, moon, the letter C, broom, jack-o'-lantern, horseshoe, shamrock, screw, witch's head, and the letter A.

EMBROIDER A POCKETBOOK

What to use:

2 squares of felt (for front and back
of pocketbook, each about the
size shown in the finished picture on page 137)
1 square of a different-colored felt (for handle)
pencil
tracing paper
scissors
straight pins
embroidery needle
6-strand embroidery floss (7 colors)
tape

What to do:

1. Tape a piece of tracing paper
over the picture on page 137.
Trace the pocketbook and all the designs on it.
Remove tracing paper. Now take a soft lead
pencil and vigorously rub it over the back of
the tracing paper. Pin the paper, penciled side
down, over one felt pocketbook square. Trace
over the lines on the paper. Remove paper. The
black lines on the felt are the designs that you
will embroider.

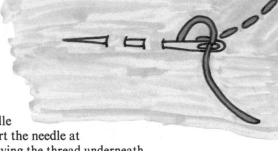

2. Here are two kinds of stitches. **Satin stitch:**
Starting from the wrong side of the felt, bring the needle
up at one edge of a design to be embroidered. Now insert the needle at
the opposite edge, and return to the starting edge by carrying the thread underneath
the felt. Make stitches parallel and close together. **Running stitch:** Insert the needle in and out
of the felt, making even stitches.

3. Embroider all the designs. Then, take your scissors
and cut all around the outside edges of the pocketbook.
This is the front. Pin it to the other square of pocketbook
felt, cut around it, and you will have the back.

4. Pin the front and back together.
Using the running stitch, sew around
the outline of the pocketbook leaving
scalloped edge open (as shown in the
finished picture).

5. Trace the handle from
the finished picture onto
tracing paper. Pin tracing to
your remaining square of
felt and cut out the handle.
Place the handle inside the
top of your two pocketbook
pieces and fasten with a few
stitches.

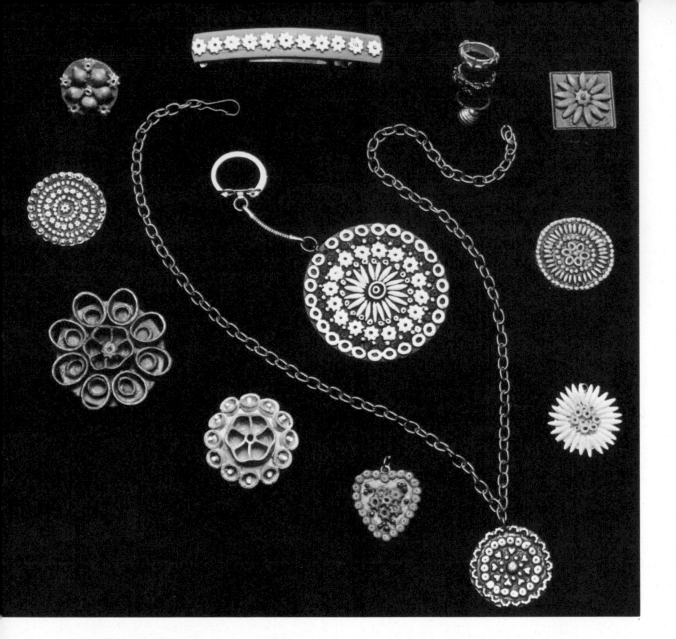

PASTE AND PASTA

It's fun. It's easy. It's inexpensive. In just a short time and with a handful of pasta, you can make toys, jewelry, and many other things. The craft is called macaroni magic . . . or noodle doodle . . . or paste and pasta.

All you have to do is take a plain object, decorate it with different kinds of pasta, and then cover it with bright paint. In this way you can change a plain piece of wood into a sign saying "My Room." A heart-shaped piece of cardboard becomes a brooch. A tin can turns into a vase or a pencil holder. A wooden building block becomes a paperweight.

Here's what you need:

• Items to decorate. These can include things made of wood, metal, plastic, stone, or glass.
• Pasta. There are almost 1,000 different shapes of pasta from which to choose. Select stars, wheels, elbows, shells, circles, squares, alphabets, or long straight spaghetti. Start with what you can find in your kitchen.
• Glue. White craft glue is good for wood, cardboard, and stone. Use model-airplane glue on glass, metal, and plastic.

• Acrylic paints.

• Acrylic spray. This seals the surface and makes the object easy to clean.

Let's turn a flat piece of wood into a paperweight. **Here's what to do:**

1) Be sure the wood is heavy enough to hold down a pile of papers and is clean.

2) Arrange pasta on the wood in any design that pleases your eye.

3) Glue the pasta—one piece at a time—onto the wood. When you have finished gluing on all the pieces, let the object stand until the glue is dry.

4) Paint the entire object. You may want to use two or more colors. For example, you could paint the entire object, including the pasta, pale green. After the first coat dries, paint the tops of the pasta dark green. (Or you may want to paint just the pasta and leave the wood natural.)

5) When you have finished painting and the paint is dry, cover your paperweight with a coat of clear acrylic spray.

There's almost no end to the items you can decorate. And even if you can't find anything to decorate, you can make something just with pasta. A necklace, for instance, by stringing together painted elbow macaroni. Or snowflakes for the Christmas tree by gluing together pasta circles of different sizes. Or a toy car from lasagna and manicotti noodles.

So get your paste and pasta, and begin!

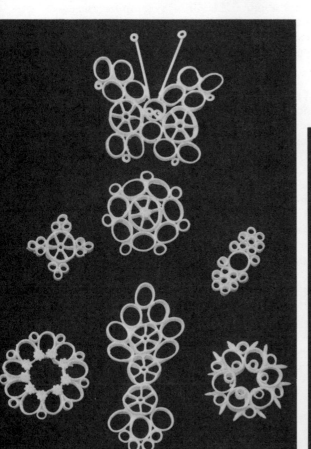

STAMP COLLECTING

A record number of stamps was issued around the world in 1977. Most of them were special stamps for collectors. But some of the new stamps issued were of higher denominations, as inflation continued to cause higher postage rates.

This same inflation also caused increases in the prices of collectible stamps. This situation brought joy to some collectors and gloom to others. Those collectors with many stamps and few spaces in their albums to fill were happy. Those with many spaces to fill—the majority of collectors—were unhappy. But however they felt, collectors had many tempting choices in 1977, including the chance to own reproductions of some of the rarest stamps in the world.

▶ ANNIVERSARY ISSUES

Two anniversaries in Britain attracted worldwide attention in 1977. One was the Silver Jubilee (25th anniversary) of Queen Elizabeth II's accession to the throne. The other was the 100th anniversary of the Wimbledon tennis championships. The Silver Jubilee was commemorated in stamps by the United Kingdom and other members of the Commonwealth, as well as by many other countries around the world.

The most interesting of the Silver Jubilee stamps was a series that was issued by a group of 24 members of the Commonwealth. The series was carefully planned, in alphabetical and chronological order, to tell the story of Elizabeth's coronation from the beginning to the end. A stamp from each Commonwealth nation depicted one important event. Thus the stamp from Ascension Island (the first member of the group, in alphabetical order) showed the first event—the departure of Elizabeth, in the gold coronation coach, from Buckingham Palace to Westminster Abbey, where she would be formally crowned. Stamps from Barbados, Belize, Bermuda, and so on, depicted other events, in sequence. Finally, the Turks and Caicos Islands stamp showed the Queen and her family waving to the crowds from the balcony of Buckingham Palace. Each of the 24 members also issued two other stamps. One showed an item used in the coronation ceremony, such as the crown or the scepter. The

other stamp commemorated a royal visit or some other link between the issuing country and Britain.

The Wimbledon anniversary prompted Britain to issue a stamp for each of the four racket sports—tennis, squash, badminton, and table tennis. All these sports developed in Britain about 100 years ago.

The United States added several stamps to its Bicentennial series. The 1977 stamps commemorated events of 1777, including Washington's victory at Princeton; the arrival of the Marquis de Lafayette from France; the drafting of the Articles of Confederation; the British surrender at Saratoga; and the valiant stand of General Nicholas Herkimer at the Battle of Oriskany.

The United States and several other countries issued stamps commemorating the 50th anniversary of Charles Lindbergh's historic transatlantic flight from New York to Paris on May 20–21, 1927. The rules of the U.S. Postal Service forbid the use of a person's name or picture on a stamp until at least 10 years after the person's death. Lindbergh died in 1974. For that reason the U.S. stamp showed only a picture of the plane, The *Spirit of St. Louis,* and the words "50th Anniversary Solo Transatlantic Flight." The French stamp for this occasion honored Lindbergh, as well as two French flyers, Nungesser and Coli. The French flyers disappeared while trying to cross the Atlantic from Paris two weeks before Lindbergh's flight.

The United States also issued a stamp honoring a century of progress in sound recording. The stamp shows the "talking machine," or phonograph, invented by Thomas A. Edison in 1877. A companion stamp commemorated the 50th anniversary of talking pictures. The design on this stamp features the equipment used to film and record *The Jazz Singer,* starring Al Jolson.

Canada and the United States each issued a stamp for the 50th anniversary of the Peace Bridge, which spans the Niagara River between Buffalo, New York, and Fort Erie, Ontario.

The 400th anniversary of the birth of the great Flemish artist Peter Paul Rubens was celebrated by beautiful stamps from Belgium, Liechtenstein, Monaco, and other countries. The Belgian stamps showed details of Rubens'

EUROPA
ESPAÑA
3 PTA
CORREOS

1977 STAMPS
FROM AROUND
THE WORLD

ESTAMPILLAS
RARAS Y FAMOSAS
1976
1959 CANADA
RUTA MARITIMA
INVERTIDA
correo 25 cts NICARAGUA
CANADA

PIERRE PAUL RUBENS (1577-1640)
60 f
RWANDA

SILVER JUBILEE
Arrival of Westminster Abbey
BARBADOS 50 c

SILVER JUBILEE
Her Majesty enters the Abbey
BARBADOS $1

ANCIENT ISRAEL LYRE
ISRAEL 2.00
1977

13 c USA
ANNIVERSARY YEAR
OF TALKING
PICTURES

SILVER JUBILEE
E R
1952 9P 1977

Surrender at Saratoga 1777 by Trumbull
US Bicentennial 13 cents

United States & Canada
Peace Bridge 1927-77
USA 13c

SILVER JUBILEE
E R
15 P
St. Helena

USA·13c
50th Anniversary Solo Transatlantic Flight

1
CANADA

2.00

SILVER JUBILEE
OF QUEEN ELIZABETH II
FIJI 10c
THE QUEENS VISIT IN 1970

UNITED NATIONS WATER CONFERENCE
25c UNITED NATIONS

3
CANADA

paintings in the museums and churches of Antwerp.

▶THE WORLD'S RAREST STAMPS

Few people can afford to buy rare stamps, and most collectors never have a chance even to see famous rarities. Now, thanks to Nicaragua, collectors can obtain exact reproductions of 12 of the world's rarest stamps. An explanation of the features that make the stamp rare and valuable is printed on the back of each one.

The reproductions appear on Nicaraguan stamps of various denominations. The 5-centavo Nicaraguan stamp reproduces the most famous U.S. rarity—the 24-cent airmail of 1918 with an upside-down airplane in the center. The 1-centavo and 3-centavo stamps reproduce stamps issued by Mauritius in 1847 with the words "Post Office" printed in error for "Postpaid."

▶OTHER STAMPS FROM AROUND THE WORLD

The United Nations issued two stamps stressing the need to preserve the world's precious supply of water. The stamps commemorate themes of the U.N. Water Conference held in Mar del Plata, Argentina, in 1977. Another set of two U.N. stamps was devoted to the theme "Combat Racism."

The highly popular Europa series, issued each year by the member nations of the Conference of European Postal and Telecommunications Administrations, featured landscapes in 1977. Each member chose a scene in its own country, taken from either a painting or a photograph.

Collectors with a special interest in nature, the arts, history—or almost any other subject —had a wealth of choices in 1977. Canada issued six stamps showing some of its most beautiful native wild flowers and three more stamps in its series depicting native trees. Butterflies native to four geographic regions of the United States adorned a block of four U.S. stamps. Taiwan also issued a series showing its native butterflies. Another U.S. block of four stamps featured Pueblo Indian pottery.

From Israel came a trio of stamps depicting its musical heritage from Biblical times. The stamps show three musical instruments—a trumpet, a lyre, and a jingle (a metal percussion instrument). All the instruments are from a museum collection in Haifa. They reflect recent archeological finds that have aided research not only in ancient music but also in the history of the Middle East.

Israel issued another interesting set of stamps during the year. These five stamps depict archeological discoveries that reveal the architecture of ancient Jerusalem, as well as the tools and implements that the ancient people used in their everyday lives. Archeological finds were also featured on stamps from many other countries, including Greece, East Germany, the Gilbert Islands, New Zealand, the Republic of Niger, and Sweden.

To celebrate its independence in 1977, the tiny African nation of Djibouti (the former French Territory of the Afars and the Issas) issued two stamps. One showed a flag and a map of the country. The other showed a flag and Djibouti's location on a map of the continent of Africa.

▶A TOPICAL COLLECTION

Collectors looking for new ideas for a topical collection—a collection built around one theme—may find an ideal subject in New Year stamps. Welcoming the New Year is one of the world's oldest and most colorful customs. And no other event has been observed in so many different ways or on so many different dates.

Some of the 1977 New Year issues are especially interesting. These include stamps from Asian countries, where 1977 was observed as the Year of the Snake, according to the ancient Oriental zodiac. Japan issued a colorful stamp showing a traditional toy snake. It is made of pieces of bamboo connected by a wire and painted green and yellow. The snake was also featured on New Year stamps from Taiwan, South Korea, and Hong Kong. Iran, which celebrates New Year's Day on March 21, issued three stamps with designs of a butterfly, flowers, and a bird with streamers. Almost from its beginnings as a nation, Israel has produced stamps celebrating the Jewish New Year, which falls in August or September according to the ancient Hebrew calendar. The Soviet Union also has been issuing New Year stamps for some time.

CHARLESS HAHN
Stamp Editor
Chicago Sun-Times

A SHELL-FLOWER PICTURE

At some time or other you've probably been to the beach, gathered some shells, and taken them home with you. You may have put them in a box and tucked them away in a drawer or closet, where they may still be sitting. Don't throw them away. You can make lovely shell-flower pictures with them.

The next time you go to the beach, gather as many shells as you can. Try to collect a variety of bivalve shells because these are perfect for creating shell pictures. (Bivalves are animals that live in shell homes formed by *two* shells,

hinged together, rather than a single, or uni-valve, shell.)

In addition to your collection of shells, you will need a background for the arrangement, and a frame. The background can be a large piece of wood or fiberboard that has been covered with material. The material should be appropriate for the frame. For instance, if you are using a fancy antique frame, you would want a background material of velvet or taffeta. A simple wooden frame would probably look best with a burlap fabric.

Start with a picture frame, a background that has been covered with fabric, and a bowl that has been sawed in half and glued onto the fabric. Here, a lace sea fan and a piece of drift-wood have been put into place first, before any of the flowers, to make the final shell-flower picture even more interesting.

You will also need a bowl to be used as the base for your seashell flowers. The bowl must be sawed in half, leaving a flat side that will fit against the background. The bowl can be of any design, size, or finish. It can be left in its natural state, painted gold, or decorated with a colorful design. When you have your fabric, frame, and bowl, you are ready to begin.

• Glue the fabric to the piece of wood or fiberboard with a thick white glue. Test thin materials first to make sure the glue doesn't go through the material and stain it. Let the fabric dry, and then glue, staple, or nail the entire piece onto the back of the frame.

• Decide where you want to position the half bowl, and glue it onto the fabric. Allow time for the glue to dry.

• Now you are ready to make your flowers. Because everyone's collection of shells is unique, the number and types of flowers made will vary from person to person. That is one of the reasons that making shell-flower pictures is a truly creative art. No two arrangements are ever the same.

• The basic materials for making the flowers are: seashells of assorted bivalves in all sizes; thick white glue; long pointed tweezers; cotton; round toothpicks; waxed paper.

• Each flower will need a "base" to support it. Use a small, rounded piece of glue-soaked cotton. The size of the piece of cotton will depend on the size of the flower you are making. For small shells, use a ¼-inch (.6 centimeter) piece, and for larger ones use pieces up to 1 inch (2.5 centimeters) across.

• Place the mound of glue-soaked cotton on a small piece of waxed paper. Then put a fairly large amount of glue on another section of the waxed paper. Holding a shell in your fingers (or with tweezers), first dip it into the glue and then push it into the gluey cotton mound. Repeat this procedure with more shells of the same type. Arrange them so that they resemble a flower, with each shell forming a petal.

• You can arrange the shells (or petals) in many different ways to make different kinds of flowers. Try overlapping the petals for a pretty effect.

• For flower centers, use small shells such as baby cups, baby whelks, lilacs, ceriths, and small flat snail shells. Colored mustard seeds are also good.

• When all the flowers are finished and the

You can make many different shell flowers. Try overlapping the "petals," and use smaller shells or mustard seeds for flower centers.

The "base" for each flower is a small, rounded piece of glue-soaked cotton. Arrange the shells on the cotton to form a flower, with the shells as petals.

Try adding a spray of flowers: glue small shell flowers onto a curved piece of florist wire.

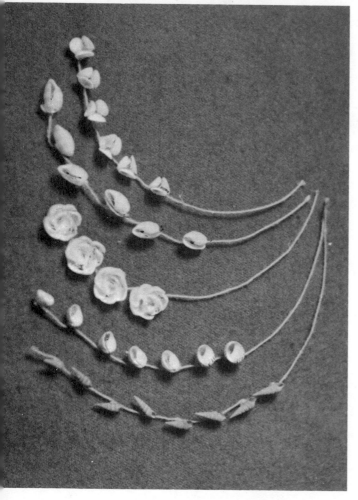

glue has dried, spray them with an acrylic lacquer spray. Or carefully paint them with clear nail polish.

• When the spray or polish is completely dry, carefully pull each flower away from the waxed paper. If there is any excess cotton you can cut it away with a small pair of scissors.

• Now you are ready to arrange the flowers on your fabric-covered background in such a way that they appear to be growing out of the bowl. Start placing the flowers and be guided by what looks best to you. Try different placements and flower combinations without gluing anything down until you are sure that the arrangement pleases you.

• A helpful suggestion in planning your arrangement is to stay with the odd numbers, 1, 3, 5, 7, and so on. For instance, three large flowers clustered together will be more pleasing to the eye than two or four. Try clustering flowers of one type together. Or scatter them throughout the arrangement. Try adding some sprays of shells for a graceful touch.

• Would you like to add some leaves to your floral arrangement? You can add greenery by using green-dyed gar scales (a very hard fish scale); cutout paper leaves from wallpaper, catalogs, or magazines; fabric leaves purchased from craft shops; plastic leaves; or even leaves you've made yourself from ribbon or fabric.

• Remember, don't glue until all the flowers have been placed. Before gluing, you may want to fill the bowl. If you have some interesting univalve shells, this would be a good place to use them. Other small leftover shells could be used here, too, as well as colorful pebbles.

• Before you begin gluing the flowers in place, it is a good idea to take your attention away from the arrangement for a while. Leave it for half an hour or so. When you return, ask yourself whether you still like it. If you do, you can begin gluing.

• Start with the larger, basic pieces of the arrangement. Slowly glue each flower into place. The outer flowers are glued next, and the sprays are added last. If you are adding leaves, tuck them into place in the appropriate spots.

• When you've finished gluing your shell-flower arrangement, step back and admire it. Aren't you looking forward to your next trip to the beach?

Here are two completed shell-flower pictures. Notice how different they are—and how very beautiful. The shell flowers above are on a fancy background in an antique frame. The shell flowers below are on a burlap fabric in a simple wooden frame. Each time you go to the beach, collect and save the seashells. In no time at all, you can make a shell-flower picture of your own.

Decorative painting: Tole work (*left*), and Pennsylvania Dutch designs showing hex signs and a milk can with a *distelfink* on it (*right*).

CRAFTS: A WORLD THAT KEEPS ON GROWING

The world of crafts is a world of continual discovery. It is a world in which you make things with your own hands, use your own imagination, and find out what materials you like best to work with.

In recent years people of all ages have discovered that handmade things have a special value and beauty that manufactured products lack. They have also learned that they can make many useful and decorative items themselves. All they have to do is obtain the necessary tools and materials and learn some basic techniques. Because of the growing interest in handicrafts, many stores have sprung up around the country that sell craft materials and give instructions in how to use them. Also, hundreds of books have been published that teach the basics of almost every craft imaginable, new and old.

There are trends and fashions in crafts just as there are in other things, and the world of crafts is a constantly changing one. Every year brings some new craft that large numbers of people are trying. Here are some crafts that were very popular in 1977.

▶ **DECORATIVE PAINTING**

For generations the Norwegians and the Pennsylvania Dutch have used a form of decorative painting to brighten furniture and accessories. This type of painting is called "tole," "folk," or "decorative" painting. Vibrant colors are used in its designs, which are usually of flowers or birds. The Norwegians call their folk painting *rosemaling* ("rose painting"), and they apply it to all kinds of useful items, even to the walls of their houses. The Pennsylvania Dutch use several different designs, but the best-known is the *distelfink*, the stylized bird seen so often on their household utensils.

Decorative painting, unlike most other types of painting, is quite easy to master. You only need to learn the basic brushstrokes and coloring techniques. Since patterns are used, drawing talent is not necessary. Items to paint abound in every home, and include almost anything made from wood or metal: boxes of all kinds, milk cans, footstools, chairs and chests, plaques, candle sconces, lamp bases.

▶ MINIATURE HOUSES AND ROOMS

Making miniature houses and rooms is a centuries-old craft. (Miniature furnishings were even found in the tombs of the ancient Egyptians kings.) People seem to be fascinated by small things—especially by tiny reproductions that are perfect in every detail. Miniatures also provide a wonderful opportunity to re-create the past. Most miniaturists work in a specific period—that is, they try to create tiny rooms of, say, the Colonial or Victorian eras.

For people who love crafts, making miniatures offers a chance to use many skills, since anything that can be made full-size can also be made in miniature. Thus furnishing a miniature room may include woodworking, painting, weaving, needlework, and metalwork. Also, assembling all the parts of the room into an attractive whole is a creative challenge.

A complete miniature house is called a "dollhouse," but it should not be thought of as a plaything. Faithfulness to scale is of great importance. If everything in the room is reduced in the same proportion, the completed setting will look exactly like its full-size counterpart. If even one detail is out of scale, the whole effect will be spoiled.

▶ WEAVING

Weaving is one of the oldest crafts known. Woven cloth has been produced by all peoples from the very earliest times.

Weaving can be done on many different kinds of looms, from the very simplest kinds to large and complicated ones. Some kinds of weaving, such as finger weaving or card weaving, can be done without any loom at all. In another kind of weaving, called backstrap weaving, the weaver's body forms part of the loom. Each kind of loom or weaving produces a different type of cloth. Most hobby weavers today start off with a fairly simple, inexpensive tabletop loom on which they weave with a relatively thick fiber. This produces very attractive heavy cloth suitable for place mats, wall hangings, purses, and ponchos. The weaver soon discovers that by using different yarns and colors, many interesting and unusual patterns can be created.

Miniatures: The Green Room of the White House.

Weavings: They can be as original as paintings.

Basketry: Baskets made by twining (*left*), and by coiling (*right*).

▶BASKETRY

Basketry, a craft that is related to weaving, was also popular during the year. Like fabric weaving, basketmaking is as old as mankind. People have always needed something to put things in. A basket is useful, but it can also be beautiful—as a visit to any museum displaying American Indian art will show you. And making a basket is fun. There are several different ways to weave a basket, but the most common are twining and coiling. In twining, strands of

material are woven in and out around several upright stakes. In coiling, rope or some similar material is coiled round and round; the rope is then joined together with yarn that is wrapped around the coils.

▶MACRAME

Weaving and basketry are both fiber crafts: that is, they are crafts that use fibers to make the finished product. Another popular fiber craft is macrame. Macrame appeals to many

Macrame: As a plant hanger (*left*), and as a wall decoration (*right*).

people because it is a simple knotting procedure using just a few basic knots—and yet it is
very creative. Macrame can be used to make
jewelry, wall hangings, belts, purses, and plant
hangers. The widespread use of houseplants in
home decorating has helped increase the popularity of macrame as a craft, for nothing holds
a pot as attractively as a macrame hanger.

Whether the items made in craft work are
fashioned mainly for their beauty or their use-
fulness, you can be sure of one thing: there is
no better time in history for learning a craft
than right now. All the knowledge and skills of
the past are available to us and so are the
materials and techniques of the modern age.
From the many craft books available, you can
choose those crafts you wish to master. Then,
before you know it, you will have the satisfaction of looking at something lovely that you
have made with your own hands.

SYBIL C. HARP
Editor, *Creative Crafts* Magazine

LIVING HISTORY

Silver Jubilee celebrations: Queen Elizabeth II leaves Buckingham Palace in the gold State Coach

A silver jubilee portrait of Queen Elizabeth.

THE QUEEN'S JUBILEE

For our Monarch and her people,
United yet and free,
Let the bells ring from every steeple
Ring out the Jubilee.

From "Jubilee Hymn" by Britain's
Poet Laureate, Sir John Betjeman

Once upon a time there was a lovely princess who lived in a faraway land across the sea. She was no fairy-tale princess, however. She was the real heir to an ancient throne. Her name was Elizabeth and her father was King George VI, ruler of the British Empire.

One day the 25-year-old Princess Elizabeth and her husband, Prince Philip, were deep in the jungle of Kenya, at the start of a trip to Britain's colonies and possessions. On that morning of February 6, 1952, word reached Elizabeth that her father, the king, had died.

She was no longer a princess—she was the queen. A little over a year later, in June, 1953, the shy, solemn young woman was formally crowned Queen Elizabeth II in a magnificent ceremony that thrilled the world.

In 1977, Queen Elizabeth and her subjects celebrated her silver jubilee—the 25th anniversary of her becoming queen.

And what a celebration it was. The year-long festivities included pomp and pageantry throughout Britain and in the many Commonwealth countries that the queen visited.

The celebration that was held in Britain was truly spectacular. British people from all walks of life joined together in a great outburst of patriotic feeling and warm affection for the woman who had been their queen for a quarter of a century.

The jubilee was officially opened on May 4, 1977, when the queen addressed both houses of Parliament in London's historic Westminster Hall. But the main festivities took place a month later.

On the night of June 6, Queen Elizabeth lit a bonfire on a hill near Windsor Castle. Within a short time, 100 other fires were lit, forming a chain from the northernmost reaches of Scotland to the Channel Islands off England's southern coast. The signal fires brought to mind the beacons that had warned the British of the approach of the Spanish Armada in 1588, during the reign of Queen Elizabeth I.

The lighting of the bonfires touched off a week of festivities that included pageants and parades, village fairs, and fireworks displays. The highlight of the Silver Jubilee was a royal procession to St. Paul's Cathedral in London, where a special thanksgiving service was held.

It was a Cinderella-like spectacle. The queen rode from Buckingham Palace to St. Paul's in

Queen Elizabeth and Prince Philip kneel in prayer during the special jubilee thanksgiving service in St. Paul's Cathedral.

the gold State Coach, which was drawn by eight gray horses. Prince Philip, wearing his medal-bedecked admiral's uniform, was at her side. Plumed cavalrymen, looking like knights of old, and a troop of Royal Canadian Mounted Police escorted the queen's coach. More than a million people lined the streets to cheer their queen.

State trumpeters sounded a fanfare as the queen entered St. Paul's to be greeted by colorfully dressed government officials, many in traditional wigs and long gowns. There were also dignitaries from all over the world.

During the service, the Archbishop of Canterbury praised the queen, citing her life as "an example of service untiringly done, of duty faithfully fulfilled, and of a home life stable and wonderfully happy."

Still more pageantry followed the next day as the queen and other members of the royal family sailed up the Thames River. They were saluted by hundreds of ships and boats of every description. And that night a brilliant display of fireworks lit up the sky over the Houses of Parliament.

In the words of one British newspaper, the jubilee week was "a jolly good party." It was also a time for the British people to reaffirm their faith in the nation's constitutional monarchy, in which the sovereign "reigns but does not rule." (The real power of government is in the hands of a prime minister and the cabinet.)

Not all Britons cheer the queen, however. Some feel that the monarchy is outdated, a relic of the past. But the overwhelming majority of the British people (nearly 90 percent according to recent polls) believe that the queen serves an important function.

The monarch is the symbol of national unity, say her supporters, and a rallying point in time of trouble. Today, when the once vast British Empire has shrunk to a few tiny possessions, the queen is a reminder of a glorious past. She provides a comforting sense of continuity in a world of rapid change.

As one British statesman put it, "The Americans have their Constitution and their flag. In addition to our flag, we have our queen."

HENRY I. KURTZ
Author, *Captain John Smith*

THE POLAR BEAR EXPRESS

"All aboard!" A conductor sings out the words as late arrivals scurry on board the Ontario Northland diesel train. It's eight o'clock on a sunny summer morning, and we're about to take a trip on a very special train—the Polar Bear Express.

Every day except Friday, from mid-June to early September, the Polar Bear Express pulls out of Cochrane, in Canada's province of Ontario. Its destination is Moosonee, a small frontier town 186 miles (300 kilometers) to the north, at the southern tip of James Bay.

So try to get a seat next to a window. We're on our way to one of the last great wilderness frontiers of North America. The Polar Bear Express is taking us on an adventure-filled journey—a journey through a region of scenic splendor, where the romance of history blends with the modern wonders of today.

With a lurch, the train starts its 4½-hour run, twisting and turning through thick woodlands. Soon we get our first glimpse of the swift-flowing waters of the mighty Abitibi River. We are traveling along a route used by French troops under Chevalier de Troyes nearly 300 years ago. Back in 1686, De Troyes and his men braved the wilderness to attack and capture the British Hudson's Bay Company post (called Moose Factory) on an island near James Bay.

Soon we'll be passing places with such colorful names as Red Sucker—where Indians still trap beaver and other animals—Big Jaw Bone River, and Otter Rapids. There's lots to dazzle the eyes—moose loping in the wild; shimmering lakes; high waterfalls; giant dams and modern power plants. See that unusual-looking bridge? That's called an "upside-down"

bridge. (It looks like an upside-down suspension bridge.) It's built that way to allow ice to pass underneath during the spring thaw.

If you get tired of looking out of the window, you might walk back to the special museum car. Here you will find fascinating exhibits tracing the history of northern Ontario. You might also look around at the people you are traveling with. Mixed in with the tourists, there are some Cree Indians. A few have brought canoes with them, so that when they leave the train, they can paddle up the river to their homes.

We're now coming into Moosonee—the "gateway to the Arctic." Some of our fellow passengers may be prospectors or geologists. They will head for the waterfront to board ships and bush planes that will take them to the far north. Beyond Moosonee, Canada's vast woodlands and tundra stretch nearly 2,000 miles (3,300 kilometers) to the Arctic Circle. This is the land of polar bears and Eskimos. It's also where geologists and prospectors are searching for gold, silver, and other valuable minerals.

While the scientists and prospectors go their way, we can take a canoe trip to Moose Factory Island. In 1673, the British set up a fur trading post there, and Moose Factory became the first English-speaking settlement in Ontario. Today, fur trading goes on, just as it has for the past 300 years.

There, too, we can wander around the Centennial Park Museum and view relics of the past. We can also visit the Indian residential school, where more than 200 Indian children go. And we can step into century-old St. Thomas' Church, with its beaded moose-hide altar cloths.

The hours slip by, and soon it is time to get back on the train for the return trip. We'll carry back with us the memory of a wonderful journey on the fabled Polar Bear Express.

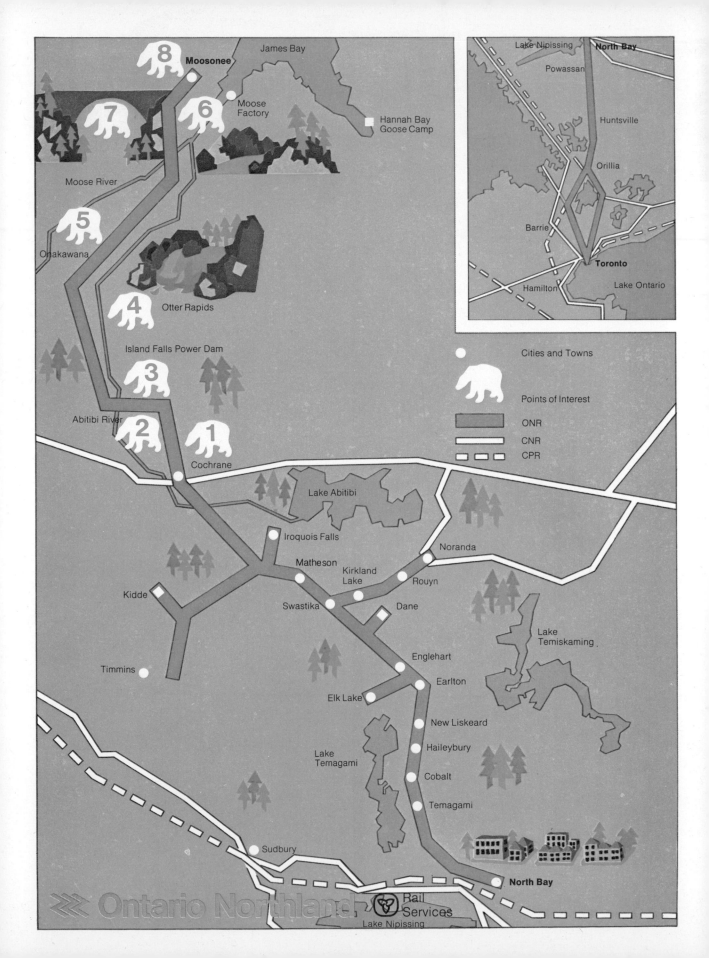

These scenes illustrate some of the exciting adventures in Daniel Defoe's *Robinson Crusoe.*

ROBINSON CRUSOE'S ISLAND

In the Pacific Ocean, about 400 miles (650 kilometers) west of Valparaiso, Chile, there is a small island that has become famous throughout the world. It is an island of magnificent beauty. Parts of it are barren rock and jagged vertical cliffs, while other parts are covered with lush greenery. The peak of the island's highest mountain is almost always hidden by churning clouds. They leap and dive against the broad face of the mountain, and then rush off to pour rain upon nearby valleys.

The island is one of a group known as the Juan Fernández Islands, named for their discoverer. But this island has become better known as Robinson Crusoe's island. For it was here that Alexander Selkirk, a sailor from Scotland, lived completely alone for four years and four months. Selkirk's experience would probably have been forgotten if Daniel Defoe had not used it as the basis for *Robinson Crusoe,* one of the world's most famous books. Because of the great popularity of *Robinson Crusoe,* Selkirk's little island has become famous too.

▶SELKIRK'S STORY

The island was discovered about 1563 by Juan Fernández, a Spanish navigator, who came upon it by accident. He settled there for a while, stocking the island with goats and pigs. However, Fernández' attempts at agriculture failed, and he soon left.

Other early settlers, the Jesuits, were also unsuccessful, and the island remained uninhabited. But it became a refuge for bands of English pirates, who found it a perfect hiding place before and after their raids. From the 16th to the 18th century, the island was a haven for many a pirate ship.

Occasionally, other ships stopped there too, but only for a short time. One of these ships was the *Cinque Ports,* an English galley that came by in October, 1704, and put off an unhappy sailor named Alexander Selkirk. Selkirk, it seemed, had quarreled with his captain. Rather than put up with the captain any longer, Selkirk asked to be put ashore. His request was granted.

Selkirk, then 28 years old, landed with the most basic of equipment—a change of clothes and two blankets; an iron saucepan and a drinking jar; an ax, a knife, a cutlass, a pistol, and a musket; and a pound of gunpowder and a bag of tobacco. He also had his Bible.

Living alone made Selkirk learn how to keep alive with nothing more than his own inventiveness and skill. He had to be a woodcutter and carpenter; a hunter, butcher, and cook; a tailor and a launderer. His many tasks probably kept him from going mad with loneliness. Yet one can imagine the terrifying hours that he must have lived through at the beginning, when the night and the ocean wrapped the island in a vast, silent darkness.

Early in his stay on the island, Selkirk spotted goats climbing nimbly among the hills and cliffs. These animals were probably the descendants of the first goats brought there by the discoverer Fernández. They provided Selkirk with food, clothing, shelter, and amazingly enough, companionship.

Selkirk built a small hut of logs and sticks. He covered the roof and sides with the hides of goats he had shot with his musket. For food, he ate their meat. But Selkirk soon ran out of gunpowder, and so his musket was useless. He then had no choice but to try to catch the goats with his bare hands.

How could a lone man catch one of those agile creatures with his bare hands? Selkirk must have been a dazzling gymnast, for only a fine athlete could have done what he did: leaping like an acrobat along the edges of cliffs, he caught the goats on the run!

One time he slipped, and rolled with his catch down a steep cliff. He blacked out. When he revived, he discovered that the little goat lay dead beneath him—like a pillow that had been placed by luck to break his fall and save his life. This accident gave him the idea of having goats live with him. To keep them from running away, he built a stockade around his hut. In that corral, the goats became tame. They reproduced, and the kids became his friends and companions. He taught them to dance and to leap, and when he went walking they followed him about.

Like anyone who must survive in the wilderness, Selkirk had to rely more on cleverness than on physical strength. He made fire by rubbing dry sticks together. He scraped sea salt from the hollows of rocks, where it had collected from dried-up seawater. For light he burned oil from sea lions, which he had killed with a club. In the rain-soaked valleys, he found wild fruits and vegetables. He fished from the beach with a net made of goat intestines. And when his clothing finally wore out, he made himself an outfit of goatskin. He sewed it with strands of rawhide, using a thinned nail as a needle.

And so this remarkable man got used to his solitary life. His beard grew long and wild. His feet grew hard from walking barefoot on the rough forest floor. He did not know if he would ever see another human again. And afraid that he might lose the ability to speak, he talked to himself or read the Bible aloud. In time, Selkirk became an "island man." He later said, "Nowhere could I be as happy again as I was on my island."

Humans are called "social animals"—they enjoy and need the company of other people. Was Selkirk different? Perhaps. But day after day, he climbed a mountain to watch the sea in hope of spotting a sail. Once he spied a ship flying the flag of France. He signaled to it, but either the sailors did not see him or they decided to ignore him. Another time, a Spanish ship anchored offshore. Unfortunately, Spain and England were enemies at the time. Selkirk was seen and chased like a wild beast. He had

Above: Selkirk, the real-life model for the fictional Crusoe. Below: Selkirk greets the captain of the *Duke*.

to flee to the forest and hide in the top of a tree.

From Selkirk's experiences, we can see that people can learn to live under the most difficult circumstances. There is no doubt that Selkirk could have survived for years and years. He did not later mention ever having been sad or bored. So far as is known, he was never sick in the four years and four months he spent on the island. He probably came to feel that time did not exist; he lived alone with the island, the sea, and the sky. And perhaps there were times when he actually stopped caring if he would ever be rescued.

In February, 1709, an English ship, the *Duke,* reached the island. The captain found Selkirk on the beach, clothed in skins and accompanied by his goats. The call of human society was too strong to resist. Selkirk went on board the *Duke* and left his island forever. Later he married and made his home in England. Ever the seagoing man, he went to sea again, with the rank of master's mate. It is possible that Selkirk met Daniel Defoe in Bristol and told the author about his adventures. *Robinson Crusoe* was published in 1719, just two years before Selkirk died. Selkirk read the book and protested that his island had been changed into a Caribbean isle with parrots! Nevertheless, his island became known as Robinson Crusoe's island.

▶ HIS ISLAND LIVES ON

One cannot blame Selkirk for protesting. Why change such a beautiful island? The climate ranges between temperate and subtropical. Showers fall in midsummer, and the loveliness of autumn is without equal. The blue-green waters surrounding the island are filled with fish. If there really is a paradise on earth, perhaps this is it.

After Selkirk left, the island remained uninhabited for many years. Sailors and soldiers came and went. The island belonged to Spain until 1818. In that year, the island passed into the hands of the newly independent country of Chile. And as the years went by, settlers came to the island and stayed.

Today, about seven hundred people live on Robinson Crusoe's island. The little town of San Juan Bautista sits on Cumberland Bay, one of the island's natural harbors. This lively town spreads among groves and orchards on a hill backed by steep mountains. In the town live fishermen, farmers, officials, and even some modern Robinson Crusoes who are looking for the solitary joy that Selkirk knew. Many tourists also come each year, drawn by the island's rich history and legendary beauty. And anyone who sees this island will understand the sorrow of Selkirk's long-ago cry:

"Oh, my beloved island, I wish I had never left thee!"

Robinson Crusoe's island: tourists flock there, drawn by its legendary beauty.

CARTOONS! CARTOONS! CARTOONS!

Practically everyone knows Charlie Brown and Snoopy. They are the leading characters in the *Peanuts* cartoon strip, which is read by millions of people every day. *Peanuts* appears in 23 languages and is read by people in many different countries all over the world. Its creator, Charles Schulz, has given us one of the most popular cartoon strips of all time.

People everywhere love cartoons. They are a unique form of art, and the "instant message" they give us is very appealing. Cartoons entertain us and make us think at the same time. Many of the most popular cartoon strips—such as *Blondie* by Chic Young, *Li'l Abner* by Al Capp, and *Beetle Bailey* by Mort Walker—have been in existence for years. They have become a permanent part of our culture.

▶ **KINDS OF CARTOON ART**

Cartoons are drawings that tell a story. The story is told quickly, sometimes in only one frame, or drawing. There are many different kinds of cartoons. Here are some of the most common:

Continuing-story cartoons. These tell an ongoing story, using many frames and little text. The cartoon stories in comic books are usually of this kind. And many of the cartoon strips in the comics sections of newspapers tell a new part of a continuing story each day. Some of the best-known cartoon characters are from continuing-story strips: Tarzan, Flash Gordon, Mary Worth, Dick Tracy, Little Orphan Annie, Li'l Abner, Superman, and Popeye.

Gag cartoons. These look at the humor of things that happen in everyday life. They have a punch line, and they tell a complete story in one or a few frames. *Hazel,* the bossy maid created by Ted Key, is an example of such a cartoon. So is *Bringing Up Father* by George McManus, which describes the problems of Jiggs and his nagging wife, Maggie. Other gag cartoons include *Peanuts, Blondie, Dennis the Menace,* and *Felix the Cat.* Two magazines that are famous for their sophisticated single-frame gag cartoons are *The New Yorker,* published in the United States, and *Punch,* published in England.

Sports cartoons. These are usually found on the sports pages of U.S. newspapers. They feature well-known athletes, coaches, and managers. In some of the cartoons the sports people are treated as heroes; in others they are criticized. Before the popularity of photogra-

An editorial cartoon. These often use caricatures, which exaggerate people's features.

A gag cartoon. It tells a complete story in one frame.

A sports cartoon by Rube Goldberg: As fighter is socked on chin, water from
glass (A) falls on sponge (B), weight of which causes string (C) to pull trigger
of pistol (D). Bullet (E) bounces off head of dumb second (F) and hits weight
(G), knocking it off rest (H). String (I) pulls tooth from mouth of resin-spaniel
(J). Dog jumps up and down with pain and works handle (K) of jack (L),
thereby jacking fighter off the floor. Boxing rules say that a fighter is not out
if his body is off the floor. If you want to argue about this go ahead—but
please don't bother us.

163

HERE ARE SOME WELL-KNOWN CARTOON CHARACTERS.
DO YOU KNOW WHO THEY ARE?

1) Donald Duck; 2) Dagwood and Blondie; 3) Flash Gordon; 4) Felix the Cat; 5) Popeye

phy and the development of television, sports cartoons were much more common than they are today. One fine sports cartoonist was Rube Goldberg. He began his cartooning career in sports. Later he branched out into other areas, becoming best known for his "Inventions," which make fun of modern technology.

Editorial cartoons. These usually make fun of politicians and other people in the news. They express an opinion about a well-known person or an important problem facing society. Their purpose is to affect the way you feel about an issue. People who draw editorial cartoons often use caricatures. Caricatures are drawings or descriptions that exaggerate people's features in such a way as to make fun of them. For example, many cartoons of President Jimmy Carter show him with very large gleaming teeth.

Advertising cartoons. These are used to sell a product or an idea. You can see them on television, in newspapers and magazines, and on posters and T-shirts.

Animated cartoons. When you watch a movie in which Donald Duck chases his naughty nephews, it looks as if the ducks are running. But what you actually see is a series of drawings, shown fast enough to fool your eyes. This is called animation. The position of each character changes slightly from one drawing to the next. When the drawings are put on film and projected, the characters look as if they are moving. The person most closely associated with animation was Walt Disney. He created many famous comic characters, among them Donald Duck, Mickey Mouse, Minnie Mouse, Goofy, Pluto, and Uncle Scrooge.

▶CARTOONS ON DISPLAY

If you want to see just about all your favorite cartoon characters, you can visit the Museum of Cartoon Art. This museum moved to a new home in 1977, a 100-year-old mansion known as Ward's Castle in Rye, New York. More than 1,000 artists are represented in the museum, which has the world's largest collection of original cartoon art. The collection traces the history of cartooning from woodcuts done in the 1800's to present-day color printing and animation.

Visitors to the museum can buy books on cartooning. They can also buy original art work by famous cartoonists.

▶COLLECTING CARTOONS

Many people collect cartoon art, so there's a great demand for it today. There are stores that deal only in this type of art. There are also conventions, usually held in big cities, where many people gather to sell, buy, and trade cartoon art.

Prices for cartoon art are often high. This is especially true for old comic books, many of which have become very rare. Perhaps the highest prices ever paid have been for single copies of *Marvel Comics* #1 (about $8,000) and *Action Comics* #1 (about $6,000). *Action Comics* #1 is the issue in which Superman first appeared. Walt Disney comic books are also valuable: a 1940 issue of *Comics and Stories* recently sold for $1,000, and *Donald Duck* #9 is also worth that much. That's a lot of money, especially when you realize that these comic books originally sold for 10 cents apiece many years ago.

Prices are also high for original cartoon art because each piece is one-of-a-kind. A 1944 *Tarzan* strip drawn by Burne Hogarth for a Sunday newspaper was recently advertised for $725. A 1933 *Krazy Kat* strip by George Herriman was offered for $1,000. Strips and single-frame cartoons drawn for daily newspapers are less expensive. A 1934 *Blondie* strip of four pictures was priced at $175.

If you collect any kind of cartoon art, it is important to keep it in excellent condition. The better the condition, the more valuable the art. For example, the comic books that get the highest prices are those that are in "mint condition." This means that they look like new, even if they are many years old. The covers are not torn or creased; none of the pages are missing; they are not stained or scribbled on; and the pages have not turned brown.

Not all cartoon art will become valuable. It's a matter of supply and demand. If people want a certain comic book and it is hard to get, the value of the book will be high. If no one wants it, it won't be worth much money—even if it is rare.

If you would like to have a collection of cartoon art, you can start by collecting comic books. Collect what you like and can afford. Even if they never become valuable, you will have a lot of pleasure reading them.

JENNY TESAR
Consultant, Curriculum Concepts, Inc.

A LITTLE FAIRY CASTLE

It's the most magnificent of castles. There are dishes made of solid gold. The chandeliers sparkle with diamonds and other precious gems. There is silver furniture, and on the walls are paintings of Snow White, Alice in Wonderland, and Old King Cole.

Does this sound like a fairy tale? Well, in a way it is. The castle is real—but it is in miniature. It measures 9 by 9 feet (3 by 3 meters), and its highest tower reaches 12 feet (3.5 meters) in height. And all the wonderful things in it are tiny—so tiny, you can hold them in your hand.

The little castle is in Chicago's Museum of Science and Industry. It was given to the museum by actress Colleen Moore as a gift to the children of the world. The castle was built on a dream, a dream we've all had—to live in a fairyland, with all the wonderful characters from the stories we have read.

So pretend you are a tiny prince or princess, only 5 inches (13 centimeters) tall. Here is your castle. Come along and take a walk through fairyland.

Step into the great entrance hall. Go over to the silver table where your gold crown is. The princess's crown is covered with pearls and has a green emerald in the center. The prince's crown and scepter are set with rubies and sapphires.

In this great hall are some of the many tiny treasures you have collected on your travels. There are the chairs of the Three Bears, the harp that Jack stole from the giant who lived atop the beanstalk, and Cinderella's glass slippers.

▶ **CINDERELLA AND KING ARTHUR**

Relax for a few minutes in the drawing room. Its walls are covered with paintings that tell the story of Cinderella. From the ceiling hangs a chandelier gleaming with diamonds, emeralds, and pearls. Its electric light bulbs, each the size of a grain of wheat, light up the room. The floor is of rose quartz and green jade, and was made in China.

Sit on a silver chair. Or perhaps you would like to play the piano. The little pieces of paper you see are sheet music—all handwritten by the composers themselves. George Gershwin

The dictionary on its stand, the diamond and emerald chair, and the gold and red leather Bible: these are their actual size, and you can hold them in your hand.

166

A little fairy castle.

gave you a copy of *Rhapsody in Blue*. Irving Berlin gave you "Alexander's Ragtime Band." Richard Rodgers gave you "Oh! What a Beautiful Morning."

Time passes quickly. Soon the "Hickory Dickory" grandfather clock tells you that it is time for dinner. As you walk into the dining hall, be careful not to break the amber vases, one on either side of the doorway. They are more than 500 years old, and actually belonged to the Dowager Empress of China.

This room looks like King Arthur's dining hall. The marble walls are covered with needlepoint tapestries that tell of the deeds of King Arthur. You sit down at the Round Table and begin eating your meal, which is served on gold plates.

Next door, in the kitchen, cooks are preparing your dessert. Water for your hot chocolate is in a kettle on a copper stove that looks just like the stove in which the wicked witch wanted to lock Hansel and Gretel!

▶ **OLD FATHER NEPTUNE AND ALI BABA**

You tell the butler that you'll have dessert in the library. This room reminds you of the great voyages you have made across the oceans to find your treasures. The copper and bronze fireplace looks like a fishnet—and holds Old Father Neptune and two mermaids in its folds. Over the fireplace is Captain Kidd, guarding his pirate chests. Over one doorway is a sculpture showing Robinson Crusoe and his man Friday. Over the other is Gulliver capturing the fleet of the Lilliputians' enemies.

Now comes the best part—your most unusual library of books. Sir Arthur Conan Doyle, F. Scott Fitzgerald, Booth Tarkington, Edna Ferber, and other well-known authors have given you special editions of their writ-

The Cinderella drawing room.

King Arthur's dining hall.

The bedroom of a prince.

ings. And every book is just the right size for your tiny hands.

Here is your book of autographs, filled with the signatures of famous people: Winston Churchill, Henry Ford, Dwight D. Eisenhower, Queen Elizabeth II, Admiral Byrd.

Is that the sound of horses? Look out the window. There's Cinderella's silver coach. It has stopped for a minute so the horses can drink from the copper fountain.

Let's go up to the treasure room. The only way to get into it is through an ironbound trapdoor. Speak the secret words, and Ali Baba, who guards the riches, will let you enter. In this room are magic rings, decanters filled with love potions, and all your souvenirs of fairyland parties.

Before you go to sleep—for even fairy princes and princesses must sleep—we'll quietly step into the chapel for a moment. Look at the lovely stained-glass window, which depicts stories from the Bible. Touch the gold and ivory organ. Here is a Bible from 1840, the smallest in the world. It is bound in gold and red leather, and contains the entire New Testament.

And now to sleep.

▶ BEDROOMS FIT FOR A KING OR A QUEEN

Here in the prince's stately bedroom is a wondrous collection of swords, including King Arthur's magical Excalibur. Two gold cannons are on a chest, and in a corner is a pair of red seven-league boots — exactly what every prince needs for his travels around the world. The carvings on the bed and chairs depict a Russian fairy tale.

As you enter the princess's room, you will notice that over the door is Peter Pan—dancing on a mushroom. The princess's room is very feminine. The walls are white, decorated with gold, and the floor is made of mother-of-pearl. A pair of diamond and emerald chairs sparkle with beauty. On the ivory dresser is a tiny gold set of comb, brush, mirror, and nail file. The canopied bed is also made of gold, and is shaped like a boat. It is the bed on which Sleeping Beauty slept for 100 years—until she was awakened by the prince.

As you lie in bed, your thoughts of the day fade into dreams. You dream that you have suddenly grown very big—as big as a human being. That might be fun—almost as much fun as being a fairy prince or princess who lives in this wonderful fairy castle.

Anne Bonny and Mary Read became very good friends.

LADIES ON THE HIGH SEAS

Today we believe that women can do whatever men can do, and go wherever men can go. But not too long ago, women were regarded as the "tender sex." They were thought to be dainty, delicate, and sensitive. Imagine how shocked people were when they heard that there were lady pirates. And that these "ladies" could be as cruel and bloodthirsty as the men!

In the early 1700's, one of the most famous of these women pirates was Anne Bonny. Anne had been born in Ireland. When she was very young, she and her parents moved to the Carolinas. Her father, a wealthy and respected planter, looked forward to the time when his daughter would make a "proper" marriage. But Anne was a rebellious teenager.

In time, Anne met a young sailor and married him—without her father's approval. Her father was so angry, he made her leave home. Anne and her husband went to New Providence, an island in the Bahamas where many sailors and pirates gathered. There, Anne's husband deserted her. But Anne did not remain alone for long. She met and fell in love with Calico Jack, a famous pirate. This handsome daredevil and his crew regularly attacked ships in the Atlantic Ocean and Caribbean Sea. Anne was completely fascinated by the

stories of his adventures. When Calico Jack was ready to return to sea, he asked Anne to go with him, and she quickly agreed.

Anne soon became very handy with her pistols and cutlass. She stood at Calico Jack's side as they boarded and plundered ship after ship. On one of the ships they captured was what appeared to be a young man. This person either volunteered or was forced to join Calico Jack's crew, and quickly became a tough and ruthless pirate. Imagine everyone's surprise when this person turned out to be a young woman—Mary Read!

Mary had been brought up in England. She had worked on a ship and had even fought in the army—always disguised as a man. When Anne Bonny discovered that the fierce pirate fighting alongside her was a woman, the two became very good friends.

Their happy but evil life on the high seas was soon to end, however. In October, 1720, the pirates were anchored off the coast of Jamaica. Suddenly a British ship appeared. Calico Jack and the other male pirates hid belowdecks, refusing Mary's demands that they come up and fight the attacking sailors. Mary and Anne bravely tried to fend off the sailors, but they were finally overpowered. All the pirates were captured, and Calico Jack, Anne,

Mrs. Ching was a brave fighter.

and Mary were convicted of piracy. As Calico Jack was led to his execution, he saw Anne for one last time. She offered little sympathy, saying she was "sorry to see him there, but if he had fought like a man, he need not have been hanged like a dog."

Anne and Mary were imprisoned. Mary caught a terrible fever and died in prison. Anne remained in prison and eventually gave birth to a child. But to this day, no one knows what finally happened to her.

▶ ONE HUNDRED YEARS LATER . . .

A much more important lady pirate lived in China, almost 100 years later. Her name was Ching Yih Saou. Mrs. Ching's husband had been a pirate in command of a fleet of 600 ships. When he was killed, his wife took over the fleet. Soon it had 800 large ships and almost 1,000 smaller ones.

Mrs. Ching was a well-organized, efficient businesswoman. She was also a smart leader and a brave fighter. Her fleet of ships was divided into six squadrons. Each was led by a lieutenant. Like Calico Jack, they had colorful names: Jewel of the Whole Crew, Frogs' Meal, Scourge of the Eastern Sea.

The pirates were allowed to have their wives on board. When the pirates attacked other ships or sailed up rivers to loot and burn villages, the women fought right alongside their husbands.

The Chinese emperor tried to end the pirates' reign of terror. In 1808 there was a big battle between Mrs. Ching's ships and a fleet of government ships. Mrs. Ching won. The government sent out a second fleet. It was quickly captured by the pirates. A third fleet was sent out. This time many of Mrs. Ching's ships were destroyed and many pirates were killed. But Mrs. Ching survived and soon was back in business. The government made a few more attempts to stop her, but none were successful.

Then the emperor tried a different approach. He offered to pardon the pirates if they would stop their terrible activities. One of Mrs. Ching's lieutenants—together with his 8,000 men and 160 ships—accepted. Mrs. Ching was angry. But when she thought more about it, the pardon seemed like a good idea, and she and her crew accepted the emperor's offer.

So Mrs. Ching stopped terrorizing the seas. But she never became a law-abiding citizen. Instead, she spent the rest of her life as the head of a big smuggling operation.

Anne Bonny, Mary Read, and Ching Yih Saou were the best-known women pirates—there were probably others. They chose and were successful in a "profession" that was believed to be for men only. And, although their acts were crimes, they achieved a certain kind of equality by being what they were—ladies on the high seas.

THE FLIGHT OF THE LONE EAGLE

Thousands of people were massed around Le Bourget airfield just outside Paris, France, on the night of May 21, 1927. They waited anxiously, all eyes focused on the dark sky overhead. Somewhere in that vast black sea of space, a lone American flier was winging his way toward Paris in a fragile, single-engined monoplane.

The man at the controls was Charles A. Lindbergh, Jr., a boyish-faced, 25-year-old former mail pilot and stunt flier. And the big question was, would he make it? Would he successfully complete his transatlantic flight from New York to Paris?

The thousands gathered at Le Bourget believed that "Lucky Lindy," as the newspapers called him, could do it. Hours went by. The night grew cold. Still they waited.

Suddenly the sound of an engine was heard. Giant searchlights lit the sky. There was a loud cheer as the crowd caught sight of a silver-gray plane. Moments later, at 10:24 P.M., Charles Lindbergh brought his plane, the *Spirit of St.*

Louis, safely down to earth. The crowd went wild. A tidal wave of people broke through a cordon of police and soldiers and rushed madly toward the plane.

Cheering Frenchmen shouting "*Lindbergh! Vive Lindbergh!*" pulled the tall, slender American out of the cockpit and hoisted him onto their shoulders. Pale and weary, the youthful aviator managed a smile as he said simply: "Well, I made it."

Indeed he had. On that memorable night in 1927 Charles Lindbergh became the first person to complete a solo nonstop flight across the Atlantic. Nicknamed the "Lone Eagle," he became an instant world hero and a legendary figure in his own lifetime.

In 1977 the United States and France celebrated the 50th anniversary of Lindbergh's incredible feat of courage and flying skill. Special events were held. Commemorative stamps were issued. And on May 20, 1977, an exact copy of the *Spirit of St. Louis* took off from a Long Island, New York, airport in a re-enactment of

The New York Times.

THE WEATHER
Generally fair today and tomorrow; moderate to fresh southerly winds.
Temperature yesterday—Max. 56, Min. 55.
Full weather report; see Page 21.
Section 1

VOL. LXXVI....No. 25,320. **** | NEW YORK, SUNDAY, MAY 22, 1927. | Including Rotogravure Picture Section in three parts—Magazine and Book Sections in Rotogravure | FIVE CENTS In Manhattan, Bronx and Brooklyn | Elsewhere TEN CENTS

LINDBERGH DOES IT! TO PARIS IN 33½ HOURS; FLIES 1,000 MILES THROUGH SNOW AND SLEET; CHEERING FRENCH CARRY HIM OFF FIELD

COULD HAVE GONE 500 MILES FARTHER

Gasoline for at Least That Much More— Flew at Times From 10 Feet to 10,000 Feet Above Water.

ATE ONLY ONE AND A HALF OF HIS FIVE SANDWICHES

Fell Asleep at Times but Quickly Awoke—Glimpses of His Adventure in Brief Interview at the Embassy.

LINDBER...

MAP OF LINDBERGH'S TRANSATLANTIC ROUTE, SHOWING THE SPEED OF HIS TRIP.

CROWD ROARS THUNDEROUS WELCOME

Breaks Through Lines of Soldiers and Police and Surging to Plane Lifts Weary Flier from His Cockpit

AVIATORS SAVE HIM FROM FRENZIED MOB OF 100,000

Paris Boulevards Ring With Celebration After Day and Night Watch—American Flag Is Called For and Wildly Acclaimed.

By EDWIN L. ...
Copyright, 1927 ...

PARIS ...
10 o'clock
dark...

LEVINE ABANDONS BELLANCA FLIGHT

...s Designer ...me Nar-...

MED

Cara-Last ...

CAPTAIN CHARLES A. LINDBERGH,
Who Flew Alone Across the Atlantic, New York to Paris, in Thirty-three and One-half Hours.

Times Wide World Photo

New York Stages Big Celebration

LINDBERGH TRIUMPH THRILLS COOLIDGE

President Cables Praise to "Heroic Flier" and Concern for Nungesser and Coli.

CAPITAL THROB...

Kellogg, New,... and Many M... Tribute

Special ...
triumph o... bergh in Paris w... mendous capital sponse and st... daring Pres... admira... through Paris fo... in person. With a this city ha... since the Wilson mi... in celebra... The exc... Johnson and w... ba...

---

the historic flight. (The original *Spirit of St. Louis* is on display at the Smithsonian Institution in Washington, D.C.)

FIFTY YEARS EARLIER

The event these activities commemorate began on the morning of May 20, 1927, when Charles Lindbergh climbed into his silver airplane and prepared to take off from Roosevelt Field on Long Island.

Lindbergh was one of many aviators who were competing for a $25,000 prize that was being offered to the flier, or fliers, who could make a nonstop trip across the Atlantic from New York to "the shores of France."

From the moment he learned of the contest, Lindbergh decided to accept the challenge. At 25, the lanky Midwesterner (called "Slim" by his friends) was already an experienced pilot. All he needed was a good plane. And thanks to a group of St. Louis businessmen, Lindbergh got the money he needed to have one built according to his own design. He named it the *Spirit of St. Louis* in honor of his backers.

Lindbergh had two main rivals for the $25,000 prize: Commander Richard E. Byrd and Clarence Chamberlain. Both these men had copilots. Lindy was the only one who would fly alone.

Rain and fog kept the competitors grounded for days. But on the morning of May 20, Lindbergh decided to chance it. With his plane loaded down with 451 gallons (1,707 liters) of fuel, he taxied onto the runway. It was a tense moment. The rain had left the field a soggy mass of mud and it wouldn't be easy to get up enough speed to lift the overweighted plane off the ground. But Lindbergh was a determined man. He pulled back the stick and felt the aircraft quiver.

Several times the plane lurched off the ground, only to drop down again. Finally, the *Spirit of St. Louis* soared into the sky—barely missing a tangled web of telephone wires at the end of the runway. The time was 7:52 A.M. The Lone Eagle was airborne.

Lindbergh had no radio on board and his only navigating instruments were a compass and a chart on which he had carefully plotted his route. Because of the way the plane was constructed—with the engine and fuel tanks in front of the cockpit—Lindbergh could not see directly ahead. He had to poke his head out of the side window or use a small periscope he had brought along.

Eleven hours after leaving Roosevelt Field, Lindbergh flew past the rocky eastern coast of Newfoundland and out over the open sea. Now he was completely on his own. He still had most of his 3,600-mile (5,800-kilometer) flight ahead of him and he would have to fly through thick fog and storm clouds much of the way. There was also the problem of staying awake during the long flight.

The plane itself helped him to stay alert. It was not a stable aircraft, and if he loosened his grip on the controls, it would drift off course, jolting him back to his senses. Other times he would stick his head out of the cockpit and let the wind and rain revive him.

Much of the time, Lindbergh flew close to the water, sometimes only 20 feet (6 meters) above the waves. His big fear was that he would run smack into an iceberg or the masts of an oncoming ship.

Occasionally, he climbed as high as 10,000 feet (3,000 meters) to avoid a storm. Once during the night hours, he flew so high that ice began to form on his wings. But Lindy spotted it before it could cause the plane to stall, and he dropped down to where the air was warmer.

By the 24th hour, Lindbergh was in a half-awake, half-asleep state. His body was numb from fatigue, his joints ached. But as darkness gave way to light on the morning of May 21, he got his second wind. In the afternoon his spirits rose when he spotted a fishing boat. Lindy brought his plane down and buzzed the little vessel. A man stared up at him from one of the portholes, and the aviator shouted: "Which way is Ireland?" The startled boatman was too stunned to answer, and Lindbergh could only hope that he was headed in the right direction. He was. Soon after this encounter, he spotted a coastline. Ireland!

At about 8 P.M. he passed over Cornwall, England. An hour later he was over the coast of France. He had done it. At that point he could have landed and claimed his prize, for the rules were that the pilot had only to reach the "shores of France." But Lindy wanted to go the whole route—to Paris. And so he continued on, landing at Le Bourget airfield shortly after 10 P.M. (Paris time). He had completed his New York to Paris flight in 33½ hours.

For Charles Lindbergh the long ordeal was over and a lifetime of fame was about to begin. Decorated by the governments of France, Britain, and Belgium, "Lucky Lindy" returned in triumph to the United States. Several million New Yorkers turned out for the traditional tickertape parade up Broadway. In Washington, D.C., President Calvin Coolidge awarded him the Distinguished Flying Cross. Until his death in 1974, Lindbergh remained the idol of millions.

▶ **FIFTY YEARS LATER**

Today the new Concorde supersonic jet can make the trip from Paris to New York in just 3½ hours—one tenth the time it took Lindbergh. But not even the Concorde's record-breaking flying time can dim the luster of "Lucky Lindy." Charles Lindbergh made his transatlantic flight alone, in a small, single-engined plane, without computers and modern instruments to guide him. His courage and endurance will never be forgotten.

HENRY I. KURTZ
Author, *Captain John Smith*

LINCOLN LORE

If you were asked to choose the greatest U.S. president, who would it be? Recently the U.S. Historical Society asked a group of leading American historians to list the top ten presidents of the United States. The 85 scholars who responded all picked Abraham Lincoln to head the list as the greatest U.S. president.

The others who ranked in the top ten were George Washington, Franklin D. Roosevelt, Theodore Roosevelt, Thomas Jefferson, Woodrow Wilson, Andrew Jackson, Harry S. Truman, James K. Polk, and John Adams.

But Abraham Lincoln stands head and shoulder above them all. More than 100 years after an assassin's bullet struck him down, he remains a towering figure in American history. To millions of Americans, the 16th president is still number one.

A beardless Lincoln. Our image of Abraham Lincoln is that of a man with a beard. Actually, he didn't grow his familiar whiskers until after he was nominated as the Republican candidate for president in 1860. Until he was 51, he had been clean-shaven.

Lincoln might have remained beardless if it had not been for an 11-year-old girl. Her name was Grace Bedell and she lived in the town of Westfield, New York. On October 15, 1860, the youngster wrote a letter to Lincoln suggesting that he grow a beard. "You would look a great deal better for your face is so thin," Grace advised. "All the ladies like whiskers and they would tease their husbands to vote for you and then you would be President."

Lincoln replied on October 19. He thanked Grace for her "very agreeable letter." As for her suggestion, he pointed out that he had never worn whiskers and if he grew them now, people might think it a "silly affectation."

However, Lincoln gave the matter more thought. And he grew the beard that he would wear throughout his presidency.

In February, 1861, while on his way to Washington, Lincoln stopped off at Westfield. Grace Bedell was among those who greeted him. Lincoln kissed her on the cheek, pointed to his new whiskers, and told her: "I grew them just for you."

The print shown here is one of the two remaining copies of a Lincoln portrait given out to delegates at the Republican National Convention in 1860.

THE INDIANAPOLIS CHILDREN'S MUSEUM

Visit a log cabin built in the 1830's. Explore a limestone cavern. Step into the tomb of an Egyptian mummy. Sit behind the wheel of a racing car that actually competed in the famous Indianapolis 500.

At The Children's Museum in Indianapolis, Indiana, there are exhibits, storytelling sessions, movies, workshops, and classes—all especially designed for young people. Here are some of the things to see and do there.

Watch toy trains puff and chug through cities and towns, over mountains, past waterfalls, and around a miniature circus. There are more than 3,000 toy trains and train accessories in the museum's collection.

Make and do things. The museum has classes that teach children to paint and make cornhusk dolls. You can also carve pumpkins, work with ceramics, play chess, learn folk dancing, make puppets, and stage your own puppet show.

Come face-to-face with *Tyrannosaurus rex,* one of the largest, fiercest predators that ever lived. It took two years to build this life-sized model, which measures 34 feet (10.4 meters) from teeth to tail.

Jump aboard a colorful, hand-carved wooden animal for a ride on the museum's carousel. Pick the animal you like best—it may be a horse, giraffe, lion, tiger, or goat. You can also see a real wood-burning locomotive, and an 1890's firehouse with a horse-drawn fire engine and a shiny brass pole.

Touch real dinosaur bones. Or open drawers filled with animal, plant, and rock specimens. You can also examine shells, bones, tree twigs, and mounted insects. There are even live animals and plants to see.

Discover the kachina doll,
which represents a spirit that
the Hopi Indians believed in.
Other artifacts in the
museum include a flint hand
ax, some beaded Indian moc-
casins, a silk Chinese robe,
and a carved African mask.

Use your imagination. More
than 500 children entered the
grand-opening poster contest
when The Children's
Museum moved to a brand-
new building in 1976. Here's
the grand prize winner, Brett
Schneider, who drew a bright
green dinosaur.

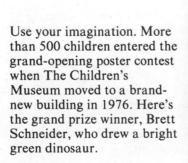

December 24, 1822: Dr. Clement Clarke Moore reads "A Visit from St. Nicholas" to his children.

THE MAN WHO INVENTED SANTA CLAUS

St. Nicholas of Myra is a patron saint of Russia. He has also been one of the patron saints of children for centuries. Legend has it that St. Nicholas brings gifts to good children on his day, December 6. There are many other legends about him too. But Santa Claus, as most North Americans have come to know St. Nicholas, was born on December 24, 1822. It was on that frosty Christmas Eve that Dr. Clement Clarke Moore, a scholar and part-time poet, penned the lines of the immortal poem "A Visit from St. Nicholas." Moore turned St. Nicholas into "jolly St. Nick," a plump, happy-go-lucky elf with a sleigh full of toys and eight prancing reindeer, and sent him flying over hill and dale to keep alive the spirit of giving. And so a new St. Nicholas legend came to be.

Here is a dramatized account of how Dr. Moore created Santa Claus.

It was a cold evening and the ground was covered with snow. Dr. Moore was on his way home to his estate in what is now the Chelsea section of New York City. He had just delivered Christmas presents to friends in Greenwich Village. Driving his sleigh was an old Dutch handyman named Peter, whose weather-beaten face seemed always to wear a smile, and who could be counted upon for a cheerful remark when the world seemed gloomiest.

Suddenly, the 43-year-old professor remembered that he had promised his children a poem as an extra Christmas present. For although he was a scholar by profession, he often wrote light verse for his family's amusement.

"By heaven, I'd nearly forgotten about that," Dr. Moore muttered to himself as old Peter, silhouetted in the moonlight, flicked his whip to spur on the horses. Dr. Moore racked his brain for an idea, turning over in his mind many possible lines of verse. But none seemed just right. Suddenly his eye fell on Peter's face, illuminated by the soft beams of the moon. The handyman's cherubic features, the pipe clenched firmly between his teeth, and the stocking cap pulled tightly over his head gave Dr. Moore an inspiration.

When they arrived home, the professor hurried to his study. "But dinner will be ready shortly," his wife protested. "Yes, yes, I know," Dr. Moore replied. "Just give me a few minutes. I have something important to do."

Alone at his desk, he began to write. The words flowed easily as his quill pen made scratchy sounds on the yellow manuscript paper. "Twas the night before Christmas," he began, "when all through the house, not a creature was stirring, not even a mouse . . ."

"Ah yes, that's exactly right," the professor announced to himself, pleased with his efforts. Quickly, he continued:

> The stockings were hung by the
>   chimney with care
> In hopes that St. Nicholas soon
>   would be there;
> The children were nestled all snug
>   in their beds,
> While visions of sugar-plums danced
>   in their heads;

By the time the family was seated at the dinner table, Dr. Moore had completed all 58 lines of his poem. After dinner he and his wife and children gathered around the fireplace for their traditional singing of Christmas carols. But the children had not forgotten their father's promise.

"You said you would give us a Christmas poem," they chorused, pulling at the sleeves of his frock coat.

At first, Dr. Moore pretended to have forgotten. "A poem? Was I supposed to write a poem?" he asked, a slight smile on his face. Then, as his children looked on with obvious disappointment, he fumbled through his pockets as if trying to find something he had misplaced. "Wait a minute!" he announced triumphantly. "Here's something."

And with a flourish, he pulled out the long yellow sheets containing the newly written verses.

While his children sat at his feet, Dr. Moore began to read. From the moment he spoke the opening lines, the youngsters were captivated.

They listened attentively as he declared: "The moon, on the breast of the new-fallen snow, gave the lustre of mid-day to objects below. When what to my wondering eyes should appear, but a miniature sleigh, and eight tiny rein-deer. With a little old driver, so lively and quick, I knew in a moment it must be St. Nick."

While the children beamed, Dr. Moore continued, describing how Santa drove his sleigh over the roofs of the buildings and called his reindeer by name: "Now, *Dasher!* now, *Dancer!* now, *Prancer* and *Vixen!* On, *Comet!* on, *Cupid!* on, *Donder* and *Blitzen!*" But it was when the professor read the lines describing the old fellow in detail, and telling how he came down the chimney "with a bound," that the eyes of his children widened in rapture:

> He was dressed all in fur, from his
>   head to his foot,
> And his clothes were all tarnished
>   with ashes and soot;
> A bundle of toys he had flung on his
>   back,
> And he looked like a peddler just
>   opening his pack.
> His eyes—how they twinkled! his
>   dimples, how merry!
> His cheeks were like roses, his nose
>   like a cherry!

His droll little mouth was drawn up
    like a bow,
And the beard on his chin was as
    white as the snow;
The stump of a pipe he held tight in
    his teeth,
And the smoke, it encircled his head
    like a wreath;
He had a broad face and a round little
    belly
That shook, when he laughed, like a bowl
    full of jelly.
He was chubby and plump, a right jolly old
    elf,
And I laughed when I saw him, in spite
    of myself;

Dr. Moore's children loved the poem so much that they immediately began to memorize the lines. But the professor himself thought little of it; to him it was just a funny story in verse. Never dreaming of its future popularity, or even of having it published, he shoved it into a desk drawer and forgot all about it.

Some months later, a family acquaintance, Harriet Butler of Troy, New York, visited the Moores. Dr. Moore read the poem aloud while they were having tea. Miss Butler was very much taken by the verses and asked permission to make copies. Later she sent one of them to her local newspaper, the Troy *Sentinel,* but failed to mention the author's name.

The Troy newspaper happily published the "anonymous" poem just before Christmas in 1823, noting in its columns: "We know not to whom we are indebted for the following description of the unwearied patron of children . . . but from whomsoever it may come, we give thanks for it."

For years afterward, the poem was often published by newspapers and magazines during the Yuletide season—but without any credit being given to Dr. Moore. In 1830 a wood engraver named Myron King produced the first illustration of St. Nick and his eight reindeer—just as they were described in "A Visit from St. Nicholas." (Santa remained a tiny elf for nearly 40 years. Only in the 1860's did he take his present-day shape of a plump gentleman of normal height, dressed in a red, fur-trimmed suit. And this was due to the American political cartoonist Thomas Nast, who drew Santa that way during the American Civil War.)

As for Dr. Moore, he finally got the credit due him when a collection of verse entitled *The New York Book of Poetry* carried the poem with his name on it in 1837. In 1844 the professor included it in one of his own books, but made it a point to note that he considered it of no more significance than "a good, honest, hearty laugh."

Certainly Dr. Moore never imagined that this little verse would eclipse all his scholarly writings on the Bible and Classical literature. And yet this is exactly what happened. Today not even the most serious scholars are more than vaguely acquainted with Dr. Moore's academic works; but millions of people throughout the world have read and been delighted by "A Visit from St. Nicholas."

The poem has now been reprinted many thousands of times, in dozens of languages. And each year at Columbia University there is a Christmas event known as the Lighting of the Yule Log. It is traditional at this ceremony to read the poem by Dr. Moore, who graduated from Columbia in 1798 at the head of his class and later became a member of its Board of Trustees.

Despite the immense popularity of his poem, Dr. Moore never earned a single penny from it. He probably would have refused the money anyway, for he was a man of independent means who preferred giving to receiving. In fact, Clement Clarke Moore was very much like the Santa Claus he wrote about—a man who quietly went about the job of bringing joy to others, and who was amply rewarded by the happiness he left in his wake. So Professor Moore might well have been describing himself in the closing lines of his time-honored poem:

He spoke not a word, but went straight
    to his work,
And he filled all the stockings; then
    turned with a jerk,
And laying a finger aside of his nose,
And giving a nod, up the chimney he
    rose.
He sprang to his sleigh, to his team
    gave a whistle,
And away they all flew like the down
    of a thistle;
But I heard him exclaim, ere he drove
    out of sight,
"HAPPY CHRISTMAS TO ALL,
AND TO ALL A GOOD-NIGHT!"

SANTA'S WORKSHOP

Now that you have read the story of how Clement Clarke Moore created the popular image of jolly St. Nick, maybe you would like to meet Santa in the flesh. Well, you can. All you have to do is take a trip to the North Pole.

No, you don't have to make a long trek across the Arctic. The North Pole we're talking about is in upstate New York amid the beautiful Adirondack Mountains, and it's the home of Santa's Workshop.

What is Santa's Workshop? It's a delightful fantasyland of quaint cottages, storybook characters, reindeer, and exciting entertainment—a place where the spirit of Christmas is celebrated six months of the year (from May through October).

There you can visit Santa in his home. And you can talk to Old King Cole, Mother Goose, Frosty the Snowman, and many of the other characters you've read about.

Santa's Workshop is actually a small village

of log cabins with high, colorfully painted peaked roofs. In the middle of the village stands the North Pole, a metal cylinder set on a stone base. Clustered around the North Pole are the workshops where Santa's helpers make all sorts of special Christmas gifts.

There's also an animal farm, with deer, lambs, ducks, and calves. And best of all, there's Santa's reindeer herd—the only one in the eastern United States. You can even take a reindeer sleigh ride through the woods.

There's entertainment and amusement rides too. A show called "Christmas Capers" is performed every day. It features Santa, Rowdy the Rascal Reindeer, Frosty the Snowman, and the North Pole Oompah Band. And you'll be amazed by the Wizard of the North, a master magician. The most popular ride is the Candy Cane Express, an old-fashioned steam train that chugs around the village. Or take a spin on the exciting "slide-a-boggan," which whirls you along at breathtaking speed.

Try to visit Santa's Workshop, the wonderful place where it's always Christmas.

A giant kite skin is stretched over a bamboo frame.

GUATEMALA'S FLYING MESSENGERS

Santiago Sacatepéquez is a small Cakchiquel Indian village in Guatemala. It is spread across a gentle hillside in the central highlands, a few miles from Guatemala City, the capital. Santiago, like many another Guatemalan village, is distinguished mainly by the costume of its women. This consists of a *huipil*, or blouse, woven on the backstrap loom, thickly brocaded with red geometrical patterns; and a dark-blue skirt held in place by a multicolored sash. But since many Guatemalan villages have their own special costumes, visitors would not be expected to flock to Santiago just to see the beautiful *huipils*. But they do flock there for something else: a colorful ceremony held every year on November 1, All Saints' Day. (All Saints' Day is a Christian religious holiday honoring the saints, both known and unknown.)

Beginning in early September of each year, for no one knows how many generations, the young men of the village have devoted their spare time and energies to an art nearly as

complicated and demanding as the weaving of the women's *huipils*. It is the art of kite making—but these are very special kites used for a very special purpose.

First a small circle of thin colored paper is placed on the floor. Then concentric rings, each with its own distinct design, are pasted around it, one after another. The kite grows outward, expanding, until it is soon too large to be fully unfolded inside the small Indian house.

The average kite skin measures 5 yards (4.5 meters) across; the biggest may be more than 30 feet (9 meters). As many as ten men work on each kite, and it takes six to eight weeks to complete one—about the same amount of time required for a woman to weave a *huipil*. But the kites will last a single afternoon, whereas the *huipil* is made to last for years.

On the morning of November 1, the women of Santiago go to the graveyard on a hillside outside of the town. There they scatter petals of wild marigold over the tombs and bare-

The finished kites are poised upright like huge shields, awaiting a strong gust of wind.

earth mounds. The people of the village call these flowers *flores de muerto* ("flowers of the dead"). Back in the village, in the courtyards of the little adobe houses, the men spend the morning stretching their giant kite skins over bamboo frames. Early in the afternoon, when breezes begin to blow over the hills, they carry the kites to the graveyard and poise them upright, like huge shields, along a fence at its downhill end. With their guy lines attached, taut, the pilots wait uphill for a westward gust of wind strong enough to take their craft aloft.

The kites are messages for the dead. Greetings. Tokens of remembrance, like the marigolds. Some kites never lift more than a few feet off the ground. Others catch strong breezes and rise high above the mountains. But these too soon come down. Some break up in the air, or, when the wind slackens, they tilt and nosedive into the groves and cornfields of the valley below. When each has been damaged beyond repair, its makers rip off the paper skin and set it afire, saving only the bamboo poles to use again the following year. And so this ancient tradition—flying messengers for the dead—lives on.

Up, up, and away—the flying messengers for the dead are carried aloft.

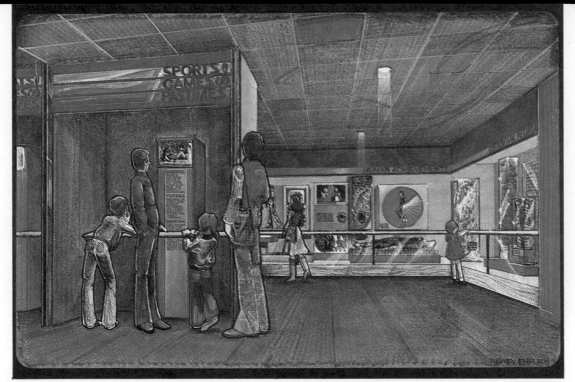

The Guinness World Records Exhibit Hall in New York City.

IT'S A WORLD RECORD!

How long was the longest beard ever grown? What is the largest seed? How much did the heaviest person of all time weigh?

In 1976 the Guinness World Records Exhibit Hall opened in New York City. And there you can see displays on all of these: the 17½-foot (5.3-meter) beard, the double coconut, the man who weighed 1,069 pounds (485 kilograms).

But you don't even have to leave your home to learn what's biggest, fastest, longest, deepest, brightest, or earliest. Just pick up the *Guinness Book of World Records*. It will tell you that Kelly Stanley of Canada needed only 36 seconds to climb a tree 90 feet (27.5 meters) tall. That Martin Luther King, Jr., was the youngest person (35) to receive the Nobel Peace Prize. That the longest telephone call was made by college students in Michigan—it lasted 1,000 hours.

This fascinating book was the idea of an executive of Guinness, a brewing company in Ireland. He thought it would be a nice gift for the company's customers. Two young men, Norris and Ross McWhirter, were hired to gather facts and write the book. The first edition came out in 1955. A new edition, with new records, is published every year. About 30,000,000 copies of the *Guinness Book of World Records* have been printed—and you can buy the book in 17 languages.

There are about 20,000 records, and countless facts about them, in the *Guinness Book*. Many can be used to stump your friends: What is the longest bone in your body? (the thighbone). Which planet has the most moons? (Jupiter, with 14). What boxer scored the most knockouts in his career? (Archie Moore, who had 141).

Some of the records are almost unbelievable. But no matter how strange they seem, they are true. Two men dropped fresh eggs from a helicopter 600 feet (183 meters) above the ground —and the eggs didn't break. A young Australian ate 63 bananas in 10 minutes. A U.S. park ranger has been hit by lightning 6 times—and has lived to tell about it.

Even you can be in the book. To become eligible, you must break a record or do something interesting that no one else has done. In 1977, for example, Samson Kimombwa ran the 10,000-meter race (10,936 yards) in 27 minutes and 30.5 seconds—setting a new world record.

Can you better that?

AMAZING RECORDS SET BY YOUNG PEOPLE

1887 15-year-old Charlotte Dod wins the women's championship at Wimbledon, the youngest person ever to win at this famous tennis tournament.

1913 11-year-old Henry Chambers is named organist at Leeds Cathedral in England, the youngest person ever to be appointed organist of a church.

1938 10-year-old Shirley Temple's wealth as a movie actress totals over $1,000,000; she is the youngest woman ever to earn that much money.

1944 15-year-old Joe Nuxhall begins pitching for the Cincinnati Reds, the youngest person ever to become a major league baseball player.

1962 4-year-old Dorothy Straight writes *How the World Began*. It's published two years later, making her the youngest person ever to have a book commercially published.

1965 12-year-old Karen Muir sets a new world record in the women's 110-yard backstroke (about 100 meters), becoming the youngest person ever to hold a major world sports record.

1970 17-year-old Sally Younger is clocked at 105.15 miles per hour (169 kilometers per hour) on water skis, the fastest any woman has ever gone on water skis.

1975 14-year-old Jim Sparks sits in a tree for more than 61 days, the longest anyone has ever sat in a tree.

1976 13-year-old Robert Knecht does 7,026 push-ups in 3 hours and 56 minutes, the most push-ups ever done at one time.

1977 19-year-old Cindy Nicholas swims nonstop across the English Channel and back in 19 hours and 55 minutes, setting a new world record. And she is the first woman ever to do it.

Robert Knecht on his way to setting a new push-ups record.

Le Carnaval de Québec: a wonderful, fun-filled celebration. The festivities include spectacular floats (*above*) and exciting canoe races across the frozen St. Lawrence River (*below*).

"Bonhomme Carnaval," the king of the *Carnaval*.

LE CARNAVAL DE QUÉBEC

Quebec City in Canada is always a lovely place to visit. But if you go there at a certain time of the year, you'll see something truly special. For every year, when winter is at its most fierce and there's a lot of snow on the ground, Quebec City holds the spectacular *Le Carnaval de Québec*—a fair, a festival, and a celebration all rolled into one.

In 1977, *Le Carnaval de Québec* was held from February 3 to February 13. Some exciting events took place a few days earlier, but they were just preparation for the actual *Carnaval*. These activities included the inauguration of Ste-Thérèse Street as Carnaval Street, and the arrival of "Bonhomme Carnaval" (the king of the *Carnaval*) and the crowning of his seven duchesses.

Then on February 3 the king and his court declared *Le Carnaval de Québec* officially open. What followed was ten days of festivities, and everyone was invited to attend. Most of the people of Quebec City and thousands of visitors from all over the world took part in a great many fun-filled events. These included colorful parades, ice hockey tournaments, canoe races across the frozen St. Lawrence River, acrobatic skiing championships, motorcycle races on ice, dog sled and snowshoe races, a treasure hunt, snow and ice sculpture contests, and even a lumberjack competition.

On February 13 the celebration was brought to a close with a spectacular final event: a glorious fireworks display. It was a fitting end to a perfect *Carnaval*.

FÊTE DES VIGNERONS

Once every 25 years or so, the small Swiss town of Vevey on the northern shore of Lake Geneva holds a spectacular celebration. It's called the *Fête des Vignerons*—the "Festival of the Winegrowers." It honors three centuries of local traditions and portrays wine growing through the changing seasons. In 1977, for the fourth and last time this century, this "once in a generation" event was held in Vevey—from July 30 to August 14.

Nearly half a million people from all over the world came to Vevey for the celebration. They saw parades, with musicians, singers, and thousands of local people dressed in historical costumes marching through the gaily decorated streets. And they witnessed colorful stage productions that showed the work in the vineyards during the four seasons.

▶ **A LONG TRADITION**

The origins of the *Fête des Vignerons* go back to the Middle Ages. A medieval religious order inspected the vineyards in the region around Lake Geneva and awarded prizes to the best local winegrowers. At the end of the ceremony, the townspeople of Vevey held a small celebration in honor of the occasion. This tradition has been carried down through the centuries.

Sometime around 1700, the Brotherhood of Winegrowers, a local "union," and the townspeople of Vevey expanded the once-modest celebration. People began to dress in costume, some of them portraying gods. One young boy dressed in a toga and recited verses about the Greeks, the Romans, and Bacchus, the god of wine. A parade was added to the festivities.

As the festival became more elaborate, the Brotherhood decided to hold it every three—and then every six—years. By the end of the 18th century, it was being held about every 25 years. Since then, the celebration has grown still bigger. Writers, musicians, and composers are commissioned to write special works for it. Artists and choreographers work with local performers to stage large production numbers in honor of the gods and the wine.

Today the pageantry of the *Fête des Vignerons* bears little resemblance to the first festival held hundreds of years ago. But it still celebrates the winegrower, his traditions, the land, and the precious wine that has been his lifeblood for centuries.

On these pages are pictures of the colorful *Fête des Vignerons* that was held in 1977.

Thomas Edison with an early version of his phonograph, which recorded sound on a tinfoil-wrapped cylinder.

ONE HUNDRED YEARS OF SOUND

One afternoon in 1877, a small group of men stood around a strange-looking device. It consisted of a metal cylinder wrapped in tinfoil, a mouthpiece, and a crankshaft to make the cylinder go around. As the others watched, one of the men turned the crank. Then he leaned toward the mouthpiece and shouted: "Mary had a little lamb. . . ."

When the speaker had finished reciting the first verse of the well-known nursery rhyme, he made an adjustment in the machine. Again he turned the crank. To the amazement of all, the machine repeated the words.

Thomas Alva Edison, the man who had spoken into the machine, beamed with satisfaction. His new device was a success. He had invented the first practical phonograph.

It was only by chance that Edison invented his "talking machine" 100 years ago. He was working on a gadget to improve the telephone. Because he was almost totally deaf, he couldn't tell how much sound was coming out of the telephone receiver. He came up with the idea of inserting a small needle in the receiver. The sound of a human voice coming over the telephone made the needle vibrate. He then could tell the amount of sound—loud or soft—that was being sent out, by the force of the needle on his finger.

That started him thinking. Could a needle be used to trace the pattern of sound waves on a solid surface so that it could be recorded and played back? Edison experimented with the idea. A disk with a needle in it was vibrated by a human voice, and a paraffin-coated paper was quickly moved under the point of the needle. The needle made prick marks in the paper.

Later he replaced the paper with a metal cylinder covered with tinfoil. Two disk-and-needle units were attached to the cylinder; one to record the sound, the other to play it back.

Edison made a rough sketch of his invention and had one of the workmen in his Menlo Park, New Jersey, laboratory make a model of it. No one was more surprised than Edison when it worked. "I was never so taken aback in my life," he said later.

The new machine was a big hit. Edison's workshop turned out 500 sets and sent them all around the United States to entertain the public. Thousands eagerly paid for an opportunity to hear the "talking machine" record and play back popular songs.

In time, a flat record, which replaced Edison's cylinder, was invented. It was played on a machine called a gramophone. Still later came long-playing records, which we now listen to on modern hi-fi stereo equipment.

All this was made possible by Edison's crude talking machine. Thanks to him, millions of music lovers can sit in the comfort of their homes listening to their favorite rock groups or classical composers on long-playing records and tape cassettes.

Edison's original "talking machine."

A gramophone.

A stereo phonograph.

A cassette tape deck.

THE BATTLE OF SARATOGA

The crackling of musket fire echoed through the thick woodlands. Cannon boomed like thunderclaps, shaking the ground. Scarlet-coated British regulars charged, their bayonets glinting in the sun. On the opposite side of the field, buckskin-clad American riflemen riddled the British ranks with well-aimed volleys.

The fighting was desperate on that cool, clear September day in 1777. For more than three hours, the rival armies punched away at each other like enraged boxers.

When the fighting was over, the Americans retreated from the clearing around Freeman's Farm, near Saratoga, New York. General John Burgoyne's British army had won the day.

But they lost the war.

For the British had suffered heavy casualties at the battle of Freeman's Farm. And a few weeks later, the badly weakened British army was defeated in the final engagement of the Saratoga campaign. On October 17, 1777, General Burgoyne surrendered the battered remnants of his army to the American forces under General Horatio Gates. The series of military events that led to Burgoyne's surrender has come to be known as the Battle of Saratoga.

Few Americans know very much about Saratoga. Yet it was the turning point of the American Revolution, and it has been called "one of the most decisive victories in the history of mankind." Fewer still know that the real hero of Saratoga was a general named Benedict Arnold—the very same Benedict Arnold who later became a traitor.

In October, 1977, the 200th anniversary of the Battle of Saratoga was commemorated by several re-enactments of the fighting near the original site of the final battles. The story of the Saratoga campaign is an important one. It is worth remembering—and retelling.

It began in June, 1777, when General "Gentleman Johnny" Burgoyne and an army of over 9,000 men marched out of Canada and invaded New York. According to the British plan, Burgoyne's column was to move south to Albany, where it would be met by General William Howe's army coming north from New York City. A third British force, under Colonel Barry St. Leger, was to strike east from Oswego, on Lake Ontario. The combined British army would then sweep all the American troops from the Hudson-Champlain Valley.

British control of the strategic Hudson River would drive a wedge between New England and the other colonies. It was the old rule of divide and conquer.

At first the campaign went well for the British. Burgoyne's army sailed down Lake Champlain and attacked the American garrison at Fort Ticonderoga early in July. The outnumbered Americans were driven from the fort. By capturing Fort Ticonderoga, Burgoyne had opened a gateway to the Hudson.

But the Americans were far from beaten. The retreating rebel troops did everything they could to delay Burgoyne's advance. They chopped down trees and dug ditches to block the forest roads. So effective were the American tactics that in 23 days, Burgoyne was able to advance only 22 miles (35 kilometers).

As the British troops plunged deeper into the rugged wilderness, their troubles mounted. Supplies were running low. Farmers loyal to the Patriot cause burned their crops and drove off their cattle so the British wouldn't have food. By early August, Burgoyne's troops were exhausted and half-starved.

In desperation the British commander sent a detachment consisting mostly of Hessians (German mercenaries hired by the King of England to fight the Americans) on an expedition to gather food and fresh horses.

At Bennington, in what is now Vermont, the Hessians ran smack into a brigade of tough New England militiamen. The Americans whipped the Hessians, killing over 200 and capturing 700 more.

Almost at the same time, the British were suffering another defeat. Colonel St. Leger's column, marching east to join Burgoyne, was repulsed (at the Battle of Oriskany) by a hastily assembled force of local farmer-militiamen.

The two American victories were bitter blows to Burgoyne. To make matters worse, the British commander received word that General Howe was not marching north to support him as he had expected. Instead, Howe had decided to attack General George Washington's army in Pennsylvania.

This painting by John Trumbull shows Burgoyne presenting his sword (surrendering) to Gates.

Historians still debate why Howe did not go to Burgoyne's aid. Some claim that Howe never received the necessary orders from his superiors. In any event, Burgoyne now found himself isolated. He had no choice but to forge ahead and try to reach Albany on his own.

Between the British and Albany were some 9,000 American troops commanded by Major General Horatio Gates and his cheif lieutenant, General Benedict Arnold. The Americans were firmly dug in on a series of bluffs called Bemis Heights.

On September 19 Burgoyne sent three columns of British troops to assault the American positions. Gates was content to fight a defensive battle. But fiery Benedict Arnold finally persuaded the overcautious Gates to allow him to attack the British in the open, at Freeman's Farm.

Led by Arnold, the American troops fought the British to a standstill. Only the arrival of reinforcements late in the day saved the British from complete defeat.

Technically, the British won the battle, but they had lost hundreds of men, and the American rebels still blocked the way to Albany. The British hastily constructed some forts and waited, still hoping that General Howe would send troops to aid them.

When three weeks passed and no help came, Burgoyne decided to gamble on another attack. On October 7, American and British troops clashed in the Second Battle of Freeman's Farm (also known as the Battle of Bemis Heights).

Again the battle was a seesaw affair. At a key moment, when the outcome was still in doubt, General Arnold galloped onto the field. Surveying the scene, Arnold discovered a weak point in the British line. He quickly gathered several American units and led them in a charge between two British redoubts (forts). Then the Americans swept into the Breymann Redoubt, the key to the British defenses, and captured it. In the fighting, Arnold was wounded in the leg. But by his bold action he had won the battle.

The British were now outflanked and had to retreat to Saratoga. There, outnumbered and surrounded, they surrendered ten days later.

The American victory at Saratoga had immediate impact. It lifted the morale of American Patriots. But most important, it led to an alliance between France and the rebelling colonies. With the aid of French troops and supplies, the American colonists went on to win their independence and to establish a new nation.

HENRY I. KURTZ
Author, *Captain John Smith*

DISCOVERING YOUR ROOTS

It's a fact of life—you have two parents, four grandparents, eight great-grandparents, sixteen great-great-grandparents . . . and so on, back to the very beginnings of human existence. You probably know who your parents and grandparents are and where they came from. But who were your great-great-grandparents? Who were your ancestors in the 17th or 18th or 19th centuries? Where did they live? How did you get here if they lived there?

These are just a few of the many questions that people everywhere have begun more and more to ask themselves. They are searching for their "roots"—for the ancestors and heritage from which they descended.

By studying family records and following other leads, some people have been able to

Alex Haley *(left)* wrote the dramatic book *Roots*. It was made into a popular TV series with LeVar Burton as Kunta Kinte *(below)*.

trace their families back hundreds of years. Most often a lot of work is involved. And finding the actual proof that shows that a particular person is really one of your ancestors is like solving a real-life mystery or a very difficult puzzle.

▶ ONE MAN'S SEARCH

Interest in family history greatly increased in 1977, thanks in large part to an American writer named Alex Haley. His book, *Roots*, told the story of Haley's nine-year-search for his family's origins. He began his search with stories that had been told to him by his grandmother in Tennessee. She had spoken of their ancestor, "the African," who left his village one day to cut wood to make himself a drum. While he was away from the village, he was captured by slave traders and shipped to the United States.

Haley's search for this ancestor took him to libraries and courthouses. It took him to London, where he studied the records of slave ships. It took him to a tiny village in Africa. There he spoke with an old man who knew the history of the village, and who told Haley about Kunta Kinte, the boy who had been captured while cutting wood—and who Haley believed was his ancestor.

Haley's dramatic book was made into an eight-part television series. It was watched by millions of Americans. (Some 80,000,000 people watched the last episode, the largest television audience in history.)

The book and the TV series inspired many people to hunt for their own roots. They enrolled in special courses given by local colleges and genealogical societies. They bought some of the many books that describe how to go about searching for one's ancestors. And they wrote or went to libraries and other places that could be of help. For example, the National Archives in Washington, D.C., received 758 inquiries in its family history services the week before the "Roots" series was televised, and then after the broadcasts, averaged 2,344 inquiries a week.

▶ WHERE TO LOOK

If you decide to search for your own roots, start at home. Talk to your relatives, especially the older ones. Ask for facts: birth dates, names of parents, names of places where they lived,

and so on. It is a good idea to prepare a fact sheet for each relative. It might look something like this:

MY ANCESTORS

Name of Person _____
Relation to Me _____
Birth Date _____ Place _____
Father's Name _____
Mother's Name _____
Brothers' and Sisters' Names _____
_____
_____
Schools Attended _____
_____
_____
Occupations _____
_____
_____
Where He/She Lived _____
_____
Spouse's Name _____
Marriage Date _____ Place _____
Children: Number _____

Name	Birth Date
_____	_____
_____	_____
_____	_____

You probably won't be able to fill in all the blanks on the fact sheet right away because you won't have all the information. But start a sheet even if all you know is the person's name. That makes him or her "real" to you. And as you go back several generations, your number of ancestors will quickly increase, causing confusion if you don't have a good system for recording information. (If you could trace your family back to the year 1600, you would be involved with about 65,000 ancestors!)

Also write down the stories that your relatives tell you— of what school was like, the games they played, the pets they had, the way they were affected by wars or elections or any other big events. You will discover that your relatives and ancestors have done many inter-

esting things. Perhaps some were famous— or infamous. One woman discovered that one of her ancestors was thought to have been a witch, and was burned at the stake in Salem, Massachusetts.

Some relatives may live far away. Perhaps you have never even met them. Write to them. Describe your project and ask for their help. Send along copies of your fact sheet and ask them to fill one out for each relative that they know of.

Ask your parents and relatives for family mementos: picture albums, family Bibles, diaries, letters, passports, birth and death certificates, marriage licenses. These things are often buried in attics or cellars, almost totally forgotten. It will take some gentle nudging on your part to get people to remember where they stored these things. But such papers can be very helpful. One woman found a letter that mentioned an uncle she didn't know existed, and a piece of property that everyone had forgotten about.

After you have gathered as much information as possible from your family, you are ready to check public records. This is where tracing ancestors begins to get especially difficult. But remember, you are a detective. And as any police detective would tell you, there's a lot of dull work involved both in the hunt for clues and in following up on the clues once you have them.

Public records include such things as land deeds, census records, wills, and military records. If, for example, you know that a great-great-grandfather settled in Sherman County, Kansas, in 1860, you could check county and town records to learn exactly where and when your ancestor bought land, what he paid for it, and how long he had it.

Churches and graveyards are also excellent sources of information. Churches have records of baptisms and marriages. Tombstones give birth and death dates, and often indicate family relationships or provide other information. This one tells us something of how a man died:

> This is the grave of Mike O'Day
> Who died maintaining his right of way.
> His right was clear, his will was strong,
> But he's just as dead as if he'd been wrong.

Public libraries have many books that tell about how to trace your roots. And some of the larger libraries have collections of old census records, newspapers, and other items that may help you.

There are also many historical societies, genealogical societies, and other groups that have collections and libraries that are devoted to the subject. One of the best of these is the central library of the Mormon Church in Salt Lake City, which has about 60,000,000 names on record, including both Mormons and non-Mormons.

Even telephone books can be helpful. One man who has an uncommon last name always checks telephone books in places he visits. If someone with the same last name is listed, the man writes or telephones the person to find out if they might be related.

▶ **SEEING FOR YOURSELF**

The information that you gather will become even more meaningful if you can visit the places where your ancestors lived. One young woman went to Czechoslovakia. There, in the city of Prague, she saw the house where her father's family had lived. She visited the church where her father had worshiped as a young boy, and she visited the hardware store where he had worked before leaving Czechoslovakia for America.

Traveling is not always an easy thing to do. It involves both time and money. But travel may be necessary to trace some of your ancestors. Knowing the language spoken by your ancestors is also helpful.

Occasionally, you will come to what seems to be a dead end. Perhaps records were lost or burned. For example, a big fire in Chicago destroyed almost all the city and county records up to 1872. Or people may have changed their names—or immigration officials changed them for them. Slaves were often given their owner's names. Names on official records may be misspelled.

But the problems will seem unimportant when compared with the joy you will feel as you learn about your family and how it survived and grew through one century after another. Tracing your roots gives history a sense of personal importance. And it tells you about yourself. As Alex Haley said, "We are what we are because of those who went before us."

JENNY TESAR
Consultant, Curriculum Concepts, Inc.

THE WORLD OF YOUTH

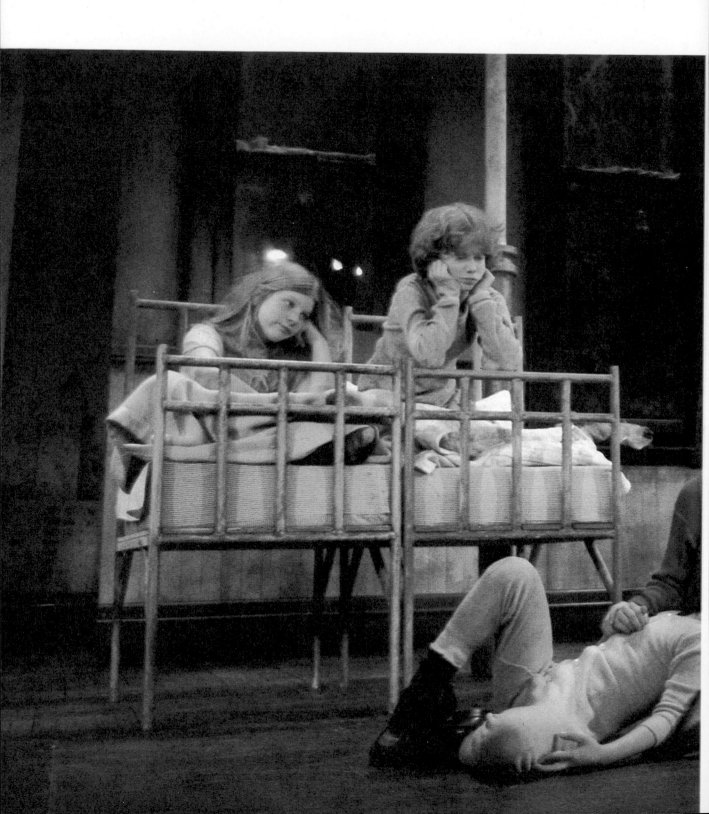

The kids in the cast of *Annie* made it one of the smash Broadway hits of 1977.

YOUNG HEADLINERS

Music lessons really do pay off! Tom and John Keane—better known as the Keane Brothers—take at least five hours of music lessons a day in several different instruments. The results? They have performed at concerts, made records, and been interviewed on TV talk shows. Best of all, the 12- and 13-year-old brothers from Encino, California, starred in their own summer television series in 1977.

By the time Ken Noda was 14 years old, he had composed three operas. And the youngster from Scarborough, New York, spent most of 1977 busily working on his fourth. His first composition, *The Canary*, was performed by the New York City Opera Company in schools as part of the opera company's education program. When he's not composing, Ken performs as a pianist with the St. Louis Symphony, the Minnesota Orchestra, and the New York Philharmonic.

Conquering the English Channel: In 1977, Cindy Nicholas (*above*), a 19-year-old Canadian, broke the world record by making a nonstop, round-trip swim in 19 hours and 55 minutes. And 13-year-old David Morgan, from Yorkshire, England, became the youngest person ever to swim the Channel. He completed a one-way trip in 11 hours and 5 minutes.

Saving energy was on the minds of New York City's junior and senior high school students in 1977. In fact, 300 of them presented their own models and diagrams of energy-producing devices. The winning entries were displayed by the Student Exposition on Energy Resources, sponsored by the National Energy Foundation. Here Frank Panicali demonstrates how to fry an egg with sunlight.

LEAPIN' LIZARDS! IT'S LITTLE ORPHAN ANNIE

Move over, Charlie Brown, Dennis the Menace, and Blondie. Look who has stepped out of the comic pages and landed on Broadway as the biggest hit of the 1976–77 theater season. It's Little Orphan Annie; her faithful dog, Sandy; and Daddy Warbucks. They're all part of a big smash musical called *Annie*.

Annie isn't an overnight sensation who came upon fame and fortune in the theater. Little Orphan Annie had a long history before she hit Broadway. For more than 50 years Annie, Sandy, and Daddy Warbucks had one adventure after another in the comic pages of daily newspapers. Annie—with her mop of curly hair, red and white dress, and huge blank saucer-shaped eyes—captured the hearts of millions of readers. Her favorite expressions, "Gloryosky!" and "Leapin' Lizards," became household words.

Now don't run off to get a newspaper to look for Annie. She's no longer there. The comic strip ended several years ago. But don't despair—Annie and her friends have come to life on the Broadway stage.

The Broadway *Annie* is not really the same as the newspaper Annie. The show uses the same characters that appeared in the comic strip, but a new story line has been added. As the curtain rises, Annie and her six little orphan friends are living in the New York Municipal Orphanage. The year is 1933 and America is in the middle of a terrible depression. Nearly everyone is poor and jobless.

But no one is unhappier than these orphans. They are watched over by the strict and wickedly funny Miss Hannigan, keeper of the orphanage. She gets angry at any sound of happiness coming from the children, and at four o'clock in the morning orders the poor little girls to scrub the floor to a high shine. And as if that isn't enough, gruff Miss Hannigan threatens to stamp out their freckles!

Ah . . . but wait. Something wonderful is about to happen. Oliver Warbucks, one of the richest men in the world, decides to invite an orphan to spend the Christmas holidays with him. Annie is the lucky one who is chosen. And the rest is pure happiness, much to Miss Hannigan's dismay. During the visit Annie charms Oliver Warbucks, and he decides to adopt her.

There are many wonderful songs and dances along the way, and of course there are some evil people who try to put a stop to the good times. But as the curtain comes down, Annie and Daddy Warbucks—and Sandy—are living happily in the Warbucks mansion.

▶ GLORYOSKY! IT'S ANDREA McARDLE

What would *Annie* be without the kids? An unthinkable situation. After all, the seven young orphans are probably the most important part of the story. The girls range in age from 7 through 14, and they are loaded with talent. In their orphanage dresses, they sing and dance their way into the hearts of the audience. But one orphan stands out. She's the one who leaves Miss Hannigan behind and steps into the wonderful world of Daddy Warbucks. She's Annie, the star of the show.

And just who is playing rags-to-riches Annie, the best Broadway role in years? Why, none other than 13-year-old Andrea McArdle of Philadelphia, Pennsylvania. Andrea has been performing since she was three years old, mostly in TV commercials and regional theaters. She also played the role of Wendy on the television soap opera "Search for Tomorrow," for which she won the 1976 award as best juvenile actress on afternoon TV.

Andrea came to the part of Annie quite by accident. She was originally cast as one of the other orphans. While the show was playing a pre-Broadway run in Connecticut, the young actress who had been playing Annie left the cast. Andrea learned the role in two days and went on to play Annie in Washington, D.C., and finally New York.

It's not easy being a leading lady, however. Living the life of a Broadway star doesn't excuse Andrea from her schoolwork. Tutors meet with Andrea and the other young members of the cast every day to go over lessons and homework assignments. The only "young person" in the cast to be excused from schoolwork is Sandy, Annie's lovable dog.

It seems that Andrea has adjusted to her new life and is settling in for a long Broadway run. She's even had her dressing room at the theater wallpapered with Little Orphan Annie cartoons!

Stepping out of the comic pages and landing on Broadway: Daddy Warbucks, Little Orphan Annie, and Sandy.

The orphans—minus Annie—sing their way into the hearts of the audience.

CAUTHEN TO WIN!

They're off! The crowds in the racetrack grandstand roar as the horses break from the starting gate. The excitement heightens as the animals go into the first turn and begin to spread out. Suddenly, as the horses reach the second turn, one rider and his mount pull into the lead. The crowds yell, urging their favorite on. A horse races across the finish line and is declared the winner. The jockey guides him into the winner's circle in front of the stands. There, a garland of flowers is draped around the horse's neck, and the prize money is presented to the owner of the horse. The jockey also basks in the glory of the moment. After all, the rider plays an important role in getting the horse to win.

In 1977 one jockey in particular—17-year-old Steve Cauthen—spent much of his time in the winner's circle. Standing 5 feet 1 inch (155 centimeters) tall and weighing 95 pounds (43 kilograms), Steve became a horse-racing teenage phenomenon.

▶ BOY WONDER

Steve Cauthen was born into a horse-racing family on May 1, 1960, in Covington, Kentucky. His father is a blacksmith, and his mother is a horse trainer (as are two uncles). When Steve was two years old, his parents gave him a pony. That special gift was probably responsible for the start of something great.

By the time he was 12, Steve began to think seriously about a career as a jockey. He studied horse-racing films to learn the techniques of various riders. He spent hours practicing his whip style by thrashing bales of hay on the family's farm in Walton, Kentucky. But most important, he spent a lot of time just watching and learning at racetracks.

On May 12, 1976, just eleven days after his 16th birthday, Steve made his debut as an apprentice jockey at Churchill Downs, the famous racetrack where the Kentucky Derby is held. Unfortunately, it wasn't a great way to start. His horse finished last. But that didn't discourage him. Five days later he rode his first winner. And THAT was the start of something great. By the time Steve started riding at the major racecourses in November, 1976, he had ridden more than 200 winners.

Then the 1977 New York racing season opened in January. Six weeks later, Steve became the first jockey ever whose horses had earned more than $1,000,000 in purse money so early in the year. In one month alone, he finished first on 59 of his 198 mounts. Once, he rode horses into the winner's circle six times in one day! And he just kept on setting records. Everything wasn't all good, however. On May 23, Steve was thrown by his horse and trampled in a three-horse spill. He suffered a concussion, a hairline fracture of his right arm, two broken fingers, and a broken rib. It took him four weeks to get well, but then he returned to ride more winners. It was back to business as usual. In June, Steve completed his term as apprentice jockey and became a full-fledged jockey. By October, Steve had become the first jockey in racing history to reach $5,000,000 in purse earnings in one season.

Steve has been at racetracks all over the United States, riding seven days a week and nine horses a day. He might ride in New York one afternoon and race at a track in California the next day. Then it's off to a racecourse in Florida. Now you might say that this kind of schedule doesn't leave much time for schooling. Wrong! Steve has been taking a high school correspondence course furnished by Eastern Kentucky University. And his grades are almost as good as his racing records.

Steve also found time to record a country-and-western album of songs called *And Steve Cauthen Sings Too!* And he has been considering the offers of book publishers bidding for his life story, and of advertisers who will pay him fantastic sums of money for endorsing their products. The future does indeed look bright for this racing whiz.

Of course, Steve's future depends on his not adding pounds and height to his small frame. But if the unthinkable should occur and he grows out of his job, Steve has other plans. He might consider a career as a horse trainer or a veterinarian. Then again, he might leave horses altogether and seek a profession in another field. But so far he's been too busy winning horse races to give much thought to a horseless future. When you're riding a winning streak, you might as well stick with it while it lasts.

Steve Cauthen weighs in for a race at Aqueduct Racetrack in New York City.

TRACY AUSTIN TAKES CENTER COURT

Who is the youngest tennis player ever to play in the famous tournament at Wimbledon, England? And who is the youngest player ever to reach the quarterfinals in the United States Open Tennis Tournament at Forest Hills, New York? There's one answer to both questions: Tracy Austin. She accomplished both feats in 1977, at the age of 14.

With her walloping two-fisted backhand and other well-learned techniques, Tracy rose to the top ranks of tennis players. But the young girl from Rolling Hills, California, made more than just tennis history in 1977. With pigtails flying and braces gleaming in the sun, Tracy captured the "teenage crown" that once belonged to Chris Evert.

It all started when Tracy was just two years old. That's when she first picked up a racket and started hitting balls. When she was three, she was playing with her older sister and three older brothers. At the age of eight, she won her first two tennis titles: the 10-and-under and 12-and-under Los Angeles city championships. After that she went on to take eleven U.S. Tennis Association titles. About the only thing left for this tennis whiz is to be the number one player in the world. And that is exactly what Tracy has in mind.

To reach that goal takes a lot of hard work. Tracy practices about three hours a day—every day—at a tennis club. She also swats the ball with her sister and brothers, and she enters every tournament she can.

Off the court, time must be made for other things. School is important to Tracy. A straight-A junior-high-school student, she often works on her homework while sitting on the sidelines at tennis tournaments. Algebra is her only tough opponent at school, and her father helps her by acting as math-teacher-by-telephone when she travels.

Tracy also likes to watch television, and she likes the Fonz most of all. Stamp collecting, making jewelry out of bubble gum wrappers, and reading Nancy Drew mysteries are her favorite hobbies.

And of course time must be set aside for her fans. After one match at the 1977 U.S. Open, Tracy rushed from the shower to answer a telephone call from an admirer—President Jimmy Carter. He congratulated her on her game and invited her to visit him at the White House. For Tracy Austin, 14 was an exciting age.

STARRING ANOTHER CASSIDY

Another Cassidy has hit the airwaves like a bolt of lightning. This time it's Shaun Cassidy who's collecting fans by the millions. Shaun is David Cassidy's (remember him?) younger half brother. In 1977, the tall, blond, 19-year-old Shaun was well on his way to becoming as successful as his famous brother. And he seemed to be following the same pattern that had brought David instant recognition all over the world: a television series, hit records, and European concert tours.

Having singer-actress Shirley Jones for a mother and the late singer-actor Jack Cassidy for a father certainly didn't hurt Shaun's chances for stardom. But they weren't the ones responsible for his success. Shaun Cassidy did it his way, and he did it on his own. Yes, there were summer tours with his mother in revivals of Broadway musicals. But that wasn't actually a career. That was just a pleasant way to spend a summer vacation. When the tours ended, it was always back to school. Chances are, however, that Shaun's "what I did on my summer vacation" reports were a lot more exciting than his classmates' stories.

After graduating from Beverly Hills High School in California, however, Shaun was on his own. Television was the first opportunity to knock at his door. Actors were being auditioned for the two lead roles in a new TV series called *The Hardy Boys,* a program based on the mystery stories by Franklin W. Dixon. Shaun was chosen to play the part of Joe Hardy, boy adventurer. The program introduced him to the public, and they were quick to respond. Fan clubs formed almost instantly all over the United States. It was a repeat of the popularity of David Cassidy's *Partridge Family,* which hit the nation several years ago.

The Hardy Boys gave Shaun the opportunity to do two of his favorite things: sing and play the guitar. "Writing and performing music is my love," he says, "and acting is my hobby."

The record companies then began knocking at his door. Shaun made several records that turned into hits—among them "Da Doo Ron Ron," a remake of a 1963 golden oldie. Other singles followed, and finally an album, *Shaun Cassidy,* hit the top ten chart.

When you're a teenage idol, word travels fast. During breaks in the filming of his TV series, Shaun went on promotional tours. His arrival sent his fans into fits of hysteria. They broke through police lines in West Germany, and mobbed a radio station in Australia, hoping to get a glimpse of their idol.

But Shaun has taken his zooming popularity in stride. He lives a relatively quiet life in California, devoting what little spare time he has to bowling and baseball, two of his favorite pastimes. He also continues to answer the door every time opportunity knocks. The last time he did so, he received an offer to star in two TV specials. There's no telling what the next knock will bring.

YOUNG PHOTOGRAPHERS

A good photograph is like a dream captured. That's what today's young photographers seem to be showing us, whether the subject is a cityscape, a rural landscape, or a purely made-up pattern. Mood and atmosphere are all-important, and if the young photographers convey these to you in their pictures, then their work is a success. The photographs on these pages are all prize winners in the Scholastic Photography Awards program of 1977. The program is sponsored by the Eastman Kodak Company.

Earthquake, by Scott Headley, 15, Rochester, New York

Aspen, by Andrew Stoloff, 16, Newton, Pennsylvania

Rock & Roll, by Curt Breusing, 17, Anaheim, California

Skyline, by John Craig, 17, Cincinnati, Ohio

Layered Forest, by Richard Oren, 17, Tucson, Arizona

Contemplation, by Alice Larson, 18, Plainview, Texas

Hair in the Air, by Charlie Clement, 18,
Hebron, Connecticut

Abandoned Reaper,
by Kevin Farrell, 17,
Oak Lawn, Illinois

HODGEPODGE

Keys. Hats. Bottle caps. Picture postcards. Sugar cubes in different wrappings. Tree roots. Put these all together and what do you have? A hodgepodge.

That was the name of a very popular exhibition at the children's museum in Karlsruhe, a city in West Germany. Hodgepodge—What Children Collect was planned and put together entirely by children. They did all the work. They even wrote texts describing their exhibits and telling why they collect the things they do.

There were 19 collections in the exhibition. They were put together by children between the ages of 4 and 14 who like to collect things.

One 4-year-old girl makes dolls from seashells. An 8-year-old boy makes pictures from bird feathers he finds on the ground. One young boy collects hats: army caps, hats from flea markets, and hats from his grandfather. Another child collects all sorts of keys.

There are many ordinary things that can be collected. Matchbooks are an example. There are many different designs on them. Corks from wine bottles are also fun. Many have words or even designs stamped on them.

Do you collect anything? If you don't, why not start? The children in Karlsruhe are sure you will find that it's a lot of fun.

YOUTH IN ART

Have you ever looked at a painting and imagined that you were in it? This dream comes true for the lucky people who are selected each year as the live models who appear in the Pageant of the Masters. In this spectacular pageant, famous works of art are re-created using people and settings that are almost exactly like the original painting or sculpture. In 1977 the show included over 40 staged masterpieces, including paintings by El Greco, Edgar Degas, Salvador Dali, Winslow Homer, and John Singer Sargent.

This unusual show is held each year in a large outdoor amphitheater in Laguna Beach, California. It is staged every evening for 45 days during the summer. The first pageant of "living pictures" was held in 1933, and since then it has become well known all over the world.

▶ RE-CREATING THE ARTWORKS

A special committee selects the artworks that are to be re-created for the pageant. Once the selection is made, photographs are taken of the paintings and sculpture. These photographs are used to guide the artists who will paint or construct huge copies of the artworks. Each copy is proportionately scaled so that it will appear human-sized on the stage.

▶ THE LIVE MODELS

About 150 live models star in the cast every night. (There are two complete casts because each person is in the show seven nights straight, and then gets a week off.) Many factors are considered in selecting the models, who are all volunteers. People of all ages are used. But a person's size and shape are more important than age, because the model must be in perfect proportion to the painted background.

To be chosen to appear in one of the masterpieces is quite an honor, and young people are often selected. In the 1977 pageant the youngest stars were 9 years old.

▶ COSTUMING

Costuming and makeup are very important. They can easily turn a boy or a girl into an old man or woman. The costumes are made from unbleached muslin cloth, which is painted to match the colors and shadows of the original artwork. The costumes are stiffened so that they will remain motionless during the performance, even if a breeze is blowing.

▶ ON STAGE

The exciting pageant is ready to begin. The announcer tells the audience about the artwork that is soon to be seen. As he speaks, stagehands are quietly arranging the settings behind the curtain. The models are helped into position, sometimes hanging onto hidden supports so they won't lose their position when the curtain is open.

Then the orchestra begins and the curtain opens. The special stage lighting focuses on the large-scale "artwork" and helps make the stage picture look like the original. The audience gasps and applauds, amazed that the "painting" or "sculpture" before them is a giant re-creation.

This is the most difficult time for the models, because they must remain perfectly still. A sneeze or cough would ruin the show. Finally, after a minute or so, the curtain closes and the models relax. They go back to the dressing room, and the next work of art prepares for its showing.

The two-hour pageant traditionally ends with a famous work that requires thirteen models. It's *The Last Supper,* a magnificent painting by Leonardo da Vinci.

▶ THE CAST SAYS . . .

The first evening of the Pageant of the Masters has ended. It's been a happy and dazzling experience for both the audience and the cast.

Let's see what one of the cast members has to say about the pageant. Dave Strauss, age 14, was chosen as a live model in 1977, when he appeared in gleaming gold body makeup. Dave was one of three models who portrayed the carved figures on a gold comb from ancient Scythia, now displayed in a Soviet museum. "The makeup is pretty messy," says Dave, "but I think being in the pageant is neat, and so do my friends."

Turn the page and you will see how the oil painting *Happy Days*, by Eugene Iverd, was re-created.

MICHELE AND TOM GRIMM
Authors, *Hitchhiker's Handbook*

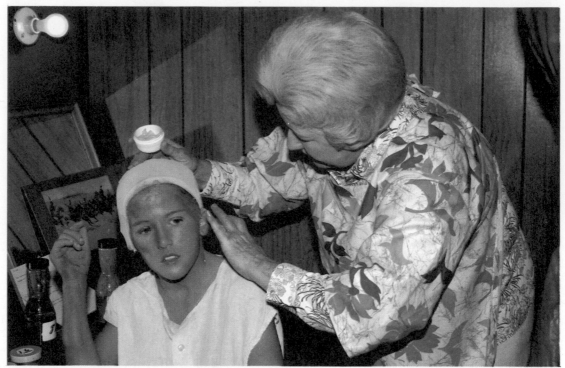

Makeup: the live models will appear very much like the people in the painting *Happy Days*.

Setting up: the models are placed against the backdrop of the re-created artwork.

The stage picture: the re-created artwork *Happy Days* as the audience sees it.

The real picture: the actual painting *Happy Days* by Eugene Iverd.

CHILDREN'S EXPRESS

The *Children's Express* newsroom starts to come to life just as thousands of offices in bustling midtown Manhattan begin to close up for the day. This is not surprising, because the staff members of *Children's Express* are schoolchildren who have been in their classrooms most of the day. When they are not close on the heels of a deadline, they are worrying about homework, playing baseball, or building up courage for the school dance.

These children have made *Children's Express* the most innovative news magazine for young people. The key to its success, and the reason for the staff's fierce loyalty to it, is that *Children's Express* is the first magazine to take kids seriously. It has shown that kids do care about more than movie star gossip. They care about saving our resources, space exploration, politics, and other important issues of the day. They are also concerned with many social issues, especially child abuse and children's rights.

Another reason for the magazine's acceptance by children all over the world is that all the articles are guaranteed to be of interest to them. Why? Because the young staff of *Children's Express* handles the stories all the way from doing the original research to writing the actual questions for the interviews.

The magazine itself is very young. It was founded in 1976 by publisher Bob Clampitt, editor Dorriet Kavanaugh, and a devoted group of reporters. From the start, the goal was to make a magazine that kids could take pride in.

The news team made its first major scoop at the Democratic National Convention in New York during the summer of 1976. The Democratic Party's nominee for president, Jimmy Carter, kept the press world in suspense by declining to reveal his choice of a vice-presidential running mate. He finally called a special news conference to announce his choice. It came as quite a surprise when *Children's Express* reporters handed out a special newspaper edition proclaiming Walter Mondale as Carter's choice—seconds before Carter announced it! The reporter who made the scoop, Gilbert (Scoop) Giles, attributed part of his success to the fact that adults didn't take him seriously and would talk as if he weren't there. They know better now!

The *Children's Express* staff then moved in on the Republican Convention, where once again they printed a special newspaper edition. This one contained an interview with Vice-President Nelson Rockefeller telling why he was supporting Gerald Ford after the incumbent president had "dumped" him. The reporters also swapped tips with TV anchormen Walter Cronkite, Dan Rather, and Harry Reasoner, who under *Children's Express* quizzing admitted the worst mistakes they had made on TV.

On their return to New York, the young reporters set up their office and began to work on the first issue of their new magazine. The busy after-school staff soon built up a bunch of investigative interviews with experts and celebrities of all kinds.

The ever-growing nationwide team of over 500 reporters—including our very own White House correspondent, Amy Carter—has cov-

Children's Express reporters (Jared Hoffman is on the left) interview Margaret Mead.

ered every topic from A to Z and has spoken to many fascinating people, including Walter Mondale, Hubert Humphrey, Jodie Foster, the Carter family, Doug Henning, Carol Burnett, and Alex Haley.

The members of this lively news team fall into two categories: reporters, who are 7 to 13 years old, and assistant editors, 14 to 17 years old. Both groups play important roles in the making of the magazine.

The reporter actually conducts the interview and asks the questions. The assistant editor is responsible for arranging the interview and organizing a team. Reporters are encouraged to work in teams led by assistant editors. The assistant editor makes sure that the reporters are thoroughly briefed on the person to be interviewed and checks their questions so that there is no repetition during the interview. Tape recorders are used to record the interview so that the reporters can concentrate fully on the discussion. After the interview the assistant editor debriefs the reporters—that is, using a tape recorder, he or she questions them to find out how they feel about what was said at the interview. This is an integral part of each article because children can hear each other's opinions on the topics.

Children from all over the world are invited to become reporters or assistant editors, and to organize news teams where they live. The most important requirement is that all major stories be cleared with the New York news center to prevent overlapping interviews.

The choices of topics are left up to the reporters and assistant editors, to encourage them to report on what they, as kids, see as interesting. Everyone is encouraged to follow up on his or her ideas and organize interesting interviews. This builds a well-deserved feeling of importance and responsibility that is too often denied to children. But, then again, that is the goal of *Children's Express.* Says reporter Jessica Trentlyon, "We're really giving our whole viewpoint on the world and what we think of it for once, not what grown-ups think of it—what we think of it. And I think that's very important that we're finally having a chance to talk out and tell the world what we really think."

• • • •

We would love to hear from you! For more information on how to be a reporter or an assistant editor, or if you are a teacher who is interested in what we are doing, write to *Children's Express* at: Children's Express, 257 Park Avenue South, New York, N.Y. 10010.

JARED HOFFMAN (age 14)
Children's Express

In 1977, the Boy Scouts of America held their 9th National Scout Jamboree in Pennsylvania.

BOY SCOUTS

The world Scouting movement was started in England in 1907 by Robert Baden-Powell. During the past 70 years, the movement has grown into a worldwide organization. In 1977 the Boy Scouts had a membership of more than 14,000,000 boys, young men, and adult leaders. In some of the 110 member countries, young women also belong to the organization.

▶ INTERNATIONAL SCOUTING EVENTS

The world Scout organization, which is headquartered in Geneva, Switzerland, continued to support community projects in developing nations during 1977. Through these projects, Scouts are involved in plans to modernize sanitation, health services, building methods, and farming and animal husbandry in their own villages, towns, and cities. Community de-

velopment projects are under way in Nigeria, Indonesia, Bolivia, Madagascar, Sri Lanka, Cameroon, and Costa Rica.

Many international Scouting events were held in 1977. Some of the highlights were the 9th National Scout Jamboree of the Boy Scouts of America; the Canadian Jamboree '77; the Iceland National Jamboree; the 6th Caribbean Jamboree, in Jamaica; and Jamborra '77, held in Ireland.

The 26th World Scout Conference, which meets every other year to set policy for the international movement, was held in Montreal in July, 1977. The Boy Scouts of Canada and L'Association des Scouts du Canada, the Scout association for French-speaking youths, were hosts of the conference.

▶ SCOUTING IN THE UNITED STATES

In August the Boy Scouts of America celebrated their 9th National Scout Jamboree at

Cub Scout activities included a safe bicycle driving project.

Boy Scouts collecting glass for recycling.

Moraine State Park in Pennsylvania. The week-long Jamboree was attended by 28,500 scouts and adult leaders, and 250 visitors from 25 other countries. Jamboree activities included games, arts and science displays, and tests in Scouting skills. And camping and other outdoor adventures were enjoyed in the huge tent "city." Scouts who were unable to attend the Jamboree in Pennsylvania joined in many of the same types of activities on a local level.

Energy conservation was one of the most important projects for the Boy Scouts in 1977. At the request of President Jimmy Carter, the Boy Scouts of America launched a major campaign in October to teach their members about energy conservation. Through education and action, Boy Scouts learned how to reduce their own energy consumption. They also learned how to help inform other Americans about the world's energy problems.

Scouting continued to promote the conserva-

tion of natural resources through their Project SOAR (Save Our American Resources). In this program, workers collected wastepaper, metals, and glass for recycling. They also upgraded and improved wildlife habitats and helped in the control of soil erosion and the prevention of litter.

The Three Programs

The Boy Scouts of America have three basic programs for their members. Cub Scouting is for boys 8 to 10 years old; Scouting is for boys 11 to 17; and Exploring is for young men and women of 15 to 20. (By the end of 1977, young women made up about 37 percent of Exploring's membership.)

In 1977 a new rank called Webelos was added to the advancement program for 10-year-old Cub Scouts. Changes were also made in the requirements for the Arrow of Light, Cub Scouting's top award.

Cub Scout summer camps were popular during the year. The camps offered recreation and learn-by-doing education through the Cub Scout advancement program. Other Cub Scout activities included a safe bicycle driving

At the Canadian Jamboree '77: Swimming, cleaning up, and making sand castles.

project, physical fitness championships, and a learn-to-swim campaign.

In its first full year of operation, Scouting's Florida High Adventure Gateway area drew about 700 older Scouts and Explorers. Locations in Florida and the Bahamas were the scene for scuba diving, subtropic canoeing, coral reef yachting, and sailing ship voyages. The Florida Gateway is the 6th national "high adventure" area of the Boy Scouts of America. Other recreation areas are in New Mexico, Wisconsin, Minnesota, Maine, and on the Kentucky-Tennessee border.

▶ SCOUTING IN CANADA

The Boy Scouts of Canada, the largest of two Canadian Scouting associations, had nearly 266,000 members in 1977. This was an increase of 10,000 new Scouts. The second organization, L'Association des Scouts du Canada, is the smaller of the two groups.

The Canadian Jamboree '77, the largest youth event ever held in Canada, was celebrated in July. Nearly 16,000 participants from all over the world met on Prince Edward Island for the 11-day encampment.

The Boy Scouts of Canada were actively involved in environmental projects in 1977. In a continuation of a nationwide reforestation project, the Canadian Scouts planted more than 2,500,000 trees. Since this project began, more than four years ago, about 5,000,000 trees have been planted in designated conservation areas across Canada.

The Boy Scouts of Canada offer separate programs for various age groups. The youngest group, 5 to 7, is called Beavers. The oldest members, with a maximum age limit of 23, are called Rovers. Between these two age groups, there are also programs for Wolf Cubs, Scouts, and Venturers.

During 1977 the Boy Scouts of Canada made new efforts to help young people who are handicapped, those who live in high-rise complexes, and those who come from one-parent families. They also helped to develop local leadership for Scouting within ethnic communities in the major cities and in the Inuit (Eskimo) communities of Canada's far north.

HARVEY L. PRICE
Chief Scout Executive
Boy Scouts of America

GIRL SCOUTS AND GIRL GUIDES

Girl Scouting and Girl Guiding is a worldwide movement with 7,300,000 members in 94 countries. The World Association of Girl Guides and Girl Scouts (WAGGGS) is the international body that oversees Girl Scout and Girl Guide groups all over the world. Each national organization operates on its own, shaping its programs to fit the needs of its country. But each national organization works as a part of the whole, with shared goals of peace and better understanding among all peoples.

▶ **THE END OF AN ERA**

For more than 60 years the Girl Scouts and Girl Guides were led by Olave, Lady Baden-Powell, the World Chief Guide. Her death on June 25, 1977, at the age of 88, ended her long years of work and travel on behalf of international Girl Scouting and Girl Guiding.

Lady Baden-Powell's interest in the movement began in 1912 with her marriage to Robert, Lord Baden-Powell, the founder of the Boy Scout and the Girl Guide/Girl Scout movements. From that time on she and her husband worked together to develop the worldwide movement for girls. As leader of this mass movement, Lady Baden-Powell was received by kings, queens, presidents and prime ministers. Many nations also honored her with their highest decorations.

Within WAGGGS, Lady Baden-Powell and her husband have been honored by a special day for the last 50 years. February 22, their joint birthday, is celebrated as "Thinking Day." On this day members hold special celebrations and think of their "sisters" throughout the world. The girls also give voluntary contributions to a Thinking Day Fund as a way to help the work of the movement. In recent years the Thinking Day Fund has helped to extend Girl Scouting and Girl Guiding in many countries.

▶ **ACTIVITIES AROUND THE WORLD**

Girl Scouting and Girl Guiding today offers many chances for girls to help change the lives of individuals, families, and even whole communities. For example, in Jamaica the Girl Guides are mounting a countrywide campaign to improve the lives of children. Under the theme "The Child and You in the Community," the Girl Guides are helping in foster homes, children's homes, and hospitals. They are also baby-sitting and giving out information about inoculation campaigns. As a special project, the Guides are helping in the national effort to register births. They have handed out to parents leaflets explaining the legal requirements and have given talks on how to register births.

Girl Guides in Pakistan are helping to improve the quality of life for women. They have formed "workshops" that take on different tasks. One group helps village women set up vegetable gardens. Another group helps to teach adults to read and write.

In Sri Lanka, the Girl Guides run a continuing family-life education project. Fifteen target areas have been set up in which work is keyed to the needs of local villages. Projects include home gardening, weaving and sewing classes, soup kitchens, courses in health and sanitation, and discussions on family health care.

In two African countries, Guiding provides the only education for some girls in remote areas. Botswana Girl Guides are now giving training in home-care to girls who have left school. Girls who have not been able to continue their formal education in school get lessons in cooking, sewing, hygiene, handicrafts, and agriculture as income-producing skills.

A similar project is being run by Girl Guides in Benin. It includes classes in home economics, reading, and writing as well as sessions on current events and local problems. The program is of special value to girls in isolated areas who would not otherwise have a chance to get any formal education.

In South America, Girl Guides in Guyana are planning some of their projects in cooperation with the government. The Guyanan Guides are involved in a "Grow Your Own Food" campaign. They are also helping to extend classroom space by making bricks for school buildings and even by making fences and school furniture.

In the industrialized countries, Girl Scouts and Girl Guides are meeting other kinds of community needs. For example, Girl Guides in Queensland, Australia, have started a cam-

Girl Guides in Pakistan help to teach adults to read and write.

Girl Guides in Australia campaigning to increase the number of kidney donors.

Girl Scouts in Kentucky inform the elderly about food stamps.

Girl Guides in Canada demonstrate friendship at the International Camp.

paign to increase the number of kidney donors. Girl Guides are stationed at shopping centers, main streets, and other busy areas to hand out kidney-donor cards and to talk about the project with passersby. The Girl Guides' effort has received so much publicity that the community has become much more aware of the need for kidney donors.

A Ranger unit of the Girl Guides in Belfast, Northern Ireland, has served the staff and patients of a mental hospital ever since 1969. The Rangers have given more than 6,000 hours of their time to help run recreational activities such as a club for patients and dancing and singing sessions.

The United States And Canada

The Girl Scouts of the U.S.A., the largest national organization of WAGGGS, gives much attention to helping members find the best ways to help their communities. For example, Girl Scouts of Suffolk County Council in New York State have planned a project at a center for juvenile delinquent girls. Aimed at helping these girls to learn to cope in society, the program will offer career workshops, sensitivity sessions, service projects, recreational and cultural activities, and educational tutoring. The Suffolk County Girl Scouts are aided in this project by a grant from the U.S. Department of Justice.

In Kentucky, another Girl Scout council has responded to a call for help by its state. Many elderly and low-income people did not know there was a government program designed to help them get food at a low price. The state asked the Girl Scouts to find and inform eligible people about "food stamps," which can be used to buy food. The Girl Scouts set up food-stamp information booths in key places to answer questions, distribute leaflets, and tell people how to apply for the stamps.

An important event for Girl Scouts of the U.S.A. in 1977 was the introduction of a new handbook, *Worlds to Explore,* combining activities for the two youngest age levels, Brownies and Juniors. The new handbook describes the first major program changes for younger members since 1963.

The most important changes covered in the new handbook are projects for girls in the fields of science and technology, and activities that help youngsters to consider a career (as well as the home) as a natural part of a woman's life.

Girl Scouts of the U.S.A. makes it possible for American members to exchange visits with members living in other countries. During the summer of 1977, American Girl Scouts traveled to South America, Europe, Africa, and Asia.

Girl Guides of Canada and Guides du Canada demonstrated international friendship in a very special way in 1977. Together they staged a massive International Camp on Cape Breton Island in the province of Nova Scotia. The International Camp was the culmination of two years of planning, involving the Guides, the Canadian government, and a number of private organizations.

More than 1,500 girls from Canada and many other countries gathered at the campsite in July for an event that was more of a "conference under canvas" than a traditional camp. Along with the usual camp activities—boating, swimming, backpacking—members took part in unusual events such as "talk-ins," in which girls discussed values and hopes for the future with noted women of achievement.

The campers also met with people from the nearby communities of Cape Breton Island. For example, "the neighbors" were invited to the camp demonstration area, where campers shared the songs, dances, and crafts of their home communities with the Cape Breton Islanders. In return, cultural and craft groups from Cape Breton communities demonstrated their skills. And the Guides made a special effort to make contact with visitors who were blind, physically handicapped, or elderly. Sighted Guides escorted blind visitors on walks along the nature trails, and other guides shared their camp experiences with "adopted grandparents for a day."

Though Canada is an industrialized country, it still has a few very remote and isolated areas. Girl Guides of Canada and Guides du Canada are seeking to serve girls on the isolated coast of Newfoundland and in the Northwest Territories. The projects include classes in hygiene, nutrition, crafts, and recreation. Day camps for children in these regions have been organized with help from the government and other agencies.

CAROL B. STROUGHTER
Girl Scouts of the U.S.A.

FUN TO READ

An illustration from the stunning picture book *Ashanti to Zulu: African Traditions*, winner of the 1977 Caldecott Award.

The Secret of the Ghost Town

From the top of Hangman's Hill, Jeremy looked west to where he could just make out the ruins of Nugget City. Once a gold-mining camp, taking thousands of dollars worth of gold from the nearby hills, Nugget City was now a lonely, empty ghost town.

"Are you really going to spend the night here in this spooky place?" asked a high, squeaky voice.

Jeremy turned to find that his friend Tom, and Mike, his camp counselor, had followed him. He nodded. "At the Frontier Hotel."

"Why?" Tom persisted. "I thought all of us at Camp Kiowa were going backpacking in the hills."

"He has his reasons," Mike said, quietly.

"Yeah, I know," Tom said. "He wants to find his great-grandfather's grave just so he can put his name on that old chart he carries around with him."

Jeremy's hand tightened on the leather folder containing the chart of a tree with branches set with blocks on which to record family names. Mike knew that this little chart was the only family Jeremy had. He had printed in the names of his missionary parents, who died of smallpox in Africa when he was two. He had also recorded the names of his grandparents who had died before he was born. Now, he had traced his great-grandfather, Jonas Lander, to Nugget City. His foster parents, the Hillmans, had arranged for him to spend the summer at Camp Kiowa—just 40 miles from Nugget City.

The counselor's voice pulled him away from his thoughts. "Be careful," Mike warned. "Remember, even though you have the Hillmans' permission to go alone to Nugget City, I am still responsible for you." He patted Jeremy's shoulder. "We'll meet you back here tomorrow evening."

"Don't get bitten by a rattlesnake," Tom called as they left.

Leaning against the hitching rail in front of the hotel, Jeremy watched his friends follow a twisting path into the hills, and he felt the loneliness of the land close in on him.

Before disappearing into the thick trees, Mike turned and waved. Jeremy waved back. Mike was a good friend. One of the reasons Mike had arranged this camping trip was for Jeremy to locate his great-grandfather's grave.

Jeremy ate bacon and eggs from a cracked blue plate in the hotel dining room and went to bed early.

A shaft of hot sun, burning a path to his bed, awakened him soon after dawn. He leaped from the bed, washed quickly, and pulled on his clothes. In ten minutes, he was clattering down the hotel's rickety stairs to buy a sandwich and a carton of milk, and then be on his way.

Over the top of his newspaper, the desk clerk gave him a friendly smile and wiped his bald head with a bandana.

"Can't imagine why a boy would want to stay behind in a broken-down hotel when he could be hiking in those cool hills with his friends," he said.

"I have something to do," Jeremy answered. "Can you tell me how far it is to Nugget City?"

Slowly the man lowered his paper, and his smile slid from his face like a mask of warm butter. "Why Nugget City?"

"Something personal," Jeremy said, reluctant to tell a stranger his problem.

The clerk's eyes narrowed. He started to say something when the screen door banged and a woman entered. She was dressed in a sun-bonnet and a brown dress, long out of fashion.

"Clyde, has anybody been out to. . .?"

"Hush, Sarah!" Clyde ordered, nodding in Jeremy's direction. "The boy, here, wants to know how far it is to Nugget City."

The woman's face hardened. "About four miles," she snapped, "but after you get there, there isn't anything to see—just rotten old buildings and rattlers. You aren't figuring on walking there, are you?" When Jeremy nodded, she said, "Don't go. It's a hot walk and there's a storm coming."

Jeremy looked past her to a blue sky.

"Don't go, boy," the clerk said. "Fact is, you don't have any business out there." His voice sounded rough.

"I'll be back by suppertime," Jeremy said.

Walking down the dusty road, he wondered about Clyde and Sarah. There was no mistaking the fact that the hotelkeepers wanted him to stay away from Nugget City. Maybe they had gold hidden there. Well, he didn't care about gold or anything. He just cared about finding his great-grandfather's grave.

Once, he looked back to see Clyde and Sarah standing in front of the hotel watching him. When he looked back a second time, he saw Clyde climb into a battered jeep and drive north in a cloud of dust.

The sun was well up into the sky when he arrived at the ghost town, with its sagging, crumbling shacks and lichen-grown fences. He walked to a cottonwood tree and shrugged off his backpack.

The water from his canteen was warm, but its wetness loosened up his dusty throat so that he could swallow his sandwich and milk. For a while he rested under the tree and wondered which shack had belonged to his great-grandfather. It was hard to imagine that Nugget City had once been a lively town. Jeremy had read about ghost towns. He closed his eyes, and in his imagination the quiet of the land around him became filled with sound.

The town probably began with someone—maybe Jonas—riding into nearby Carson shouting, "Gold! Those hills are bulging with gold! Come on, grab yourselves a claim!" The people would run to gather up spades and picks and gold pans and head for the hills—great-grandfather Jonas no doubt showing the way. The news of the gold strike would leak to the outside world and a gold rush would be on. Into this sagebrush-and-jackrabbit land would come prospectors, surveyors, and storekeepers who would sell flour at 70 dollars a sack and bacon at 3 dollars a pound, and hotelkeepers who would charge 2 dollars for a dirty blanket and space on the floor to sleep. A laundryman would hang out a shingle and wash the miners' clothes for 5 dollars a load, and Wells Fargo would set up a bank to take care of all the miners' gold. The prospectors would bring their families and build homes.

Then, the streets would ring with children's laughter, and men would gather to talk, and someone would play "My Darling Clementine" on a harmonica. This would go on until the mines petered out, and, one by one, the families would pack their belongings in a wagon and move on. Their houses would fall to pieces, and the town would become a ghost town.

"Get out of here! Leave now!" The words came in a hollow wailing sound, and, for a drowsy moment, Jeremy thought the voice had come out of the dead past of Nugget City. He opened his eyes and sat up, frightening a brown lizard that had been sunning itself on a nearby rock. Again, the quiet closed in around him. Had he imagined the words? He looked up at the hills behind him. There were thickets and trees where a man could hide. Uneasy, he remembered the warnings of the hotelkeeper to keep away from Nugget City.

Shouldering his pack again, he struck out across the sagebrush to where he could see what resembled a cemetery. "They're not going to scare me away," he said stubbornly.

When he reached the area, Jeremy saw it was an old cemetery where fences lay crumbling on a bed of sage and thistles. For about 15 minutes he searched the headstones trying to read the names carved onto the splintered and sandblasted markers. "Elvie Millett, born 1842, died of a bullet 1863," one read. "Mary Crawford, died age three of lung fever," read another. But search as he might, he found no marker bearing the name of Jonas Lander.

He crossed to what appeared to be the town's main road. On his right, a dilapidated wooden building looked about to crumble onto the desert floor. He looked inside where a nest of rats had taken up residence, and he was glad to move on. Ahead was a false-fronted building of sandstone. Jeremy could just make out the words, "Wells Fargo and Company."

He was just leaving the Wells Fargo building when two shots rang out. Instinctively he ducked down behind a pile of rubble. For a moment all was quiet, then a voice shouted, "Get out! Leave here or you'll be sorry!" Another shot blasted the air.

More angry than frightened, Jeremy yelled, "I'm not getting out until I get what I came for!"

"There is no gold! Nugget City's mines petered out years ago!"

So someone thought he was after gold. But if there was no gold, why should someone be so anxious to keep him away?

"I'm not looking for gold!" he shouted back. "I'm here to find my great-grandfather's grave!"

"Why in tarnation didn't you say so?" From around one of the leaning shacks emerged Clyde. Belatedly, Jeremy saw the nose of the jeep protruding from behind a building a short distance away.

The bald-headed clerk walked toward him, his rifle tucked under his arm.

"You could have saved us all a lot of trouble if you hadn't been so closemouthed back there at the hotel," he said. "Whose grave are you looking for, and why do you think it's here?"

Jeremy noted that the hostility had dropped from the man's face.

"I found a letter from my grandmother that said her father-in-law had refused to budge from Nugget City in Nevada, even though the gold was gone from the hills. He must have been the last survivor with no one to bury him, because I couldn't find his marker.

"What's his name, son?"

"Jonas. Jonas Lander."

Clyde's eyes widened. "Jonas Lander!" He started to laugh so hard that Jeremy thought he might have a stroke right there in the hot sun. "Oh, son, the joke is on you! Come on, get in the jeep!"

"I'm not leaving until I've looked this place over!"

"Come on. We're not going far."

The jeep followed a winding road leading over the hills to a small shack.

"Hello, in there! It's me—Clyde!" the man called.

The door of the shack opened and an old man came out, blinking against the bright sun. He wore a full beard, soft and silky white. His white hair fell to his shoulders. His shoes were broken and grayed with dust, and his clothes were faded but neatly mended.

"Son," Clyde said, "meet your great-grandfather."

Jeremy sat in the jeep in stunned silence, as Clyde walked over to talk to the old man. A moment later Jonas returned with Clyde.

"You must be Carrie's boy," he said in a voice as soft as his beard. "She wrote to me from Africa when you were born—thought you were still there. Come in the house, boy, we've got lots to talk about."

By the time Jeremy and Clyde got back to the hotel, the boys were lined up on the porch of the Frontier Hotel. "Hey, where you been?" Tom yelled.

"Nugget City—talking to my great-grandfather."

His counselor held him by both shoulders and looked into his face. "Did I hear you right? You did say talking to your great-grandfather?"

Jeremy nodded. "He's alive, Mike! He just discovered a big vein of gold! That's why Clyde and Sarah wanted to keep me away from the ghost town. They were afraid a stranger might find out about the gold before he had a chance to stake his claim. But his claim is already recorded."

"Jeremy, that's great! That is really great!"

"Grandfather Jonas wants me to go to school in Carson, so I can be with him on weekends and in the summer."

"You'll have a real family like other people," Mike said softly. "I'm so glad for you, Jeremy. Well, get your gear and climb in the bus. You'll be wanting to go back to Ohio to tell the Hillmans. I have a feeling they will want you to be with Jonas."

In the bus, Jeremy told his friends about his adventure, but he didn't forget to wave out the back window of the bus to his friends Clyde and Sarah, who had promised to look after his great-grandfather at Nugget City until Jeremy could get back to do it himself.

Ten Miles
at Each Step

Once upon a time in Denmark, there lived a very poor man named Sven who often went to a beech forest to pick up firewood. He had a wife and children at home, but the family had little to eat and not much wood to burn on the hearth.

One morning as Sven wandered in the forest, a stranger stepped out from behind a very large tree. This stranger was very tall, and his eyes smoldered like live coals. He wore elegant black clothes, a fine hat covered his head and shadowed his face, and a very long cloak concealed his feet.

"My poor man, what are you doing here on this very cold day?" asked the tall man, with a strange smile.

"Oh, I came here hoping to find some firewood to take home to keep my family warm. I have both wife and children, but we have little to eat and scarcely enough wood to burn."

"Too bad, too bad," the stranger remarked dryly. "You do lead a dog's life. But if you want to change it, you can do so easily. Perhaps I can be of some help."

Sven answered sadly, "I certainly must keep my family from starving or freezing to death. I would do anything in my power to change our lives for the better!"

"Then all you have to do," remarked the stranger, "is promise to give me that living creature who is now in your home this very moment, but whom you have never seen or heard of. Can such a creature mean anything to you?"

"No, of course not. I'll go along with that!" cried the woodsman. Already his existence seemed a little brighter.

The stranger went on: "In return for this living creature, you will find your home always filled with food and drink and firewood— even more than you need. In fact, you can ask for anything necessary for your comfort and well-being, and it will be right under your nose as soon as you make the wish."

"This man must be crazy or a sorcerer," thought Sven to himself. "But what can I lose? I own nothing at all. The live creature this stranger wants to own must be a cat or a dog, or perhaps a pixie who has been hiding under the boards of the floor. Why should I keep it?"

So the bargain was made and Sven agreed. "I'll keep my promise," he said slowly and with a grave face. Then he offered his hand to clinch the pact.

But the hand of the stranger seemed to burn him.

"Remember, from this hour you can never break your vow," the stranger said. "The living creature you have pledged to me is your very own son who lies sleeping in his mother's womb. She has not told you anything about him, because she does not want to add to your worries."

At these dread words, Sven's stomach seemed to drop down into his boots; his head whirled about. But he had made his vow and he had clinched it with a handshake. So what was he to do?

Meanwhile, the stranger kept on speaking in his metallic voice: "I'll let you keep him at home until he is fourteen years old. But on the very day he is fourteen, you must bring him here to this spot. But I warn you, don't send him to priest, pastor, or teacher; let him stay at home or wander in the woods by himself. I shall write whatever I want on his soul."

These last words frightened the woodsman. Yet what could he do? "A poor man like me has small choice," he muttered to himself, looking down in embarrassment. When he lifted his eyes again, the stranger had vanished.

When Sven arrived at his cottage, the house was warm, lamps were brightly lighted, and a feast lay spread on the table. His wife was weeping for joy, and his children were so busy gobbling the food that they did not even stop to greet their father.

From that day on, Sven's table was always filled with the tastiest food, his hearth was always bright with fire, his lamps were lit, and fine clothes hung in the one and only clothes closet. A horse and some cows appeared in their stable, and in their yard were geese and chickens and ducks.

About six months later, Sven's wife gave birth to a son, who was baptized with the curious name of Dom. He grew into a bright little boy and was way ahead of other boys of his age. According to the bargain with the stranger, the lad was not placed in school. He stayed at home and soon learned how to take care of himself. But no matter how little attention was paid to him, the boy learned to read and write. He devoured every book he could beg or borrow, even from the pastor, although he was not allowed to go to the pastor's school.

In short, when he was thirteen years of age, Dom knew a lot more than his father had ever known. This made his father feel even worse when he realized what a wonderful lad he had promised to give away to a complete stranger.

A year had almost passed, and Dom would soon be fourteen years old. To Sven's amazement, some time before his birthday, the lad said to his father, "Please take your sheath knife and carve a three-legged chair and a three-legged table to stand in front of the chair. I know that you have promised me to the Devil. Why, in dreams I've seen a chair waiting for me in Hell. To save me from this fate, you must not use any tool other than your steel sheath knife. And be sure you have these two objects ready by my fourteenth birthday— because each time you carve off a piece of wood for the chair *here,* in Hell a piece is cut off the chair waiting for me *there.* If we are clever, I may never need to suffer in Hell."

Sven was so happy, he cut and he carved both day and night until the chair and table were ready. Then on Dom's birthday, father and son carried table and chair into the forest to the very same spot where Sven had met the stranger some fourteen years before. Right there the lad took a long, sharp stick and drew a very large circle in the earth.

"What are you doing that for?" asked his father.

"This is white magic I learned from the pastor's book. If you stay inside this circle, the Devil cannot touch even a hair of your head," answered Dom with a solemn face. "But you must remain inside this circle for twenty-four hours, or else its blessing will not protect you. When that time has passed, then you can go home and no harm can come to you."

"But what about you?" asked Sven, turning his eyes away.

"Well, it's not going to be so easy for me," admitted Dom. "I'll draw a circle just like the one that protects you. I'll sit inside it, but for how long I cannot tell. For I have to remain there until everyone knows that I am waiting to be saved."

"But what do people care what happens to a poor lad like you?" cried Sven.

"Wait, and I shall explain! When the news reaches every crack and corner of the whole world, perhaps then a pure maiden with a loving heart will come to me, lift me in her arms, and carry me off to her home where we shall be safe and happy all our years. But if that pure maiden with the loving heart never appears, then I belong to the Devil, and I shall just have to sit and sit here until he comes to fetch me."

238

Hearing these grave words, Sven had nothing to say. He went to his circle and sat down on a hillock. The lad walked a way through the forest, where his father could hear but not see him. In this spot, the lad drew another wide and perfect circle, and right in the middle of it he placed the three-legged chair and in front of that, the three-legged table. Then he sat down on the stool, and on the table he placed a book of white magic that he loved to read.

Not an hour passed before the stranger appeared and bowed to Dom. The lad examined the stranger with keen eyes. He could see that horns pushed up his elegant hat, and that the hem of his long cloak swayed back and forth revealing cloven hoofs.

After greeting Dom, the Devil (for of course it was he) walked a short space through the woods to greet the lad's father. He bowed, then said in his harsh metallic voice, "My day has come. Your son is fourteen years of age. Now you must turn him over to me!"

"Take him yourself, you have seen him!" answered Sven, his face red with rage. How could he have failed to know fourteen years ago that this same stranger was Satan himself?

Now the Devil walked back to the circle where Dom was sitting with his nose in his beloved book.

"No more nonsense! *No book in the world can save you!* So prepare for your journey to Hell!"

The lad paid no attention whatever. He just kept on reading.

Then the Devil tried to place his hoofs inside the circle, but to no avail. He could not move a muscle. He just stood fixed as if made of wood.

Finally, in a rage, he wrenched loose and marched back to Sven and tried to lure him out of his circle by wiles and by threats. But Sven was faithful to his son's warning, and he would not move an inch.

Soon the Devil was rushing from father to son, begging, pleading, threatening, to get them out of their circles. All to no avail! Finally, with a shriek of fury, he disappeared, leaving only a cloud of smoke and the smell of sulfur behind to show that he had been there.

Dom remained sitting on his three-legged stool with his nose in the book. He waited and waited and wondered if in all the world there lived a pure and lovely girl who would be willing to break the spell that kept him bound. He really did not know how long he stayed there, but it seemed a very long time indeed—weeks, months, maybe years.

When he had almost given up all hope, on a bright sunny morning he heard a rustling of wings above his head. And before he knew what was happening, he was gathered into the arms of a lovely, smiling young girl who seemed to him like an angel. She picked him up as if he were thistledown, and before he could collect his wits to ask who she was and where they were going, off they flew—a long, long way until at last they reached a castle that lay south of the sun, east of the moon, and in that silent place round which the winds play their wild games.

At last, safe in this castle, the young girl explained to Dom that she had heard about him, how he had been pledged to the Devil even before he was born. She had determined therefore that no matter how dangerous the journey, she would fly to save him from his awful fate.

"And I am willing to marry you. I can decide for myself, for I am the princess here!"

How great was his joy that he had escaped being chained in Hell forever! How happy he was that this pure and beautiful girl loved him! So their wedding was planned.

Then a strong longing took hold of Dom. He wanted to see once more his humble cottage near the beech forest.

"I must go back to visit my parents once more," Dom pleaded with the princess. "I feel certain they have been grieving about me for a long time."

"Very well," said the princess, "I shall carry you home to see your parents, and you can stay as long as you like. I shall put this ring on your finger. It is our engagement ring. If you want to be with me again, then just turn the ring and say to yourself, 'I must fly back to my sweetheart!' Then you will be here with me in no time at all.

"But do not say: 'I want my sweetheart to come here to me!' I am no mortal maid. I shall not run after you no matter how much I love you. Never forget my words, or all our happiness will come to an end."

"I promise I shall do as you say," said Dom.

At once Dom was taken back to his parents' cottage on the edge of the forest. The princess set him down just outside his own home and then she vanished.

When Dom stepped into his childhood home, his mother and father rose to their feet in amazement. They could scarcely realize that this handsome, well-clad young man was their very own son.

"But it's truly me!" cried Dom. "I've come back on a visit to prove to you that I am not chained down in Hell as the Devil wanted. I am happy and in love with a lovely princess who lives in a castle south of the sun, east of the moon, and right in the middle of the wind."

"That is a very strange place to live, and we never heard of it before," remarked his parents. "But wherever it is, and whoever she is, we are happy and grateful that you have come for a visit."

They ate and drank and had a merry time.

"But why can't your princess come here so we can see her and thank her for saving you?" asked his parents over and over. And after some days Dom began to wonder if his sweetheart would not take pity on his old parents and show herself at least once under their roof.

Early one morning he walked out under the trees, pondering this. He recalled his vow to her that he would do as she wished in all things. But then, of course, she was not like other girls. Perhaps he could never really understand her. And maybe his life with her in that faraway castle was nothing but a dream.

At last he determined that if she truly loved him she would come to him. So he turned the engagement ring on his finger and whispered softly, "Dear Princess, do come to me and prove your love by forgetting your pride."

With that he heard a quick rushing of air about him and the rustle of wings. He felt the arms of his beloved near him. In a trice, she twitched the ring off his finger, and away she flew in a cloud.

And there he stood, quite alone, and he knew at once that he had thrown away all his happiness. Now the ring was gone, and it would not change matters at all if he tried to find his princess. From now on he had to remain there and be just as lonely as he had been as a child.

After some weeks, he realized he could no longer stay with his parents. His father looked unhappy when he gazed at his son. His

parents could not understand why the young girl Dom loved would not come to visit them.

Early one day Dom bade them farewell and wandered out into the world to try to recover his lost paradise. He walked and he walked. He really didn't know where he was going, or exactly what he expected to find.

At twilight one day, he happened to be in a very thick forest. And there before him, in a small clearing among the trees, he spied two demons who seemed to be haggling with each other.

As Dom drew near he saw that on the ground between them lay a pair of old boots.

"What are you haggling over, demons?" asked Dom as he came closer.

"Oh, we are haggling over these boots. They are not just old boots, they are magic, for each boot can carry a traveler ten miles at each step."

"This is a silly matter for demons to be haggling over," observed Dom. "Each of you take one boot, and that will settle the matter justly."

"Oh, no, that won't do at all!" they cried. "We each want *both* of them so we can go as fast as the fastest wind. One boot is not enough!"

"Here's how to settle this matter," began Dom. "You will have to run a race for them. See that round, gray stone over yonder? When I say 'Go' you must run, and the first one to get there and back will win the boots."

The demons agreed to this, so when Dom shouted 'Go,' off they went at such a clip that the dust from the forest seemed to stand up round their very ears.

"How stupid can demons be!" thought Dom, as he quickly stuck his feet into the boots. In a trice he was far away, so that when the two demons came back to the spot where they had started, they found no sign of boy or boots.

All that day Dom seemed almost to fly over the earth, so fast did the magic boots carry him. Near nightfall he came to a castle where the king of all the birds lived.

He was warmly welcomed to the castle, and in a vast room painted light blue like the sky, the king bade Dom tell his errand.

"What can I do for you, my lad?" asked the Bird King.

"Can Your Majesty, or any of your subjects, tell me how to reach that castle that lies south of the sun, east of the moon, and right in the middle of the wind? For there lives my beloved, and through my own fault I have lost her. But I must find her again. She is my lost paradise."

"Stay here overnight," said the king. "By evening all the birds will come home to roost and to rest. I shall ask if any of them ever heard of the castle you seek."

Toward evening, the king sent a message to all the birds who had come home to roost and to rest. The birds were asked if they had ever seen or heard of the wonderful castle that was south of the sun, east of the moon, and right in the middle of the wind. But not one bird, not even the oldest crow, had ever seen or heard of that castle.

So the king called Dom into the blue hall again, and he said, with a sad look, "I'm sorry, I cannot help find your beloved. But do take this letter to my brother who rules over all the winds of the world. The winds go where no bird can find his way, so maybe one of my brother's subjects can help you find the castle where your princess lives. But my brother lives far from here, and I am not certain you will ever find him."

"Oh, yes, I will!" declared Dom. So he bade the king goodnight, and he went to his own room, and there he slept in peace. Early the next morning he was on his way, with the letter in his pocket and the magic boots on his feet. For each step he took, he covered ten miles, and by evening he had reached the castle of all the winds of the world. There, in a drafty gray hall that seemed to be whirling about like a top, sat the king. He was so old that his hair looked like gray moss, and his whiskers were waving east, west, north, and south.

"Here is a letter from your brother, king of all the birds," explained Dom, as he stepped to the throne and handed him the letter.

The king read it at a glance, and then spoke in a voice that was kind, though as deep as a drum. "I'm sorry to tell you, young traveler, that the castle you dream of is one I have never seen or heard of. And I am king of all the winds, so I should know. However, soon my winds must come home to rest; then I shall send my messenger to ask them if they have heard of your castle."

Toward evening a hurricane rushed in from all directions, and the king's messenger then asked the winds if any of them had ever seen or heard of that strange castle which lies south of the sun, east of the moon, and right in the middle of the wind.

No, not one had ever seen it or heard of it. When the king was given this message, and gazed at the sad face of Dom, he sent his messenger to ask, "Are all the winds here, every one?"

A little breeze from the South whispered, "The Northwest Wind has not come home, but should be here soon."

At this very moment the Northwest Wind blustered in. He rushed forward, then suddenly lay down with such haste he sounded like thunder.

The king's messenger shouted, "Northwester, you must know where the castle lies which our friend is seeking. It lies . . ."

"Of course I know it!" muttered the Northwest Wind. "But it's a horribly long way off, and I seldom bother to go there."

"But you are going tomorrow with Dom!"

"Nonsense!" shouted the great wind. "You expect *me* to slow down to a pace that a lad walks? Never! He will only hold me back, so I shall never reach that castle."

When the king heard about this arrogant answer, he himself raged down to the Northwest Wind, shouting, "No more ridiculous roaring from you about being held back by a lad who merely walks. This lad wears magic boots of which you know nothing. Tomorrow morning you will set off with him, and don't come back here to rest until you have shown him the castle south of the sun, east of the moon, and right in the silent center round which all you whirly winds blow."

Hearing this command, the Northwest Wind sulked. But he had to obey his king. So the next day, the wind started off at a fast clip, but Dom in his magic boots soon rushed ahead of him.

"That's strange, he's no ordinary lad," thought the Northwester to himself. "I'd better use a little more haste." So he turned into a storm, but even then he had a hard time keeping up with the lad in his wonderful boots.

It was just dinnertime when they came into sight of the marvelous castle. Now the Northwester was so tired he begged leave to lie down in the woods nearby to get a little rest. Indeed, in order not to make the poor wind feel more miserable, Dom took off his boots and walked the final distance in his socks, for otherwise his pace would have carried him right past the castle.

With his boots in his hands, and his eyes glowing with hope, Dom ran round the castle. There, in a rose garden, picking sweet roses, was his very own princess!

"Oh, I never thought you would come all this way to find me!" she cried in her sweet young voice.

After they had embraced, they made plans for their wedding, which was held a week later in great joy and splendor. It is believed that the princess and her sweetheart still live there happily.

As for the Northwester? He slunk back home, and has never again blown as hard as he did on that long, strange journey he made with the lad who wore marvelous boots that carried him ten miles at each step.

a Danish story from *Scandinavian Stories*
by MARGARET SPERRY

POETRY

TUMBLING

In jumping and tumbling
    We spend the whole day,
Till night by arriving
    Has finished our play.

What then? One and all,
    There's no more to be said,
As we tumbled all day,
    So we tumble to bed.

ANONYMOUS (c. 1744)

THE FIRST TOOTH

Through the house what busy joy,
Just because the infant boy
Has a tiny tooth to show!
I have got a double row,
All as white, and all as small;
Yet no one cares for mine at all.
He can say but half a word,
Yet that single sound's preferred
To all the words that I can say
In the longest summer day.
He cannot walk, yet if he put
With mimic motion out his foot,
As if he thought he were advancing,
It's prized more than my best dancing.

CHARLES AND MARY LAMB
(1775–1834)   (1764–1847)

HOW TO WRITE A LETTER

Maria intended a letter to write,
But could not begin (as she thought) to indite;
So went to her mother with pencil and slate,
Containing "Dear Sister," and also a date.

"With nothing to say, my dear girl, do not think
Of wasting your time over paper and ink;
But certainly this is an excellent way,
To try with your slate to find something to say.

"I will give you a rule," said her mother, "my dear,
Just think for a moment your sister is here,
And what would you tell her? Consider, and then,
Though silent your tongue, you can speak with your pen."

ELIZABETH TURNER (1775?–1846)

THE SPIDER AND THE FLY

"Will you walk into my parlour?" said the Spider to the Fly,
" 'Tis the prettiest little parlour that ever you did spy;
The way into my parlour is up a winding stair,
And I have many curious things to show you when you are there."
"Oh no, no," said the little Fly, "to ask me is in vain,
For who goes up your winding stair can ne'er come down again."

"I'm sure you must be weary, dear, with soaring up so high;
Will you rest upon my little bed?" said the Spider to the Fly.
"There are pretty curtains drawn around, the sheets are fine and thin;
And if you like to rest awhile, I'll snugly tuck you in!"
"Oh no, no," said the little Fly, "for I've often heard it said,
They never, never wake again, who sleep upon your bed!"

Said the cunning Spider to the Fly, "Dear friend, what can I do,
To prove the warm affection I've always felt for you?
I have within my pantry good store of all that's nice;
I'm sure you're very welcome—will you please to take a slice?"
"Oh no, no," said the little Fly, "kind sir, that cannot be,
I've heard what's in your pantry, and I do not wish to see."

"Sweet creature," said the Spider, "you're witty and you're wise;
How handsome are your gauzy wings, how brilliant are your eyes!
I have a little looking-glass upon my parlour shelf,
If you'll step in a moment, dear, you shall behold yourself."
"I thank you, gentle sir," she said, "for what you're pleased to say,
And bidding you good morning now, I'll call another day."

The Spider turned him round about, and went into his den,
For well he knew the silly Fly would soon come back again;
So he wove a subtle web, in a little corner sly,
And set his table ready, to dine upon the Fly.
Then he came out to his door again, and merrily did sing:
"Come hither, hither, pretty Fly, with the pearl and silver wing;
Your robes are green and purple—there's a crest upon your head;
Your eyes are like the diamond bright, but mine are dull as lead."

Alas, alas! how very soon this silly little Fly,
Hearing his wily, flattering words, came slowly flitting by;
With buzzing wings she hung aloft, then near and nearer drew,
Thinking only of her brilliant eyes, and green and purple hue;
Thinking only of her crested head—poor foolish thing! At last,
Up jumped the cunning Spider, and fiercely held her fast.
He dragged her up his winding stair, into his dismal den,
Within his little parlour—but she ne'er came out again!

MARY HOWITT (1799–1888)

BEYOND CONFUSION

My mother says yes;
My father says no.
I say yes;
My brother says maybe so.
I don't know where;
I don't know how,
That's why I'm confused here and now.
How do I know if I'm an elf?
What do you think of me?
I don't think I was meant to be! I think
I'm going to calm down,
And get rid of my frown,
Why did I think I wasn't myself?
And I'm certainly not an elf!
I'm me!
I was meant to be!
That's why I was confused there and then,
And I don't think I'll be ever again!

LAURA CREIGHTON
age 9
Phoenix, Arizona

FALL

I am a leaf and
I live on a tree. Then
I fell and I died.
Then I came back to
life and I blew
for days and days and
I blew to Canada,
to Maine and back
where I started
from and I got
picked up for
a game.

JIMMY BIDWELL
age 9
Wilmot, New Hampshire

WHO AM I?

The rain may fall,
but I won't stall!
I may bail hail,
but I won't fail!
The sun may scorch,
but I'll get to your porch.
Can you guess who I am?
The Mailman!

JON HEATH
age 9
St. Clair Shores, Michigan

YELLOW DRAGON
(Road work machines)

Big yellow dragon
belching down the street
Sighing as it eats the road
Robot centipede with eleven feet
Eats the stones, spits them out
Sits on them, squashing them

GARRI MANTESE,
age 9
Mt. Waverly, Victoria, Australia

SKY BOOK

Silver jet
Soaring,
Penciling a
Polished sky
with wobbly
words.

KRISTIN MILLER
age 7
Ottawa, Canada

WHAT IS YELLOW?

Sun in the sky is partly yellow.
So is the color of lemon Jell-O.
Lightning is yellow when it rains.
Yellow is flowers on the window panes.
Eberhard Faber makes yellow pencils,
And I wish Georg Jensen made yellow utensils
For eating things like bananas and squash
And keeping them yellow right after you wash.
Crayola makes crayons that sometimes are yellow.
It seems like yellow is quite a fellow.
Yellow brightens up your day
In an extraordinary way!

MARGOT S. HEILIGMAN
age 11
Syracuse, New York

IF I COULD ONLY BE . . .

If I were only one inch tall,
A pebble could be my bowling ball.
Or think how fun it could be,
If I were as tall as an evergreen tree.
Maybe it would be even better,
If I were only as light as a feather . . .
And a piece of fuzzy could be my bed,
If I were as light as I just said.
But if I were 25 feet tall,
I wouldn't fit in a bed at all!
If I were hollow, all inside,
I'd float like a bubble with the tide.
But what if I were big and fat?
I don't think I'd care for that.
If I were as thin as the page of a book,
I'd hide in places you'd never look!
If I were only two inches or three,
I would climb up a flower instead of a tree.
But I guess I'd rather be me.

JEANNE WELCH
age 12
Lake Forest, Illinois

LIFE

Galloping through the streets,
It's as though I were riding on air.
Riding my beautiful black stallion,
Flying through the trees and enjoying
    the breeze,
Letting all my time fly by me,
Ignoring all my duties of life,
Letting out all the strife,
I shall not ignore this fact,
But life has its times for this and that.

DAWN HUBBARD
age 11
Whitesboro, New York

It starts with willow wands: a Pomo woman begins to weave a basket.

A Basketmaker's Story

This is a true story. It is the story of a woman of the Pomo Indian people of northern California—a people famous for their fine basketmaking. And it is a special kind of history, oral history. Large sections of this story are in the actual words of the basketmaker herself. A researcher made a tape recording of this woman's voice as she remembered the past. Then the recording was transcribed into written form so people could read it. Oral history works the magic of capturing the voices of the past for all time.

I am a native American—an Indian. I was born in Northern California just as the twentieth century began. All my life I have lived between two worlds. I am like a person who tries to ride in two canoes at the same time—a foot in each of them. As a working woman and a citizen, I belong to the white man's world. But in my heart, and in my work as a fine basketmaker, I belong to the world of my people, the Pomos.

For many years before my birth, the wagon trains of the white settlers headed west rolled into our coastal mountain forests. The wagons often brought war, destruction, and disease with them. My people were reduced to little bands of men, women, and children, struggling to stay alive. The Pomos worked at shearing sheep for ranchers, chopping wood, and picking hops in the hop fields. (Hops are the buds of the hop plants; when they are dried, they are used to flavor beer and other beverages.) Many Pomos were rounded up and placed on an Indian reservation near Covelo, in Mendocino County, California. Others—my family among them—managed to stay free. We lived in little family settlements called *rancherías*—the old Spanish word for small farms or ranches.

My immediate family are Southern Pomos. (There are also Central and Northern Pomos in California. These groups speak slightly different dialects of our language.) My father died when I was small. But I had a good mother and an especially wonderful grandmother. A wise grandmother is the greatest blessing a Pomo girl can have. Since a grandmother's responsibility for raising and feeding her own children is over, she has time to teach her grandchildren the ancient skills of our people.

When I Was Young...

When I was young, we lived in the hills, far from any town. I had no playmates of my own age. The forest was my playground. It also provided my toys. I built little houses from rocks and leaves. And I made my own dolls. The woody stalks of the wormwood plant made excellent dolls. If the stalk I chose had young, leafy shoots on it, I could bend the tips of them over and they looked like hair. And I climbed the great, red madrone trees to gather their leaves. When insects had nibbled at the leaves, they looked like lace, and I made gowns for my dolls with them.

Sometimes I ran for hours through the brush, following the animal trails or playing hide-and-seek with my mother's fox terrier. I loved to splash through the swift, cool waters of the creeks, looking for cattail grass and special roots. I gave names to the willow and elderberry trees and talked to them as if they were people. It might sound like a lonely life—but it wasn't.

When I was young, I was baptized a Christian in the Roman Catholic church at Santa Rosa. But we seldom saw a priest. We mixed our old Pomo customs with our new religion. Fasting—not eating for periods of time—is a religious custom among both Roman Catholics and Pomos. Pomos always fasted to purify themselves so that the Great Spirit would help them with their work. We fasted before we began to weave a complicated feather basket. I remember how my grandmother would work many long hours making baskets, weaving bright woodpecker feathers and myrtle hawk feathers with reeds and redbud strips. I watched her closely and tried to help by bringing materials to her as she needed them. When we could no longer bear our hunger, we would break our fast and eat. Today, when I weave my own baskets, I remember exactly how my grandmother looked as she wove her baskets many years ago. In a way it is as if she had never died, for I am carrying on her life by practicing the art that was so much a part of it. My basket weaving brings me close to her and to our past.

White men's diseases made the Pomo very ill. We had no resistance to them. When I was five I nearly died of measles—a disease that is usually not serious when white children have it. Burning with fever, I thought I saw giant roosters walking over me, crowing. I screamed with terror and struggled to escape. We had no white doctors to help in those days. My grandmother nursed me in the Pomo way—with healing herbs. Soon I was well again.

After my experience with measles, my grandfather decided I needed extra protection. Grandfather was a Pomo singing doctor— the name we used for our medicine men. He held a special ceremony to protect me against disease in the future. He built a very hot fire, sang prayers to the Great Spirit, and performed many ancient rites. As a part of the ceremony, he mixed a potion for me to drink that had the blood of a turtle in it. It was awful to think about and awful to taste—but I had to drink it if I wanted to get well.

Singing doctors like my grandfather were also Pomo priests. Even our dances had religious meaning, with every movement guided by ritual. Today some white doctors have begun to study Indian herbal medicines and healing techniques. They have begun to discover the scientific reasons for some of the cures our singing doctors were able to bring about.

We Move North

My mother married again when I was nine. My stepfather was good to me. Soon he took us to live near Hopland, in a rancheria where many of our family were. My uncles worked in the vineyards, or helped with the cows and horses on the bigger ranches in the area. My grandmother did the washing for a nearby resort where rich white people came. My mother hid me whenever white people came by our rancheria. She had heard tales of Indian children being kidnapped and sold as workers to ranchers, and she had no intention of taking any chances with my safety.

During Northern California's winter rainy season we lived in a small wooden house. But in the summer we moved down by the river and built a traditional Pomo house. It was actually a hut made of woven willow branches and covered with leaves. We had two bedrooms. In one, my grandmother built me a bed of woven willow branches held high off the ground by four wooden stakes. It had a mattress stuffed with dried cornhusks. I had to climb up on a box to get into bed. I loved my high bed—but it had a practical purpose, too. It kept me out of the reach of rattlesnakes, which were common in the area.

And in summer we made our annual pilgrimage to the sea—to the Pacific. This was a joyous vacation for all of us at the rancheria. We traveled in horse-drawn wagons, going along the river valleys to the coast. When we reached the beach, the women gathered kelp and

"In the summer we moved down by the river and built . . . a Pomo house."

other seaweed. They also collected our year's supply of salt from hollows in the rocks. When the tide was high and waves dashed against the rocks, spray collected in the natural hollows and depressions in the rocks. When the sun beat down on the rocks, the salt water in the hollows evaporated, leaving salt crystals. The men fished for salmon or gathered mussels and abalone near the shore. Everybody picked blackberries, huckleberries, elderberries, and manzanita berries.

Then the men built fires on the beach, slit the salmon open, hung them on twigs, and smoked them slowly over the fires. I remember, too, how good the shellfish tasted after they had been roasted under the hot ashes of the fires. We dried most of our beach harvest for winter. We would eat the dried seaweed, kelp, and berries then, and make soup from the dried abalone.

In the winter rainy season we also gathered food. There were many kinds of edible mushrooms that grew in winter in our part of California. The men hunted deer then, too, and brought home the meat. And acorns from the oak trees of our forests were the staff of life for us. My mother and grandmother spent long hours preparing acorn mush. Acorns aren't easy to prepare for eating. You have to gather them, shell them, dry the kernels, and when they're dry, pound them into flour. Then the flour has to be soaked several times in water to take away all the bitterness. When all these steps have

The old ways: a woman grinds dried acorns into flour for making mush.

been taken, the acorn flour can be cooked into a delicious mush. I love acorn mush so much that even today I gather sacks of acorns in the fall.

The Indian School

My life was a happy one until I was eleven. The year I was eleven an agent of the United States Government came to see my mother. He persuaded her to send me away to school. There was a school on the Indian reservation at Covelo, California. I had never gone to any kind of school and I was terrified at the thought of leaving my home and my family.

Covelo was about 80 miles (130 kilometers) north of the rancheria. It took two days of hard travel to get there because much of the way was through the wilderness. They gathered all the Pomo children who were to go to school—including me—and loaded us on a wagon. When we came to the end of the wagon trail, there was a railroad. We were loaded onto a flatbed railroad car that took us through steep canyons thick with forests of pine and fir. Then we got off the railroad car and boarded a horse-drawn stagecoach. We made an overnight stop along the way. The next day we continued our journey in another wagon. I was afraid of the rushing Eel River when we reached it. And we were in redwood country. I was afraid that the gigantic trees would fall down on us. In fact, I felt that my whole world was collapsing around me.

That year at the Indian school was a nightmare. I was put in a dormitory with other Pomo girls—but I only knew one of them. And the girl I knew was older than I was and in a different class. I spoke no English, and we were not supposed to speak our own languages. This meant that I never understood what anyone said to me. Because I couldn't understand, I couldn't follow the rules of the school about dressing, eating, and doing chores. I often was punished for failing to do my work, or for doing the wrong chore at the wrong time.

The teachers tried to teach us to sew by giving us cards with designs on them picked out with holes. We were supposed to "embroider" them by twisting lengths of colored yarn through the holes. It seemed pointless to me and not half as interesting as basketmaking. I often cried myself to sleep at night.

One night our dormitory burned down. All the clothes my mother had packed so lovingly for me were burned. The girls had to move into a boys' dormitory. We even had to wear boys' clothes until they could get dresses for us. And when the dresses came, they were all alike. Each dress had a name tag sewn inside with the name of the girl who was to wear it. But since I couldn't read, I couldn't understand what the labels said. Sometimes I put on another girl's dress and got into trouble for it. I learned to wait until everyone else had finished dressing. Then I knew that the dress that was left had to be mine.

An older girl, a Pomo like myself, made friends with me. But she soon took sick with tuberculosis. Tuberculosis was another disease of the white man that Indians had no resistance to. My friend grew so ill that she had to stay in bed all the time. I took care of her and brought her meals to her. I was always hungry in those days because I was too shy to grab food the way the other students did. So I was able to eat the leftovers from my friend's tray. Despite my nursing duties, I never caught the disease from my friend. I believe I really was protected by my grandfather's medicine ceremony.

A New Life

At last the terrible year at the Indian school was over. I was so glad to come home! I never went back to that school. When I was thirteen, the government opened a school at our rancheria. I attended it for three years. I learned to speak English from a kind, patient teacher. Then I was able to learn to read and write.

I had worked in the hop fields every summer since I was ten. But I began to dislike doing it. It was hot, tiresome work. I thought I should be able to do something better now that I could speak English and read and write. When I was eighteen I went to a Roman Catholic priest I knew in Ukiah, California, and asked for help. He took me to San Francisco, where we visited St. Joseph's Hospital—a wonderful place. I wanted very much to work there. But the priest took me to some old people who needed help. They were willing to pay me $35 a month and give me room and board. In return, I was expected to do the housework and care for them. The only trouble was they would never let me go out. Soon I began to feel like a deer in a cage. I packed my suitcase and told them I wanted to leave. Furious, they flung open the front door and said, "Get out!"

Alone on the streets of San Francisco, the only big city I had ever seen, I felt lost and frightened. But I found my way to a streetcar stop. A policeman told me how to get to St. Joseph's Hospital. It was the only place in San Francisco I knew about. This was in 1918, the last year of World War I. Hospitals were short of help. I had no trouble getting a job in the hospital kitchen. I worked there happily for several months. I was given the task of taking other employees to church and to Golden Gate Park for picnics. My employers had gotten the idea that I knew my way around the city. I didn't, of course. But I got along by asking policemen for directions.

A Basketmaker Once More

In 1919 I married the man who is still my husband. After a Christian wedding in the Roman Catholic Church, we went to my husband's rancheria for a Pomo wedding. His family—who were Northern Pomo people—gave my family many blankets that they had woven themselves. In return, my relatives gave baskets filled with Indian clamshell money. The shells were pierced so they could be strung to make necklaces. Other gifts exchanged included belts made of beads or of shells and feathers, and baskets heaped with dried fish and acorn flour. We had a grand feast, too.

We moved to a Pomo settlement near the ranch where my husband worked. In the next ten years, we had four children. There were two girls and two boys. My husband and I, remembering the problems we had had because of the language barrier, spoke only English to our children. Today we feel a little sad that we never let them learn their native tongue. In 1932 we voted to let our children go to school with the white children. This was an experience that my husband and I had never had. But we felt that our children belonged more to the white world than we ever did.

Those were busy years for me—raising children, harvesting crops to make extra money, and, later, taking part-time work in a laundry. But always, deep inside, I longed for only one thing. I wanted to go back to my Pomo basketmaking.

I kept remembering how, as a child, I had gone with my mother and my grandmother to gather materials for baskets. We gathered sedge roots and bullrushes in the swamps. We cut willow wands beside the streams. And we had gone up into the western hills to find the redbud switches that were used to make the red designs in our baskets. We also brought back fern roots from the hills. The fern roots were dyed black to create some of the black patterns in our baskets. The sedge roots had to be peeled, dried, and scraped before they could be used. My grandmother taught me to put the fern roots

"I find feathers dropped by wood-peckers and hawks...I find soft green feathers from the heads of wild ducks...I walk through the foothills in search of redbud twigs..." All these things, and a great deal more, went into the decoration of these Pomo baskets from the early 1900's.

257

Pomo women once used sturdy work baskets (like the one in this old photograph) when they gathered acorns and supplies for basketmaking.

in a container that had black mud, water, and rusty nails in it. This awful mixture turned the delicate roots jet black. It also made them very dirty. So my grandmother also taught me how to clean the mess off the roots before I used them. From her I learned to split and carve and shape the heart of the redbud wands. And she taught me where to find bright red feathers for feather baskets. I wanted to do all these things once more myself.

Even when I was first married, I had wanted to make baskets. But I was very busy and I had little time. Then my grandmother died. I lost not only her help but also her fine examples of basketmaking.

According to our Pomo custom, her baskets were buried with her. The first little basket I had made for her after my marriage was buried with her, too.

My mother had more modern ideas. She was proud of her basketwork and wanted to be remembered for it. She made me promise that her baskets wouldn't be buried with her when she died. She wanted me to keep them as an example—as guides to help me in my own work. And she wanted me to have them as a remembrance of her. So when she died, years later, I kept my promise not to destroy her work. Many of my people were angry because I had broken a sacred tradition.

I finally went back to serious basketmaking when I was past 60. And, although I am an old woman now, I have never stopped. I go out to the swamps and dig sedge roots, and I cut the willow switches along the streams. I find feathers dropped by woodpeckers and hawks. Sometimes I find the soft green feathers from the heads of wild ducks. In the fall I walk through the foothills in search of rosy redbud twigs. Never let anyone tell you a Pomo woman ever grows too old for this work.

I make baskets as small as a dime. I make big baskets for storage. I make the traditional Pomo feather baskets that are famous all over the world. It is a thrill to feel these baskets grow under my hands like living things.

I have to admit with sadness that some people, even in my own family, tell me I should stop my work. They say we should let the old ways die. Perhaps they feel my basketmaking lets white people laugh at us as "ignorant, primitive Indians." I say we should all be who we are. Or do my people fear that others will learn the ancient skills and get rich from our Pomo art? Museums do pay well for fine baskets.

Whatever their reasons, I believe that those who would stop me from working in the old ways are wrong. I wish more of my own people would feel pride in creating the kind of art that we have always made. I hear that some native Americans are beginning to realize the importance of teaching the young to value their heritage.

So now I teach basketweaving in the coastal village of Mendocino, California. In spring I take my students on weekend trips to gather the reeds and roots. Later, I show them how to cure and dye the materials and how to weave their baskets. Unfortunately, I don't have many Indian girls in my classes. I wish I had more. Nowadays, they don't like to dig in the mud.

Basketmaking requires great patience and skill. Even though we no longer fast when we weave our baskets, it is still a craft that must be done with special love and reverence. We are honoring the great weavers of the past when we work in the traditional ways. We are honoring all of those—my grandmother included—who are buried now with their beautiful baskets and their loving wisdom.

a historical story by
ELISABETH MARGO

Beatrix Potter created *The Tale of Peter Rabbit*, one of the world's best-loved children's stories.

HAPPY BIRTHDAY, PETER RABBIT

"Once upon a time there were four little Rabbits, and their names were—Flopsy, Mopsy, Cotton-tail, and Peter. They lived with their Mother in a sand-bank, underneath the root of a very big fir-tree."

And so begins one of the world's best-loved children's stories—*The Tale of Peter Rabbit*. Its hero is as much a little child as he is a young rabbit. He is mischievous: he disobeys his mother and goes into Mr. McGregor's garden. Mr. McGregor chases him all over the garden and in the tool-shed, giving Peter a dreadful fright.

Is it possible that little Peter Rabbit is 75 years old? Yes, it is, because 1977 marked the 75th anniversary of the first publication of his story.

Peter's creator was a woman named Beatrix Potter, who was born in London in 1866. A great naturalist, she had an active imagination and a wonderful artistic talent. As a young girl, she drew whatever she saw—animals, flowers, stones, woods, streams. She developed for herself a complete fantasy-world in nature.

In 1893, Miss Potter sent a letter to a young boy. In it, she told the story of a little rabbit named Peter. She included some drawings.

Some years later she expanded the story and added more drawings, and in 1902 she published *The Tale of Peter Rabbit*.

Other books followed, containing more characters—little animals with some very human qualities. There is Squirrel Nutkin, who teases Old Brown the Owl and very nearly loses his tail. There is Johnny Town-Mouse, who finds country life too quiet, and his friend Timmy Willie, who finds city life very disturbing. And there are others, such as Pigling Bland, Mr. Tod the fox, Mrs. Tiggy-Winkle the hedgehog, and Jemima Puddle-Duck. The tales, 23 in all, are simple but strike a note of truth in all of us. The drawings are clever and charming in their detail. They seem to show how the world looks through the eyes of a child.

Peter Rabbit will always be the most famous of all of Beatrix Potter's creatures. And he will always live in a world where no one ever grows old. May Peter have many more happy birthdays, and may he always outrun Mr. McGregor!

Among the special events of the year observing Peter's anniversary was the publication of *Peter Rabbit's Natural Foods Cookbook*. Here is a recipe from it.

MR. McGREGOR'S
SCRUMPTIOUS PUREED BEETS

EQUIPMENT
small sharp knife
saucepan with lid
measuring cup and spoons
blender

INGREDIENTS
3 medium-sized beets
1 tablespoon chopped onion
2 tablespoons lemon juice
½ teaspoon salt
1 teaspoon honey
⅓ cup plain yogurt

Cut the roots and tops from the beets and wash the beets thoroughly. Cook them in slowly boiling water until tender—from 1 to 2 hours. Drain and cool. Slide off the skins, chop the beets into small pieces, and put them into the blender. Add the remaining ingredients to the blender, put on the lid, and run the blender until all the ingredients are well mixed. Serve hot or cold.
 Serves 4.

Backstroker's Challenge

Lisa Hunt stepped out of her mother's car and ran around the gym to the pool. It had been a bad Monday, and she was somewhat out-of-sorts. She dropped her towel and hurried to the edge of the pool, twisting a rubber band around her long, blonde hair.

"Lisa, over here." It was Ron Allen, the coach. Beside him stood two strangers. "I want you to meet Pam and Johnny Martin. They've just joined the team."

"You mean, just lost our minds," Pam said, shivering in the chill wind. "Our folks thought swimming would help us get acquainted. We moved here last week. Johnny's experienced, but I've never been on a team."

"Lisa will show you the ropes," the coach said. Then he shouted, "Everybody in the water! Two thousand warm-up."

"Did he say 'two thousand'?" Pam whispered. "Is he kidding?"

"You can do it," Lisa said encouragingly. "Just stay a length behind me and keep to the right side of the lane." She dove in and started swimming down the 25-yard pool. Just before she reached the end, she flipped, hit the wall with her feet, and pushed off with a powerful snap of her legs.

After a couple of strokes, she looked back at Pam and saw her do an open turn. "Oops," she thought, "that will put the coach in a nasty frame of mind." Nothing made him angrier than swimmers who didn't flip.

Lisa continued her laps, her disposition returning to its normally cheerful state as she churned up and down the pool. On the next turn, she noticed that Pam was keeping up well, although she was still doing open turns.

After they finished the warm-up, the coach started them on the backstroke. Lisa smiled because she loved this stroke. She knew that she could win the backstroke event in the meet with North City Aquatics Club two weeks from now, and she was counting on winning a medal in the championships. If only they had another girl for the 15- to -17-year-old division—a good freestyler—then they could enter two relays. She wondered if Pam's freestyle was good enough.

Lisa watched Pam gliding past her in the other direction with a smooth, beautiful stroke. Then Pam reached the wall, and did another open turn. That would ruin her time!

The coach halted Lisa when she reached the end of the lane. When Pam touched the wall, he shouted at her to stop. "Lisa, I told you to show Pam the ropes," he said. "Didn't you tell her we flip every turn?"

Lisa reddened. "I'm sorry, Coach. It's so automatic, I—"

Pam interrupted. "Don't blame Lisa. She told me to do what she did, but I can't flip."

Ron Allen groaned. "Try, anyway. Everyone flips on this team."

"I don't know how," Pam protested.

"Come on," Lisa said. "We're behind now. Just turn as fast as you can."

After practice, Lisa learned that Pam lived just a block from her. They walked outside where they found their mothers talking. Lisa waved good-bye to Pam and Johnny and got into the car.

During the drive home Lisa was silent, wondering how good Pam would be if she learned to flip.

"Lisa," her mother's voice broke into her thoughts, "I've arranged with Mrs. Martin to share the driving. I'll bring all of you to the pool, and she'll pick you up. Is that all right?"

"Sure," Lisa agreed. "Pam seems nice, and Johnny's cute."

Mrs. Hunt laughed. "You girls. Always thinking about boys!"

Lisa had other things on her mind during the rest of the week. She worried about the meet. Johnny Martin was a top swimmer, and with Mike Jackson, the older boys were strong. But the younger swimmers were weak, so it was up to the older girls to make some points. If only they had someone to do the freestyle, they would have a relay. But Lisa was sure Pam's freestyle wasn't strong enough. And she couldn't flip.

The next Saturday afternoon, she hurried down to Mike Jackson's house. It was a warm day, almost hot for early May, and just perfect for a swim in Mike's pool.

She spread her towel out at the edge of the pool and grinned at Mike.

"Come on in!" he shouted.

"Not yet. I want to work on my tan."

Mike climbed out and sat down beside her. "The coach is coming over. He wants to talk to us."

"Any idea why?"

"No," said Mike, "but he'll be here soon." Mike stretched out on his back. "Ever notice Pam Martin's eyes?" he asked dreamily. "I've never seen a girl with green eyes before. Do you think she would go to the Soph Hop with me, if I asked her?"

A sharp pain tightened Lisa's throat. She turned her face away, glad that Mike was lying down and couldn't see her. She and Mike had been friends since kindergarten, and they usually went to all the school dances together. She'd just assumed they would go to the Soph Hop. You don't own him, she told herself. Mike's got a right to have a date for the dance if he wants.

The door opened and Ron Allen came out. The coach's face was serious as he sat down beside them.

"What's the problem, Coach?" Mike asked. "You look upset."

"It's the meet," Ron said. "We need an older girls' free and medley relay. The only way we can do that is to teach Pam Martin to flip before next Saturday. Then she can do the backstroke. Lisa can do the free leg."

Lisa sputtered as she stared at her coach. "But, but—"

"I know you're our best backstroker, but I've timed Pam, and I think she'll be almost as fast if she flips. She's too slow in freestyle to anchor the relay. With Helen doing the butterfly and Jackie in the breaststroke, we can win. We need those points."

Mike nodded. "I sure would like to beat North City. They made us look like dog paddlers last year."

"Would it be all right with your parents, Mike, if Pam and Lisa used your pool for an hour each morning?" The coach turned to Lisa. "If you'll teach Pam to backflip, we'll have a chance."

Lisa smiled gamely. "I'll give it a try."

· · ·

When her alarm went off, Lisa almost hit the clock. She was tempted to go back to sleep, but instead forced herself out of bed. She grumbled all the way to Mike's house that morning and all the rest of the week. Getting up early tired her, and she had homework every day so she couldn't rest before practice. Deep inside, a feeling of resentment built up. Why was she doing it, she wondered. The backstroke events had always been hers. Now Pam would have that part of the relay. The new girl worked hard and she had mastered the flip, Lisa admitted grudgingly to herself on Friday afternoon when Pam backflipped each turn during practice.

On the day of the meet, the team arrived at the North City pool early. After the warm-up, Coach Allen gathered his swimmers around him and told them to do their best. "This year it's our turn," he said.

The score seesawed back and forth from the first event. Lisa stood behind the blocks watching Pam start the medley relay. Her stroke was smooth and strong, and she soon had a lead. Lisa held her breath as Pam neared the wall, then smiled proudly when she flipped and came out of the turn ahead of her opponent. She watched intently while Jackie lost ground in the breaststroke. Then Helen dove in for the butterfly leg, but the North City flyer was good.

Lisa stood on the block knowing she'd be about half a length behind when she hit the water. She leaned forward watching Helen closely, determined to get a good start. The North City freestyler dove in; then Helen touched, and Lisa was off with a good dive.

The turn came up almost before she knew it, and she flipped and started back, concentrating on her pull. She caught a glimpse of North City's swimmer and knew she was gaining. Her legs felt like worn-out rubber bands, and her lungs were on fire as she reached for the wall. She touched and leaned forward, dropping her head while she fought for breath.

Then she looked over at the judges. She had lost! Pulling herself out of the pool, she walked over to the coach, still breathing hard.

Ron Allen smiled. "Your split was 27.6, Lisa. That's your best time. I'm proud of you."

Lisa shook her head. "We lost."

She sat down on her sleeping bag, angry with herself. She had lost by two inches. She should have been able to make that up! It seemed only seconds before it was time for the backstroke. Still tired, she dove into the pool for the start.

She took a deep breath, reached for the rung on the starting block, and pushed back hard when the gun sounded. At the end of the first 50 yards, she and Pam were ahead. She knew it had been a fast 50 because her arms were tired. When she hit the wall on the 75, she saw that Pam was right beside her and that they'd lengthened their lead.

She pulled hard for the finish, catching a glimpse of Pam inching ahead of her. When she touched the wall, she knew that Pam had reached it first. Pam turned to her with a bright smile. Lisa ignored her, climbed out of the pool, and walked to her sleeping bag without stopping to ask for her time.

She sat down and buried her face in her arms. She hated the coach for asking her to teach Pam to flip. She hated herself for doing it, and she hated Mike who was taking Pam to the Soph Hop. Right then, she decided that she hated swimming, too. She'd quit. The team didn't need her. Pam could do the backstroke events, and she didn't care whether they had a relay or not.

She heard a roar from the crowd, and then Mike and Johnny sat down beside her. "What was that about?" she asked.

"Score tied," Mike said with a wide grin. "Johnny won the backstroke for five points, and my second place gave us three more. With the points you and Pam made, it's all even."

Johnny pulled out a chocolate bar and handed Lisa half. "Have some energy. You've got to win the 100 free."

Lisa shook her head. "No chance. That North City girl beat me in the relay, and then Pam beat me," she said bitterly.

Johnny studied her thoughtfully. "You know, you did a great thing when you taught Pam to flip," he said. "But it seems to me that you should be faster than you are. I don't think your underwater push is strong enough. I had the same trouble." He turned to Mike. "Would it be all right if we kept on working in your pool in the mornings? Pam needs practice with her flips, and I'd like to help Lisa with her stroke."

Mike agreed with a big smile. "Great. I'm sure my folks won't mind. I'll make breakfast so we can eat together before school. If you change at my house, we'll have an extra fifteen minutes. And the practice will be good for all of us."

• • •

When Lisa walked up to the blocks for the freestyle, the score was still tied. Her face was serious as she waited for the starter's gun, but inside she was smiling. No matter how this race turned out, no matter what the final score was, she knew she was part of a team, and a team worked together. Her face burned as she realized that it had taken a new boy to make her understand. She took a deep breath and looked at the starter, wondering if Johnny would like to go to the Soph Hop.

LOOKING AT BOOKS

HEY, KID!

"I have this thing. It's white and black and gray. I'm gonna let you have it, Kid. Today's your lucky day." Thus begins this funny tale written by Rita Golden Gelman and illustrated by Carol Nicklaus. The girl who receives the big friendly pet named Sam is delighted— at first. But she soon learns that Sam never stops talking or singing. He talks and sings all day long and right through the night. Finally, the girl can't take it any longer. She packs Sam in a crate and takes him far, far away.... Then she meets a boy. And she says, "Hey, Kid! I have this thing. It's white and black and gray. I'm gonna let you have it, Kid."

HOW DJADJA-EM-ANKH SAVED THE DAY

A Tale from Ancient Egypt

This story was written 3,500 years ago in ancient Egypt. It has been translated and illustrated by Lise Manniche. It tells about King Seneferu. One day the king is very bored. He asks the court magician, Djadja-em-ankh, what he should do. Djadja-em-ankh suggests that the king watch some girls rowing on the palace lake. "Watching them row up and down will cheer you up," he says. The king arranges the boating party, and he is happy. But then a charm worn by one of the girls to ward off evil falls into the lake. The king says he will give her another one, just like the original. But the girl refuses: "I want my own, not another one!" The king sends for Djadja-em-ankh. The magician says some magic words and folds the water from half the lake right on top of the water in the other half of the lake—sort of like folding an omelet in half. The girl's charm is found and returned to her, and the magician returns the water back to the way it had been before. Everyone is happy once again and the king rewards Djadja-em-ankh.

The original story was written in hieroglyphics, a kind of writing that uses pictures instead of the letters of an alphabet. It was written on a scroll made of fibers from the papyrus plant. This scroll can still be seen; it's in a museum in Berlin. The new translation is also made in the form of a scroll. You unroll the scroll and read the story from right to left, just as the ancient Egyptians did.

Roll of Thunder, Hear My Cry

This novel about Cassie Logan and her family was awarded the 1977 John Newbery Medal, the highest award for a book for young people. Written by Mildred D. Taylor, the story takes place in Mississippi during the Depression of the 1930's. Cassie is a young black girl who grows up in a strong and loving family. But her pride and courage are often tested by white people who think Cassie is inferior because of the color of her skin. School buses pass her by, shopkeepers ignore her, and her father is shot and injured by white men. The story describes the many episodes in the life of Cassie and her brothers as they and their parents fight to live on their own land.

ASHANTI TO ZULU

This wonderful picture book was the winner of the 1977 Caldecott Medal for excellence in illustration. Written by Margaret Musgrove and illustrated by Leo and Diane Dillon, it introduces us to 26 African tribes—one tribe for each letter of the alphabet. We learn that the Ikoma (*shown below*) gather honey with the help of tiny birds. The Kung store water in ostrich eggshells. The Xhosa wear copper-colored blankets and smoke long pipes. The book shows that people have many different customs: they live in different kinds of places, eat different foods, and raise their children in different ways.

WORLD OF SPORTS

The great Pelé has helped make professional soccer a major sport in North America.

Reggie Jackson slams home run number 3 in the sixth and final game of the World Series. The Yankees took the Series from the Dodgers, four games to two.

BASEBALL

When the New York Yankees were trying for a return to baseball glory in 1976, they were stopped in the World Series by the Cincinnati Reds. But that was just a one-year postponement. In 1977 the Bronx Bombers were once again triumphant.

Since 1920, when Babe Ruth arrived, the Yankees have won 31 American League pennants and 21 World Series. And the 1977 win was achieved in a way that reminded people of Ruth's incredible batting power.

In the final game of that Series, Reggie Jackson, in true Babe Ruth fashion, slammed three home runs and drove in a total of five runs. The Yankees won the game, 8–4, from the Los Angeles Dodgers and captured the World Series, four games to two.

More than 56,000 people in historic Yankee Stadium, and millions more watching television, saw Jackson wallop his three homers in successive times at bat. Only Ruth had ever hit as many as three in a single Series contest. He did it twice, in 1926 and 1928. Jackson's total of five homers for the Series set a new record.

For the Yankees, the Series triumph was the climax to a season filled with turmoil. They had fought with each other and with their manager, Billy Martin, as often as with their opponents on the field. They had won the Eastern Division title after a tense, three-way struggle in which the other two contenders, the Baltimore Orioles and the Boston Red Sox, finished in a tie for second, two and a half games behind the Yankees.

While the Yankees were struggling for their division success, the Kansas City Royals were landing the Western title, beginning with a sixteen-game winning streak in September. They coasted home with an eight-game margin over the Texas Rangers. Kansas City's 102–60 record was the best among the four divisions in the two leagues.

New York's victory over the Royals in the five-game playoff for the league championship was almost a repeat of the two teams' post-season meeting in 1976. In 1976, Chris Chambliss's ninth-inning homer defeated the Royals in the fifth and decisive playoff game. And in 1977, a three-run burst in the top of the ninth changed a 3–2 deficit into a 5–3 Yankee triumph.

Lou Brock of the St. Louis Cardinals steals the 893rd base of his career, breaking Ty Cobb's record. By the end of the season, Brock had stolen 900.

In the National League, the Dodgers easily won over the Reds in the Western Division—a surprise, since Cincinnati had won the two previous World Series. Los Angeles, under a new manager, Tom Lasorda, captured 17 of their first 20 games to gain a commanding lead over the Reds. They kept the advantage throughout the season and finished 10 games in front. And they became the first team in major league history to have four of their players hit 30 or more homers—Steve Garvey (33), Reggie Smith (32), Dusty Baker (30), and Roy Cey (30).

The Philadelphia Phillies, after a second straight Eastern Division title, lost to the Western winner again. The Dodgers ended up with three victories in four engagements.

Contrary to tradition, the two Most Valuable Player awards went to players who were not members of the championship teams—Rod Carew of the Minnesota Twins in the American League, and George Foster of the Cincinnati Reds in the National. Carew won his sixth league batting crown with a .388 average. It was the highest in twenty years, matching Ted Williams' 1957 mark. Foster collected 52 home runs and 149 runs batted in. Only three other National Leaguers have surpassed 50 homers in one season, Hack Wilson, Ralph Kiner, and Willie Mays.

The Cy Young Awards for outstanding pitching were captured by Sparky Lyle, the relief hurler for the Yankees, in the American League, and by Steve Carlton of the Phillies in the National. Lyle played in 72 games, posted a 13–5 won–lost mark, and was given credit for saving 26 other contests.

		R	H	E	Winning/Losing Pitcher
1	New York	4	11	0	Sparky Lyle
	Los Angeles	3	6	0	Rick Rhoden
2	Los Angeles	6	9	0	Burt Hooton
	New York	1	5	0	Jim Hunter
3	New York	5	10	0	Mike Torrez
	Los Angeles	3	7	1	Tommy John
4	New York	4	7	0	Ron Guidry
	Los Angeles	2	4	0	Doug Rau
5	Los Angeles	10	13	0	Don Sutton
	New York	4	9	2	Don Gullett
6	New York	8	8	1	Mike Torrez
	Los Angeles	4	9	0	Burt Hooton

1977 WORLD SERIES RESULTS

FINAL MAJOR LEAGUE BASEBALL STANDINGS

AMERICAN LEAGUE

Eastern Division

	W	L	Pct.	GB
*New York	100	62	.617	—
Baltimore	97	64	.602	2½
Boston	97	64	.602	2½
Detroit	74	88	.457	20
Cleveland	71	90	.441	28½
Milwaukee	67	95	.414	33
Toronto	54	107	.335	45½

Western Division

	W	L	Pct.	GB
Kansas City	102	60	.630	—
Texas	94	68	.580	8
Chicago	90	72	.556	12
Minnesota	84	77	.522	17½
California	74	88	.457	28
Seattle	64	98	.395	38
Oakland	63	98	.391	38½

NATIONAL LEAGUE

Eastern Division

	W	L	Pct.	GB
Philadelphia	101	61	.623	—
Pittsburgh	96	66	.593	5
St. Louis	83	79	.512	18
Chicago	81	81	.500	20
Montreal	75	87	.463	26
New York	64	98	.395	37

Western Division

	W	L	Pct.	GB
*Los Angeles	98	64	.605	—
Cincinnati	88	74	.543	10
Houston	81	81	.500	17
San Francisco	75	87	.463	23
San Diego	69	93	.426	29
Atlanta	61	101	.377	37

*pennant winners

MAJOR LEAGUE LEADERS

AMERICAN LEAGUE

Batting
(top 10 qualifiers)

	AB	R	H	Pct.
Carew, Minnesota	616	128	239	.388
Bostock, Minnesota	593	104	199	.336
Singleton, Baltimore	536	90	176	.328
Rivers, New York	565	79	184	.326
LeFlore, Detroit	652	100	212	.325
Rice, Boston	644	104	206	.320
Bumbry, Baltimore	518	74	164	.317
Fisk, Boston	536	106	169	.315
Brett, Kansas City	564	105	176	.312
Cowens, Kansas City	606	98	189	.312

Pitching
(top 5 qualifiers, based on ERA)

	W	L	ERA
Tanana, California	15	9	2.54
Blyleven, Texas	14	12	2.72
Ryan, California	19	16	2.77
Guidry, New York	16	7	2.82
Palmer, Baltimore	20	11	2.91

Home Runs

	HR
Rice, Boston	39
Bonds, California	37
Nettles, New York	37
Scott, Boston	33
Jackson, New York	32
Gamble, Chicago	31
Thompson, Detroit	31

NATIONAL LEAGUE

Batting
(top 10 qualifiers)

	AB	R	H	Pct.
Parker, Pittsburgh	637	107	215	.338
Templeton, St. Louis	621	94	200	.322
Foster, Cincinnati	615	124	197	.320
Griffey, Cincinnati	585	117	186	.318
Simmons, St. Louis	516	82	164	.318
Rose, Cincinnati	655	95	204	.311
Hendrick, San Diego	541	75	168	.311
Luzinski, Philadelphia	554	99	171	.309
Oliver, Pittsburgh	568	75	175	.308
Smith, Los Angeles	488	104	150	.307

Pitching
(top 5 qualifiers, based on ERA)

	W	L	ERA
Candelaria, Pittsburgh	20	5	2.34
Seaver, N.Y.–Cincinnati	21	6	2.59
Hooton, Los Angeles	12	7	2.62
Carlton, Philadelphia	23	10	2.64
John, Los Angeles	20	7	2.78

Home Runs

	HR
Foster, Cincinnati	52
Burroughs, Atlanta	41
Luzinski, Philadelphia	39
Schmidt, Philadelphia	38
Garvey, Los Angeles	33
Smith, Los Angeles	32

Chiang Chen-jung at bat. Chiang led the Taiwanese to victory over the team from El Cajon.

LITTLE LEAGUE BASEBALL

The 31st Little League World Series was held at the Lamade Stadium in Williamsport, Pennsylvania, in 1977. Once again, the Far East dominated the Series. In the championship game, the team from Taipei, Taiwan, defeated the team from El Cajon, California, 7–2. It was Taiwan's sixth world title since 1969. The finale was watched by 23,000 spectators and by a national TV audience.

Chiang Chen-jung, a muscular 12-year-old, led the Taiwanese to victory with his pitching arm and his bat. As the pitcher in the final contest, he limited the El Cajon batters to four hits, struck out nine, and walked two. At the plate, he contributed three hits in four times at bat.

On their way to the championship, the Taiwanese defeated Canada, 19–0, and Mara-caibo, Venezuela, 9–2. The overwhelming defeat of the Canadians included a no-hit effort by pitcher Tsai Tsung-hien and 18 hits by the Taiwanese team. Only two Canadians reached base, one on an error, the other because he was hit by a pitched ball.

During the three games played in Williamsport by Taiwan, Chiang was the third baseman when he wasn't pitching. He collected 10 hits in 12 times at bat, including three home runs and two doubles, and drove in 10 runs. His .833 batting average was a record for Series play, over the .733 mark made by Chen Pai-sheng in the 1973 Series.

The El Cajon team advanced to the climactic meeting with Taiwan by turning back the teams from Hattiesburg, Mississippi, 3–1, and Rotterdam, New York, 6–3.

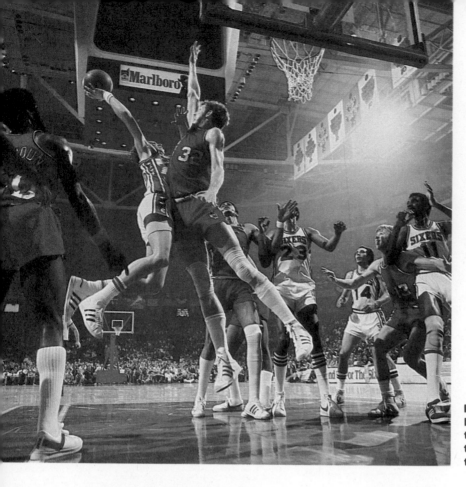

Portland's Bill Walton tries to block a shot by Philadelphia in the playoff finals. Portland won the NBA championship, 4 games to 2.

BASKETBALL

In the 1976–77 season, the National Basketball Association (NBA) produced a "Cinderella" winner—the Portland Trail Blazers. Portland had joined the NBA in 1970, and this was only their seventh season of play. So it came as a surprise to many when they defeated the heavily favored Philadelphia 76ers in the championship playoff series, 4 games to 2. The Trail Blazers made a rare recovery in the series. They were defeated in the first two contests, and then won four in a row. Cheered on by a wildly excited Oregon audience, they ended the competition with a breath-taking 109–107 victory.

Before the regular season began, the NBA had expanded to 22 teams (in 4 divisions). It had picked up four teams from the disbanded American Basketball Association (ABA)— the New York Nets, Denver Nuggets, San Antonio Spurs, and Indiana Pacers.

During the pre-season shuffle of talent, the Nets traded Julius Erving (Doctor J) to the 76ers. He had been the ABA's outstanding performer, and possibly the best in either league. Erving helped make the 76ers into a superpower during the regular season. They led the Atlantic Division with a 50–32 record, and they had a 6-game margin over the defending league champions, the Boston Celtics.

In the Pacific Division, the Los Angeles Lakers had the best regular-season log in the NBA, 53–29, with a 4-game bulge over Portland. Portland's 49–33 record was their best ever, and put the team into the playoffs for the first time.

Led by former UCLA all-American Bill Walton, Portland reached their peak during the playoffs. They eliminated Chicago, Denver, and Los Angeles (in a 4-game sweep) on the way to the final struggle with Philadelphia. The Trail Blazers lost the first two games of the playoffs, on Philadelphia's home court, and it didn't seem as if they could go on to win. But their excellent teamwork, as taught by their coach, Jack Ramsay, enabled

FINAL NBA STANDINGS

EASTERN CONFERENCE

Atlantic Division

	W	L	Pct.
Philadelphia	50	32	.610
Boston	44	38	.537
New York Knicks	40	42	.488
Buffalo	30	52	.366
New York Nets	22	60	.268

Central Division

	W	L	Pct.
Houston	49	33	.598
Washington	48	34	.585
San Antonio	44	38	.537
Cleveland	43	39	.524
New Orleans	35	47	.427
Atlanta	31	51	.378

WESTERN CONFERENCE

Midwest Division

	W	L	Pct.
Denver	50	32	.610
Chicago	44	38	.537
Detroit	44	38	.537
Kansas City	40	42	.488
Indiana	36	46	.439
Milwaukee	30	52	.366

Pacific Division

	W	L	Pct.
Los Angeles	53	29	.646
Portland	49	33	.598
Golden State	46	36	.561
Seattle	40	42	.488
Phoenix	34	48	.415

NBA Championship: Portland Trail Blazers

COLLEGE BASKETBALL

Conference	Winner
Atlantic Coast	North Carolina
Big Eight	Kansas State
Big Ten	Michigan
Ivy League	Princeton
Mid-American	Miami (Ohio)
Missouri Valley	Southern Illinois
Pacific Eight	UCLA
Southeastern	Tennessee; Kentucky (tied)
Southern	Virginia Military
Southwest	Arkansas
West Coast Athletic	San Francisco
Western Athletic	Utah

NCAA: Marquette

National Invitation Tournament: St. Bonaventure

Marquette's Butch Lee was the outstanding player in the championship game of the NCAA tournament.

Walton, Maurice Lucas, and others to overcome the individual brilliance of the 76ers' Erving. Erving was the leading scorer in the six games, with 182 points, including 40 in the last game. But Walton's leadership of a Portland team that had confidence and a great defense earned him the playoffs' most valuable player award. In the 31-year history of the NBA, only one other team (Boston) had erased a 2–0 deficit to win the championship. But only Portland achieved it in four straight games.

In college play, Milwaukee's Marquette University triumphed. They beat the University of North Carolina, 67–59, in the championship game of the NCAA tournament. The success of the Marquette Warriors was a fitting parting gift to Al McGuire, who retired after thirteen years as their head coach. It was a goal that Coach McGuire had not been able to reach in eight previous NCAA tournaments. The outstanding player for the Warriors was Butch Lee, a Puerto Rican–born youngster who lives in the Bronx.

In the National Conference championship game, Dallas quarterback Roger Staubach (12) led the Cowboys to victory over the Minnesota Vikings, 23–6.

FOOTBALL

Professional football's 1978 Super Bowl paired the old and the new—the Dallas Cowboys, who had been there three times before (and won once), and the Denver Broncos, who had never been in a playoff game of any kind in their eighteen years of existence. The Broncos and the Cowboys went into the Bowl with identical regular-season records, 12–2, the best in the National Footbal League (NFL). But Dallas proved to be the better team and captured the Super Bowl, 27–10.

The Cowboys, who had reached the postseason competition in eleven of the last twelve seasons, had captured the National Conference championship with a 23–6 romp over the Minnesota Vikings. Led by skillful quarterback Roger Staubach, the Cowboys outrushed and outpassed the Vikings. And an aggressive defense forced the Vikings into five fumbles, three of which the Cowboys recovered.

In addition to Dallas and Minnesota, the National Conference playoff qualifiers were the Los Angeles Rams (10–4), and the Chicago Bears, the wild-card entry with a 9–5 mark that matched Minnesota's. For the once mighty Bears, it was the first playoff appearance in fourteen years, but they were overwhelmed by Dallas, 37–7, in the opening post-season skirmish. In the other conference playoff preliminary, the Vikings, with Bob Lee substituting at quarterback for the injured Fran Tarkenton, scored a surprising 14–7 triumph over the Rams.

In the American Conference title contest, the Broncos dethroned the defending Super Bowl champion Oakland Raiders, 20–17. Haven Moses led Denver into football's promised land by catching touchdown passes of 74 yards and 7 yards from quarterback Craig Morton, who had previously played with Dallas and the Giants. Denver and Oakland had divided their two regular-season meetings, the Broncos winning in Oakland and losing at

Denver's Haven Moses caught touchdown passes of 74 and 7 yards in the American Conference championship game. The Broncos beat the Oakland Raiders, 20–17.

home. The Raiders, with an 11–3 record, had been the wild-card entry for the playoffs.

The Baltimore Colts and the Pittsburgh Steelers had also reached the playoffs in the American Conference. In one of the two playoff preliminaries, Oakland and Baltimore waged the third longest battle in football history. Tied at 31–31 at the end of regulation time, the Raiders won in the 43rd second of the second overtime period when Ken Stabler threw the third touchdown pass of the day to his tight end, Dave Casper, for a 37–31 decision. Denver joined Oakland in the American Conference championship final with a 34–21 victory over Pittsburgh, through a late surge that broke a 21–21 deadlock.

Individually, Walter Payton, the Chicago Bears' running back, was the NFL's outstanding performer with 1,852 yards rushing, the third highest total ever in the league. He fell just 151 yards short of O. J. Simpson's record of 2,003 yards, set in 1973.

In the Canadian Football League, the Mon-treal Alouettes trounced the Edmonton Eskimos, 41–6, for the Grey Cup.

▶ COLLEGE PLAY

A wild scramble to be named college football's No. 1 team ended in a series of astonishing results in the New Year's bowl games, from which Notre Dame emerged as "the best." The Irish record of 11–1 was equaled by four other major teams, Texas, Alabama, Arkansas, and Penn State. Notre Dame was chosen on the basis of its Cotton Bowl win, a stunning 38–10 triumph over Texas, the team previously ranked first. Among Notre Dame's achievements was its success in stopping Texas running back Earl Campbell, who had been awarded the Heisman Trophy as the nation's outstanding college player.

Also surprising were the tallies in other bowls: Washington over Michigan in the Rose Bowl, 27–20; Alabama over Ohio State in the Sugar Bowl, 35–6; and Arkansas over Oklahoma in the Orange Bowl, 31–6.

Texas running back Earl Campbell was awarded the 1977 Heisman Trophy.

FINAL NFL STANDINGS

AMERICAN CONFERENCE

Eastern Division

	W	L	T	Pct.	PF	PA
Baltimore	10	4	0	.714	295	221
Miami	10	4	0	.714	313	197
New England	9	5	0	.643	278	217
Jets	3	11	0	.214	191	300
Buffalo	3	11	0	.214	160	313

Central Division

	W	L	T	Pct.	PF	PA
Pittsburgh	9	5	0	.643	283	243
Cincinnati	8	6	0	.571	238	235
Houston	8	6	0	.571	299	230
Cleveland	6	8	0	.429	269	267

Western Division

	W	L	T	Pct.	PF	PA
Denver	12	2	0	.857	274	148
Oakland	11	3	0	.786	351	230
San Diego	7	7	0	.500	222	205
Seattle	5	9	0	.357	282	373
Kansas City	2	12	0	.143	225	349

Conference Champion: Denver Broncos

NATIONAL CONFERENCE

Eastern Division

	W	L	T	Pct.	PF	PA
Dallas	12	2	0	.857	345	212
Washington	9	5	0	.643	196	189
St. Louis	7	7	0	.500	272	287
Giants	5	9	0	.357	181	265
Philadelphia	5	9	0	.357	220	207

Central Division

	W	L	T	Pct.	PF	PA
Minnesota	9	5	0	.643	231	227
Chicago	9	5	0	.643	255	253
Detroit	6	8	0	.429	183	252
Green Bay	4	10	0	.286	134	219
Tampa Bay	2	12	0	.143	103	223

Western Division

	W	L	T	Pct.	PF	PA
Los Angeles	10	4	0	.714	302	146
Atlanta	7	7	0	.500	179	129
San Francisco	5	9	0	.357	220	260
New Orleans	3	11	0	.214	232	336

Conference Champion: Dallas Cowboys

1978 Super Bowl Winner: Dallas Cowboys

COLLEGE FOOTBALL

Conference	Winner
Atlantic Coast	North Carolina
Big Eight	Oklahoma
Big Ten	Michigan; Ohio State (tied)
Ivy League	Yale
Mid-American	Miami
Pacific Eight	Washington
Southeastern	Alabama
Southern	VMI; Tennessee–Chattanooga (tied)
Southwest	Texas
Western Athletic	Brigham Young; Arizona State (tied)

Cotton Bowl: Notre Dame 38, Texas 10
Gator Bowl: Pittsburgh 34, Clemson 3
Orange Bowl: Arkansas 31, Oklahoma 6
Rose Bowl: Washington 27, Michigan 20
Sugar Bowl: Alabama 35, Ohio State 6

Heisman Trophy: Earl Campbell, Texas

Hollis Stacy blasts out of a sand trap, on her way to winning the U.S. Women's Open.

GOLF

Lanny Wadkins wins the World Series of Golf.

PROFESSIONAL	Individual
Masters	Tom Watson
U.S. Open	Hubert Green
Canadian Open	Lee Trevino
British Open	Tom Watson
PGA	Lanny Wadkins
World Series of Golf	Lanny Wadkins
U.S. Women's Open	Hollis Stacy
Ladies PGA	Chaku Higuchi
	Team
World Cup	Spain
Ryder Cup	United States

AMATEUR	Individual
U.S. Amateur	John Fought
U.S. Women's Amateur	Beth Daniel
British Amateur	Peter McEvoy
British Women's Amateur	Angela Uvielli
Canadian Amateur	Rod Spittle
Canadian Ladies Amateur	Kathy Sherk
	Team
Walker Cup	United States

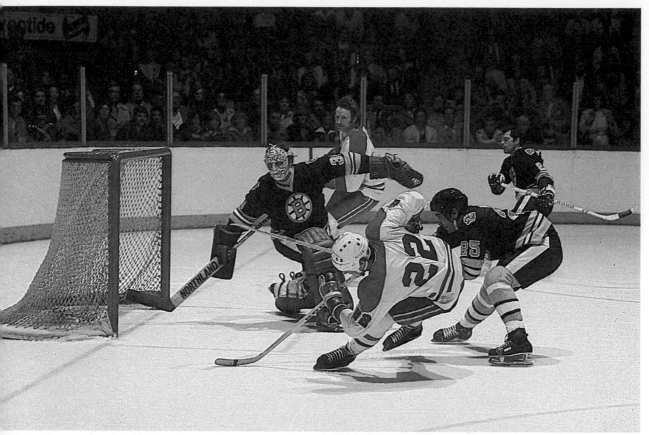

The Montreal Canadiens battle the Boston Bruins in Stanley Cup play. Montreal trounced Boston in four straight games.

HOCKEY

The Stanley Cup, the symbol of the National Hockey League championship, was captured by the Montreal Canadiens in 1977. It was their second consecutive win, and their 20th Cup triumph. There's no question about the Canadiens' superiority over the other current major league hockey clubs. They are even being compared to great hockey teams of the past. Montreal's star performer, Guy Lafleur, has been called the equal of his legendary predecessor, Maurice "The Rocket" Richard. And the team as a whole is thought to be as good as the championship teams that were led by The Rocket.

In the 1977 final playoff series (best-of-seven), the Canadiens skated to four straight victories over the Boston Bruins—repeating their sweep over the Philadelphia Flyers in the Stanley Cup final in 1976. After gaining decisions over the Bruins by 7–3, 3–0, and 4–2, in the first three games, the Canadiens were held even, 1–1, in regulation time in the fourth engagement. But the delay was only a short one, as Jacques Lemaire produced the decisive goal for a 2–1 decision in 4:32 of the sudden-death overtime period.

The Canadiens erased all their post-season competitors in 14 games, only two over the minimum. They captured four in a row from St. Louis, four out of six from the New York Islanders, and the four straight from the Bruins. Their record during the regular, 80-game season showed 60 victories, 8 defeats, and 12 ties. Including the playoffs, they lost a mere 10 decisions through the long campaign, and only two of those on their home ice, the Montreal Forum.

In addition to his share of the team's prize money, Lafleur collected a caseful of post-season silverware. Included were the Art Ross Trophy as the league's scoring champion; the Conn Smythe Trophy as the most valuable player in the Stanley Cup competition; the Hart Trophy as the most valuable player during the regular season; and a gold puck for being a member of the All-Star team, onto which he was unanimously voted.

Other Canadiens who won post-season honors were Larry Robinson, who was awarded the Norris Trophy as the league's best defenseman, and Ken Dryden and Michel Larocque, who shared the Vezina Trophy as best goalies. Willi Plett of the Atlanta Flames was chosen for the Calder Trophy as the rookie of the year; and Marcel Dionne of the Los Angeles Kings received the Lady Byng Trophy for combining gentlemanly play with excellence on the ice.

The title in the financially troubled World Hockey Association went to the Quebec Nordiques. In the final series for the Avco Cup, they defeated the Winnipeg Jets, four games to three, thus dethroning the 1976 champions. The seventh and decisive engagement was an 8–2 romp for the Nordiques, who earned their first championship in the WHA's five-year history. That final series was the first such all-Canadian contest of major league hockey teams since Montreal played Toronto for the 1967 Stanley Cup.

Robbie Ftorek of the Phoenix Roadrunners won the Gordie Howe Trophy as the league's most valuable player—but his team had gone out of business after the season ended. In another unusual twist, the celebrated Howe family, father Gordie and sons Mark and Marty, left the Houston Aeros and signed contracts with the New England Whalers.

In 1977 world play, eight teams competed at the international tournament held in Vienna, Austria. Czechoslovakia retained its world hockey title, Sweden placed second, the Soviet Union third, and Canada fourth. They were followed by Finland, the United States, West Germany, and Rumania.

The Quebec Nordiques defeated the Winnipeg Jets, four games to three, for the Avco Cup title.

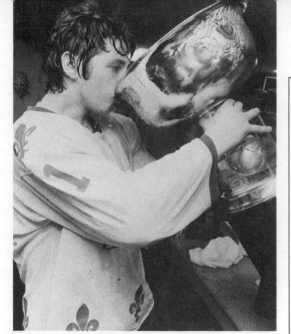
Drinking champagne from the Avco Cup.

FINAL WHA STANDINGS

East Division

	W	L	T	Pts.
Quebec	47	31	3	97
Cincinnati	39	37	5	83
Indianapolis	36	37	8	80
New England	35	40	6	76
Birmingham	31	46	4	66

West Division

	W	L	T	Pts.
Houston	50	24	6	106
Winnipeg	46	32	2	94
San Diego	40	37	4	84
Edmonton	34	43	4	72
Calgary	31	43	7	69
Phoenix	28	48	4	60

Avco Cup: Quebec Nordiques

OUTSTANDING PLAYERS

Scorer	Real Cloutier, Quebec
Rookie	George Lyle, New England
Goalie	Ron Grahame and Wayne Rutledge, Houston
Most Valuable Player	Robbie Ftorek, Phoenix
Sportsmanship	Dave Keon, New England
Defenseman	Ron Plumb, Cincinnati
Avco Cup play	Serge Bernier, Quebec

FINAL NHL STANDINGS

CAMPBELL CONFERENCE

Patrick Division

	W	L	T	Pts.
Philadelphia	48	16	16	112
N.Y. Islanders	47	21	12	106
Atlanta	34	34	12	80
N.Y. Rangers	29	37	14	72

Smythe Division

	W	L	T	Pts.
St. Louis	32	39	9	73
Minnesota	23	39	18	64
Chicago	26	43	11	63
Vancouver	25	42	13	63
Colorado	20	46	14	54

WALES CONFERENCE

Norris Division

	W	L	T	Pts.
Montreal	60	8	12	132
Los Angeles	34	31	15	83
Pittsburgh	34	33	13	81
Washington	24	42	14	62
Detroit	16	55	9	41

Adams Division

	W	L	T	Pts.
Boston	49	23	8	106
Buffalo	48	24	8	104
Toronto	33	32	15	81
Cleveland	25	42	13	63

Stanley Cup: Montreal Canadiens

OUTSTANDING PLAYERS

Calder Trophy (rookie)	Willi Plett, Atlanta
Conn Smythe Trophy (Stanley Cup play)	Guy Lafleur, Montreal
Hart Trophy (most valuable player)	Guy Lafleur, Montreal
Lady Byng Trophy (sportsmanship)	Marcel Dionne, Los Angeles
Norris Trophy (defenseman)	Larry Robinson, Montreal
Ross Trophy (scorer)	Guy Lafleur, Montreal
Vezina Trophy (goalie)	Ken Dryden and Michel Larocque, Montreal

Guy Lafleur, winner of three major NHL trophies, was Montreal's star player.

Quebec's Serge Bernier was the most valuable player in the Avco Cup playoffs.

Charles Tickner, the U.S. Men's Champion.

World Cup ski champ Lise-Marie Morerod.

ICE SKATING

FIGURE SKATING
World Championships

Men	Vladimir Kovalev, U.S.S.R.
Women	Linda Fratianne, U.S.
Pairs	Irina Rodnina/ Alexander Zaitsev, U.S.S.R.
Dance	Irina Moiseyeva/ Andrei Minenkov, U.S.S.R.

United States Championships

Men	Charles Tickner
Women	Linda Fratianne
Pairs	Tai Babilonia/Randy Gardner
Dance	Judi Genovese/Kent Weigle

SPEED SKATING
World Championships

Men	Eric Heiden, U.S.
Women	Vera Bryndzey, U.S.S.R.

SKIING

WORLD CUP CHAMPIONSHIPS

Men	Ingemar Stenmark, Sweden
Women	Lise-Marie Morerod, Switzerland

CANADIAN-AMERICAN TROPHY SERIES

Men

Downhill	Robin McLeish, Canada
Slalom	Mike Durtschi, U.S.
Giant Slalom	Phil Mahre, U.S.
Overall	Raymond Pratte, Canada

Women

Downhill	Gail Blackburn, U.S.
Slalom	Heidi Preuss, U.S.
Giant Slalom	Heidi Preuss, U.S.
Overall	Heidi Preuss, U.S.

U.S. ALPINE CHAMPIONSHIPS

	Men	Women
Slalom	Cary Adgate	Christin Cooper
Giant Slalom	Phil Mahre	Becky Dorsey
Combined	Cary Adgate	Christin Cooper

Two record setters: Ulrike Tauber (*above*) in the 200-meter individual medley; and Christiane Knacke (*right*) winning the 100-meter butterfly.

SWIMMING

WORLD SWIMMING RECORDS SET IN 1977		
EVENT	**HOLDER**	**TIME**
	Men	
400-meter freestyle	Brian Goodell, U.S.	3:51.56
100-meter breaststroke	Gerald Moerken, W. Germany	1:02.86
100-meter butterfly	Joe Bottom, U.S.	54.18
200-meter individual medley	Graham Smith, Canada	2:05.31
	Women	
400-meter freestyle	Petra Thumer, E. Germany	4:08.91
800-meter freestyle	Petra Thumer, E. Germany	8:35.04
1,500-meter freestyle	Alice Browne, U.S.	16:24.60
100-meter butterfly	Christiane Knacke, E. Germany	59.78
200-meter individual medley	Ulrike Tauber, E. Germany	2:15.85

Wimbledon glory: Queen Elizabeth looks on as Virginia Wade reigns as the Women's Champion.

TENNIS

Major glory in tennis in 1977 was shared by players from many nations: by Virginia Wade of Britain and Björn Borg of Sweden in Britain's Wimbledon tournament; and by Chris Evert of the United States and Guillermo Vilas of Argentina in the U.S. Open.

Wimbledon celebrated its 100th anniversary as the legendary center of world tennis competition. And with Queen Elizabeth as a spectator, it was fitting and proper that a native of Britain should win the women's singles crown. It was the first time in eight years that a Britisher had won a Wimbledon singles title. In her finest hour, Wade defeated Betty Stove of the Netherlands, 4–6, 6–3, 6–1. In the semifinal, Wade had stunned the defending champion, Chris Evert, 6–2, 4–6, 6–1.

In the men's final, Borg repeated his 1976 Wimbledon success by conquering a familiar opponent, Jimmy Connors of the United States. In one of the greatest duels ever seen on Wimbledon's center court, Borg emerged with the trophy after 3 hours and 14 minutes of play. The scores in the five-set match, which enthralled 15,000 spectators, were 3–6, 6–2, 6–1, 5–7, 6–4.

Connors had beaten Borg in the 1976 U.S. Open final. But another meeting at Forest Hills was made impossible when Borg injured his shoulder during an early match and did not play in the rest of the tournament. Connors had clear sailing until the final, when he again encountered a stubborn foe. This time it was Argentina's Guillermo Vilas. The match was almost as thrilling as the Wimbledon encounter between Connors and Borg, as Vilas recovered from a slow start and won in four sets, 2–6, 6–3, 7–6, 6–0.

For Evert, the victory at Forest Hills was her third straight in the U.S. Open. It was achieved with a 7–6, 6–2 triumph in the final over Wendy Turnbull of Australia. The last woman to win three consecutive singles titles at Forest Hills was Maureen Connolly (from 1951 through 1953). Even more remarkable was Evert's four-year record of having been undefeated in 113 consecutive matches on clay courts (Wimbledon is grass).

TOURNAMENT TENNIS

	Australian Open	French Open	Wimbledon	U.S. Open
Men's Singles	Roscoe Tanner, U.S.	Guillermo Vilas, Argentina	Björn Borg, Sweden	Guillermo Vilas, Argentina
Women's Singles	Kerry Reid, Australia	Mimi Jausovec, Yugoslavia	Virginia Wade, Britain	Chris Evert, U.S.
Men's Doubles	Arthur Ashe, U.S./ Tony Roche, Australia	Brian Gottfried, U.S./Raul Ramirez, Mexico	Ross Case/Geoff Masters, Australia	Bob Hewitt/ Frew McMillan, South Africa
Women's Doubles	Dianne Fromholtz/ Helen Gourlay, Australia	Pam Teegaurden, U.S./ Regina Marsikova, Czechoslovakia	Helen Gourlay, Australia/ Joanne Russell, U.S.	Betty Stove, Netherlands/ Martina Navratilova, U.S.

Davis Cup Winner: Australia

Karin Rossley of East Germany, setting a world record in the 400-meter hurdles.

TRACK AND FIELD

WORLD TRACK AND FIELD RECORDS SET IN 1977

EVENT	HOLDER	TIME, DISTANCE, OR POINTS
Men		
100-meter run	Harvey Glance, U.S.	9.8
800-meter run	Alberto Juantorena, Cuba	1:43.43
5,000-meter run	Dick Quax, New Zealand	13:12.9
10,000-meter run	Samson Kimombwa, Kenya	27:30.5
20,000-meter walk	Daniel Bautista, Mexico	1:23.32
50,000-meter walk	Enrique Vera, Mexico	3:56.39
110-meter hurdles	Alejandro Casanas, Cuba	13.21
400-meter hurdles	Edwin Moses, U.S.	47.45
High jump	Vladimir Yashchenko, U.S.S.R.	7'7¾''
Women		
1-mile run	Natalie Maracescu, Rumania	4:23.8
3-mile run	Jan Merrill, U.S.	15:13.3
100-meter run	Marlies Oelsner, E. Germany	10.88
500-meter run	Rosalyn Bryant, U.S.	1:11.8
5,000-meter run	Natalie Maracescu, Rumania	15:41.4
10,000-meter run	Peg Neppel, U.S.	33:15.1
50-meter hurdles	Jane Frederick, U.S.	6.56
400-meter hurdles	Karin Rossley, E. Germany	55.63
High jump	Rosemarie Ackerman, E. Germany	6'6¾''
Javelin	Kathy Schmidt, U.S.	227'5''
Shot put	Helena Fibingerova, Czechoslovakia	73'2¾''
Pentathlon	Nadyezhda Tkachenko, U.S.S.R.	4,839 points

Batter up! Sculptor Claes Oldenburg's "Batcolumn" is a new addition to Chicago's impressive skyline. Many people think that "Batcolumn" is an unusual work of art. But Oldenburg feels that the latticed steel sculpture, which is 100 feet (30 meters) high, symbolizes nothing more than what it is —a baseball bat. The sculptor (*on the right*) has dedicated it as "a monument both to baseball and the construction industry."

Muhammad Ali retained his world heavyweight boxing title in a championship match on September 29, 1977, at Madison Square Garden. The judges awarded Ali a unanimous decision over his opponent, Earnie Shavers, in a tough fight that went the full 15 rounds.

The America's Cup, awarded by the New York Yacht Club, is the most sought after international sailing trophy. The famous race, which takes place every three years, was held again in 1977. The U.S. entry *Courageous* was the defending champion, and it beat the yacht *Australia* in a four-race sweep in the best-of-seven series.

Twenty-eight-year-old Toller Cranston starred in one of Broadway's biggest hits in 1977. But it was not a drama, a comedy, or a musical. It was his "The Ice Show," a blend of figure skating, dancing, and theater. The enthusiastic audiences were thrilled by his unique style. Born in Ontario, a province in Canada, Cranston began skating at an early age. He has won many figure-skating championships, and placed third at the 1976 Winter Olympics.

SOCCER: THE NEW KICK IN NORTH AMERICA

"It can't happen here!"

That's what everyone said. Everyone said that soccer would never become popular in North America. "Football is big. So is baseball, and hockey, and basketball. Soccer? Forget it!"

But everyone was wrong.

For many years, soccer has been hugely popular in more than 100 countries. In South America and Europe, crowds of over 100,000 people have jammed stadiums for important games. In Britain, fans of rival teams have started fights with each other. And when the World Cup matches are held—once every four years—businesses close down all over the globe as people head home to switch on their television sets. It is estimated that 1,000,000,000 (billion) people will follow the 1978 World Cup matches. Imagine—one *billion* soccer fans! And until recently, only a very few of them lived in North America.

But very suddenly it seems, soccer *has* happened here. The year 1977 will probably be remembered as the year in which soccer "took off" in North America, especially as a spectator sport. However, even though it was not until 1977 that soccer achieved great popularity in North America, the sport has been played here for a long time. And a number of years of groundwork were necessary before soccer could become as popular as it has. A number of years of groundwork, and one very special player.

How did it all happen?

▶ THE GROUNDWORK

People have been playing soccer in North America since the time of the American

294

Revolution, 200 years ago. In cities with large immigrant populations, you could always see a soccer game in a park on a nice weekend day. Within the past few decades, many colleges and high schools have fielded soccer teams. Then in 1967 two professional soccer leagues were formed. But North American sports fans weren't ready for professional soccer. People didn't attend the games in large numbers. The leagues failed.

The leagues tried again in 1968. This time they joined together to become one league, the North American Soccer League (N.A.S.L.). But the N.A.S.L. didn't fare much better than the two original leagues had. At the end of the season, twelve of the seventeen teams in the league dropped out. Again, lack of fan support and money were the problems.

Yet despite these rather poor beginnings, the groundwork had been laid. In the late 1960's and early 1970's, more and more people began noticing soccer. In particular, the young people of North America were getting involved in the game. They were getting involved in the best way possible: they were playing it. And as more and more young people began playing soccer, the N.A.S.L. began to do a little better. Many of those youthful participants were also money-paying fans. So each year new teams came into the N.A.S.L.

▶ ONE VERY SPECIAL PLAYER

By 1975 it was obvious that interest in professional soccer was growing. And more and more young people were playing on organized soccer teams. But soccer in North America still seemed to be missing something. It still needed something special before it would be considered a big-time sport.

Soccer found what it needed: a superstar, a player who could capture the attention of the fans, the newspapers, and the television cameras. His name? Edson Arantes do Nascimento, better known to the world as Pelé (pronounced pay-lay).

Although Pelé was discovered by North American soccer only in 1975, he had been known throughout the soccer-playing world since 1956. In that year, he began playing with the Santos team of Brazil (his native country) and very quickly became its star. No player alive could match his skills. Whether dribbling, shooting, passing, or "heading" the ball,

Pelé, the "Black Pearl," was the best. He was soccer's Babe Ruth: the great player beloved by all fans of the game. He was soccer's Muhammad Ali: a fabulous showman whom people came to watch even if they knew little about the sport. Pelé was just what North American professional soccer needed. In 1975 the owners of the New York Cosmos of the N.A.S.L. went after him with a $4,700,000 contract. Pelé had been ready to retire, but he signed on to play for three years.

It was not just money that brought Pelé here. He was already a wealthy man. But loving the game as much as he did, Pelé came because he wanted to help make soccer popular on this continent.

Pelé played his first game for the Cosmos in June, 1975. Since then, game by game, soccer's popularity has grown and grown. In 1977 record-setting crowds and nationwide television coverage have indeed proved that professional soccer has become a major sport in North America.

▶ THE TURNSTILES ARE CLICKING

The Cosmos set a U.S. attendance record on June 19, 1977, when 62,394 fans passed through the turnstiles into Giants Stadium in East Rutherford, New Jersey. They saw Pelé score three goals as the Cosmos beat the Tampa Bay Rowdies, 3–1. Pelé says he cried that day—the sight of all those soccer fans had thrilled him to tears. "This," he said, "is what I came for."

However, that attendance record didn't stay on the books for long. On August 14, 1977, 77,691 people roared as the Cosmos trounced the Fort Lauderdale Strikers 8–3 in a playoff game. It was the largest crowd ever to attend a soccer match in North America.

Soccer is a team sport, and the Cosmos are a great team. They had other excellent players in addition to Pelé, including Italian star Giorgio Chinaglia and the masterful West German, Franz Beckenbauer. On August 28, in Portland, Oregon, the Cosmos faced the Seattle Sounders for the N.A.S.L. championship. The game, called the "Soccer Bowl," was televised in eleven countries including the United States. Seattle, a strong team, pressed the Cosmos from the opening kickoff. But the Cosmos held on to win, 2–1.

Steve Hunt, a 21-year-old Englishman, was

Pelé and Steve Hunt: The Cosmos are the champions!

the Cosmos' most valuable player that day. And goalie Shep Messing made some tough saves. For the Cosmos, winning the championship was the perfect way to finish the season. Overall, in 1977 the Cosmos drew an average attendance of 39,000 people per game.

The N.A.S.L. has eighteen teams, and five or six more are expected to join the league for the 1978 season. Despite the success of the Cosmos, not all the other teams are doing well. In 1977 the N.A.S.L. had an average attendance of 13,300 per game. Toronto, the 1976 champion, averaged only about 5,000 per game. And another league, the American Soccer League, with eight teams, averaged under 3,000 per game.

The people who run the professional soccer leagues are well aware of these attendance figures. They know, however, that as more and more young people take up the game, league

attendance will naturally increase. So the professional soccer leagues have encouraged youth soccer leagues as much as possible.

▶PELÉ'S FAREWELL

On October 1 the great Pelé played his final game. It was an exhibition match between the Cosmos and the Santos of Brazil, Pelé's first team. Pelé played the first half for the Cosmos and scored a goal. At halftime, he changed into a Santos shirt. He wanted to retire as a member of the Santos team.

After the game, which the Cosmos won, both teams declared that no player would ever again wear Pelé's number, 10, for either team. Pelé's great career was over.

With Pelé gone, will soccer continue to grow in North America? Undoubtedly it will. All the young people playing the game are sure that soccer has "made it."

More and more boys and girls are playing soccer—the game the whole world loves.

▶ THE BALL KEEPS MOVING

Indeed, youth soccer leagues are attracting hundreds of thousands of boys and girls each year. Youth soccer may soon have more participants than Little League baseball. And peewee football hasn't got a chance against the popularity of youth soccer.

What is it about soccer that draws so many young people to it? There are several things:

1. Anyone can play. Soccer is not only for the tall, strong, and heavy, as are football and basketball. Size doesn't matter. The smaller player can be just as good as the bigger player. And there are many leagues for girls as well as for boys.

2. There isn't much chance of injury in soccer, mostly because there is little body contact. In hockey and football, on the other hand, injuries are frequent.

3. Soccer doesn't require a lot of equipment; only a ball is necessary. Therefore, setting up a team is inexpensive. Parents of young hockey and football players have always complained about the costs of uniforms and protective padding and helmets. There is no such problem with soccer.

4. Playing soccer is excellent for getting into good physical condition. For 90 minutes, it's run, run, run. As one young player put it, "The ball keeps moving." And as the ball moves, the players must move after it. Compare this with the many delays and time-outs of football and basketball!

Most of all, soccer is a game that is filled with magic. It offers drama, excitement, and breathtaking speed. It's the game the whole world loves.

DANIEL J. DOMOFF
Consulting Editor
Educational Developmental Laboratories

SKATEBOARDING: SURFING ON WHEELS

In the early 1960's some California teenagers attached roller skates to wood boards so they could practice "surfing" on the sidewalk. This skateboarding fad was short-lived because bumpy roads and stones stopped the small skate wheels and sent the sidewalk surfers sprawling. That wasn't much fun, so the skaters went back to surfing in the sea.

A few years later, however, someone made bigger and wider wheels out of polyurethane plastic. These were softer than the roller-skate wheels, and they rolled over stones and bumps and gave excellent traction. These wheels were mounted to special shock absorbers, called trucks, which made the boards easier to maneuver. The boards, too, were improved.

With the new equipment, skateboarding really caught on, and the number of skateboarders grew every year. Today, more than 20,000,000 people are regular riders—in the United States, Canada, Japan, Venezuela, France, Switzerland, Brazil, and many other countries.

▶ COMPETITIVE SKATEBOARDING

Skateboarding has come a long way since the 1960's. In addition to the millions who are skateboarding just for fun, there are people who are skating to win. Today skateboarding is a competitive sport—for both professionals and amateurs.

Professional skateboarders compete, both individually and in teams, for big prize money. They also give demonstrations, endorse products, and appear in television commercials. Most of these athletes are in their teens or twenties, but the skateboarding star of one Pepsi commercial was only five years old.

A few of these athletes are making very good livings as professional skateboarders. Eighteen-year-old Ty Page, an outstanding skateboarder with the nickname "Incredible," was expected to make nearly $100,000 in 1977 by winning contests and endorsing skateboard equipment. And 16-year-old Laura Thornhill expected to earn $60,000 in a year as a pro skateboarder.

These pro skateboarders are competing in the men's slalom.

Not all competitive skateboarders are pros. Some are keeping their amateur status so they can compete in the Olympics—if skateboarding is accepted as an Olympic event. These youngsters can join any of the amateur teams that are forming and competing with each other.

THE BIG CONTESTS

Competitive skateboarders can enter several championship categories, including downhill speed racing, slalom, cross-country, and freestyle.

The men usually prefer downhill racing, competing against each other or against the clock. They also like slalom—weaving at breakneck speeds around plastic cones, just as slalom skiers do around poles.

The women seem to enjoy freestyle most. To music, each competitor performs her own ballet on a skateboard. She designs the routine to show her skill and skateboarding style. Her routine often includes high jumps; handstands; and 360's—which means turning around in circles on one pair of wheels, similar to an ice skater pirouetting on skates.

Safety equipment is very important in competitive skateboarding. The athletes always wear helmets, elbow pads, knee pads, socks and shoes, gloves, and sometimes wrist bracers. If a skateboarder falls, the safety equipment will prevent serious injury. One skateboarder was especially thankful he was wearing padded leather gloves when he lost his balance during a pro competition. His hands hit the pavement at over 50 miles per hour (80 kilometers per hour), but he walked away from the spill unhurt. Some downhill speed racers are now wearing all-leather suits during competition, which make them look more like motorcycle racers than skateboarders.

SKATEBOARD PARKS

It is often difficult to find a large, smooth, and safe area in which to skateboard. For this reason, special skateboard parks are being opened everywhere. In California alone, more than 25 outdoor skateboard parks were under construction in 1977. And in some places, these special parks are being built indoors so that people can skateboard in the winter months.

A young skateboarder takes her turn in the women's freestyle high jump.

These parks have concrete hills, bowls, and flat areas where skateboarders can practice wheelies, 360's, kick turns, tail slides, handstands, and other maneuvers. Some parks even have long courses for cross-country practice.

After learning how to keep their balance and make some easy maneuvers, skateboarders like to zoom around the concrete bowls. The higher you climb toward the upper edge, the more you seem to defy gravity. (During some championship competitions, teammates encourage each other to "hit the lip"—ride as close as possible to the top of the bowl without shooting over its edge.)

Skateboard parks are great places to have lots of fun. They are also excellent places to practice if you want to become a professional or amateur competitor.

▶SKATEBOARD MODELS

There are many different skateboard models. You have a choice of wood (oak, ash, teak, mahogany, or layers of maple veneer), as well as plastic, fiberglass, or aluminum. Prices range from $10 to $110. Or you can buy blank boards, trucks, and wheels separately, and assemble your own custom model.

Some skateboards have been adapted for other kinds of enjoyment. One model is fitted with handlebars so it can be used as a scooter. On another model, you can attach a mast and sails to the board, using wind power to skate. You can even buy a motorized skateboard.

▶SAFE SKATEBOARDING

Follow these rules for safe skateboarding:

• Always wear shoes when skateboarding; athletic shoes are best because they give you a good grip on the board.

• Wear a helmet, gloves, knee pads, and elbow pads, even for skateboarding around the neighborhood.

• If you fall a lot and usually land on your hands, wear wrist guards. If you keep landing on your hips, wear hip pads. Or wear skateboarding pants with padding sewn in the seat.

Safety equipment is very important for skateboarders. This youngster wears a helmet, elbow and knee pads, shoes and socks, and gloves.

• Take good care of your equipment and inspect it before you ride. Check the board for cracks or splits and make sure all nuts and bolts are tightened. Be certain that the trucks are adjusted properly and that wheels and bearings are turning freely.

• Try to skate in areas designated for skateboarding, such as skateboard parks.

• If you are allowed to skateboard on the sidewalk, watch out for pedestrians.

• When skateboarding in the street, obey traffic signals and signs, and all traffic regulations.

• Never skateboard in a busy street, or in a street where it is difficult for motorists to see you.

• Never allow a bicycle, car, or other moving vehicle to tow you while you are on a skateboard.

• Always be courteous to other skateboarders and people you meet while skateboarding.

• Set a good example so you do not give skateboarding a bad name.

▶ **FOR MORE INFORMATION**

There are three magazines devoted to the sport of skateboarding: *Skateboard World, Skateboarder,* and *Wide World of Skateboarding.* The magazines feature interviews with the pros, discuss the latest equipment, describe the newest skateboard parks, and announce upcoming contests.

The International Skateboard Association is trying to promote safe skateboarding throughout the world, and to establish skateboarding as an accepted recreational and competitive sport. If you would like to learn more about pro and amateur skateboarding, as well as how to go about setting up a skateboard park where you live, write to the International Skateboard Association, 711 W. 17th Street, Costa Mesa, California 92627.

If you live in Canada, you can write to the Canadian Skateboard Association, 102 Bloor Street West, Toronto, M5S 1M8.

MICHELE AND TOM GRIMM
Authors, *Hitchhiker's Handbook*

THE CREATIVE WORLD

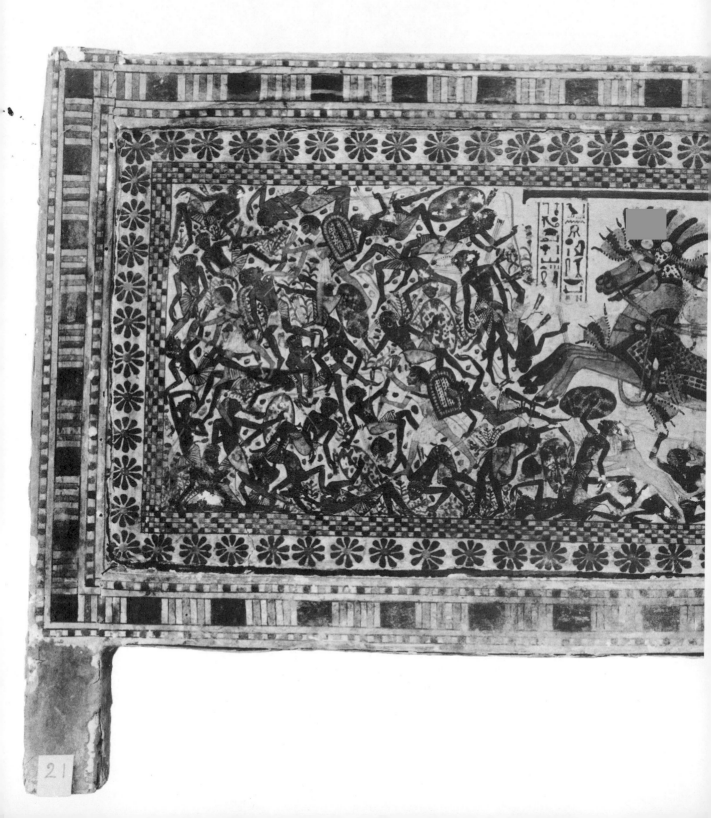

A decorated chest was among the incredible treasures found in the tomb of King Tut, the young king of ancient Egypt. In 1977 these treasures were shown in museums in many parts of the United States.

Jason Robards (best supporting actor) in *All the President's Men.*

1977 ACADEMY AWARDS

CATEGORY	WINNER
Picture	*Rocky*
Actor	Peter Finch *(Network)*
Actress	Faye Dunaway *(Network)*
Supporting Actor	Jason Robards *(All the President's Men)*
Supporting Actress	Beatrice Straight *(Network)*
Director	John G. Avildsen *(Rocky)*
Foreign Language Film	*Black and White in Color* (Ivory Coast)
Song	"Evergreen" *(A Star Is Born)*
Documentary Feature	*Harlan County, U.S.A.*
Documentary Short	*Number Our Days*
Cinematography	Haskell Wexler *(Bound for Glory)*

Sylvester Stallone and Talia Shire in *Rocky* (best picture).

Faye Dunaway (best actress) in *Network.*

ARTISTS OF THE CANADIAN ARCTIC

The Canadian Arctic is a cold, barren land. Vast fields of snow and ice are broken by glacier-covered mountains. In the dead of winter the sun never shines. At the height of summer it shines 24 hours a day—yet the ground remains permanently frozen.

But there is life here. Billions of birds make their nests in this land. Caribou herds move across the plains. Seals and walruses swim in the waters. And there are human beings—the Eskimos, descended from people who first came to the Canadian Arctic some 5,000 years ago.

They came from Asia, across the Bering Strait. These early people were nomadic—they didn't live in towns but wandered from place to place. They were hunters who followed the caribou herds, searched for the birds' nesting grounds, and caught fish and seals and walruses. They were people who used every part of whatever they took from their environment. For example, a walrus provided them with food (its meat); clothing (its skin); and tools for sewing and cutting (made from its bones).

During the endless winter nights, when a family rarely left its house of snow, the people carved bones into useful items. Perhaps a small mask or a tiny figure of an animal or person would be fashioned from the bone. These sculptures probably had religious value or were used in the practice of magic.

It wasn't until the 19th century that the Eskimos came into regular contact with white men. Most of the white men who traveled into the Canadian Arctic were traders. They wanted furs. Sometimes an Eskimo would carve something to sell or give to the traders. However, rarely was anything intentionally carved as "art."

But life was changing. White people moved farther north, building towns and bringing industry where caribou once roamed. White hunters killed huge numbers of caribou. The Eskimos found the wandering existence more and more difficult, because there wasn't enough game to feed all the people.

By the late 1940's it became obvious that new ways of survival had to be found. It was then that the economic value of Eskimo art was realized and that people were encouraged to create sculpture and other artifacts that could be sold in the outside world.

Today, art—especially carving, but also printmaking—is a major source of income for some Eskimos. The sculptures are carved primarily in whalebone, walrus ivory, and stone. They usually depict three major subjects.

Animals and the hunt. Eskimo artists often carve powerful polar bears, sleek seals, swimming sea birds, and watchful caribou. They make carvings of the men who spend long hours trying to catch the animals: a hunter standing over a hole in the ice, waiting for a seal to come up for a breath of air; a man lying in wait on the frozen ground, his harpoon close at hand; a fisherman carrying his catch of fish; a man with a dead fox slung over his shoulders.

Family and community. The family is very important to Eskimos, and one of the most common subjects of their art is a mother and her child. A sculpture might show the mother holding a child in her arms. Or the child might be nestled on the mother's back, in a special pouch in her parka hood.

Fantasy. Many carvings depict spirits, myths, and legends of the Eskimo people. There are carvings of sea goddesses and the merman, bear spirits and sea spirits, priests and sorcerers. Sometimes a sculpture shows an Eskimo with a spirit. For example, there is one in which an Eskimo is removing lice from the spirit's fur.

Almost all Eskimo art shows traditional scenes and beliefs. But life in the Canadian Arctic has changed in recent years. Dogsleds are giving way to snowmobiles. Snow houses and tents of animal skins have been replaced by prefabricated plywood homes. Instead of caribou meat, people eat canned foods.

There are other influences of the white people, especially on the children, who go to English-speaking schools. There are comic strips and radios and airplanes. The children learn about Santa Claus and television and lands where it is always warm.

Will today's young artists of the Arctic continue to depict the same subjects that were important to their parents and grandparents? Or will their art reflect the mixed white and Eskimo world they are now growing up in?

An Eskimo family after the hunt.

Eskimos playing a stick game.

Mother and child.

An Eskimo hunter.

THE MUSIC SCENE

The biggest news of the popular music scene in 1977 was the death of two music giants—Bing Crosby and Elvis Presley. Each singer represented an era of his own, offering a style and presence that was imitated by hundreds of other entertainers but never duplicated.

In October, Bing Crosby, a man whose popularity spanned several decades and who starred in many fields of entertainment, died at the age of 73. Crosby made over 850 records, including "White Christmas," a single that sold almost 40,000,000 copies, making it the largest selling single record of all time.

The most upsetting news to hit the rock world came in August, when Elvis Presley died at the age of 42. His death caused a tremendous outpouring of fan adoration and grief. Nothing else that happened in the popular music field in 1977 could compare to the hysteria that followed the death of "the king."

Two "greats" passed from the music scene: Bing Crosby, whose artistry spanned many decades . . .

. . . and Elvis Presley, who was the idol of "the rockin' 50's."

308

Newsmen from all over the world rushed to Presley's home in Memphis, Tennessee, to report on every detail of the last months of the entertainer's life, his death, and his funeral. The media spoke of the "end of an era," but the symbol of that era would not disappear. Elvis suddenly was big news again. He was the subject of hour-long TV news documentaries and special newspaper supplements. His films took over the airwaves. Fans clamored for his recordings, emptying record stores around the country in a matter of hours. They also bought Presley memorabilia—anything associated with the king—at the highest possible prices. And in Memphis, plans were being made to erect a bronze statue of Elvis on a bluff overlooking the Mississippi River.

Presley's last recordings, "Way Down" and *Moody Blue*, zoomed onto the Top Ten charts. They were, however, almost overshadowed by several tribute records to Elvis. "The King Is Gone," composed and recorded by Ronnie McDowell, sold over 2,000,000 records within weeks of its release. Among the many other memorial records was "Elvis Has Left the Building." The unusual title of the record was taken from the announcement always made at the end of Presley's live appearances. This recording was the work of J. D. Sumner, a gospel singer who toured with Elvis during the 1970's.

▶ **THE BEGINNING OF A NEW ERA?**

Presley's death did indeed signal the end of an era. But 1977 failed to produce any new charismatic personalities or fresh sounds that would start a new long-range musical trend.

However, there were some new stars and albums that were hailed by the critics and the record-buying public. Blond and boyish Peter Frampton sold over 13,000,000 copies of his album *Frampton Comes Alive!* This milestone surpassed the sales of Simon and Garfunkel's *Bridge over Troubled Waters* and Carole King's *Tapestry* of a few years past. *Frampton Comes Alive!* became the biggest selling album of all time. His new album, *I'm in You*, appears on its way to becoming as successful.

Barry Manilow, a singer of soft, romantic pop, had happy news for his fans during the year. He had gold singles with "Weekend in New England" and "Looks Like We Made It." Manilow also had superhits with his *Live* album and his spectacular TV special.

Barry Manilow in concert.

The Steve Miller Band's *Fly Like an Eagle* won the *Rolling Stone* magazine award for Best Rock Album of the Year. The band followed this success with a new single, "Jungle Love," and a new album, *Book of Dreams*.

Poetic Joni Mitchell climbed to new heights in her career. Her album *Hejira* was widely applauded as a "masterly piece of work" that achieved the perfection of art songs. "Amelia," one of the songs from the album, was singled out as "one of the best songs of the entire folk-rock era."

But despite the tremendous appeal of these singers, none of them had the charisma or the individuality of Presley, the Beatles, or Bob Dylan. After the troubled times of the late 1960's and early 1970's, it seems Americans are much more concerned with togetherness. Perhaps that's why the mellow tones of today's musicians became the sound of 1977.

▶ **A GROUP EFFORT**

News about musical groups would have to begin with Fleetwood Mac, the group of groups. Their hit singles "Dreams" and "Don't Stop" were preludes to *Rumours*, one of the most popular albums of all time. *Rumours* remained number one on the charts for a record-breaking six months. This success fol-

Fleetwood Mac, the group of groups in 1977.

lowed their *Fleetwood Mac* album, which has sold a tremendous 3,000,000 copies.

The slow, country-style Los Angeles sound of the Eagles also attracted quite a following. They added to their popularity with their album *Hotel California* and their singles "One of These Nights" and "New Kid in Town."

Musical groups with an impressive past also contributed to the music scene during the year. The soft-rock group Bread, which disbanded in 1973, rose to the top of the charts again in a 1977 reunion. With hits such as "If" and "Baby, I'm-a Want You" behind them, David Gates (the lead singer) and Bread prepared for the future with the hit album and single *Lost Without Your Love*.

The Bee Gees, who originally made it big with sweet melodies and smooth vocal harmonies, staged a surprise comeback by adding disco rhythms to their balladry. Barry Gibb, one of the Gibb brothers (who are, in reality, part of the Bee Gees), said that "we used to have a lot of message songs. But I think people are far more interested in themselves now. The important thing is, you're supposed to have a ball." And with those words said, the Bee Gees put it all together and came up with the bubbling *Children of the World*.

Another group that made news in 1977 has really been making news for two decades. The Beach Boys, creators of the '60s carefree surfin' sound of Southern California, brought those sounds up-to-date with a new album, *Love You*. And to show that their popularity has not lessened over the years, they continued to draw enormous crowds to their infrequent U.S. concerts.

KC and The Sunshine Band extended their string of disco-danceable singles with "I'm Your Boogie Man." And Crosby, Stills and Nash used their soft harmonies and energetic instrumental abilities to produce the top album *CSN*.

▶**JAZZ—A REBIRTH**

It had to happen. In a 1977 *Newsweek* cover story, it was noted that ten years ago there were fewer than 10 jazz clubs in New York City; now there are 80. In Boston, the number has grown in seven years from 1 to 21. And on the West Coast, Los Angeles has twice as many jazz spots as there were three years ago.

The sale of jazz record albums made incredible gains, and the number of people who attended the Newport Jazz Festival in New York "broke all records." It was as if some-

Look again . . . it's not the Beatles, it's their lookalikes, Broadway's *Beatlemania.*

thing entirely new had marched onto the music scene. And, in a sense, it had. A generation of rock 'n' rollers finally "heard" the fresh sounds of Herbie Hancock's V.S.O.P. quintet, and the "free jazz" of pianist Keith Jarrett and saxophonist Anthony Braxton. It was an enthusiastic discovery—and a long-awaited rebirth.

▶ **MUSIC FROM BROADWAY AND FILMS**

Broadway still rocked with the sound of nostalgia. *Grease*, using the sounds and spirit of the "innocent" 1950's, continued to be Broadway's longest-running show. *Hair*, "the" theatrical experience of the 1960's, was brought back to Broadway for another run. And one of the biggest surprises of the theater season was the appearance of *Beatlemania*. In this new production, four young men, who look somewhat like the originals, performed the many songs associated with the Beatles. It wasn't really the same, but it was close enough and the ever-present Beatle fans flocked to the theater.

Three movies led to best-selling albums: the sound tracks of Sylvester Stallone's surprise smash hit *Rocky*; the sensational and indescribable *Star Wars*; and the Streisand/Kristofferson version of *A Star Is Born*.

▶ **AND THEIR SOUND CONTINUES**

It was a big year for Barbra Streisand. Not only did she have a hit with "Evergreen," the love theme from *A Star Is Born*, but she also won an Oscar as the song's co-writer (along with Paul Williams). Barbra's new album, *Superman*, became a Top Ten seller, as did one of its songs, "My Heart Belongs to Me."

Children of the World, the bubbling new album by the Bee Gees.

Debby Boone became a star with her first record.

Man" and his album *JT* both added to his superstar status.

Linda Ronstadt, a prime mover behind the Southern California country-rock sound, recorded a new album, *Simple Dreams*. One of the cuts from the album, "Blue Bayou." was an overnight sensation.

Other established artists whose popularity continued were Natalie Cole (hailed as today's Queen of Soul) with her new single "I've Got Love on My Mind"; and Marvin Gaye, whose *Live at the London Palladium* made him an important force in the recording business.

▶ NEW VOICES

The charts were filled with the names of newcomers. Mary MacGregor's overnight hit "Torn Between Two Lovers" was written by Peter Yarrow (of Peter, Paul, and Mary fame). Nineteen-year-old Andy Gibb, youngest of the Gibb brothers but not part of the Bee Gees, made a name for himself with the number-one single "I Just Want to Be Your Everything." British-born singer Leo Sayer had two top-flight singles in "You Make Me Feel Like Dancing" and "When I Need You," and the hit album *Endless Flight*.

One of the brightest new stars on the horizon has a name from the past. She is Debby Boone, daughter of Pat Boone. Debby recorded "You Light Up My Life" from the film of the same name, and it was an instant hit. She just might be someone to watch out for in the future.

Kris Kristofferson and his wife, Rita Coolidge, sang separately on records, but toured the concert circuit together. Kris had a winner with his *Songs from Kristofferson* album. And Rita had one with *Anytime . . . Anywhere*, which includes the hit song "(Your Love Has Lifted Me) Higher and Higher."

Another couple, Carly Simon and James Taylor, competed in the husband-and-wife record race. Carly did it her way with "Nobody Does It Better." James's record of "Handy

---

1977 GRAMMY AWARDS

Record of the Year	*This Masquerade*	George Benson, artist
Album of the Year	*Songs in the Key of Life*	Stevie Wonder, artist
Song of the Year	*I Write the Songs*	Bruce Johnston, songwriter
New Artist of the Year		Starland Vocal Band
Pop Vocal Performance—female	*Hasten down the Wind*	Linda Ronstadt, artist
Pop Vocal Performance—male	*Songs in the Key of Life*	Stevie Wonder, artist
Rhythm and Blues Vocal Performance—female	*Sophisticated Lady*	Natalie Cole, artist
Rhythm and Blues Vocal Performance—male	*I Wish*	Stevie Wonder, artist
Country Vocal Performance—female	*Elite Hotel*	Emmylou Harris, artist
Country Vocal Performance—male	*Stand by My Woman Man*	Ronnie Milsap, artist
Original Score for a Motion Picture	*Car Wash*	Norman Whitfield, composer
Score from an Original Cast Show	*Bubbling Brown Sugar*	23 composers
Classical Album	*Beethoven: The Five Piano Concertos*	Artur Rubinstein, with Daniel Barenboim conducting the London Philharmonic
Recording for Children	*Prokofiev: Peter and the Wolf/ Saint-Saëns: Carnival of the Animals*	Hermione Gingold, narrator; Karl Böhm conducting the Vienna Philharmonic

HEART *Little Queen*

Two of the most popular new groups on the music scene: ABBA and Heart.

Television again made its contribution to the ranks of hit singers. Tall, blond, and handsome David Soul stepped out of his detective role in the "Starsky and Hutch" TV series and recorded a hit single "Don't Give Up on Us," and a new album *Playing to an Audience of One*.

Shaun Cassidy of the "Hardy Boys" TV series (and younger half-brother of David Cassidy) also moved successfully from the tube to the disc. "That's Rock 'n' Roll" and "Da Doo Ron Ron" were two of his runaway best-selling singles, while *Shaun Cassidy* became a smash album.

New groups also made the charts in 1977. Boston, Kansas, the Commodores, and the Swedish group ABBA all had big hits during the year. Heart, a sextet led by sisters Nancy and Ann Wilson, stood out as a group to watch. Their first album, *Dreamboat Annie*, sold 2,500,000 copies. They followed this success with *Little Queen* (both a single and album) and a rousing single, "Barracuda."

The Floaters, a Detroit group that climbed to the Top Ten chart with "Float On," produced a curious debut album in which each member of the group announced his own astrological sign. This "gimmick" also seemed to work quite well as a drawing card at their live performances.

▶ SOMETHING DIFFERENT

New trends continue to come and go on the music scene. One such trend, the so-called Punk Rock, has attracted attention as the New Wave in music. Punk Rock originated in Britain among unemployed working-class youths. The rock-and-shock music is expressed in a primitive form that is supposed to reflect the disturbed feelings of these deprived young people. In their live performances, some Punk Rockers are abusive and angry. They also tint their hair in unusual colors, paint their faces in odd designs, and wear T-shirts and torn jeans.

The American version of Punk Rock—while stressing less of the sociological cause and more of the musical sound—can be seen and heard in the performance of Kiss, and the strange antics of Alice Cooper.

Fans of Punk Rock view it as the effort of a new generation to find its own identity by shocking the older generation. In their crude-and-rude music, Punk Rockers are turning away from the slick, studio-produced rock of groups like the Eagles and Fleetwood Mac. Critics of Punk Rock dismiss the development as a cultural and musical dead end. It's too soon to tell if Punk Rock will develop into an accepted music trend.

ARNOLD SHAW
Author, *The Rock Revolution*

313

MOVIES MADE FOR YOU

You are far away from home, in a foreign country. You are with two friends when you discover that your uncle plans to kidnap you!

What do you do? Where can you go? Will your friends be able to help you?

These problems face Thomas Okapi in the movie *On the Run.* All ends happily, but before the movie is over there is lots of excitement and adventure for Thomas and his friends.

On the Run was made especially for children. So were *The Sky-Bike* and *Robin Hood Junior.* These films and many others are seen by children all over the world—in movie theaters at Saturday matinees and on television. There are even special mobile units that bring the films to schools, libraries, and other places.

These films were made by the Children's Film Foundation. This British group has been making movies for young people for over 25 years. The purpose of the movies is to entertain —to make children happy. To be sure that the films are interesting and enjoyable, the producers watch how children react when they see the films. Do the children laugh and pay close attention to the story? Or are they bored and restless?

Young people everywhere seem to have the same likes and dislikes when it comes to movies. They like movies with animals, such as dogs, cats, and horses. They like movies in which children play important roles. They like funny movies and cowboy movies. And they like adventure movies—like *The Flying Eye,* in which a boy detective helps stop thieves from stealing a secret formula.

Some of the Children's Film Foundation movies are based on books. *On the Run* is based on a book of the same title by Nina Bawden. Another movie, *The Secret Cave,* is based on a story by the famous novelist Thomas Hardy.

Many of the movies are made in Great Britain. But some have been filmed in Australia, Egypt, Libya, Morocco, the Netherlands, and other countries.

In real life, the young people who star in Children's Film Foundation movies are like typical kids—the kind you would like for friends and schoolmates. Most of them study acting at drama schools. Some of them have gone on to become well-known adult actors and actresses.

But before they grow up, they have lots of fun making movies filled with adventure, comedy, and mystery. And their audiences have lots of fun watching them.

The Sky-Bike. An eccentric inventor wants to win the prize for the first man-powered flying machine. He invents the sky-bike, a strange contraption that is powered by pedaling, and enters it in the contest. The inventor's young friends get the sky-bike airborne and compete against a crooked gang in the exciting race. (Amazingly, in 1977 a young man actually flew a pedal-driven plane over a 1.4-mile [2.3-kilometer] course—the first sustained man-powered flight of a mile or more.)

On the Run. Thomas Okapi, the son of an important African, is staying with his uncle in London. He discovers that his power-mad uncle is going to kidnap him. With the help of two friends, Thomas heads for the seaside—with his uncle in hot pursuit. The youngsters hide in a cave, but Uncle Joseph soon discovers their hideout. The police get there just in the nick of time to save them.

Robin Hood Junior. The year is 1190, and the place is England. In an exciting series of adventures, Robin Hood Junior and his friends battle it out with the wicked Baron de Malherbe and his henchmen.

WHAT DO YOU SEE IN THIS PICTURE?

Paul Revere looks as though he might step right out of this portrait and tell us about his historic horseback ride in April, 1775. But he delivered his warning about the British attack *after* John Singleton Copley did this painting, which was completed sometime between 1765 and 1770.

Here, Paul Revere holds a delicately rounded teapot, smooth and glistening, which he, as a silversmith, had made. He is in shirt sleeves, typical dress of a craftsman in colonial America. The flowing lines of the white shirt show the artist's careful use of detail. Revere's hand is also depicted precisely, with strict attention to the shape of each finger. Copley's feeling for paint, applied thickly and richly, softens the hard lines and slickness of the surface. The artist's use of the tiniest details gives a magic realism that makes the figure in the portrait come alive.

Paul Revere's clear eyes reflect an inner strength that made him a great and popular hero in American history. The air of calm about him bespeaks a man who would fear no danger. This portrait shows a real person. No record tells how many times Paul Revere sat for this portrait, but Copley early showed a great concern for being careful and accurate. He worked with his subjects as many as fifteen or sixteen sittings, at about six hours a stretch. Can you imagine what it would be like to sit still for almost a hundred hours to have your portrait painted!

The way John Singleton Copley could paint individuals so that they actually looked like real people made his personal style very popular. He ranks as the number one portrait painter of colonial America. He was, in fact, the first outstanding artist in the American colonies. Other artists before him had lacked the skill to do beautiful pictures with fine, artistic qualities.

Copley painted in this new country when people were busy establishing homes and towns and farming the land. There were no schools that taught art. He had to figure out his own ways of handling paints on canvas. He did study the work of the few colonial painters he could find. In this way he picked up something of the local flavor that was especially American. Copley showed the dignity of the craftsman and a respect for simplicity in his portrait of Paul Revere. Europeans preferred finer people in their portraits, dressed in elegant satins and laces and jewels.

Copley started painting as a teenager in Boston, where he was born on July 3, 1738. Peter Pelham, his stepfather, taught him engraving (cutting lines into metal). Copley carried the careful use of line over into painting. When Copley was fifteen, he painted *The Gore Children,* stiffly posed with somewhat blank facial expressions. But it was a start.

At eighteen, he painted *Ann Tyng (Mrs. Thomas Smelt).* This and other early pictures made Copley the talk of artistic circles. How pleased he must have been to know he was painting as well as much older Boston painters! He was working all the time, improving his techniques. Bodies began to look more natural. Precise outlining showed that he recorded all the details he observed with much care. He painted many Yankee housewives and many somber merchants and businessmen making good in the New World. One was John Hancock, first signer of the Declaration of Independence.

Around 1766—ten years before the signing of the Declaration of Independence—Copley's career received a great boost. His work *The Boy with the Squirrel* won praise in a London art exhibit.

In 1774, five years after his marriage, Copley went first to Italy and then settled in London. In addition to portrait painting, he turned out canvases of historical events. For about ten years the transplanted American artist continued to win fame.

Then his luck began to run out. For about the last twenty-five years of his life, Copley lost his strength and good health. He could no longer capture events and people in art works. He was unable to earn the money he needed for a living. Maybe good fortune might have lasted longer if he had stayed in America and painted portraits of Americans. *Paul Revere* shows what excellent and typically American work Copley was able to produce. This type of work placed him among the greatest American painters.

Self-portrait. Rubens painted this when he was about 60 years old.

THE PAINTER OF ANTWERP

In the early 1500's, Antwerp was a busy, happy city, an important port and diamond-trading center in what is now Belgium. But by 1568 it was torn apart by religious differences. Among the people who fled the city to avoid death for their beliefs were Jan and Marie Rubens. They eventually settled in Siegen, a small town in what is now West Germany. There, on June 28, 1577, Marie Rubens gave birth to Peter Paul, who would someday be called the Painter of Antwerp.

Peter spent the first ten years of his life in Siegen. It was only after Peter's father died that Marie Rubens was able to return to Antwerp with her children, of whom Peter was the youngest. The city was to be Peter's home for the rest of his life. He traveled widely and spent eight years studying in Italy—but he always returned to the city he loved.

The whole world loves and respects Rubens and the wonderful art he created, and this was made clear in 1977 when the 400th anniversary of his birth was celebrated. But nowhere is he loved more than in Antwerp, which cele-

brated the anniversary with exhibits of his paintings and also of life in that city during the 1600's. There were special foods for the anniversary: Rubens beer, Rubens sauces, and Rubens ice cream. And of course there were many souvenirs for the people who came from all over the world to see the paintings.

The major art exhibits were in museums. But Rubens' paintings were also to be seen in many other places: in Antwerp Cathedral, where he worshiped; in his home, on what is now known as Rubens Street; in the Church of Saint Jacques, where he is buried.

▶ HIS ART

As a teenager Rubens worked as an apprentice to three Antwerp painters. Then in 1600 he went to Italy to study Renaissance art. This was a fairly common practice for artists from northern Europe. Most of these artists became skilled at copying the styles of their teachers. But Rubens went much further. He developed his own style—one that showed the influence of both northern and southern European art

Rubens' chalk sketch of his son Nicholas, done about 1625.

but was at the same time very different from that of earlier artists.

His paintings were full of life. They were large, sometimes covering an entire wall or ceiling. He once wrote, "I confess that I am, by natural instinct, better fitted to execute very large works than little curiosities."

Rubens was a happy man, who enjoyed life; his paintings reflect this. He loved to paint people—romantic couples, playful children, and beautiful women. He used members of his family as models for many of his paintings. Drama and excitement also played important roles in many of his works. He painted men at war, snarling tigers, dogs attacking wild boars, galloping horses.

Mythology provided many subjects for Rubens. He enjoyed painting Greek gods and goddesses in scenes taken from ancient stories. One, for example, shows the sons of Zeus kidnapping the daughters of King Leucippus. Another shows a sad goddess of love and an aloof little cupid; it is based on a Latin saying: "Without gods of wine and corn, love languishes and the goddess of love is chilled."

Religion was another major theme. Rubens was a devout Catholic who went to church every morning. His paintings of the Holy Family, saints, angels, and Adam and Eve were in great demand throughout Europe.

Then there were his portraits. Many of the important businessmen and great leaders of that time commissioned Rubens to paint their pictures. His friendships with important people led to a second career for Rubens—that of diplomat. Because of his fame, his charming personality, and his desire for peace, he was frequently sent on missions between countries. His ability to speak seven languages—Latin, Flemish, English, French, German, Spanish, and Italian—also helped. He worked to bring peace to the Netherlands and, later, to stop the fighting between Spain and England. "For my part," he wrote, "I should like the whole world to be at peace and that we should live in a century of gold and not of iron."

▶ **HOW HE LIVED AND WORKED**

Rubens married in 1609, a year after returning to Antwerp from Italy. His wife, Isabella, bore him three children. She was a gentle, quiet woman and Rubens loved her very much. Thus it was a shock when she died of the plague in 1626.

Tournament near a castle. Knights in armor
battle as the sun sets over a lovely landscape.

Rubens often painted family portraits. Here he strolls in
the garden with his second wife and one of his sons.

Negro heads. Rubens never ceased to study and paint the human anatomy.

Four years later, in 1630, Rubens married again. His new bride, Helena Fourment, was a niece of his first wife. Though she was only 16 years old, she was considered the most beautiful woman in Antwerp. She served as a model for Venus, the Virgin Mary, and other women featured in Rubens' art. And she and Rubens had five children.

The family lived in a large house that Rubens had bought about 1610. In that year—when he was 33—he had already become the best-known painter in his country and one of the most famous painters in Europe. In the course of time he had a two-story studio added onto the house. There he, his assistants, and his pupils could work on the large paintings that had been commissioned by people from many countries.

Sometimes Rubens would make a drawing in chalk. The assistants would use this as a guide as they painted a large work of art. When the assistants were finished, Rubens would look at and improve their painting, adding brushstrokes of color here and there to make it what he had envisioned. The price of the painting would depend on how much work Rubens himself had done on it.

Most of the assistants who worked in his stu-dio never became well-known in their own right. When they left Rubens to set up their own places, they didn't paint masterpieces like those created at Rubens' studio.

Occasionally Rubens would work with other well-known artists, such as Anthony van Dyck or Jan Brueghel. Or he would have a specialist do a particular part of a painting. For example, in a large painting of the Greek god Prometheus, an eagle is painted by Frans Snyder. In a painting of a bear hunt, Paul de Vos painted the animals.

It is believed that Rubens produced about 1,800 paintings during his life. He always worked hard. Even after he was rich and famous, he continued to get up at four o'clock every morning. After going to church, he would work until five in the afternoon.

In general, he enjoyed good health. But as he grew older, he developed gout, a painful, crippling disease of the joints. This finally led to his death on May 30, 1640, shortly after his 63rd birthday.

"It is not important to live long, but to live well," he once said. Rubens lived well. And his name has lived long—through 400 years during which his art has given great pleasure and inspiration to many millions of people.

TUT, THE BOY KING

The ancient Egyptians believed that "you *can* take it with you." In fact, they believed that you *had* to—if you wanted to be ready for your next life.

And so royalty and other wealthy people built large burial tombs. These contained not just the body of the dead person but all sorts of things the person might need or want in the next life: furniture, weapons, jewelry, religious objects, food, sandals, musical instruments, and incense. The more important the person, the bigger the tomb and the richer its contents.

We cannot say if this practice helped the dead. But it was a wonderful practice as far as people living today are concerned. Objects buried in tombs, if they were not stolen by grave robbers, were preserved and kept safe for thousands of years. When the tombs were discovered in the 19th and 20th centuries, they revealed important information about what life was like in ancient Egypt.

The richest discovery of all was the most recent. This was the discovery in 1922 of the tomb of Tutankhamen, a king who ruled Egypt more than 3,300 years ago—probably from about 1334 B.C. to about 1325 B.C. Some 5,000 objects were found in his tomb. Fifty-five of the most splendid of these objects are now touring the United States in an exhibit called "Treasures of Tutankhamen."

Tutankhamen—or Tut, as he is now often called—was only 9 years old when he ascended the throne. While still a child, he married Ankhesenamen, a daughter of Nefertiti. And then suddenly, when he was only 18 or 19, King Tut died. The cause of his death is not known. However, his skull is somewhat damaged, which suggests that he might have been assassinated.

It was the practice in ancient Egypt to mummify the body. This involved several steps. First, all the internal organs except the heart were removed. A mineral called natron was used to dry the body. Then oils and other substances were used to embalm it. Finally, the body was wrapped in linen and placed in a coffin. King Tut's body was actually placed in three coffins, one inside the other. The innermost coffin—that closest to the body—was made of solid gold.

King Tut's internal organs were embalmed separately. The liver, lungs, stomach, and intestines were placed in four miniature coffins, each guarded by a golden statue of a goddess.

The ancient Egyptians buried their royalty in an area along the Nile River called the Valley of the Kings. There, probably after a lavish funeral, King Tut's mummy and belongings were placed in a tomb, which was then sealed. Not too long afterward, robbers broke into the tomb. They stole some gold and jewels and the precious oils and unguents (ointments) that filled vases and jars. But most of the tomb's contents was left behind. As time passed, the sands of the hot, windy valley covered the tomb, hiding it from later bands of robbers.

In the 19th century, archeologists began digging in the valley, looking for tombs. They found more than 30 royal tombs. All of them had been robbed, so they contained relatively few treasures. By the beginning of the 20th century, most archeologists believed that all the tombs in the valley had been discovered. But one young archeologist disagreed.

Howard Carter believed that the tomb of King Tut was somewhere in the Valley of the Kings. He based this belief, in part, on several earlier finds: a cup bearing King Tut's name; a group of pottery jars bearing Tut's seal; and a small tomb containing pictures of Tut and his wife.

Carter convinced a fellow Britisher, Lord Carnarvon, to finance a search for the tomb. In 1918, work began. By 1922, Carnarvon became discouraged. He said he would not finance another year of sifting through sand. Carter pleaded for one last season, and Carnarvon agreed.

On November 4, 1922, the Egyptians who worked for Carter discovered the beginning of a staircase. As they cleared away the overlying material, they came upon a door sealed with the seals of the royal burial place. Carter telegraphed Carnarvon, telling him of the discovery and urging him to come to Egypt.

Carnarvon arrived in Egypt on November 20. By November 26, the door was removed, revealing a passageway that ended in another sealed door. Carter drilled a small hole in the second door and looked in.

"Can you see anything?" asked Lord Carnarvon. "Yes, wonderful things," replied Carter.

This death mask is made of gold, inlaid with semiprecious stones and blue glass. It was placed over the head and shoulders of Tut's mummy, outside the linen bandages that surrounded the entire body. It is thought to be a good likeness of the young king's features.

Carter was looking into the antechamber, the first of four small rooms in the tomb. It was piled high with all sorts of objects— thrones, beds, boxes, weapons, even chariots.

Slowly the men made their way through the antechamber, the annex, the burial chamber, and the treasury. Each room contained priceless treasures.

"The period to which the tomb belongs is in many respects the most interesting in the whole history of Egyptian art," Carter wrote, "and we were prepared for beautiful things. What we were not prepared for was the astonishing vitality and animation which characterized certain of the objects."

The most beautiful of all the objects was found in Tut's coffin. There, covering the King's mummy, was a death mask made of solid gold and inlaid with stones and glass. Its features are those of the young king who lived so very long ago: narrow eyes edged with black, a slender nose, fleshy lips.

The mummy itself was in poor condition. The oils used to preserve the body had partly destroyed it. But we must be thankful for the riches with which the body was surrounded. If the Egyptians hadn't believed that utensils, ornaments, and furnishings were needed in the afterlife, we could never have learned so much about young King Tut and his time.

This elegant statue of the goddess Selket is made of wood covered with gold. On her head is her emblem, a scorpion. The Egyptians believed that Selket had magical powers. The statue was placed in Tut's tomb to protect his mummy against evil.

This small chair is made of ebony and decorated with ivory and gold. Its legs are shaped like the paws of a lion. The chair was probably made for Tut when he was a young boy.

The ancient Egyptians liked ornate jewelry. This beautiful pendant is made of gold, semiprecious stones, and glass. The yellowish scarab in the center is a symbol of the sun god. The scarab has the wings, tail, and hind legs of a falcon, another symbol of the sun god.

A lion sits atop this cosmetic jar that contained scented oils and unguents. Perhaps the lion was meant to suggest the character of King Tut. Or it may represent the god Bes, who was a god of pleasure. The contents of such jars were considered very precious and were removed by ancient robbers who broke into Tut's tomb.

The real stars of *Star Wars* are the brilliant special effects and the extraordinary sets. Fierce spaceship battles in a starry galaxy and the intricate workings of the interior of a spaceship—plus one very strange-looking crew member—are just some of the reasons *Star Wars* is a smash hit.

STAR WARS

If you're going to see *Star Wars* for the first time—or the tenth—be prepared for a spectacular event. And get your hisses, boos, and applause ready, because this is the kind of movie that you will want to react to—out loud. It's all about the good guys against the bad guys, with a princess thrown in for good measure. And it all adds up to total entertainment.

George Lucas, the director of *Star Wars*, describes his film as a "space fantasy." It takes place a long, long time ago in a galaxy thousands of light years from Earth. This galaxy is ruled by the cruel Galactic Emperor and his evil lieutenants, Grand Moff Tarkin and Lord Darth Vader. These are the bad guys, and they are engaged in a war against the good guys—rebel forces on the planet Tatooine. The rebels are determined to rid themselves—and the galaxy—of their cruel masters. But it is not an easy task. The Galactic Emperor has a horrible weapon at his fingertips. That secret weapon is the dreaded Death Star, a huge planet-sized armored battle station that glides through space destroying rebel planets with a single devastating ray. Planets explode into billions of pieces once Death Star has struck. There is no escape.

But don't lose hope. A beautiful rebel princess, Leia Organa, has escaped from the Galactic Empire in her spaceship. She has with her the complex plans of the construction of Death Star. The plans detail all the strengths and the weaknesses of the armored battle station. If the plans can be delivered to the rebel forces, the good guys might be able to launch a successful attack against Death Star.

Grand Moff Tarkin, aware that Princess Leia has fled the empire with the plans, sends Darth Vader and a force of Imperial storm troopers to capture her. Just before the villains' spaceship overtakes the princess' ship, Leia hides the secret plans of Death Star in a robot named Artoo-Deetoo. Then she launches Artoo-Deetoo and his companion robot See-Threepio toward the friendly planet Tatooine in search of help. Shortly after the capsule carrying the two robots blasts off into space, Princess Leia is taken prisoner by Darth Vader and brought to Death Star, and into the hands of wicked Grand Moff Tarkin.

While the evil forces torture brave Princess Leia to make her tell what she has done with the plans, See-Threepio and Artoo-Deetoo safely land on Tatooine in their capsule. There they enlist the help of Luke Skywalker, Han Solo, and Ben Kenobi.

A rescue of Princess Leia and the destruction of Death Star are the objectives of the heroes, but it isn't going to be easy. The good guys know this, but nothing will deter them from their mission. The suspense builds as Han Solo, his copilot the Wookiee Chewbacca (a huge apelike creature), Luke, and Ben Kenobi guide their spaceship into outer space. The journey is a perilous one. The good guys encounter the bad guys and fight a furious laser-bolt battle in space. The good guys win the battle, but they know that more difficult problems will await them if they reach Death Star.

Will their venture end in success or failure? Will they rescue Princess Leia? Will Luke, Han, and Ben Kenobi be able to destroy the terrible Death Star before it can wield its destructive powers? Will the good guys rule the galaxy in peace and harmony, or will the cruel Galactic Emperor, the evil Grand Moff Tarkin, and all the other bad guys continue to hold power over the universe? The last half hour of the film answers these questions in some of the most exciting and suspenseful action ever seen on the motion picture screen.

▶ **BEHIND THE SCENES**

Harrison Ford (Han Solo), Mark Hamill (Luke Skywalker), Carrie Fisher (Princess Leia), Alec Guinness (Ben Kenobi), and Peter Cushing (Grand Moff Tarkin) are the leading actors in *Star Wars*. But the audiences seem to enjoy the extraordinary special effects more than anything else in the film.

In all, there are more than 350 special effects in *Star Wars*, ranging from star-studded outer space to arid planets, to monsters, robots, and galactic weapons. How in the world—or out of the world—did the makers of the film do it? Perhaps the easiest part was finding an arid planet that resembled Tatooine. Fortunately the movie crew didn't have to leave planet Earth for that. They found just what they were looking for in southern Tunisia, on the edge of the great Sahara desert in Africa. The construction crew worked for eight weeks

These two men are up to no good. The villainous Grand Moff Tarkin and Lord Darth Vader control the Galactic Empire by using the force of the dreaded Death Star.

Good guy Luke Skywalker questions Artoo-Deetoo and See-Threepio about their mission on Tatooine.

to turn the desert and towns into a faraway planet. The people who live in that remote area of Tunisia make their homes in caves cut into the sides of craterlike holes in the ground. These underground homes—used as protection from the scorching heat of summer and the bitter cold of winter—were perfect settings for the planet Tatooine.

The rest of the special effects weren't as easy to produce. Many of the effects were taken care of with trick photography, difficult camera work, and extravagant costumes. However, the spaceships, the interstellar flights, the blazing space battles, and the hand-to-hand duels with laserlike sabers were another matter. So were the robots, the Sand People, and the other strange characters in the film. But it really wouldn't be fair to give away all the secrets of *Star Wars*. However, we can reveal one little and one big secret. The two robots, See-Threepio and Artoo-Deetoo, are played by real people—one short actor and one tall actor.

Whatever the secrets, *Star Wars* is one of the biggest, most exciting films of the year. Just sit back, hiss the villains and cheer the heroes, and wonder at the magic that unfolds on the screen before your eyes. And above all, let your imagination run free. That's the real secret of *Star Wars*.

It's a chilling moment when the evil Imperial storm troopers on Tatooine question Luke and his friend Ben Kenobi about the two robots.

The situation appears hopeless as Princess Leia, Han Solo, and Chewbacca find themselves trapped on Death Star. Will the heroes escape? You'll have to see *Star Wars* to find out!

Mikhail Baryshnikov and Natalia Makarova, dancing in *Sleeping Beauty*, are ballet superstars.

BALLETOMANIA

A 600-year-old art has recently been "discovered." This very popular art is ballet. Millions of people attend ballet programs each year. Ski champions and football players are taking ballet lessons to improve balance and develop stronger bodies. Teenagers are copying the fashions worn by dancers—bulky leg warmers, stretchy leotards, the layered look. People lined up outside movie houses to see *The Turning Point,* a film about the ballet world in which some of today's leading ballet dancers are featured.

The craze is called "balletomania." And the people who spend many of their evenings in the theater watching their favorite dancers are called "balletomanes." They cheer loudly as the dancers execute an especially graceful passage. They shower the dancers with bouquets of roses and demand curtain call after curtain call.

What has caused the great rise in interest in this art? Why is it suddenly so popular?

Television, for one thing, has helped. First, it has increased our interest in visual forms of communication, as opposed to verbal forms, such as talking and reading. This is especially true for younger people, who have grown up with television. It may help explain why young people dominate so many ballet audiences.

Second, television has broadcast a number of beautiful ballets in recent years. After seeing the graceful dancers in *Giselle* and the comic mice in *The Nutcracker* on a small TV screen, people are anxious to see what the ballets look like on stage. And once they have seen ballet on stage, they're hooked.

Much of the increased interest in ballet is also due to such superstars of dance as Rudolf Nureyev and Mikhail Baryshnikov. These two men were born in the Soviet Union. Both were well-known dancers before defecting to the West. Nureyev left the Soviet Union in 1961, Baryshnikov in 1974. Another outstanding Soviet dancer, Natalia Makarova, also defected to the West. These three dancers received a great deal of publicity when they left the Soviet Union. Photographs of them dancing appeared in newspapers and on television. They were interviewed, written about, and talked about. Before long, Nureyev became as well-known as Joe Namath, and people were as anxious to see the dancer perform as they were to watch the football quarterback in action.

(In fact, there are definite similarities between a dancer such as Nureyev and a football

The lovely and romantic *Giselle* is one of the oldest and best-loved ballets.

player such as Namath. Both are involved in a very demanding physical activity. Both started with great natural talent and worked very long and hard to reach the top of their profession.)

Most of the top dancers began studying ballet when they were only eight or nine years old. Before long, they were spending many hours a week in class and many additional hours practicing on their own. And the study and the practice never end. Although they are among the world's best dancers, Nureyev, Baryshnikov, and Makarova continue to take lessons and to practice every day.

Great dancing is more than technical skill. It involves artistry, grace, and style. When a dancer leaps into the air, the height of his jump is only one thing to look at. How did he prepare for the jump? How does his body look as he moves—are his arms in the proper position, his legs stretched, his toes pointed? Does he land gracefully?

Why did the Soviet dancers come to the West and to the United States? "We had to come to America because the standards of dancing are the highest and the choreography beyond anywhere else," said Baryshnikov.

Choreography is the arrangement of a dance. It tells each dancer what steps he or she must do. It describes how the dancers are ar-

ranged, both in relation to one another and to the space in which they are dancing.

The choreographer—the person who "composes" the ballet—must relate the dancers' movements to the music and to the story or idea of the ballet. Since words are rarely spoken in ballets, the dancers must express moods as well as actions by the way they move. Unless they do this well, the audience won't understand what is happening. The stage setting and the costume design must also be appropriate. Thus, four arts are involved in putting together a ballet: dancing, music, drama, and decor.

Choreographers often create ballets for specific dancers. They sense a dancer's strengths and bring them out. Twyla Tharp saw Baryshnikov's potential for comedy and so she wrote *Push Comes to Shove* for him, a ballet that gently makes fun of the world of classical dance.

Almost any theme may be the basis of a ballet. Many of the oldest and best-loved ballets, such as *Giselle* and *Swan Lake,* have romantic themes. Others have a comic or a patriotic theme. George Balanchine's *Stars and Stripes,* for example, which is danced to the marches of John Philip Sousa, is a tribute to the American way of life.

Swan Lake tells the story of Odette, the Swan Queen.

La Fille Mal Gardée is a comic ballet with a very happy ending.

Three sailors on shore leave spend a night on the town in *Fancy Free.*

Here are brief descriptions of some popular ballets that you would probably enjoy:

Giselle. This ballet is based on a legend about what happens to girls who are engaged to marry but die before their wedding takes place. According to the legend, their spirits return at night to dance in the moonlight. Giselle is a peasant girl who discovers that the man she loves is not a peasant as he had pretended, but a nobleman, and engaged to a noblewoman. She dies of a broken heart, or, in some versions, by killing herself.

That night, she and the other spirits rise from their graves. The nobleman sees Giselle and joins her. The other spirits try to kill him. But Giselle saves him by dancing with him until dawn, when she and the other spirits must return to their graves. This is one of the greatest and most important ballets ever written. All the world's great ballerinas have danced Giselle.

La Fille Mal Gardée. This comic ballet was first produced in 1786. It is one of the oldest ballets still danced. It tells the story of a young girl, Lise, whose mother wants her to marry the son of a rich neighboring farmer. But Lise outwits her mother (in very funny episodes) and marries the boy she loves.

Rodeo. Choreographed by world-famous Agnes de Mille, this ballet takes place in the American Southwest. At a Saturday-night dance, all the men ignore a cowgirl dressed in jeans. She leaves and changes into a pretty dress. When she returns, all the men cluster around her. The ballet, set to music by Aaron Copland, includes a square dance, complete with caller and hand clapping.

Swan Lake. Danced to the music of Tchaikovsky, this is the story of Odette, the Swan Queen. Odette is really a princess who has had a spell cast on her by a wicked magician. At night she is human but during the day she is a swan. The spell can be broken only by a man who loves her, and her alone. Prince Siegfried falls in love with Odette. The magician wants to prevent his spell from being broken. So he has his own daughter, Odile, impersonate Odette. Prince Siegfried is fooled at first, but then he realizes his mistake. In some versions, the Prince fights with the magician and defeats him, thus breaking the spell. In other versions, the broken-hearted Odette must return to the lake. *Swan Lake* is one of the most popular ballets ever danced.

Fancy Free. This is a humorous story about three sailors on shore leave. The sailors spend an enjoyable evening dancing and flirting with three girls. The ballet combines classical choreography with jitterbug and modern dance steps.

Young dancers practice at the *barre* at the American Dance Center school.

A VERY SPECIAL SCHOOL

"Pull in your stomachs!"

"Straighten the back!"

"Bring those shoulders forward!"

It's Saturday morning. Some 25 youngsters at the American Dance Center in New York City are working at the *barre* and listening to teacher Tom Stevens. This very special school teaches ballet. And the boys and girls in the class are just a few of the hundreds of thousands of children who are taking ballet classes today.

"Eyes focus forward!"

"Pull the thighs up!"

"Toes on the floor!"

These children know that the most important thing a young dancer must learn is discipline. Dancers must be able to pay attention and to work within a structure. Steps must be practiced again and again until they are exactly right. It's not just a matter of putting the feet in the right place. Every part of the body must be held and moved correctly.

Ballet training should begin when children are between the ages of 8 and 12. When they are older, their bodies are not as flexible, and it's much more difficult for them to develop the combination of grace, strength and agility that are needed to perform the various steps.

Most dance schools exist on their own. But some schools are connected with dance companies. The American Dance Center, for example, is the school of the Alvin Ailey American Dance Theater. When the students at this school are about 14 years old, they may try out, or audition, to enter a special program. After one or two years in this program, the best students can join the Alvin Ailey company, and perform on stages around the world.

That is the dream of the students in Tom Stevens' class. But they all know that it will take a great deal of work even to hope that their dream may come true.

Stephanie is the real-life subject of the book *A Very Young Dancer.*

A VERY YOUNG DANCER

"My name is Stephanie. . . . I've been taking [ballet] lessons since I was six. I'm ten now. My sister Andrea, who is twelve, started when she was eight. We both go to The School of American Ballet. She's taking toe this year and she lets me try on her slippers. Next year I'll take toe for five minutes at the end of each class. Andrea says it makes you feel big but that's just in the beginning. After a while it just hurts. You get blisters and bunions. Her feet are a mess. You should see them."

This is in the opening of the book *A Very Young Dancer,* by Jill Krementz. It tells all about the real-life Stephanie and her dancing. In pictures and text, the book describes what it is like to study ballet and to dance a lead role in a famous ballet.

The book begins with a photograph of Stephanie working at the *barre*—something a dancer does every day of her or his life. There are 28 students in her class, which meets three times a week.

Most of the young students in her school want to be in the New York City Ballet's production of *The Nutcracker.* They audition on a Saturday afternoon in the fall. Stephanie is nervous when it's her turn to audition. But she does well, and is chosen to dance the part of Mary—a starring role.

The following weeks are very busy. Stephanie has about five rehearsals every week. She has to be measured for costumes and fitted for shoes.

Finally, it's opening day. Stephanie's family comes to watch. So does her very first ballet teacher. After the ballet is over, many people go backstage to congratulate her, and some people even ask for her autograph.

Stephanie, a very young dancer, may one day be a famous ballerina.

Then again, she might decide to do something with horses. She really likes horses, too.

THE NUTCRACKER

It's Christmas Eve. A little girl named Mary is having a wonderful time at her family's party. She and her friends are playing games and dancing. Soon the presents are given out. Mary's godfather gives Mary a wooden Nutcracker doll dressed in a uniform of red and blue. Mary loves her Nutcracker doll, even though it isn't very handsome.

After the party is over, the family goes to sleep, but Mary leaves her bed and goes back to the living room, where she has left her Nutcracker. Cradling it in her arms, she falls asleep on the sofa.

Suddenly, noises awaken her. She opens her eyes and sees that the Christmas tree is growing taller and taller. Her toys are growing too, and soon they are as big as she is. A group of giant mice rush into the room, scaring Mary.

The Nutcracker has also grown. He and the toy soldiers have come to life, and they battle the mice with swords and a cannon. Just as the Mouse King tries to attack Mary, the Nutcracker kills him. The other mice run away.

The living room fades away. Mary finds herself in a beautiful forest. Coming toward her is the Nutcracker, who has changed into a handsome Prince. Hand in hand, they walk off into the distance.

As morning comes, Mary and the Prince reach the Land of Sweets—a wonderful place where the streets are made of candies and the buildings are of fancy cakes and cookies. Traveling in a ship made of gilded walnut shells, the young travelers sail down rivers of lemonade and orange juice to the palace of the Sugar Plum Fairy.

The fairy invites the children to sit on a throne made of white icing. They are given cakes and ice cream and many other delicious things to eat. And they are entertained by dancing food from all over the world: chocolates from Spain, teas from China, coffee from Arabia. Even the Sugar Plum Fairy and her handsome Cavalier dance for them.

But it's time to leave. Mary and her Prince fly off in a sleigh pulled by reindeer. As they leave, the Sugar Plum Fairy and all the other wonderful people in the Land of Sweets wave good-bye.

And so ends *The Nutcracker,* one of the world's favorite stories. Each year, hundreds of dance groups perform this fairy-tale ballet. Sometimes the story is slightly different. For example, in some versions the little girl's name is Clara. She wakes up at the end, as if the whole adventure had just been a dream.

Many of the parts in *The Nutcracker* are danced by young people, including the party guests, the soldiers, the mice, and, of course, Mary and the Prince.

The Nutcracker is an enchanting experience —for the children on stage as well as those in the audience. It's just what each of us wishes would happen on Christmas Eve—or any other night of the year.

Mary loves her wooden Nutcracker doll, which she received as a Christmas gift.

The Nutcracker and the toy soldiers have come to life and battle the mice.

Dancing foods from all over the world perform in the Land of Sweets.

Eyes and mouths are drawn on pads of paper. With a flick of the page, the expressions on these characters' "faces" change.

MUMMENSCHANZ

Two people are on a stage. Their faces seem to be made of modeling clay. One person molds the clay and re-arranges his face— making it more and more handsome. The other person has no such luck. No matter how he molds the clay, he only makes himself look worse. He becomes very upset, especially as he watches the other person. Then the two people slam into each other, head-on. The two faces merge into one big gray blob.

No words are spoken while this takes place. Nor are words spoken by another performer who wanders into the audience and tears off her eyes and mouth. A 10-year-old from the audience rushes over to put a new face on the performer's boxlike head. With adhesive tape, the youngster makes eyes, a nose, and a crooked, grinning mouth. Another youngster adds hair of colored wool.

These are some of the funny, strange, and unusual things that are done by three performers in a show called *Mummenschanz*. The performers do everything in mime. This is an art that uses only movements of the body to communicate ideas and feelings. Words are never spoken.

The group's name comes from two German words—*Mummen,* meaning "game" or "play" and *Schanz,* meaning "chance." The name is based on two traditions. One dates from the Middle Ages, when gamblers wore masks so that other people couldn't tell by looking at their faces if they held good card hands or poor ones. The other is a Swiss folk tradition in which people taking part in village celebrations wore masks to hide their identities.

The performers dress in black leotards in almost every skit. It is the incredible masks that provide new costumes for each new skit. The performers make their own masks, often using common everyday objects. Pads of notepaper and rolls of toilet paper become eyes and mouths. Soap bubbles stream from a character's mouth. Sometimes a performer tears the mask off another performer—but there is always another mask underneath. "What is it?" cries someone in the audience. Trying to guess is half the fun.

When the show is finished, the actors take a curtain call to great applause. And at last, the audience sees their faces. But the audience never hears their voices.

In the spring of 1978, *Mummenschanz* will tour many U.S. cities. See it if you can. It's a very special show.

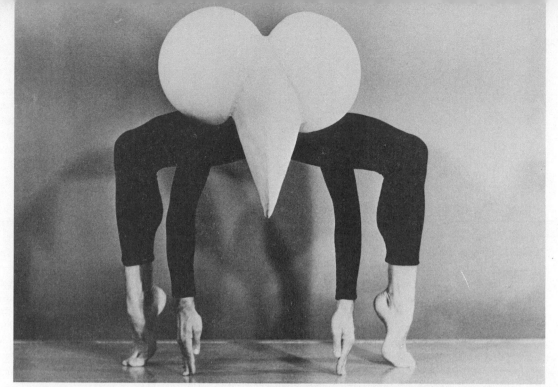

A simple mask, plain black leotards: Is it a bird? . . . an insect? . . . or is it something else? What do you think?

Soap bubbles and uncurled party favors are used to show how disturbed and agitated this character is.

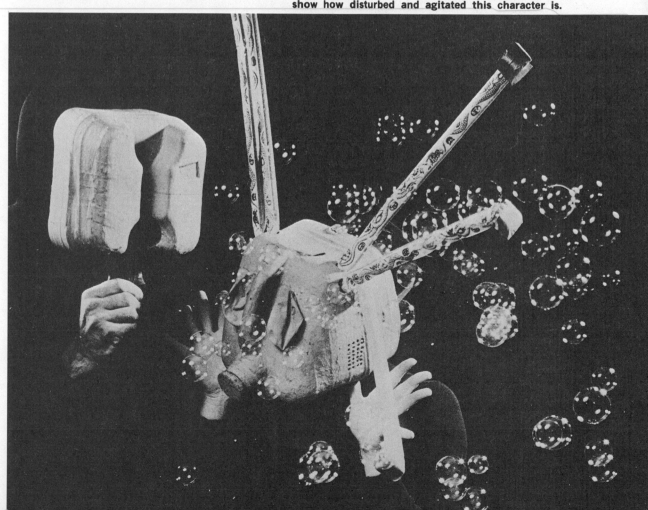

THE DYER'S ART

Each spring nature produces an abundance of plants—in the fields, in the forests, even high up in the mountains. If we pay close attention to these gifts of nature, we can learn many things. Stop by the roadside and look carefully at the goldenrod, the tansy, some Queen Anne's lace, or the pokeberry bush that you may see growing there. Years ago such plants played an important part in people's lives. Some were used as food, some for medicine, and some for the beautiful colors they produced when they were prepared as dyes.

When you visit a museum, you may admire the colorful embroidery work made by the ancient Egyptians, the Indians of North and South America, and the early American colonists. The colors you see came from many different plants. These colors have held fast on the fabrics for hundreds, even thousands, of years.

Today there is a renewed interest in dye plants. Many people are experimenting with plants to produce unusual colors on wool, cotton, silk, linen, angora, and other natural fibers. (It is only on natural fibers that these natural colors will "hold fast.")

▶ WHERE DYES COME FROM

Some of the plants that today's "nature dyers" use can be found close to home. They may be common weeds, such as goldenrod, dandelion, yarrow, and plantain; or garden flowers, such as dahlias, roses, marigolds, and irises. People who live in the city can invade their kitchens for onion skins, carrot tops, beets, and frozen or canned blueberries, all of which make good dyes. There are also some rather more unusual dye sources, many of which come from faraway places.

• If marigolds are used as a dye plant, the orange or yellow blossoms should be snapped off just before they start to fade. The flower heads should then be "de-petaled." The petals can be used fresh or placed on a screen to dry in the sun for a few days. If they are dried, they can then be stored in jars or plastic bags. They will dye just as pretty a yellow, orange, or green after being stored for six months as they will when freshly picked.

• A person who goes on a walk through the early autumn woods may find the maple-leaf viburnum. This is a small bushlike tree (usually found growing near maple trees) that bears tiny blue-black berries. These berries give a good range of colors: purple, violet, black, brown, and green. The colors fade

Pokeberries

Orange day lilies

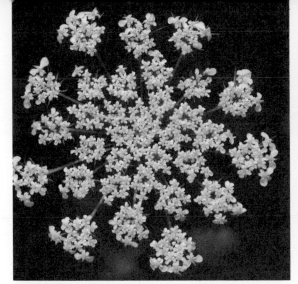

Queen Anne's lace

Maple-leaf viburnum

Irises

Marigolds

Dahlias

Dandelions

Picking pokeberries.

Squashing the berries to release the dye juices.

Dyeing the wool in the pokeberry dyebath.

Hanging the pokeberry-dyed wool on a tree to dry.

quickly though, actually changing overnight. But this is still an interesting plant to work with, for even the faded colors are very pretty.

• For a silvery-gray color, look for the staghorn sumac tree with its clusters of fuzzy red berries. This usually grows in sunny places at the edge of woods or vacant lots. Be sure not to go near the white-berried sumac, though, because it is poisonous.

Sumac dyes best when it has been hung up in bunches and dried out like hay. Some branches should be cut off (leaves, berries, and all), tied in small bunches, and hung in a garden shed or attic. Once the sumac has dried, chop up the whole plant for use in the dyeing process.

• An unusual dye source is a lichen that clings to rocks high up in the mountains. This is the umbilicaria, which strongly resembles a flattened-out, dried-up mushroom top. Umbilicaria yields brilliant fuschia, purple, maroon, violet, and pink colors. But it will not yield any color at all unless it is soaked in ammonia for fifteen to thirty days.

• Another unusual dye source is the cochineal bug, which produces a rich scarlet dye color. This tiny, scaly bug thrives in parts of South America, where it feeds on cactus plants. (Cochineals are being bred today in the American Southwest, which is also cactus country.) Once these bugs are collected and dried, they are pounded into a powder for dyeing purposes.

Until South America was conquered by Spain, the red dye of the cochineal bugs was known only to the South American Indians. Their kings and priests wore beautiful red and purple robes colored by the cochineal dyes. When the Spanish conquistadors arrived in South America, they admired the vivid robes of the Indian noblemen. On learning that their wonderful colors came from bugs, the Spaniards shipped thousands of the little cochineals back to Spain along with their gold and silver plunder.

• Logwood is another interesting dye source. This comes from South America in the form of small brownish-red pieces of woody bark from the logwood tree. The dye extracted from this bark can be either rose-brown or black in color. Logwood is so hard that the Indians of South America, who know it well, call it "the hatchet breaker."

• Then there is madder root, which comes from Australia. Madder root gives colors that range from red to soft apricot. The dye is extremely strong and lasting. In fact, madder root is so strong and penetrating that the sheep that eat it regularly are found (on being butchered) to have red bones.

COLORS AND MORDANTS

The story of the art of dyeing is the story of colors. But it is also the story of substances called mordants, which must be used in the dyeing process to make the colors "hold fast" to the yarn being dyed. If mordants are not used, the colors being transferred to the yarn will usually fade away in the sunlight or run away in the wash water or the rain.

Most mordants are metallic salts, such as the salts of chrome, iron, copper, and tin. Alum is another mordant, and it is especially effective when mixed with cream of tartar. Still other mordants are vinegar; sea salt; and tannic acid, which is found in nuts, roots, and tree bark.

Some mordants do more than just make the color of the plant juice hold fast to the yarn being dyed. They produce an interesting change in the color. For example, goldenrod is known for its lovely yellow dye, which is drawn forth by a mordant of alum mixed with cream of tartar. However, goldenrod will also produce a stunning orange color if the yarn is first "mordanted" with chrome salts. And a pretty green shade emerges if iron salts are used.

Tin salts, when added directly to the dyebath (the big pot in which the plant juice and the yarn are being cooked), will brighten whatever color the yarn is being dyed. For example, a skein of wool being dyed with cochineal will turn a brighter red with the addition of a small amount of tin salts. If you want to darken or dull your dye, however, an addition of iron salts will do the job. In colonial times, women would "sadden," or darken, their wools by adding rusty nails to the dyebath.

STEPS IN DYEING

Only natural dye sources (mainly plants) and natural fibers (obtained from either animals or plants) are used in "nature dyeing." The very best natural fiber for a beginner at the dyeing art is wool, because it takes dye colors beautifully and is quite easy to work with. Natural wool comes in several different shades, but you should use either fleece or white yarn that has not been chemically treated. The steps by which skeins of wool yarn are dyed are similar to the steps used for most other animal fibers, with the exception of silk. (Silk has its own special, and different, "dyeing lore.")

Preparing the plants. The first step in dyeing is to gather and prepare (this often means "chop up") the plants you want to use. Some plants are best used fresh, but others are best used after being dried for weeks or sometimes even months.

The mordant bath. The next step is to mordant the wool. Use a 4-gallon (15-liter) enamel pot for your mordant bath, and put 3 gallons (11 liters) of rainwater or softened tap water in it. Then dissolve the mordant in a little warm water and add it to the pot. Next add one pound (.4 kilograms) of *thoroughly wet* wool yarn. Simmer the bath for one hour. Then remove the wool and place it in a rinse bath of hot water. After rinsing, remove the wool and place it on a board or tray to drain.

Now the wool is ready for dyeing. Chrome-mordanted wool should be dyed right away, but wool mordanted with other substances can be stored for some time.

Preparing the dyebath. First soak the plant materials you have already prepared. Use a 4-gallon (15-liter) enamel pot (the "dyepot") three quarters full of "plant stuff" and filled to the top with water. Depending on the firmness of the plant stuff, the soaking time can vary from overnight (for flower petals) to a week or more (for twigs and tree bark). After the soaking, the plant stuff and its water must be boiled from one to two hours. Add more water from time to time if any boils away. You now have your dyebath. You may leave the plant stuff in the dyepot during the next step, the dyeing.

Dyeing. Now put 1 pound (.4 kilograms) of *wet* wool yarn into the dyebath *all at once*. When the wool is in, push it down gently under the dye juice. Make sure you leave enough room in the pot so that the wool isn't packed in and can float a little.

Simmer the wool in the dyebath for one hour. If the color you want develops before the hour has passed, stop dyeing and start rinsing the wool. You can use the same dyebath for a second and third batch of wool, but each succeeding batch will be a paler shade.

After the dyeing, the wool skeins must be rinsed in hot water until the rinse water is clear, and then hung up to dry. The drying will take place quickest outdoors in the sunlight—but at this point the most delicate dyes will fade somewhat. Still, it may be better to have them fade now rather than after the wool has been woven into cloth.

▶EXPERIMENTING WITH AN ONION

For a quick adventure in dyeing, you might start with the skins of an onion. But do bear in mind that this is not quite like regular dyeing because the processes take place much faster and the wool does not need to be mordanted in advance in the usual way.

First get the dried skins of five or six large onions. Place the skins in a 4-quart (3.7-liter) enamel pot. Cover the skins with water and simmer for fifteen minutes. Add one heaping teaspoonful of salt and stir. Now add a small skein of wet wool yarn. Simmer the onion skins and the wool for about fifteen minutes, after first bringing the dyebath to a brief boil. In just these few minutes, your wool will turn a lovely yellow-orange color, and you will have had your first success at the dyer's art.

▶IF YOU BECOME A DYER

To become a dyer is to become a naturalist, a cook, and a chemist. The naturalist in you will be able to recognize many different plants at all the different stages of their growth. You will learn just where the plants can be found and at what time of the year they are best picked to make the best dye colors. As a cook, you will get the knack of filling your dyepot the best way, stirring your wool skeins with a practiced hand, and of simmering the wool and plant stuff together just the right amount of time. And the chemist in you will be in charge of just which mordants will marry best with which plants to create the loveliest colors.

A wonderful moment will come at the end of the dyeing when you look at your colorful wool skeins hanging in the sunlight. How proud you will be that it was your skill, matched to nature's bounty, that brought forth this little bit of the rainbow.

RUTH AGAR CASTINO
Author, *Spinning and Dyeing the Natural Way*

THE NEW BOOK OF KNOWLEDGE
1978

The following articles are from the 1978 edition of *The New Book of Knowledge.* They are included here to help you keep your encyclopedia up to date.

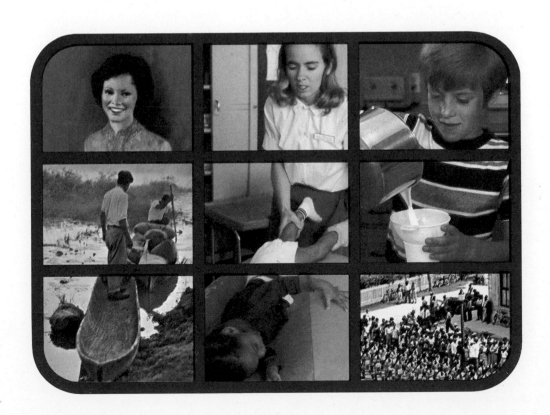

DJIBOUTI

The Republic of Djibouti is one of Africa's newest nations. Formerly known as the French Territory of the Afars and the Issas, it became independent in 1977. Djibouti is a small, sparsely populated desert land with virtually no natural resources. Its chief assets are its strategic location at the southern entrance to the Red Sea, its port and capital, also called Djibouti, a railroad, and French military bases.

▶ THE PEOPLE

Estimates of the population of Djibouti vary considerably, since many of its people are nomads. Their existence in an inhospitable land depends on constant traveling in search of

The Great Mosque in the city of Djibouti. Almost all the people of the country are Muslims.

pasture for their herds of camels and flocks of goats and sheep. Often the herdsmen cross into neighboring countries seeking new pasture. It has been said that there are about twice as many goats in Djibouti as people, who number approximately 125,000. About half the population lives in the city of Djibouti.

The two main ethnic groups are the Afars, who have close ties to neighboring Ethiopia, and the Issas, who are related to the people of nearby Somalia. There are also some Europeans, chiefly French, and Arabs in the coastal towns. Except for the Europeans, almost all the people are Muslims. Languages spoken include French, Afar, Somali (spoken by the Issas), and Arabic. The coming of independence has little affected the nomadic people of the interior, who still live much as their ancestors did.

▶ THE LAND

Djibouti has an area of 8,800 square miles (23,000 square kilometers). It is located in northeastern Africa, just north of the landmass known as the Great Horn. It is bordered by Ethiopia on the north, west, and south, by Somalia on the southeast, and by the Gulf of Aden on the east.

Most of the country consists of arid plains, but there are mountains that rise to a height of 5,000 feet (1,500 meters). A narrow coastal plain lies along the Gulf of Aden. The land is barren and desolate with sharp cliffs and deep ravines. About 90 percent of the country is classified as desert. Most of the rest is pastureland. The vegetation is made up largely of thorn shrub, cactus, and sparse grasses, which provide meager grazing for the herds and flocks of the nomads. There are a few irrigated orchards and palm groves. Overgrazing of the land has led to soil erosion throughout most of the country.

▶ THE CLIMATE

The climate is very hot. From May to October temperatures average 92° F (33° C), and temperatures as high as 113° F (45° C) have been recorded. The weather is only slightly cooler between November and April. Through part of the year, winds blowing from the Arabian desert across the Gulf of Aden bring dry air and no moisture. Rainfall is scanty.

THE ECONOMY

Djibouti has no useful mineral deposits or other natural resources except for livestock. About half the population lives by animal herding. There is some fishing, and a few people make their living from the soil. With practically no arable land, almost all the country's food must be imported. There is almost no manufacturing except for soft drink bottling companies and meat processing plants.

The mainstay of the economy is the port of Djibouti, which lies in a natural harbor on the Gulf of Tadjoura, an inlet of the Gulf of Aden. It is a free port, which means that no customs duties need be paid. Djibouti owes much of its importance to its location on the waters leading to and from the Suez Canal, and the city is a port of call for ships using the canal. Many of the people in the city work on the docks and in ship repair shops.

A second important source of income is the railroad, which links Ethiopia with the port of Djibouti. The port is Ethiopia's main outlet to the sea and is thus vital to that country's economy. Over 50 percent of Ethiopia's imports and exports pass through Djibouti by way of the railroad.

The French military garrison, which remained in Djibouti after independence, also provides some revenue. In addition, France contributes an annual subsidy to keep the economy going.

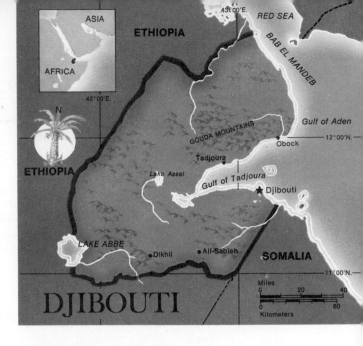

DJIBOUTI

FACTS AND FIGURES

REPUBLIC OF DJIBOUTI is the official name of the country.

CAPITAL: Djibouti.

LOCATION: Northeastern Africa. **Latitude**—10° 52' N to 12° 43' N. **Longitude**—41° 48' E to 43° 25' E.

AREA: 8,800 sq mi (23,000 km²).

POPULATION: 125,000 (estimate).

LANGUAGE: French, Afar, Somali, Arabic.

GOVERNMENT: Republic. **Head of state**—president. **Head of government**—prime minister. **International cooperation**—Arab League.

ECONOMY: Agricultural products—livestock, dates, garden vegetables. **Industries and products**—transit trade, ship's supplies, hides, soft drink bottling, meat processing. **Chief exports**—hides, cattle, coffee (in transit from Ethiopia). **Chief imports**—food, cotton goods, cement, chemicals. **Monetary unit**—Djibouti franc.

HISTORY AND GOVERNMENT

Because of its nearness to the Asian continent, Djibouti was long an arrival point for migrations from Asia to Africa. Between the 8th and 10th centuries Arabs converted the people of the region to Islam. The French became interested in the area in the 19th century and signed treaties with the local chiefs. The French wanted influence in the region to counter British influence in Aden—now Yemen (Aden)—across the Red Sea. After the Suez Canal was opened and Britain became active in Egypt, France claimed a protectorate over the area—in 1885. The colony was known as French Somaliland. It remained a protectorate until 1958, when it became a French overseas territory.

The name French Territory of the Afars and the Issas was adopted in 1967 after the people voted to keep their country an overseas territory of France. Ten years later, however, the people voted for independence, which was declared on June 27, 1977.

The two problems facing Djibouti are the lack of a true economic base upon which to develop the country, and the claims of its larger neighbors, Ethiopia and Somalia. Ethiopia regards the railroad link with Djibouti as vital to its interests. Somalia has traditionally claimed the land in which the Issa people live. Djibouti's future depends on whether these problems can be solved.

HUGH C. BROOKS
St. John's University

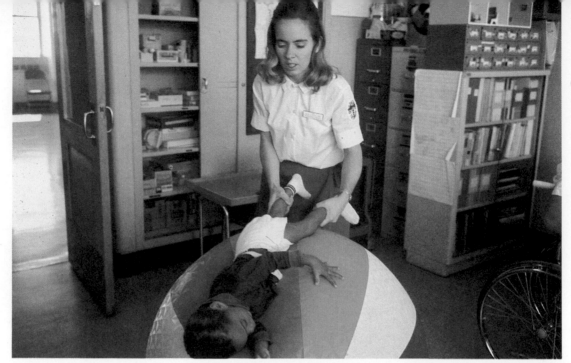

In a specially equipped schoolroom, an occupational therapist works with a disabled child to improve his co-ordination and balancing skills.

OCCUPATIONAL THERAPY

Most people can walk, write, dress, and feed themselves with no help from others. In fact, most of us do these and countless other things almost without thinking about them.

There are many people, however, who have disabilities, or handicaps, that make it difficult for them to perform even the easiest tasks. Some disabilities, often those that are present at birth, are permanent. Disabilities that are a result of an accident or an illness may be temporary. Disabled people may be paralyzed (unable to move parts of the body), crippled, blind, or deaf. They may have lost an arm or a leg, or the ability to control certain muscles.

These physical problems often lead to emotional ones. Frequently, disabled people become depressed because they cannot do what they once did, or what their friends and members of their family can do. Sometimes the emotional problems are as difficult to cure as the physical ones.

Occupational therapy is a form of treatment that helps the handicapped lead happier lives. Through a carefully planned program, occupational therapists teach the disabled to perform the activities that are part of self-care, school, work, and leisure.

▶ HOW OCCUPATIONAL THERAPY HELPS

The chief goal of occupational therapy is to help patients through a program of "curing by doing." The more patients can do by themselves, both physically and creatively, the faster their boredom and depression are overcome.

Planning the Program

The first thing a therapist does is to evaluate the patient's physical ability. After studying such things as muscular strength, sight, hearing, and motor coordination, the therapist knows how much the patient can do alone and when help is needed.

Next, the therapist must find out how the patient gets along with others. The therapist studies the patient's ability to work and share with other people, and to enjoy their company and learn from them.

The planning of the overall therapy program is usually worked out with the patient, the members of the patient's family, and professional people such as the family doctor and a vocational counselor. This joint planning helps to make certain that all the patient's needs will be met.

Treatment

Often therapists use activities, or in some cases special crafts, to improve a patient's control of weak or damaged muscles. When the muscles are strong enough, the patient is ready for the next stage. The therapist breaks difficult physical activities down into single-step tasks, or small, simple steps. As the patient learns each step, the therapist gradually adds more difficult steps.

Sometimes therapists will suggest special aids and equipment to make physical activity easier. For example, a therapist might be asked to help a child who has cerebral palsy. Children with this disease cannot control their muscles. As a result, they may have trouble sitting up, which makes schoolwork, reading, and eating difficult to do.

The therapist might suggest that a special chair be designed to improve sitting balance. Other equipment, such as an adjustable reading table, might be provided to make doing homework easier.

A therapist might plan a program for an elderly person, possibly one who has arthritis, a disease that attacks the joints of the body. The therapist teaches such patients how to cook, clean, and take care of themselves. Mechanical aids might be provided to make these tasks easier.

The occupational therapist uses selected activities so that patients are able to return to productive living. For example, amputees (people who have lost a leg or an arm) can learn how to drive a car. People with sight or hearing loss can be trained to do some kind of office work. Many can learn to do important work in factories.

Where Do Therapists Work?

Occupational therapy can be practiced in homes, schools, factories, and offices. Whenever it is possible, familiar places are used so that patients can see how many activities they can learn to do alone, and how much their dependence on others is decreasing.

When it is not possible to use a real-life setting, therapists use hospital clinics that have simulated settings, or models. Most of these clinics have a model kitchen, dressing room, bedroom, and dining room, as well as work and play areas. There may also be space for exercise equipment.

▶ HISTORY OF OCCUPATIONAL THERAPY

Early in the 20th century the disabled were taught by crafts teachers. Occupational therapy as a profession began during World War I when thousands of wounded soldiers needed help. Britain offered one of the earliest training programs for therapists.

In the United States, the American Occupational Therapy Association was founded in 1917. By 1952 there were enough national Associations to form the World Federation of Occupational Therapists. The international organization held its first meeting in Scotland in 1954.

Today, people are becoming more and more aware of the special needs of the disabled. Therapists and the handicapped have joined together to press for greater understanding and for more laws to benefit the disabled. In 1973 the U.S. Congress passed a Vocational Rehabilitation Act for the mentally and physically handicapped. The Education for All Handicapped Children Act, giving disabled children the right to a free public education, was passed in 1975.

▶ CAREERS IN OCCUPATIONAL THERAPY

The first requirement for someone seeking a career in occupational therapy is a deep desire to help others. Like teachers, occupational therapists must be patient and friendly, and able to communicate with others.

Over 60 colleges and universities in the United States have programs in occupational therapy. At the undergraduate level, training includes four years of study, followed by practical experience in a clinic. Courses in anatomy, biology, psychology, and creative skills are stressed. There are also programs in certain special fields at the master's and doctoral level. Candidates who successfully complete the basic program use the initials O.T.R. (Occupational Therapist, Registered) after their names.

The Certified Occupational Therapy Assistant (C.O.T.A.) is a high school graduate or the equivalent who has completed a program in occupational therapy. Courses focus on physiology, daily tasks and skills, and at least two months of supervised field work.

Shirley A. Zamora
Program Specialist
Children's Center, Washington, D.C.

Recently elected to the Hall of Fame: Clara Barton and George Washington Carver.

THE HALL OF FAME FOR GREAT AMERICANS

The Hall of Fame for Great Americans is an institution honoring American citizens who have been truly outstanding in the arts, the sciences, government, the military, or other career. It was founded in 1900 by Henry Mitchell MacCracken, the Chancellor of New York University. MacCracken had studied halls of fame in several countries, and he wanted Americans who have greatly influenced their country to be honored in a similar way.

Members of the Hall of Fame are chosen by a board of electors made up of more than 100 prominent citizens from every state. After an election is held, sculptors are chosen to create bronze busts of the persons elected. The busts are then placed on display in the Hall of Fame colonnade. The colonnade, designed by the architect Stanford White, stands on a bluff overlooking the Harlem River in New York City. It is an open-air corridor, semicircular in shape, on the campus of Bronx Community College of the City University of New York.

Each bust occupies its own niche in the colonnade. Under each bust is a bronze plaque, bearing the name and the dates of birth and death of the person honored, along with a quotation by her or him.

The first election was held in 1900, for which more than 1,000 nominations were received from the public. The electors finally voted on 234 nominees. Of these, 29 were elected, including some of the nation's founders—George Washington, Thomas Jefferson, Benjamin Franklin, and John Adams.

Under an early rule, only native-born citizens were eligible for election to the Hall of Fame. But that rule was changed, and naturalized citizens became eligible. Women have always been eligible. The first three to be elected were the astronomer Maria Mitchell and the educators Mary Lyon and Emma Willard. Black members include the scientist and educator George Washington Carver and educator Booker T. Washington.

Until 1970, elections were held every five years. Since that time, they have been held every three years. The public is invited to nominate candidates. All candidates must have been dead for at least 25 years, and must be important historically in one of five categories—arts, sciences, humanities, government, or business and labor.

In 1973, Louis D. Brandeis, George Washington Carver, Franklin D. Roosevelt, and John Philip Sousa were elected to the Hall of Fame. The 1976 members were Clara Barton, Luther Burbank, and Andrew Carnegie.

The future of the Hall of Fame is uncertain. In 1977, New York University and the City University of New York, which have jointly financed and maintained the Hall, had to withdraw their support. The 1979 elections have been suspended for the present. The universities are trying very hard to find new funding for the Hall of Fame. But it is possible that the 97 bronze busts will be moved to a new home—away from the handsome colonnade that was specially designed to display them.

YOGURT—A NATURAL FOOD

The exact origin of yogurt is not known. But we do know that this important dairy product dates back to biblical times—and beyond. Yogurt was probably first eaten in the Middle East. In that region's hot climate, milk spoils rapidly. For this reason yogurt, which does not spoil easily, was a welcome discovery. Yogurt no doubt developed sometime in the distant past when certain bacteria accidentally got into some stored milk.

That is what yogurt is today—milk in which two friendly strains of bacteria have been grown. The names of these micro-organisms are *Lactobacillus bulgaricus* and *Streptococcus thermophilus.*

How is yogurt made? In its most common form, yogurt is made from cow's milk. Much of the fat is often removed and nonfat milk solids with extra protein are added. The milk is homogenized, pasteurized, and then injected with the bacteria. Sometimes fruit preserves and other ingredients are added. But in natural yogurts, no artificial flavor, color, or preservatives should be used.

The milk, now containing the bacteria, is piped into machines that fill the yogurt cups you see in the stores. These cups are then stored in incubators until the product reaches a custard-like thickness. Throughout this process, temperatures must be carefully controlled for the yogurt to develop properly.

Yogurt is a food with many uses. It is a good source of protein, calcium, certain B vitamins, and minerals. Because of its nutritional value, many people eat yogurt as a supplement to their regular diet or as a snack between meals. It can be enjoyed by itself or combined with other foods, such as peanut butter or dry cereal. Many cooks use yogurt in recipes for salad dressings, party dips, desserts, and main dishes.

Yogurt is a popular food in many parts of the world. In Finland it is called *glumse,* in Norway *kyael meelk,* and in Russia *prostokvasha.* In India, the Balkans, and the Middle East, yogurt is used in many dishes.

Food markets in the United States offer different types of yogurt. There is the sundae-style yogurt, with fruit on the bottom; Swiss-style, with fruit throughout; and western-style, with fruit on the bottom and fruit coloring and sweetening on top. Two of the most popular types of yogurt are frozen yogurt on a stick and soft-frozen yogurt served in cups or cones from machines.

Some people make yogurt at home with their own yogurt machine. The instructions, which come with the machine, must be followed carefully. For example, unless the milk is kept at the right temperature, the bacteria cannot live. The result would then be sour milk, not yogurt.

JUAN E. METZGER
Chairman, Dannon Milk Products

Making yogurt at home—so easy that two children can do it.

353

BELIZE

Belize is a small self-governing British dependency on the east coast of Central America facing the Caribbean Sea. It is bounded on the north and west by Mexico and on the west and south by Guatemala. Once known as British Honduras, the dependency was renamed Belize in 1973.

▶ THE PEOPLE

The population of about 140,000 is made up of many different peoples. The largest group are the Creoles, who are the descendants of African slaves once brought to cut the valuable trees in the forests. There is also a large group of mestizos, people of mixed European and Indian descent. The rest are Maya and Carib Indians, East Indians, Chinese, Europeans, and others. All these various peoples generally get along well together.

English is the official language. It is spoken as a local dialect containing many Creole words, and so is difficult for other English-speaking people to understand. Spanish is spoken as a mother tongue or a second language by many. Schooling is free and compulsory for children from age 6 to 14. The great majority of people can read and write.

Most of the people live along the coast. About a third of the population lives in Belize City, the chief port and former capital. The present capital, Belmopan, has a population of about 3,000.

▶ THE LAND

Belize has an area of 8,867 square miles (22,965 square kilometers). The swampy coast is fringed by many small islands known as cays. The low coastal plain rises gradually toward the interior. In the south are the Maya Mountains and the Cockscomb Mountains. Victoria Peak, in the Cockscombs, rises to 3,681 feet (1,122 meters). This peak is the highest point in Belize.

The hot and humid climate is cooled along the coast by northeast trade winds. In the south there can be over 170 inches (4,300 millimeters) of rainfall a year. The country lies within the Caribbean hurricane belt, and storms have caused great damage to people and property in the past. The new capital, Belmopan, was established inland because the former capital, Belize City, had been devastated twice by hurricanes.

There are many rivers, most of them shallow and none very long. The Belize River is the most important. Much of the country's timber is floated downriver to the coast. A large part of the country is forest land, and for two centuries lumbering was the major industry. Mahogany, cedar, rosewood, and other woods

Royal Welsh Fusiliers parade in Belize City, the country's chief port and largest city.

were the chief exports, but now sugar has become the leading export. It is followed by citrus fruits (chiefly oranges and grapefruit). Corn, rice, and beans are grown, mostly for local use. Fish are abundant and lobsters are a valuable export.

▶ HISTORY AND GOVERNMENT

Belize was once part of the Maya Empire. In 1638 British sailors who were shipwrecked off the coast became the first European settlers. Other British settlers followed and set up communities.

Spain, which governed the neighboring territories (now Mexico and Guatemala), tried in vain to drive the British out. When Guatemala became independent in 1821, it claimed Spain's right to the land. Guatemala and Britain have tried over the years to settle the long-term dispute. But to this day they have never agreed on the boundary between Belize and Guatemala.

Belize, then known as British Honduras, became self-governing in 1964. It has a prime minister, an elected House of Representatives, and an appointed Senate. The governor, chosen by the British monarch, oversees foreign affairs.

Many Belizeans want independence. However, to be self-supporting, Belize must raise the level of its economy. With its entrance into the Caribbean Community and Common Market (CARICOM), it is hoping to sell more of its products overseas. It is making more land available for agriculture and is improving farming methods. And, in view of the beauty of its scenery, it hopes to expand its tourist industry.

The dispute with Guatemala over its claim to Belize must be resolved. Once that is done, Belize can move forward in its quest for independence.

Reviewed by SIR PETER STALLARD
Former Governor, Belize

FACTS AND FIGURES

BELIZE is the official name of the dependency.

CAPITAL: Belmopan.

LOCATION: East coast of Central America. **Latitude**—15 ° 54' N to 18 ° 30' N. **Longitude**—88 ° 11' W to 89 ° 13' W.

AREA: 8,867 sq mi (22,965 km²).

POPULATION: 140,000 (estimate).

LANGUAGES: English, Spanish, Indian dialects.

RELIGION: Roman Catholic, Protestant.

GOVERNMENT: Self-governing British dependency. **Head of state**—British monarch, represented by governor. **Head of government**—prime minister. **International cooperation**—Commonwealth of Nations.

ECONOMY: Chief agricultural products—sugar, citrus fruits, rice, corn, beans. **Industries and products**—hardwoods and wood for pulp, citrus fruits (canned, juice, and concentrates), sugar refining. **Chief exports**—sugar, citrus fruits, mahogany, cedar and pine. **Chief imports**—foodstuffs, machinery and transport equipment, petroleum, manufactured goods. **Monetary unit**—Belize dollar.

Village produce is carried to market in dugout canoes.

ROSALYNN SMITH CARTER

Rosalynn Smith Carter was born in Plains, Georgia, on August 18, 1927. Her father, a Plains mechanic, died of leukemia when Rosalynn was 13. While her mother supported the family of four children by sewing for other people and working at the post office, Rosalynn helped by sewing and working in a beauty parlor. She attended high school in Plains and went to Georgia Southwestern College in nearby Americus, where she took a two-year general program in interior decorating.

Rosalynn and Jimmy Carter were married in 1946 immediately after Carter's graduation from the U.S. Naval Academy. During their first seven years of marriage, the Carters had three sons. (A daughter, Amy, was born in 1967.) Because her husband was often away for long tours of duty as a submarine officer, Rosalynn Carter reared the boys and managed the household.

When Carter left the Navy, he and Rosalynn returned to Plains to run the family farm and peanut business. Later, when Jimmy entered politics, Rosalynn continued to keep the books for the family business. She emerged as a public figure in her husband's second campaign for the governorship of Georgia. It was during this time that she became deeply interested in mental health, retardation, and the care of the aged. Her husband, as governor, placed her in charge of his administration's mental health program. Mrs. Carter became active in making legislative recommendations, recruiting volunteers, and informing the public of the necessity for mental health. She helped establish a statewide network of mental health centers.

Mrs. Carter is a rather shy and private person. Still, she became one of the most popular and sought-after speakers during her husband's two-year presidential campaign. A slender woman, with slightly curling brown hair, bright hazel eyes, and a warm engaging smile, Mrs. Carter captivated audiences wherever she traveled.

Perhaps her most significant role as first lady is that of adviser to her husband. Shortly after his election to the presidency in November, 1976, she took part in strategy sessions. She also joined in the discussions held to select presidential appointees, such as the cabinet officers. While she is not a policy-maker, the president does seek her ideas and advice on many issues.

Within the first few months of her husband's inauguration, Mrs. Carter set the tone for her role as first lady by appointing a "projects director" to help her carry out her ambitious and far-reaching plans. She does not limit her activities to hosting White House dinners, but takes a more active approach to her duties as the wife of a president. She does important work as a traveling ambassador for her husband, visiting those states and foreign countries that he is unable to visit. She also continues to play an important role as a political adviser in the Carter administration, and she works on mental health and problems of the elderly. Mrs. Carter serves as honorary chairperson of the President's Commission on Mental Health.

Reviewed by MARGARET B. KLAPTHOR
Smithsonian Institution

MAO TSE-TUNG

Mao Tse-tung, revolutionary leader and poet, was the founder of the People's Republic of China and its ruler for nearly 30 years. He was born on December 26, 1893, in Shao Shan, a village in Hunan province, South China. His father, a stern man, was a successful rice merchant and farmer.

Mao went to a nearby primary school. When he was thirteen, his father made him give up schooling for farm work. By that time the boy already had a great love for books—especially those books filled with adventures and rebellions.

Mao worked on the farm for three years and then returned to school, where he was a brilliant but rebellious student. When the Chinese revolution against the Manchu dynasty broke out in 1911, he joined the revolutionary army. Mao stayed in the army for six months and then resumed his schooling. He was not happy with the new Chinese Republic and thought the revolution had not won needed reforms. At school Mao headed a group of students who debated how to achieve those reforms.

In 1918 Mao went to Peking. He worked in the Peking University library as a fetcher of newspapers, but he also edited his own monthly paper. On May 4, 1919, the Peking students rebelled against the government. An associate of Mao's was the guiding spirit of this movement, which protested the transfer of former German lands, or "concessions," in China to Japan. Though most of these students were Socialists, a few called themselves Communists.

In July, 1921, Mao was one of the founding members of the Chinese Communist Party, which met in Shanghai. Within six years he had become one of the party's most important members.

The Communists joined forces with the Kuomintang, China's chief party of reform. But suddenly, in 1927, Chiang Kai-shek, leader of the Kuomintang, turned on the Communists and began to massacre them. Mao and his followers set up a base in the mountains of Kiangsi province and fought off five Kuomintang attacks. Then, with Chou En-lai and Chu Teh, the Commander-in-Chief of the Red Army, he led the Communist armies on the Long March. This 6,000 mile (9,700 kilometer) trek took them to the borders of Tibet and then north to the valley of Yenan, where, in 1936, they set up a power base.

In the following year the Japanese invaded China. For a time the Kuomintang and the Communists united against the common enemy—but this unity did not last long. Chiang Kai-shek's armies were forced to retreat while the Communist guerrilla armies fought on behind the Japanese lines. By the time the Japanese were defeated in 1945, it was clear that the Communists had more support among the Chinese people than did Chiang Kai-shek's forces. A civil war followed, ending in a Communist victory in 1949.

In Peking, on October 1, 1949, Mao proclaimed the People's Republic of China. The landlords were stripped of their holdings, the government took control of industry, and communes (communities where everything is owned in common) were set up. The entire country came under the control of the Communist Party. The control was so rigid that Mao feared the revolutionary spirit would die out. At various times, without much success, he tried to lessen the power of the Communist government officials. The Great Proletarian Cultural Revolution in the late 1960's, led largely by Mao's wife, Chiang Ching, was an effort to cleanse the government by giving power to young soldiers called Red Guards.

Mao's health began to fail in the late 1960's. He died in 1976 at the age of 82.

ROBERT PAYNE
Author, *Mao Tse-tung*

INTERNATIONAL STATISTICAL SUPPLEMENT
(as of December 31, 1977)

NATION	CAPITAL	AREA (in sq mi)	POPULATION (estimate)	GOVERNMENT
Afghanistan	Kabul	250,000	19,800,000	Mohammed Daud Khan—president
Albania	Tirana	11,100	2,500,000	Enver Hoxha—communist party secretary Mehmet Shehu—premier
Algeria	Algiers	919,593	17,400,000	Houari Boumédienne—president
Angola	Luanda	481,351	6,800,000	Agostinho Neto—president
Argentina	Buenos Aires	1,072,158	25,700,000	Jorge Rafael Videla—president
Australia	Canberra	2,967,900	14,100,000	Malcolm Fraser—prime minister
Austria	Vienna	32,374	7,500,000	Rudolf Kirchschläger—president Bruno Kreisky—chancellor
Bahamas	Nassau	5,380	210,000	Lynden O. Pindling—prime minister
Bahrain	Manama	240	260,000	Isa bin Sulman al-Khalifa—head of government
Bangladesh	Dacca	55,126	83,000,000	Ziaur Rahman—president
Barbados	Bridgetown	166	250,000	J. M. G. Adams—prime minister
Belgium	Brussels	11,781	9,900,000	Baudouin I—king Leo Tindemans—premier
Benin (Dahomey)	Porto-Novo	43,483	3,200,000	Mathieu Kerekou—president
Bhutan	Thimbu	18,147	1,200,000	Jigme Singye Wangchuk—king
Bolivia	La Paz Sucre	424,163	5,800,000	Hugo Banzer Suárez—president
Botswana	Gaborone	231,804	700,000	Sir Seretse Khama—president
Brazil	Brasília	3,286,478	110,000,000	Ernesto Geisel—president
Bulgaria	Sofia	42,823	8,800,000	Todor Zhivkov—communist party secretary Stanko Todorov—premier
Burma	Rangoon	261,789	30,800,000	U Ne Win—president U Maung Maung Kha—prime minister
Burundi	Bujumbura	10,747	3,900,000	Jean-Baptiste Bagaza—president
Cambodia (Kampuchea)	Pnompenh	69,898	8,400,000	Pol Pot—communist party chairman Khieu Samphan—head of state
Cameroon	Yaoundé	183,569	6,500,000	Ahmadou Ahidjo—president
Canada	Ottawa	3,851,809	23,200,000	Pierre Elliott Trudeau—prime minister
Cape Verde	Praia	1,557	300,000	Aristides Pereira—president
Central African Empire	Bangui	240,535	2,600,000	Bokassa I—emperor

NATION	CAPITAL	AREA (in sq mi)	POPULATION (estimate)	GOVERNMENT
Chad	N'Djemena	495,754	4,100,000	Félix Malloum—head of government
Chile	Santiago	292,257	10,500,000	Augusto Pinochet Ugarte—president
China	Peking	3,705,396	852,000,000	Hua Kuo-feng—communist party chairman
Colombia	Bogotá	439,736	24,400,000	Alfonso López Michelsen—president
Comoros	Moroni	838	310,000	Ali Soilih—head of state
Congo	Brazzaville	132,047	1,400,000	Joachim Yombi Opango—president
Costa Rica	San José	19,575	2,000,000	Daniel Oduber Quirós—president
Cuba	Havana	44,218	9,400,000	Osvaldo Dorticós Torrado—president Fidel Castro—premier
Cyprus	Nicosia	3,572	640,000	Spyros Kyprianou—president
Czechoslovakia	Prague	49,370	14,900,000	Gustáv Husák—communist party secretary and president Lubomír Štrougal—premier
Denmark	Copenhagen	16,629	5,100,000	Margrethe II—queen Anker Jorgensen—premier
Djibouti	Djibouti	8,800	125,000	Hassan Gouled—president
Dominican Republic	Santo Domingo	18,816	4,800,000	Joaquín Balaguer—president
Ecuador	Quito	109,483	7,300,000	Alfredo Poveda Burbano—president
Egypt	Cairo	386,660	38,000,000	Anwar el-Sadat—president Mamdouh Salem—premier
El Salvador	San Salvador	8,260	4,100,000	Carlos Humberto Romero—president
Equatorial Guinea	Malabo	10,830	320,000	Francisco Macías Nguema—president
Ethiopia	Addis Ababa	471,777	28,700,000	Mengistu Haile Mariam—head of state
Fiji	Suva	7,055	580,000	Ratu Sir Kamisese Mara—prime minister
Finland	Helsinki	130,120	4,700,000	Urho K. Kekkonen—president Kalevi Sorsa—premier
France	Paris	211,207	53,000,000	Valéry Giscard d'Estaing—president Raymond Barre—premier
Gabon	Libreville	103,346	530,000	Albert B. Bongo—president
Gambia	Banjul	4,361	540,000	Sir Dauda K. Jawara—president
Germany (East)	East Berlin	41,768	16,800,000	Erich Honecker—communist party secretary Willi Stoph—premier
Germany (West)	Bonn	95,976	61,500,000	Walter Scheel—president Helmut Schmidt—chancellor
Ghana	Accra	92,099	10,300,000	Ignatius K. Acheampong—head of government
Greece	Athens	50,944	9,200,000	Constantine Tsatsos—president Constantine Caramanlis—premier
Grenada	St. George's	133	100,000	Eric M. Gairy—prime minister

NATION	CAPITAL	AREA (in sq mi)	POPULATION (estimate)	GOVERNMENT
Guatemala	Guatemala City	42,042	6,300,000	Kjell Laugerud García—president
Guinea	Conakry	94,926	4,500,000	Sékou Touré—president Lansana Beavogui—premier
Guinea-Bissau	Bissau	13,948	530,000	Luiz de Almeida Cabral—president
Guyana	Georgetown	83,000	800,000	Arthur Chung—president Forbes Burnham—prime minister
Haiti	Port-au-Prince	10,714	4,700,000	Jean-Claude Duvalier—president
Honduras	Tegucigalpa	43,277	2,800,000	Alberto Juan Melgar Castro— head of state
Hungary	Budapest	35,919	10,600,000	János Kádár—communist party secretary György Lazar—premier
Iceland	Reykjavik	39,768	220,000	Kristján Eldjárn—president Geir Hallgrimsson—prime minister
India	New Delhi	1,266,598	610,000,000	Neelam Sanjiva Reddy—president Morarji R. Desai—prime minister
Indonesia	Jakarta	735,269	139,600,000	Suharto—president
Iran	Teheran	636,294	33,400,000	Mohammed Reza Pahlavi—shah Jamshid Amouzegar—premier
Iraq	Baghdad	167,925	11,500,000	Ahmed Hassan al-Bakr—president
Ireland	Dublin	27,136	3,200,000	Patrick Hillery—president Jack Lynch—prime minister
Israel	Jerusalem	7,992	3,500,000	Ephraim Katzir—president Menahem Begin—prime minister
Italy	Rome	116,303	56,200,000	Giovanni Leone—president Giulio Andreotti—premier
Ivory Coast	Abidjan	124,503	6,700,000	Félix Houphouët-Boigny—president
Jamaica	Kingston	4,232	2,100,000	Michael N. Manley—prime minister
Japan	Tokyo	143,750	113,000,000	Hirohito—emperor Takeo Fukuda—premier
Jordan	Amman	37,738	2,800,000	Hussein I—king Mudar Badran—premier
Kenya	Nairobi	224,959	13,800,000	Jomo Kenyatta—president
Korea (North)	Pyongyang	46,540	16,200,000	Kim Il Sung—president Li Jong-ok—premier
Korea (South)	Seoul	38,022	35,900,000	Park Chung Hee—president
Kuwait	Kuwait	6,880	1,000,000	Jaber al-Ahmed al-Sabah—head of state
Laos	Vientiane	91,429	3,400,000	Souphanouvong—president Kaysone Phomvihan—premier
Lebanon	Beirut	4,015	3,000,000	Elias Sarkis—president Selim al-Hoss—premier
Lesotho	Maseru	11,720	1,200,000	Moshoeshoe II—king Leabua Jonathan—prime minister

NATION	CAPITAL	AREA (in sq mi)	POPULATION (estimate)	GOVERNMENT
Liberia	Monrovia	43,000	1,800,000	William R. Tolbert—president
Libya	Tripoli	679,360	2,500,000	Muammar el-Qaddafi—president
Liechtenstein	Vaduz	61	24,000	Francis Joseph II—prince
Luxembourg	Luxembourg	999	360,000	Jean—grand duke Gaston Thorn—premier
Madagascar (Malagasy Republic)	Antananarivo	226,657	8,300,000	Didier Ratsiraka—president
Malawi	Lilongwe	45,747	5,200,000	H. Kamuzu Banda—president
Malaysia	Kuala Lumpur	127,316	12,300,000	Yahaya Putra ibni al-Marhum—paramount ruler Hussein Onn—prime minister
Maldives	Male	115	122,000	Ibrahim Nasir—president
Mali	Bamako	478,765	6,000,000	Moussa Traoré—president
Malta	Valletta	122	320,000	Sir Anthony Mamo—president Dom Mintoff—prime minister
Mauritania	Nouakchott	397,954	1,500,000	Moktar O. Daddah—president
Mauritius	Port Louis	720	900,000	Sir Seewoosagur Ramgoolam—prime minister
Mexico	Mexico City	761,602	62,300,000	José López Portillo—president
Monaco	Monaco-Ville	0.4	25,000	Rainier III—prince
Mongolia	Ulan Bator	604,248	1,500,000	Yumzhagiyn Tsedenbal—communist party secretary
Morocco	Rabat	172,413	17,800,000	Hassan II—king Ahmed Osman—premier
Mozambique	Maputo	302,329	9,400,000	Samora Machel—president
Nauru	—	8	8,000	Bernard Dowiyogo—president
Nepal	Katmandu	54,362	12,900,000	Birendra Bir Bikram Shah Deva—king Kirtinidhi Bista—prime minister
Netherlands	Amsterdam	15,770	13,800,000	Juliana—queen Andreas A. M. Van Agt—premier
New Zealand	Wellington	103,736	3,100,000	Robert D. Muldoon—prime minister
Nicaragua	Managua	50,193	2,200,000	Anastasio Somoza Debayle—president
Niger	Niamey	489,190	4,700,000	Seyni Kountche—head of government
Nigeria	Lagos	356,668	64,800,000	Olusegun Obasanjo—head of government
Norway	Oslo	125,181	4,000,000	Olav V—king Odvar Nordli—prime minister
Oman	Muscat	82,030	800,000	Qabus ibn Said—sultan
Pakistan	Islamabad	310,403	72,400,000	Fazal Elahi Chaudri—president Mohammed Zia ul-Haq—head of government

NATION	CAPITAL	AREA (in sq mi)	POPULATION (estimate)	GOVERNMENT
Panama	Panama City	29,209	1,700,000	Omar Torrijos Herrera—head of government
Papua New Guinea	Port Moresby	178,260	2,800,000	Michael Somare—prime minister
Paraguay	Asunción	157,047	2,700,000	Alfredo Stroessner—president
Peru	Lima	496,223	16,100,000	Francisco Morales Bermúdez—president
Philippines	Manila	115,830	43,800,000	Ferdinand E. Marcos—president
Poland	Warsaw	120,724	34,600,000	Edward Gierek—communist party secretary Piotr Jaroszewicz—premier
Portugal	Lisbon	35,553	8,800,000	António Ramalho Eanes—president Mário Soares—premier
Qatar	Doha	4,000	150,000	Khalifa bin Hamad al-Thani—head of government
Rhodesia	Salisbury	150,803	6,500,000	John Wrathall—president Ian D. Smith—prime minister
Rumania	Bucharest	91,700	21,400,000	Nicolae Ceausescu—communist party secretary Manea Manescu—premier
Rwanda	Kigali	10,169	4,300,000	Juvénal Habyalimana—president
São Tomé and Príncipe	São Tomé	372	81,000	Manuel Pinto da Costa—president
Saudi Arabia	Riyadh	829,997	9,200,000	Khalid bin Abdul-Aziz—king
Senegal	Dakar	75,750	5,100,000	Léopold Senghor—president
Seychelles	Victoria	107	59,000	France Albert René—president
Sierre Leone	Freetown	27,700	3,100,000	Siaka P. Stevens—president
Singapore	Singapore	224	2,300,000	Benjamin H. Sheares—president Lee Kuan Yew—prime minister
Somalia	Mogadishu	246,200	3,300,000	Mohammed Siad Barre—head of government
South Africa	Pretoria Cape Town	471,444	26,100,000	Nicolaas Diederichs—president B. John Vorster—prime minister
Spain	Madrid	194,897	36,000,000	Juan Carlos I—king Adolfo Suárez González—premier
Sri Lanka (Ceylon)	Colombo	25,332	14,300,000	William Gopallawa—president Junius R. Jayewardene—premier
Sudan	Khartoum	967,497	16,100,000	Gaafar al-Numeiry—president
Surinam	Paramaribo	63,037	435,000	Henck A. E. Arron—prime minister
Swaziland	Mbabane	6,704	500,000	Sobhuza II—king
Sweden	Stockholm	173,732	8,200,000	Carl XVI Gustaf—king Thörbjorn Fälldin—prime minister

NATION	CAPITAL	AREA (in sq mi)	POPULATION (estimate)	GOVERNMENT
Switzerland	Bern	15,941	6,300,000	Willi Ritschard—president
Syria	Damascus	71,586	7,600,000	Hafez al-Assad—president Abdel Rahman Khleifawi—premier
Taiwan	Taipei	13,885	16,600,000	C. K. Yen—president Chiang Ching-kuo—premier
Tanzania	Dar es Salaam	364,898	15,600,000	Julius K. Nyerere—president
Thailand	Bangkok	198,456	43,000,000	Bhumibol Adulyadej—king Kriangsak Chamanad—premier
Togo	Lomé	21,622	2,300,000	Gnassingbe Eyadema—president
Tonga	Nuku'alofa	270	90,000	Taufa'ahau Tupou IV—king Prince Tu'ipelehake—prime minister
Trinidad & Tobago	Port of Spain	1,980	1,100,000	Sir Ellis Clarke—president Eric Williams—prime minister
Tunisia	Tunis	63,170	5,700,000	Habib Bourguiba—president
Turkey	Ankara	301,381	40,200,000	Fahri Korutürk—president Bulent Ecevit—premier
Uganda	Kampala	91,134	11,900,000	Idi Amin—president
U.S.S.R.	Moscow	8,649,512	258,000,000	Leonid I. Brezhnev—communist party secretary and president Aleksei N. Kosygin—premier
United Arab Emirates	Abu Dhabi	32,278	230,000	Zayd bin Sultan—president
United Kingdom	London	94,226	55,900,000	Elizabeth II—queen James Callaghan—prime minister
United States	Washington, D.C.	3,615,123	215,800,000	James Earl Carter, Jr.—president Walter F. Mondale—vice-president
Upper Volta	Ouagadougou	105,869	6,200,000	Sangoulé Lamizana—president
Uruguay	Montevideo	68,536	3,100,000	Aparicio Méndez—president
Venezuela	Caracas	352,143	12,400,000	Carlos Andrés Pérez—president
Vietnam	Hanoi	128,402	46,500,000	Le Duan—communist party secretary Ton Duc Thang—president Pham Van Dong—premier
Western Samoa	Apia	1,097	151,000	Malietoa Tanumafili II—head of state
Yemen (Aden)	Madinat al-Shaab	112,000	1,700,000	Salem Ali Rubaya—head of state Ali Nasir Mohammed—prime minister
Yemen (Sana)	Sana	75,290	5,300,000	Ahmed Hussein al-Ghashmi—head of government
Yugoslavia	Belgrade	98,766	21,700,000	Josip Broz Tito—president Veselin Djuranovic—premier
Zaïre	Kinshasa	905,565	25,600,000	Mobutu Sese Seko—president
Zambia	Lusaka	290,585	5,100,000	Kenneth D. Kaunda—president

INDEX

A

B

C

D

G

Guinness Book of World Records, reference book 186–87
Guinness World Records Exhibit Hall, New York City 186
Guyana 360
    Girl Guides 224

Hai Bar Reserve, Israel 63
Haiti 360
Haley, Alex, American author 197; picture 196
Hall of Fame for Great Americans, New York City 352
Hamill, Mark, American actor 327
Handicapped, rehabilitation of the 350–51
Handicrafts *see* Hobbies, handicrafts, and projects
Happy Days, painting by Iverd
    re-creation by live models, pictures 216–17
Harlan County, U.S.A., documentary motion picture 304
Harris, Julian, American artist 130
Hart Trophy, hockey trophy 285
Hattiesburg, Mississippi
    Little League baseball team 277
Hazel, cartoon strip 162
Headley, Scott, American winner in scholastic-photography program
    Earthquake, photograph 210
Heart, American musical group 313
Heating
    fuel shortage in United States 93–94
Heisman Trophy, football 281
Herding of livestock
    Djibouti 348, 349
Herriman, George, American cartoonist 165
Hessians, German mercenaries, hired by the King of England to fight
    the Americans in the Revolutionary War 194
Hey, Kid!, book, picture 268
Hickory horned devil, caterpillar, picture 75
Highlands, light-colored areas on the surface of the moon 97, 98, 100,
    103
Hijacking of trains
    terrorism of South Moluccans in the Netherlands 21
Hobbies, handicrafts, and projects 148–51
    building a vivarium 58–61
    decorating objects with pasta 138–39
    dyeing 340–46
    embroidering a pocketbook 136–37
    making a shell-flower picture 144–46; pictures 147
    mural created by high school students, picture 124–25
    starting a kids-only club 126–29
    topiary gardening 122; pictures 123
    tracing a family genealogy 196–99
Hockey, sport 284–87
Hoffman, Jared, American reporter, picture 219
Hogarth, Burne, American cartoonist 165
Holidays
    New Year stamps 143; pictures 142
Honduras 360
Honeybee, insect
    Smithsonian Institution Insect Zoo's honeybees, picture 75
Horn of Africa, northeastern Africa 38–39
Horse racing
    Cauthen, Steve, American jockey 206–7
Horses
    Seattle Slew, picture 57

Hospitals
    Girl Guide project in Belfast mental hospital 227
    occupational therapy 351
How Djadja-em-ankh Saved the Day, Egyptian story, picture 269
Howe, Gordie, Canadian athlete 285
Howe, Mark, American athlete 285
Howe, Marty, American athlete 285
Howe, William, English general 194–95
Howitt, Mary, British writer
    Spider and the Fly, The, poem 247
Hudson River, New York
    Battle of Saratoga 194
Huipil, blouse worn by Mexican and Central American Indian women
    184
Hummingbird
    bee hummingbird 73
Humor
    cartoons 162
Hungary 360
    return of the Crown of St. Stephen 32
Hunt, Steve, British athlete 295–96
Hunting
    endangered species 62, 64, 66
Huntsville, Alabama
    Alabama Space and Rocket Center 120–21
Hyena, animal
    predator of wildebeests 71

I

Ice, picture 94
    snowflakes 95
Icebergs
    source of fresh water for Saudi Arabia 115; pictures and map 114
Icebreaker, ship with special hull to force a path through ice
    Arktika 26
Iceland 360
Ice skating 288
    Cranston, Toller, picture 293
Igneous rock, rock formed by cooling of molten lava
    moon rock 97; pictures 98
India 360
    Bengal tigers 63–64
    cyclone in Andhra Pradesh 33
    government of Indira Gandhi 46–47
    parliamentary elections 16
Indianapolis, Indiana
    Indianapolis Children's Museum 176–79
Indians, American
    Alaskan native claims 105
    Basketmaker's Story, A, historical story 250–59
    Cakchiquel Indians 184–85
    cochineal dye, use of 345
Indonesia 360
    terrorism of South Moluccans in the Netherlands 20
Influenza, disease 110
Insects
    cochineal bug 345
    monarch butterfly 54
    Smithsonian Institution's Insect Zoo 74; pictures 75

M

Mauritania 361
Mauritius 361
Maze, puzzle 134
McArdle, Andrea, American actress 204; picture 205
McDade, Joseph E., American scientist 110–11
McDowell, Ronnie, American singer 309
McGuire, Al, American basketball coach 279
McManus, George, American cartoonist 162
McWhirter, Norris, Irish author 186
McWhirter, Ross, Irish author 186
Mead, Margaret, American anthropologist, picture 219
Meade, James E., British economist 31
Medicine
 Girl Guide project to increase kidney donors 224, 227; picture 225
 legionnaires' disease 110–11, 13
 Nobel prize 31
 occupational therapy 350–51
 organ transplants 14
Memphis, Tennessee
 Presley, Elvis, death of 309
Mestizos, people of mixed European and Indian descent
 Belize 354
Metallic salts, chemical compounds
 use as mordants in dyeing process 345
Meteorites
 moon 99, 100
Metric system, of measures
 Canada 28
Mexico 361
 coin honoring José María Morelos y Pavón 131
 monarch butterfly 54
Miami, Florida
 snowfall 93; picture 92
Mice, rodents
 Old World harvest mouse 72
Microvision, pocket-size television set 12
Middle East 11
 diplomatic relations 34
 Ismailia conference 35
 Sadat's visit to Israel 42–43, 33
Mime, the art of portraying a character by body movement only
 Mummenschanz 338; pictures 339
Mines and mining
 control of the ocean's resources 48–49
Miniatures, small-scale reproductions of objects 149
 miniature castle 166–69
Minimum wage 32
Minneapolis, Minnesota
 below-zero weather, picture 94
Minnesota
 below-zero weather in Minneapolis, picture 94
 eastern timber wolves 67
Minnesota Vikings, football team 280, 282
Mississippi
 Hattiesburg's Little League baseball team 277
Mitchell, Joni, American composer and performer 309
Mobutu Sese Seko, Zaïrian leader 38
Mojave Desert, California and Arizona
 Landsat photograph 82
Mojsov, Lazar, Yugoslavian diplomat 29
Moluccas, islands, Indonesia
 terrorism of South Moluccans in the Netherlands 21
Monaco 361
Monarch, butterfly 54
Mondale, Walter F. ("Fritz"), U.S. vice-president 13
 Children's Express 218
Money
 coin collecting 130–31
Mongolia 361
Monkeys, animals
 space exploration 121
Montreal, Canada
 World Scout Conference 220

Montreal Alouettes, football team 281
Montreal Canadiens, hockey team 284–85, 286
Moon 96–103
 Lunar Odyssey, ride that simulates a journey to the moon 121; picture 120
Moore, Clement Clarke, American scholar 180–82
Moore, Colleen, American actress 166
Moose Factory, Ontario 156
Moped, motorized bicycle 90
Mordant, substance used to fix dyes 345, 346
Morelos y Pavón, José María, Mexican priest and patriot 131
Morerod, Lise-Marie, Swiss athlete, picture 288
Morgan, David, British athlete, picture 203
Morocco 361
Morton, Azie Taylor, U.S. treasurer 130
Morton, Craig, American athlete 280
Moses, Haven, American athlete 280
Mostel, Zero, American actor 29; picture 28
Motion pictures
 Academy Awards 304–5
 animated cartoons 165
 Chaplin, Charlie, death of 35
 Children's Film Foundation 314–15
 commemorative stamp 140
 Crawford, Joan, death of 20
 Mostel, Zero, death of 29
 music from films 311
 Star Wars 326–329
Mott, Nevill F., British physicist 31
Movies *see* Motion pictures
Mozambique 361
Muir, Karen, South African athlete 187
Mummenschanz, mime show 338; pictures 339
Mural painting
 mural created by high school students, Nyack, New York, picture 124–25
Murder
 death penalty as punishment 45
 "Son of Sam" 26
Museum of Cartoon Art, Rye, New York 165
Museums
 Alabama Space and Rocket Center 120–21
 Indianapolis Children's Museum 176–79
 Guinness World Records Exhibit Hall, New York 186
 Museum of Cartoon Art, Rye, New York 165
Musgrove, Margaret, American writer
 Ashanti to Zulu, book, pictures 228–29, 271
Music 308–13
 Crosby, Bing, death of 30
 Presley, Elvis, death of 26
 Stokowski, Leopold, death of 29
Musical comedy
 Annie 204; pictures 200–1, 205
 music from Broadway 311
Mystery, detective, and suspense stories
 Secret of the Ghost Town, The 230–35

N

Nabokov, Vladimir, Russian-born American author 24
NASA *see* National Aeronautics and Space Administration

O

S

U

Y

Z

The following list credits or acknowledges, by page, the source of illustrations and text excerpts used in THE NEW BOOK OF KNOWLEDGE ANNUAL. Illustration credits are listed illustration by illustration—left to right, top to bottom. When two or more illustrations appear on one page, their credits are separated by semicolons. When both the photographer or artist and an agency or other source are given for an illustration, they are usually separated by a dash. Excerpts from previously published works are listed by inclusive page numbers.

12 Sinclair Radionics
13 Edward Hausner—*The New York Times*
15 *The New York Times;* Brent Jones
16 Wide World
17 NASA
18 John Wilford—*The New York Times*
19 Courtesy Canadian Consulate
20 Courtesy of *The Boston Globe*
21 *London Daily Express* / Pictorial Parade
22 Wide World
23 UPI
24 Wide World
25 Wide World
27 Wide World
28 Wide World
29 Wide World
30 Central Press / Pictorial Parade
32 UPI
33 UPI
34 Wide World
35 UPI
37 UPI
38 UPI
39 Wide World
40 Jerry Darvin
41 Dan Baliotti
42 Henri Bureau—Sygma; William Karel—Sygma
44– Reprinted by permission of *Junior Scholastic,*
45 © 1977 by Scholastic Magazines, Inc.
45 Bert Dodson
46 UPI
47 UPI
49 UPI
51 Carl Frank—Photo Researchers
52– Tom McHugh—Photo Researchers
53
54 Tom McHugh—Photo Researchers
55 Martha Swope
56 Wide World; UPI
57 National Audubon Society / Photo Researchers; UPI; Harry Morris—*The New York Times*
59– From *Great Pets* by Sara Stein. Published by
61 Workman Publishing Company, Inc. © 1976 by Sara Stein
63 Tom McHugh—Photo Researchers
64– Sullivan & Rogers—Bruce Coleman; Kenneth
65 Fink—National Audubon Society / Photo Researchers
66 Russ Kinne—Photo Researchers; G. Ronald Austing—National Audubon Society / Photo Researchers
67 Allan D. Cruickshank—National Audubon Society / Photo Researchers; Karl Maslowski—Photo Researchers
69 Courtesy Riverbanks Zoological Park
70 Leonard Lee Rue—National Audubon Society / Photo Researchers; Chaumeton—Jacana; Russ Kinne—Photo Researchers
71 Text adapted from *Predators Are a Part of Nature* by George W. Frame. © 1975, Highlights for Children, Inc., Columbus, Ohio. By permission of the publisher.
72– Paul Harvey
73
74 Kjell Sandved
75 Kjell Sandved
76 Tom & Michele Grimm
77 Tom & Michele Grimm
78 New York Zoological Society Photo
79 New York Zoological Society Photo
80– Courtesy Alyeska
81
82 Goddard Space Flight Center / NASA

83 Goddard Space Flight Center / NASA
85 Francois Colos
86 Courtesy Binney & Smith
87 Martha Roberts—Monkmeyer
88 Jet Propulsion Laboratory—California Institute of Technology
89 Wide World; NASA
90 Russ Kinne—Photo Researchers
91 Shell Maritime Française
92 Sepp Seitz—Woodfin Camp
93 UPI
94 UPI
95 The American Museum of Natural History
96 NASA
98 NASA
101 U.S. Dept. of Geological Survey
104 *The Christian Science Monitor*
106 R. Norman Matheny—*The Christian Science Monitor*
107 Courtesy Alyeska; UPI
108 Courtesy Alyeska
110 Wide World
111 Courtesy Center for Disease Control, Atlanta, Ga.
112 Peter Tatiner—Liaison
114 Harry Carter
115 Peter Tatiner—Liaison
116– Thomas Garcia
117
118 Courtesy Harry Goldsmith
119 Courtesy Harry Goldsmith
120 Courtesy Alabama Space and Rocket Center
122 Jenny Tesar
123 Jenny Tesar
124– Marjorie Pickens
125
126– From *The Kids-Only Club Book* by Shari Lewis
129 © 1976. Published by J. P. Tarcher, Inc.
130 Courtesy Krause Publications, Inc.
131 Courtesy Krause Publications, Inc.
133 Adapted from *Pocket Calculator Fun & Games* by Ross and Pat Olney. Text © 1977 by Ross R. Olney, illustrations © 1977 by Gretchen Lopez. By permission of Franklin Watts, Inc.
134 Jacques Chazaud

135 © 1976 Highlights for Children, Inc., Columbus, Ohio.
136– Judith Hoffman Corwin
137
138 Courtesy *Creative Crafts* magazine
139 Courtesy *Creative Crafts* magazine
144– Courtesy *Creative Crafts* magazine
147
148– Courtesy *Creative Crafts* magazine
151
152– P. Marlow—Sygma
153
154 Peter Grugeon—Camera Press / Photo Trends
155 UPI
156 Courtesy Ontario Northland Transportation
157 Commission
158– Adapted from "Robinson Crusoe's Island," by
161 Enrique Bunster, in November–December, 1971, issue of *Américas,* monthly magazine published by the General Secretariat of the Organization of American States, in English, Spanish, and Portuguese. Adapted by permission.
158 Mansell Collection
160 Courtesy O.A.S. *Américas*
161 W. H. Hodge—Peter Arnold
162 © 1959 United Features Syndicate Inc.
163 Pat Oliphant, © 1976, *The Washington Star.* Reprinted with permission, Los Angeles Times Syndicate; Mal in *The Christian Science Monitor* © 1977 TCSPS; © Rube Goldberg, permission granted by King Features Syndicate Inc.
164 © 1954 Walt Disney Productions; © 1978 King Features Syndicate, Inc.; © 1978 Felix the Cat Productions, Inc.
166– Courtesy Public Relations, Museum of Science
169 and Industry, Chicago
170 Rare Book Division, The New York Public Library
171 From *The History of Piracy* by Philip Gosse. Reprint 1968 Burt Franklin (Publishers). Courtesy of the publisher.
172 Ryan Aeronautical Library
173 © 1927 by The New York Times Company. Reprinted by permission.
175 UPI
176– Courtesy The Children's Museum
179
180 Jane Latta—Columbiana Collection, Columbia University
181 Courtesy Columbiana Collection, Columbia University
183 Courtesy Santa's Workshop, Inc.
184– Adapted from "Guatemala's Flying Messengers,"
185 by Erskine Lane, in October, 1976, issue of *Américas,* monthly magazine published by the General Secretariat of the Organization of American States, in English, Spanish, and Portuguese. Adapted by permission. Photos, Erskine Lane
186 Courtesy Sterling Publishing Co., Inc.
187 *Minneapolis Tribune*
188 Courtesy Quebec Government House, N.Y.
189 Michael Philip Manheim—Photo Researchers
190– Luis Villota
191
192 U.S. Dept. of the Interior, National Park Service, Edison National Historic Site
193 U.S. Dept. of the Interior, National Park Service, Edison National Historic Site; The Bettmann Archive; Courtesy Panasonic
195 Yale University Art Gallery
196 UPI; Courtesy The Wolper Organization, Inc., and Warner Bros. Television Distribution, Inc.

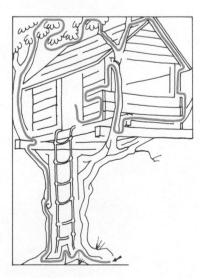

198 Susan Swan
200– Martha Swope
201
202 Tony Korody—Sygma; Richard Howard—Camera 5
203 *London Daily Express;* UPI; National Energy Foundation
205 Chicago Tribune–New York News Syndicate; Martha Swope
206 Ken Korotkin—*The Daily News*
207 UPI
208 UPI
209 ABC-TV
210– Courtesy of Scholastic Photography Awards,
213 conducted by Scholastic Magazines, Inc., and sponsored by Eastman Kodak Company
214 Courtesy Staatliche Kunsthalle Karlsruhe
216 Tom & Michele Grimm
217 Tom & Michele Grimm; © 1932 Catalda Fine Arts Inc., N.Y.C.
218– Courtesy *Children's Express*
219
220 Boy Scouts of America
221 Boy Scouts of America
222 Boy Scouts of Canada; Boy Scouts of Canada
223 Boy Scouts of Canada
225 Girl Scouts of the U.S.A.
226 Dept. of Human Resources, Commonwealth of Kentucky
228– From *From Ashanti to Zulu.* Text © 1976 by
229 Margaret Musgrove, pictures © 1976 by Leo and Diane Dillon. Published by The Dial Press, N.Y.
230 Charles McVicker
235 Charles McVicker
236– From *Scandinavian Stories* by Margaret Sperry.
243 Illustrated by Jenny Williams. © 1971 by Franklin Watts, Inc. Used by permission.
248– Reprinted by permission from *The Christian*
249 *Science Monitor,* © 1977 The Christian Science Publishing Society. All rights reserved.
250 The American Museum of Natural History
253 Museum of the American Indian
254 The American Museum of Natural History
257 The Brooklyn Museum, Gift of Mrs. Frederick B. Pratt; The American Museum of Natural History; Museum of the American Indian
258 The American Museum of Natural History
260 Courtesy Frederick Warne & Co., Inc.
261 From *Peter Rabbit's Natural Foods Cookbook.* Text © 1977 Arnold Dobrin, illustrations © 1977 Frederick Warne & Co., New York and London. By permission of Frederick Warne & Co., Inc.

262 Charles McVicker
265 Charles McVicker
268 From *Hey, Kid!* by Rita Golden Gelman, © 1977. Illustrations by Carol Nicklaus. Published by Franklin Watts, Inc., N.Y.
269 Illustration from *How Djadja-em-ankh Saved the Day: A Tale of Ancient Egypt.* Translated from the original Hieratic, with illustrations and commentary, by Lise Manniche. © 1976 by Lise Manniche. Reprinted by permission of Thomas Y. Crowell Company.
270 From *Roll of Thunder, Hear My Cry* by Mildred D. Taylor, frontispiece by Jerry Pinkney. © 1976 by The Dial Press, N.Y.
271 From *From Ashanti To Zulu.* Text © 1976 by Margaret Musgrove. Pictures © by Leo and Diane Dillon. Published by The Dial Press, N.Y.
272– Curt Gunther—Camera 5
273
274 Wide World
275 Wide World
277 Vannucci Foto Services
278 Walter Iooss—*Sports Illustrated,* © Time Inc.
279 Sports Information Bureau / Marquette University
280 UPI
281 UPI
282 UPI
283 Wide World
284 Denis Brodeur
285 UPI
286 UPI
287 Dan Baliotti; Quebec Nordiques
288 Wide World
289 Eastfoto; Wide World
290 Art Seitz—Liaison
291 Eastfoto
292 UPI
293 Wide World; Wide World; Martha Swope
294 Central Press / Pictorial Parade
296 Wide World
297 Mimi Forsyth—Monkmeyer
298 UPI
299 Tom & Michele Grimm
300 Tom & Michele Grimm
301 Tom & Michele Grimm
302– Harry Burton—The Metropolitan Museum of
303 Art
304 © by Warner Bros. Inc. All rights reserved.
305 Wide World; Wide World
307 The American Museum of Natural History; The American Museum of Natural History; The

American Museum of Natural History; Courtesy Canadian Consulate General
308 Wide World; UPI
309 UPI
310 Courtesy Warner / Reprise Records
311 Martha Swope; Courtesy RSO Records, Inc., photo by Ed Caraeff
312 Courtesy Warner Bros. Records, Inc.
313 Courtesy Atlantic Records; Courtesy Portrait Records
314 Courtesy Children's Film Foundation Ltd.
315 Courtesy Children's Film Foundation Ltd.
316– Text adapted from *A Real American Artist*
317 *Paints a Real American,* by Louise D. Morrison. © 1976, Highlights for Children, Inc., Columbus, Ohio. Photo, Boston Museum of Fine Arts
318 Editorial Photocolor Archives
319 Albertina
320 Scala / Florence; Scala
321 Giraudon
323– Lee Boltin
325
326 © 1977 Twentieth Century-Fox Corp. All rights reserved.
328– © 1977 Twentieth Century-Fox Corp. All rights
329 reserved.
330 Martha Swope
331 Martha Swope
332 Martha Swope; Jack Vartoogian
333 Jack Vartoogian
334 Jenny Tesar
335 From *A Very Young Dancer.* © 1976 Jill Krementz. Published by Alfred A. Knopf, Inc.
336 Martha Swope
337 Martha Swope
338– Courtesy *Mummenschanz*
339
340 Marjorie Pickens
341 Marjorie Pickens
342 Marjorie Pickens
343 Marjorie Pickens
344 Marjorie Pickens
348 Alain Nogues—Sygma
349 George Buctel
350 American Occupational Therapy Association
352 Culver Pictures; Courtesy Tuskegee Institute
353 Ann Hagen Griffiths—DPI
354 Tom Hollyman—Photo Researchers
355 George Buctel; Charles R. Meyer—Photo Researchers
356 George Sottung
357 UPI